THE SOUTH SAXONS

Frontispiece: Remains of Pevensey Castle (*Photo*: Robin Skinner)

THE
SOUTH SAXONS

edited by

Peter Brandon

Phillimore

1978

Published by
PHILLIMORE & CO. LTD.
London and Chichester
Head Office: Shopwyke Hall,
Chichester, Sussex, England

ISBN 0 85033 240 0

Printed in Great Britain by
UNWIN BROTHERS LIMITED
at The Gresham Press, Old Woking, Surrey
and bound by
THE NEWDIGATE PRESS LIMITED
Book House, Dorking, Surrey

CONTENTS

LIST OF PLATES

Remains of Pevensey Castle (*frontispiece*)

Between pages 150 and 151

LIST OF FIGURES

FOREWORD

This volume originated with a proposal made in 1974 to the Friends of the University of Sussex Library by the late Cmdr. R. B. Michell, O.B.E., D.S.C., that the 1500th anniversary of the founding of the Saxon kingdom of Sussex should be celebrated as an event of no less consequence than the Norman Conquest which brings the Saxon period of English history to an end. A Co-ordinating Committee was appointed under Cmdr. Michell's chairmanship to organise a number of events in Sussex on the theme of 'Aelle and after', including a Colloquium held at the University of Sussex in November 1977.

In the discharge of the task of editing this volume I have been greatly assisted by a Publication Committee comprising Mrs. Joyce Giles, Miss Eileen Hollingdale, Dr. Angus Ross and Messrs. Martin Bell, Peter Lewis (chairman), Kenneth Neale, Lionel Philips and Robin Reeve. I am also grateful to Ann Ollis and to the clerical staff of my department for help with the typescript; to Elizabeth Dawlings and Robin Skinner, also of my department, for help with illustrations; and to Ann Winser for compiling the index and for much general help. It is a particular pleasure to recall the friendly and lively discussions with members of the Friends of the University of Sussex Library and with the contributors to this volume which encouraged yet another excursion into the problematic Saxon past of one of the great scenes of human existence in Britain.

PETER BRANDON

Kingston Buci,
May, 1978

The Friends of the University of Sussex Library wish to acknowledge with gratitude grants and donations towards the cost of this publication from the following:

South East Arts Association; Alliance Building Society, Hove; American Express International Banking Corporation, Brighton; Ansvar Insurance Company Limited, Eastbourne; Barclays Bank Limited, Brighton; Charles Clarke (Haywards Heath) Limited; Gateway Building Society, Worthing; ITT Creed Limited, Brighton; John Wiley & Sons Limited, Chichester.

Permission of the Editor, *Medieval Archaeology*, to reproduce Figs. 1 and 2 is gratefully acknowledged.

I

INTRODUCTION: THE SAXON HERITAGE

Peter Brandon

ACCORDING TO the folk-memory version of the event in the *Anglo-Saxon Chronicle*, the year 1977 marked the fifteen hundredth anniversary of the landing on the Sussex coast by the first Saxons under Aelle. Modern scholarly opinion does not accept this dating and, on the basis of more reliable European evidence, prefers to bring forward Aelle's attack by some 20 years.[1] Nevertheless, it seemed fitting to recall the traditional anniversary by reconsidering the Saxon heritage of Sussex between the mid-fifth century A.D. and the making of Domesday Book in 1086 (which is, in effect, the record of Anglo-Saxon land making between these dates). This is a period still standing greatly in need of interpreters. Few human beings can have left behind them such scanty and fleeting details of their own lives and actions as the Saxons. Partly in consequence of this, much of Saxon enterprise is overshadowed by the impressive monuments of Roman practical genius and new sources of wealth and creative energy released by Normanisation. In fact, the six centuries of the Saxon Age, when our speech, our village names, our Church and many of our other present institutions originated, are the least understood and the most under-rated of all the contributions to the whole long process of the making of Sussex.

A preliminary reassessment of Saxon Sussex is now overdue. The Saxon period is being illuminated by the aid of ever-increasing evidence provided by archaeology and scholars are reinterpreting the difficult and scanty historical sources. It thus seems appropriate to move deeper into questions about the Saxons' response to the land of Sussex and to measure the stature of their actual achievements. Also important is the need to identify some of the gaps in our knowledge and to urge for research along new lines of enquiry. Accordingly, contributions were invited from nine scholars who have approached the period from their own specialist standpoint, but who in combination, it is hoped, present something towards a co-ordinated view of the total environment of Saxon Sussex and an outline of Saxon social and religious organisation.

1

Northern Europe between the fifth and seventh centuries A.D. was astir as it probably never had been before. The Saxons, to take only one Germanic tribe on the North German plain, were swarming westwards to Drenthe in present Holland and across the North Sea to Britain, southwards towards Westphalia and eastwards into Jutland. Aelle's founding of his small, independent, Saxon nation of Sussex is but one of the results of an expansive impulse which sent Saxons bursting out of their original narrow quarters between the rivers Weser and Elbe.[2]

It was formerly the popular historical theory that the various people bound together under Aelle's leadership by the single interest of land-seeking, massacred or drove westwards the conquered inhabitants of the hitherto small but prosperous canton of the *Regni* and made a fresh start in farming and settlement. The many previous settlements abandoned on the higher and steeper parts of the downland seemed to corroborate this conjecture. Anglo-Saxon life in England, drawn on very simple lines, was assumed to have been a copy of life on the North German plain transplanted into the shadow of ruined Romano-British towns and villas. Many scholars now speculate on a course of development strikingly different. It is suggested that the great feudal estates found in later Saxon and Norman Sussex, consisting of scattered farmlands and wooded wastes governed from a single headquarters, may be not the work of Germanic enterprise but the result of a gradual evolution from as far back as the British Bronze Age. This is only one of the deeper perspectives of the Dark Age which now make the period such a challenge and fascination. Interweaving the fabric of life of Saxon Germany into the warp and woof of communities living in Sub-Roman Britain is one of the radical revisions of long-accepted views for which we must now be prepared. What was once a plain and simple tale based on liberal interpretations of such late sources as the *Anglo-Saxon Chronicle* has now necessarily become a highly complex major reassessment using all the resources of scientific archaeology, the analytical study of the humanised landscape, based on the work of Professor W. G. Hoskins, and of such important aids as place-names.

Unfortunately, the countryside the Saxons inherited and adapted in Sussex is not yet delineated clearly enough for us to know much about the size, distribution and organisation of the late Romano-British population. Consequently, we still lack a datum against which we can measure the advance and retreat of settlement. The Saxons should be studied against the division of Sussex into the Weald, on the one hand, and the coastal plain and downland, on the other. This duality of environment, with its contrasting challenges and opportunities, is a fact of nature to which man in Sussex has had to adapt himself throughout time. It is this interaction between man's will and his varying environment which brings most of the significance to the study of human existence in south-eastern England. The old opinions and beliefs about the origin of Saxon Sussex, supported the notion that all at the outset was frontier, a mere strip of settlement stretched precariously upon the sea-edge of the wild, the supposedly untouched forest and marsh of the Weald. We had a picture in our mind's eye of men from across the North Sea set upon a new coast to do the work of pioneers. As the history of human effort was added to by one generation after another, Sussex was perceived as developing as a spreading wedge into the iron-bearing wooded hinterland of the river ports. This was considered to have been an extremely slow-moving process, very much incomplete when the sixteenth century came to an end, and consequently the Saxon rôle in this long-term movement was regarded as a comparatively small one. To what extent, if at all, are these older beliefs still tenable?

In the attempt to grasp the whole reality of the Dark Ages, their history is now increasingly being studied at two quite different levels—the deep-seated forces at work in the complex arena of warfare and politics (these give rise to the most dramatic changes) and also the 'submerged' history of man in the mass and his relationship to his environment, 'a history in which all change is slow, a history of constant repetition, ever recurring cycles', in fact an almost timeless history, often pulsing with barely perceptible rhythms. Many scholars now suspect that when Sussex became a small independent Saxon nation some of its already multi-centuried features of human existence changed only slowly, or hardly at all. By reason of the woods, marsh and sea that confined it, Sussex was naturally segregated from the outside world and sealed in a seclusion which has tended ever since to preserve these old layers of culture. Consequently, much of the ancient, accumulated past of Sussex still flows very much alive into the present. So gradual has been the process of change that even in this century Hilaire Belloc could write of Sussex as the 'resistant county'. Its ancient man-made landscape, revealing the relationships between men, their land and buildings, is the kind that William Morris had in mind when he wrote that in such scenes 'we have before us history in its most delightful and . . . instructive shape'.[3]

The scientific study of the humanised landscape of Sussex is, in fact, showing how almost every environment is a palimpsest, bearing the marks of man in stage after stage of previous occupation. This evokes in the mind an endless succession of ever-changing pictures from dates so remote, or so indefinite, as to be almost beyond chronology and lends support to Hoskins's aphorism that 'everything is older than we think'. This is certainly true of the coastal plain and downland which has responded to many centuries of previous human effort before Aelle's landing, and which archaeologists are steadily rendering more intelligible to us. Furthermore, the recent study of prehistoric peoples has shown that their intellectual and physical capabilities were much greater than formerly supposed. We have new information, some of it of a surprising kind, of the labour resources available in prehistoric south Britain and of evidence that points to the slow accumulation of tradition rather than any violent breaks with the past. The old idea that Iron Age communities struggled to live by means of a precarious subsistence farming will probably need considerable qualification. Archaeology has hitherto produced many thousands of ground plans, but it has had too little to tell about how men actually lived. The Iron Age skills now being revived by means of experimental archaeology at the Ancient Farm Research Centre, Butser, may overturn many of the old-established theories, e.g.,

concerning the yield of corn. Iron Age and Romano-British 'huts', as built at
Butser, were not the crude, flimsy structures often previously imagined, but
solid, well-built dwellings with rafters weighing up to 10 tons bearing an equal,
or greater, weight of thatch. Barns were similarly built to last. Around the
farmsteads were well-tended hedgerows and coppices. In short, farmsteads in
fifth-century *Britannia* would not have been given up lightly.[4]

Of greater relevance to the present discussion is the growing evidence that
Britain in the Iron and Romano-British periods was also very populous. Professor
Cunliffe's estimate of the population in Roman Britain of four millions at its
peak in the late second century, compared with the estimate of only 1½ millions
in 1086, and a rise to four millions again by 1348,[5] will reopen the debate on the
multiple relationships between early man in South-East England and his
activities and the environment. Hypothetical as these estimates must be
regarded in the light of our present knowledge, and however inadequate such
figures are as a frame on which to hang a regional study of population, it is hard
to escape the conclusion that the population increase in the Iron and Roman
periods led to a gradual settlement ever more deeply in the Weald. Conversely,
the dramatic decline in population between the third and seventh centuries can
have scarcely failed to have left its mark on the abandonment of the more
marginal land in the Weald, and elsewhere, previously opened up. We should
perhaps no longer regard many of the woodland clearances between the eighth
or ninth and the thirteenth centuries as assaults on *virgin* lands, but as a *recovery*
of previously lost farmland when a rising population was turning back upon its
old paths and filling up again some of the spaces abandoned centuries earlier.

It is in the light of this recent research that we broadly have to reconsider the
Saxon contribution to the making of England. In the hearts of its sons and
lovers Aelle has long been the true founder of Sussex. If in the full perspective
of history he appeared to have created a kingdom of less consequence in the
heritage of England than that of Kent, or Northumbria, or Wessex, he was
thought to have created something of a little land by itself, peculiar to the
South Saxons themselves, which has ever since been endowed with a more than
average strength of local consciousness. Yet the heart alone is as treacherous
as the mind alone, and we have to face the probability that the Romanised
population of Sussex was absorbed into the new Saxon state and that a
continuous occupation exists between some of their rural settlements and those
of the new men. The formidable Roman masonry in the curtain walls and
bastions of the Saxon shore fort of Pevensey (*Andredesceaster*) is a living
monument to both Aelle's victorious warriors and their brave resistors
(*Frontispiece*).

When we trace, albeit fragmentarily, the slow, but ultimately successful
agrarian settlement which was the territorial basis of the early South Saxon state,
its most memorable beginnings were in the coast and downland part of Sussex
(Fig. 1). From the tenth century, when this vanished world can be recaptured
in rather greater detail, we find the South Saxons confronting a new destiny,
self-absorbed in the further challenge of wresting a living from the interior

forest, far from the landing places and homes of the first settlers. When reassessing the place of Aelle and his successors in the beginnings of our civilisation there are few more fitting figures to re-discover than the under-rated Saxon ploughman cultivating on the edge of the Forest-waste and daily, bit by bit, wearing his way into it. *Har holtes feond,* 'the old enemy of the wood', is how the Saxon poet addresses the man who drove the plough.[6] The very name Weald (O.E. *Wald,* a forest) still renders a remote, but palpable, sense of its former uncultivated wildness and its perpetual challenge to those who wanted to make a new farm and a new and freer life. We may come to conclude that the partial winning of new land in the Weald was one of the main gifts of the South Saxons to posterity. In the coastal scene of their action, a tempting prize to a farming folk, the South Saxons were the destroyers of the Roman material culture implanted there during the four previous centuries. Contrastingly, the Saxon Wealdsman may properly be said to have been creative and to have taken a new lead in the rough first work of civilisation. The simple-hearted swineherds, cattle-drovers and woodmen who every summer drove their herds northwards to browse in the wooded Weald (so beginning to wear down into deep hollows the intricate pattern of half-forgotten by-ways still surviving as greenways) were amongst the first to appraise the Weald, to test its strength and to learn its lore. In plying their axes to clear patches of the forest and to fence off their rough huts, they were inaugurating a new epoch in Sussex history. It was probably their discovery that the Sussex Weald generally was too poor to be cultivated without some preliminary improvement. Only after centuries of further effort was the rank clay of the Weald gradually rendered fertile, and each generation had added a little to the family stock. This has been largely the achievement of smallholding farmers, hard, bold, sturdy, unsophisticated, as strong as the soil they worked upon and with a sense of freedom and independence that came from holding the handles of their own ploughs. Even at the beginning of the nineteenth century they still retained a cheerful sense of a community, all but inaccessible to strangers, living on close terms with the soil and holding their own in the well fortified self-sufficiency which was for generations a condition of survival.

The uninterruptedness which is the mark of Wealden colonisation between the eighth or ninth and the early fourteenth centuries, the pivotal period of this enterprise, makes it impossible to draw a firm line between the Saxon and the succeeding woodland clearance. The evidence for a considerable Saxon clearance is considered below.[7] Put summarily, the woodland clearance of the twelfth to the early fourteenth centuries, transforming the use and appearance of extensive tracts of Sussex countryside, mark the culmination of a process which had steadily been in operation over at least the three previous centuries and which silently nibbled away as much, or an even larger area, than the later and better documented era following. Little research has yet been turned to the men who faced the wildness and sought to make something out ot if. The would-be pioneering lords and peasants faced new conditions in which they could not ply their traditional farming skills or live as they had been accustomed.

In learning new ways of living they were not merely destroyers of the wild, but also finders of new ways of coming to terms with a relatively hostile environment, thereby making a permanent contribution to our civilisation. These new lands, new men, new thoughts, warrant further study and so does the extent to which the woodmen moulded the wild to their own needs and in turn were moulded by the nature of their environment.

Few people realise how ancient is the Sussex landscape around them, how little it has been explored, and what scope there is for further discovery. We can the better, in the words of Maitland, think the thoughts and know the men of this remote age a little better through the medium of the extensive network of routes woven by men travelling to and from the principal centres of coastal manors and their numerous outlying pastures. It is readily observable that the general direction of the close net of Sussex by-roads is from north to south. On closer examination it will be found that most of the villages and hamlets lining the fertile strip at the foot of the Chalk escarpment, and also settlements nearer the coast, have a direct connection by road with places in the deep Weald. That some of these routes, or parts of them have become totally unnecessary, is indicated by their present unmetalled condition. If we now take, by way of example, the roads and trackways within the triangle bounded by Littlehampton, Horsham and Brighton, it is found that many of these by-ways are still traceable over quite remarkably long distances.[8] It is a road system which suggests that the local necessity of settlers in the oldest developed parts of Sussex was not so much connections between neighbouring settlements as between each one and its outlying woodland pasture. We have, in fact, before our eyes actual witness to the pattern of old droving roads developed by a large number of anciently self-contained communities, the old arteries through which ran Sussex life into the Wealden appanage. It brings very vividly to the eye and mind the comings and goings of men over a passage of time now almost forgotten. These roads are perhaps the most striking survival of the age of frontiersmen left in Sussex. It has hitherto been assumed that this system of long-distance droving based on scattered woodland-pasture 'outliers' is of Saxon origin. The possibility is that the custom of droving and the agrarian ground plan which developed from it may take us back into remote pre-history. One day we may be nearer to a solution to this enigma, but this will require the detailed reconstruction of the old road system, a most neglected aspect of field archaeology.

Although the physical appearance of few parts of England have been more utterly changed since Aelle's landing than the great expanse of woodland, scrub and marsh which bore the name of *Andredeswald* there is still identifiable in the present-day landscape surviving woodland once familiarly known to Saxon man. One of these fragments of rough, uncultivated, land is Mens wood, a woodland-common, now a Nature Reserve of 358 acres located in the remotest corners of three parishes in the heart of the West Sussex Weald—Wisborough Green, Fittleworth and Kirdford. In thirteenth-century manorial records its name is rendered *Mennesse,* a word derived from Old English *ge-maennes* and used of the joint or common tenancy of land. This tract of woodland was thus originally called simply 'common-land'. Ruth Tittensor identifies the Mens wood with swine-pastures called *Palinga Schittas* ('sheds or swinecotes of the people of Poling' [a place between Arundel and Littlehampton]) because mentioned in the same Saxon charter of 953 A.D. are *Boganora* (Little Bognor Farm) and *Hidhurst* (Idehurst) which are places south and north of the Mens itself. From Saxon times the Mens has had an unbroken history as a woodland-common to the early years of this century.[9] Generally speaking, every Wealden manor or 'outlier' of a coastal manor in the Weald, has retained patches of woodland-common which has survived both the attack on the surviving woodland ending in the early fourteenth century, and the 'clearing up' enclosures of the eighteenth and early nineteenth centuries. These relict woodland-commons are an important part of the Saxon heritage of Sussex for they recall the many centuries in man's more primitive Sussex existence when the coastal inhabitants found in the distant forest all the resources they needed which the fields themselves did not produce. Man took from the forest wood for heating, for building and for fencing; he found forest grazing for his livestock and acorns for his pigs, as well as game and honey. 'It was to the peasant so complete an assistance that human life seemed to be linked to the existence of these wooded masses; and in primitive epochs the villagers of the Middle Ages continued to live near the edge of its forests, as on a shore, where its origin and its needs, as well as secret inclinations, held it fast'.[10]

Those who look long and closely on the Sussex scene will know that a day's journey across fields and hills can still bring one into close contact with the Saxon past through the medium of the numerous simple churches with their 'almost miraculous continuity of structure and function' that tend to prevail in downland communities which did not greatly expand after Domesday and often steadily dwindled from the later middle ages. In the late eighteenth century we find Gilbert White of Selborne writing of the smallness, or 'meanness' as he expresses it, of 'Sussex houses of worship (with) little better appearance than dovecotes . . .'.[11] Fortunately, these little Saxon churches have been cherished for a century or more for aesthetic rather than for practical reasons and we are able to remain in direct touch with some of the early makers of Sussex. Coming readily to mind are the churches of Bishopstone, near Seaford, with its fine Saxon nave and its *porticus* bearing a sundial in memory of Eadric and that of Worth which in its large scale and boldness is a reminder of early successful woodland clearing in the deep Weald.

Another way of recapturing something of Saxon Sussex is to perambulate in the wake of the Saxons the bounds of landed property whose landmarks are recorded in Anglo-Saxon charters. One charter that responds to this technique is a charter of King Canute dated 1018 A.D. by which he granted to the Archbishop of Canterbury a 'grove called *Haeselerse* in the famous forest of *Andredeswealde*' (*quiddam silvule nemus concedo in famosa silva Andredes-wealde*).[12] Treading the bounds indicated on this charter we journey along water courses, so recovering their Saxon names, and follow the still-surviving earthen banks thrown up to mark the property boundary. Another illuminating Saxon charter is the document assigned to 772 A.D. and relating to the Bexhill district.[13] The landmarks mentioned as bounding the 'inland' (the most intensively farmed part of the estate) are still readily identifiable natural features. We can also, with little difficulty, tread the Saxon bounds of the 'outland', marshy and low-lying tract in the Pevensey Levels. One of the most valuable pieces of information which can be gleaned from this charter is that the 'outland', even at this early date, has become permanently farmed and settled.[14]

By detailed studies of this kind, with the aid of place-names and by careful visual observation of actual sites, we shall be able to recover something of the essence of the Saxon landscape of Sussex and by this reconstitution we shall be better informed both as to the Saxons themselves and to the scale of their enterprise. Disregard of the actual geographical conditions at the time, frequently robs arguments of their point. The reconstruction of the Sussex coastline in Saxon times is particularly important for it greatly differed from that which we see today. Resulting from a submergence of the land initiated in Roman times, the now minute alluviated streams (rifes) on the coastal plain were wide, watery obstacles; Selsey and probably Felpham were islanded by salt-water; the drowned lower valleys of the Sussex streams formed wide estuaries; Pagham, Bognor and Broadwater were then wide inlets and low-lying tracts such as the Pevensey and Willingdon Levels were inundated. E. M. Yates has recently summarised the old appearance of the coastal plain in the neighbourhood of Chichester: 'Perhaps it is not too fanciful to visualise the landscape of the Dark Ages as resembling parts of Friesland and Saxony with settlements on low rises separated by strips of alluvium, giving rich grazings but periodically inundated, resembling, that is, the original homeland of the South Saxons'.[15]

A primary task in the reconstruction of the Saxon setting, will be the broad delimitation of tracts of woodland, marsh, heath and cultivated land. We still know too little about the distribution of early Saxon woodland. Although the strongest physical contrast in Saxon Sussex was that between the still thickly wooded clays of the Weald, where settling more land meant woodland clearance, and the more open and habitable fringes of downland and plain, the latter region carried much woodland, especially in west Sussex. The Sussex-Hampshire border, with its wide inlets and inaccessible islands and peninsulas, was particularly well wooded. Bede tells us that the seventh-century Irish priest Dicul had a monastery at Bosham 'all compassed about with woods and the sea'.[16] West of Chichester on the poorer gravels, we find Bishop Ralph in the early thirteenth century hacking and hewing fresh fields out of his wooded wastes[17] and in the Manhood peninsula (although a Sussex cradle of Sussex Romano-British civilisation) extensive woodland-common lay astride the present road between Chichester and the Witterings as the sprinkling of place names in *-leah* inform us. This common-woodland (its name is derived from *maene-wudu*, 'common wood', so giving its name to the whole peninsula) functioned like the Mens wood mentioned previously and it was not finally obliterated until 1793 when 650 acres of common were enclosed by Acts of Parliament.

We now need to examine the question as to how far the Romano-British plan of settlements and fields was modified by the South Saxons in the course of their folk migration. The old explanation for the apparent contrast in lowland England between the 'traditional' nucleated villages of the Anglo-Saxon landscape and the dispersed farms, hamlets, villas and occasional villages which is the archaeological evidence for Roman Britain was a total discontinuity. It was, for example, J. N. L. Myres's opinion that the English conquest 'involved a complete break with the agricultural past'.[18] According to this view the Saxons drove away or wiped out most of the natives and then settled in the best places in large nucleated settlements amongst the abandoned Romano-British farmsteads. As far as coastal Sussex is concerned, the existence of numerous hamlets and their servile attributes, greatly helps to remove some of the alleged contrasts between the agrarian institutions of the Romano-Britons and the incoming Saxons. Those who postulate that, in the main, the Anglo-Saxons took over estates as going concerns and embarked on the land clearing of previously deserted places will find coastal Sussex a fascinating arena for their historical detection. The hamlet geography of Sussex and Kent has already attracted much attention. It was the subject of an elegant monograph in 1933 by J. E. A. Jolliffe[19] who pronounced it, and the structure of fragmented (multiple or discrete) estates, including their Wealden outliers, as Jutish. In his review of this work, J. N. L. Myres noted the similarity of the multiple estate and its institutions to the organisation in Celtic countries and, in words which have a prophetic ring today when a continuity between Roman and Saxon Britain is favoured, remarked 'can we be sure that he (Jolliffe) has not taken us back to something still older than the Jutes to the Celtic organisation?[20] In the light of current opinion it is interesting to recall the remarkable prescience of W. D. Peckham, a Sussex antiquary, who in 1925 regarded the hamlets near Chichester as survivals of Celtic *clachans* and discovered that some of the fields were measured in units similar to Roman *jugera*.[21] G. R. G. Jones has recently revived the suggestion of Celtic territorial survivals in the Saxon countryside and has suggested that the multiple estate and its hamlet structure of settlement evolved around the focus of hillforts in the millennium before the coming of the Romans.[22] Some of his conjectures are specifically based on Sussex agrarian patterns. We are still far from clear how the small 'Celtic' fields, typically arranged on downland in lynchetted blocks and of sub-rectangular appearance evolved into the long, thin ploughlands associated with Saxons. It is possible that ordered studies of aerial surveys will help to give us fairly definite answers to these matters. Many of the Sussex hamlets became deserted or considerably shrunken in the period between the fourteenth and the sixteenth centuries, leaving fossil imprints and mere shells of what were once lively settlements. One or two of these would probably greatly repay archaeological investigation.

There is a tremendous gap in our knowledge concerning South Saxon fields and field systems. Since the nature of an adopted field system strongly influenced the pattern of rural settlement the two aspects are inseparably linked and together make a highly complex problem. In this matter we are all guessers, groping in a dense fog. It was the old surmise that on the downland and coastal plain the Saxon farmed in a little village collectively with long, thin ploughlands worked within a communal type of land exploitation, whereas in the Weald one of the peasants' precious freedoms of isolation was the cultivation of fields enclosed within their own ring fence from the very beginning. This conjecture is still useful as a working proposition but fresh thinking and wide-ranging field surveys, as well as archaeological investigation, are now needed.

When coastal Sussex emerges into the stronger light of the thirteenth and fourteenth centuries we find peasants working unfenced strips of common arable (the lord's demesne being invariably separately fenced off). The territorial basis of the common-fields was not the parish, nor even the manor, but the *tything,* i.e., the cluster of dwellings making a township (*toun*) for fiscal and administrative purposes. Even a small downland parish such as Alciston or Bishopstone made room for a smaller, subsidiary, and self-contained set of common fields (Tilton and Norton respectively) additionally to that of the main cluster of farmsteads around the parish church. The parish of Ringmer contained four separately differentiated common-field systems at each of its anciently-settled hamlets of Ashton, Middleham, Norlington, and Wellingham, whilst the parish of West Firle, east of Lewes, also comprised four sets of common-fields at the big nucleated village of Firle itself, the 'head' of the parish, and at three neighbouring hamlets—Charleston, Compton, and Heighton, now reduced to single farms. Further examples can be quoted. Burpham parish was composed of the three tythings of Burpham, Wepham, and Peppering; Climping included Atherington and Ilesham (since destroyed by the sea); Offham was a separate tything in the parish of South Stoke, and Rackham, Cootham, and Buddington were similarly organised within Amberley, Storrington, and Steyning respectively. It is noteworthy that several of these named places are separately recorded in Domesday Book and that the others have early place-name suffixes. Identical, or very similar, patterns recur again and again on the coastal parts of Sussex. It must be remembered that coastal Sussex is agriculturally rich and was crowded with large medieval estates and closely-spaced peasant communities.

In the light of this general picture of tenurial conditions in the later middle ages it is difficult to resist the inference that the multiplicity of common-field systems functioning as distinct local units and based on hamlets interspersed between larger 'head' settlements represents the bones of an agrarian structure of great antiquity which is older than the institution of the parish, which appears in coastal Sussex to have been introduced for ecclesiastical purposes. It seems scarcely possible that the rural ground plan we have been selectively analysing could have altered in its fundamentals since the upheavals caused by the Saxon invasions.

In the instances mentioned large central or 'head' villages are a major element in the rural pattern. If we now consider another aspect of Saxon Sussex, the large estates, those in south-west Sussex seem never to have comprised large central villages, but contained many dispersed hamlets housing land holders who performed labour services on the demesnes. We know most about the great ecclesiastical estate with which St. Wilfrid was endowed in the Selsey peninsula by a king of the South Saxons in the seventh century. This was worked by a force of 250 slaves and by bondmen dwelling at various named settlements which can be identified with existing places such as Bersted, North Bersted, Crimsham, the Mundhams, and Shripney. When the estate is the subject of detailed documents in the thirteenth century the compact fields of the demesne are found to be worked by villeins and cottars dwelling in several of the appendant communities named in the seventh-century charter. These were mostly hamlets. For the large royal manor of Bosham no Saxon charter evidence has survived, but an identical pattern of small dispersed groups of servile cultivators is traceable from the early Middle Ages. Place-names help to confirm the antiquity of the topographical and social basis. Walton is considered to be derived from the Old English *wealh* and *tun,* meaning the vill of the native Britons. This would appear to be one of the places where the humble natives, who supplied most of the labour, had their quarters. Creed is another interesting hamlet. Its name means 'garden' or 'small enclosure'. In the thirteenth century and later no large fields existed there, the occupiers being only cottars. This again seems to confirm the ancient existence of a servile society living in hamlets. By way of further examples it is instructive to consider the three Sussex *Charltons,* each of them small settlements and sited on outlying parts of great estates at Domesday—the archbishop's estate of Pagham, the once royal estate of Steyning, and the estate formerly held by Earl Godwin at Singleton. The place-name is derived from Old English *Ceorls-tun,* 'the peasant village', and they would seem also to be specifically places for dependent labourers.

The hamlet is thus a dominant feature of the rural ground plan of medieval Sussex, even to the exclusion in some places of the 'traditional' large central villages. It is reasonable to suppose that, being peripherally sited, the plough-lands of the hamlet-dwellers did not intermingle with the lord's and that the consolidated demesnes we encounter in the thirteenth century are of long standing. This agrarian organisation—of which we have glimpses back to the seventh century—bespeaks a high level of efficiency and an economically advanced institution. It may not be too fanciful to perceive in the Saxon ground plan the deep roots of the precociously developed agriculture of coastal Sussex documented in the later middle ages. A further clue to a highly developed demesne agriculture by the late eleventh century are the large renders of legumes made by the archbishop's estate at Pagham.[23] In the thirteenth century the coastal demesnes in Sussex are intensively worked on the basis of soil-renewing rotations using extensively sown legumes.[24] There is only scanty documentation for farming techniques for the earlier centuries, but the scraps of evidence we have been considering are not inconsistent with the conjecture that the basic elements of its high farming so amply recorded in the later middle ages had been already adopted in the far-off Saxon period. Do we see in these clearly articulated estates an even earlier stamp of Romanised ingenuity and planning? Certainly in Saxon times the easy access to seaborne commerce would have removed an insuperable barrier to economic development and the rich soils of the plain and the great sheepwalks on the downland would have provided one of the most favourable natural environments in England. All this would go far to explain the great concentrations of landed estates on the coastal plain in the hands of the Crown, the Church, and the great Saxon lay magnates, notably Earl Godwin.

Despite the fitful glow of light, the contributors to this volume have added many fresh perspectives to the beginnings of civilisation in Sussex. Yet nothing reveals more the great weaknesses of the present archaeological record than that almost nothing is currently known of what must have been one of the most important South Saxon environments, that of the sea. Anglo-Saxon literature reflects an intimate maritime knowledge and experience. The storms, toils and dangers stir the poet's imagination and the Saxon pride in ships and their spirit of adventure is conveyed by many apt turns of phrase, as in *The Seafarer*:

> His mind dwells not on the harmonious harp,
> On ring-receiving, or the joy of woman,
> Or worldly hopes, or anything at all
> But the relentless rolling of the waves.[25]

The information on Saxon ships and shipping is so meagre that we still cannot see the English Channel of the tenth and eleventh centuries. A major task in the reconceiving and reorganising of the life of Saxon Sussex will be to fill in this picture of its ships and of the seamen who probably turned peasant with the seasons.

Thus deepening enquiry into the South Saxons and their setting is raising fresh problems and there are a host of remaining difficulties. We are, in Leslie Alcock's phrase, 'only on the eve of discovering how Roman Britain became Anglo-Saxon England'.[26] It is to be hoped that the discoveries and interpretations recorded in this group of essays and Professor Cunliffe's suggestions for fresh approaches will make the final task of lightening the Dark Ages on both a larger and a smaller canvas a little easier. As for the Saxon heritage of Sussex, this deserves to be more widely known and admired. For this reason this book will have served one of its main purposes if it induces local teachers and historians to turn with a greater readiness to the South Saxon past.

EARLY ANGLO-SAXON SUSSEX: FROM CIVITAS TO SHIRE

Martin G. Welch

THE 'coming of the Saxons' in the fifth century was one of the crucial events in the formation of modern Britain. New kingdoms were set up by the German-speaking settlers from Scandinavia and Germany, replacing the Roman provincial organisation in much of Britain. Our English language is the most obvious debt we owe to the Anglo-Saxons, but it does not stand alone. Until the recent reorganisation of local government, the English counties were still essentially the same as the shires of the tenth century kingdom of England. The modern counties of West and East Sussex owe their existence to the fifth-century creation of the kingdom of the South Saxons.

Our theme is the brief history of this kingdom to its decline and final absorption into the West Saxon kingdom of the ninth century. Scattered pieces of information of varying degrees of reliability must be put together rather as in a jigsaw, though unfortunately more pieces than is desirable have been irretrievably lost or still await discovery.

The main Anglo-Saxon written sources are the Venerable Bede's *Ecclesiastical History of the English Nation*[1] completed in 731, the *Life of St. Wilfrid*[2] attributed to Eddius Stephanus and used by Bede as a source, and a set of annals first compiled in the West Saxon kingdom in the ninth century, the *Anglo-Saxon Chronicle*[3]. British sources include the sermon *Concerning the destruction and conquest of Britain*[4], apparently written in the middle of the sixth century by Gildas and used by Bede, and the *History of the Britons*[5] attributed to Nennius. The latter, a ninth-century compilation, contains a valuable account of the settlement of Kent, which provides an historical context for the Sussex settlement.

The bare outline of events given in these and other written sources must be understood in the context of the archaeological evidence for Anglo-Saxon settlement. Burials furnished with weapons, jewellery, and other grave finds repay detailed study. The houses, outbuildings, and enclosed yards of their settlements, however, have not been located as frequently as the cemeteries. The Christian conversion of the seventh century resulted in a simplified burial rite, while the eighth century saw the end of the practice of depositing grave finds. The archaeologist's loss is the historian's gain, for the Church sought to safeguard the extensive lands granted to it by recording the transactions in writing. Not surprisingly the earliest charters drawn up by the Papal missionaries owe much to Italian documents. The last category of evidence to which we will turn are place-names. Anglo-Saxon names in maps and documents can be traced back through the Middle Ages to the *Domesday Book* of 1086 and even to earlier written sources. The place-name experts are able to suggest the probable meaning of the name and the date of its formulation from their study of the development of the Old English language. Place-name evidence, if used in conjunction with the historical and archaeological evidence, can add to our understanding of Anglo-Saxon England.

The geography of Roman and Saxon Sussex

Sussex is divided into three distinct physical zones: the coastal plain in the south-west; the chalk upland of the South Downs to its north; and the Weald beyond that (Figs. 1 and 2). The most fertile regions are the loamy soils of the coastal plain and a belt immediately north of the Downs, consisting of the Upper Greensand formation and downwash from the chalk. It is here that we find most of the Roman villas and some early Saxon settlement. The Downs are a dry region with no springs or flowing water except in the lowest valleys, whose thin soils were better suited to pasturage than to cultivation. The farms, hamlets and villages of the Romano-British peasantry are found here, but not the villas. The majority of Saxon cemeteries occur on downland hilltops or on their upper slopes. The discovery of a settlement on Rookery Hill, Bishopstone, above the contemporary cemetery, suggests that in many cases we can expect to locate a Saxon settlement close by its burial ground.

With the exception of the fertile belt close to the Downs, the Weald must have formed an intractable region. Sands and gravels, which covered much of it, probably supported oak and birch forests and heathlands. A band of heavy clay covered by a dense oak forest was interposed between the fertile loams and the sands and gravels. This forest of *Andredeslea,* as it is named in the *Anglo-Saxon Chronicle*[6], is described by Wilfrid's biographer,[7] who also comments on the rocky coastline. Here he was presumably thinking of the chalk cliffs between Brighton and Eastbourne. The coastline must have had an appearance rather different from its present one in the Roman and early Saxon period. Much of the alluvium in the river flood plains had not yet been deposited, and the tidal estuaries extended further inland. The extent of coastal erosion which has taken place can only be guessed, but it has been estimated that the coastal plain may have been at least a mile broader.

The extent of the lands governed by the magistrates of *Noviomagus Regnensium* (Chichester) is not precisely known.[8] The *civitas* of the *Regni* or *Regnenses* was derived from the pre-conquest Atrebatic kingdom of Verica. Verica's kingdom seems to be the coastal region of Hampshire east of the River

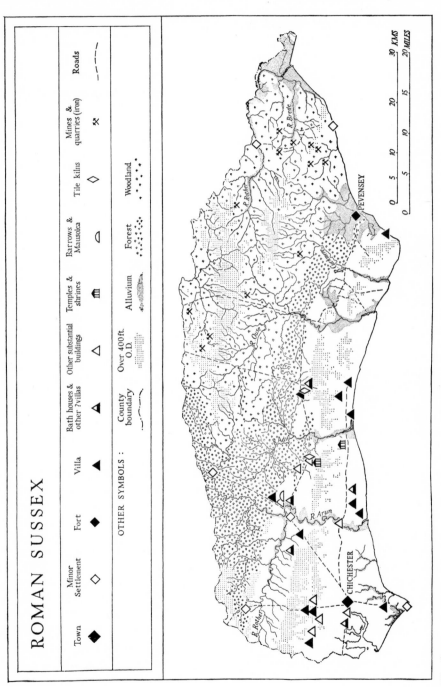

ROMAN SUSSEX

Town ◆

Minor Settlement ◇

Fort ◆

Villa ▲

OTHER SYMBOLS :

Bath houses & other villas ◀

Other substantial buildings ◁

Temples & shrines ⬚

Barrows & Mausolea ◖

Tile kilns ◇

Mines & quarries (iron) ✕

Roads ⌐ ⌐

County boundary

Over 400ft. O.D.

Alluvium

Forest

Woodland

Fig. 1

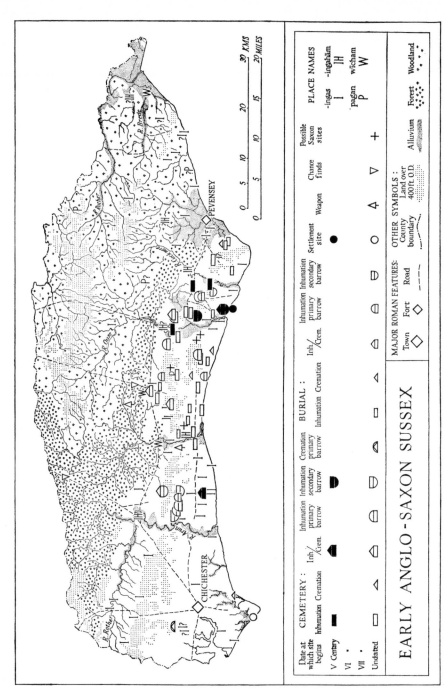

EARLY ANGLO-SAXON SUSSEX

Fig. 2

Meon and Sussex west of the River Ouse. As a loyal ally of Rome, this kingdom was enlarged under Cogidubnus, but may have subsequently been reduced again. The possible extent of the territories of the *civitates* of *Venta Belgarum* (Winchester) and *Calleva Atrebatum* (Silchester) must be taken into account. As elsewhere in Britain, the villas concentrated around the capital at Chichester. Most are found within a fifteen-mile radius, but it is difficult to be certain where in the west the villas of the *Regnenses* end and those of the *Belgae* begin. In the east, there are two villas isolated from the main group. Part of what may have been a villa, abandoned in the second century, has been excavated recently at Newhaven,[9] and there was an undated villa at Eastbourne.

The Sussex Weald was exploited industrially in the form of iron workings, mainly dating to the first and second centuries. The discovery of tiles with the inscription CLBR at several of these sites suggests state ownership exercised by the *Classis Britannica* (British fleet). This may well imply that the greater part of eastern Sussex lay outside the *civitas*. At Footlands, near Battle, production continued into the fourth century, but the majority of the sites had been abandoned in the third, and it has been suggested that the Forest of Dean took their place.[10] A single radiocarbon date suggests the possibility of iron workings in the early Saxon period. A small bloomery site at Turner's Green, near Heathfield, produced a date of A.D. 567 ± 45,[11] which must be treated with caution until it can be confirmed.

Late Roman Sussex

The eastern and southern coasts of Britain came under attack in the third century for the first time since the Roman conquest. Contemporary sources name the pirate raiders as the Franks. They are apparently the same people of Germanic origin living on the North Sea coasts of the Netherlands and North-West Germany, whom earlier Roman writers termed Chauci and Frisians, and fourth-century Romans called Saxons. As a result Eutropius, writing in the third quarter of the fourth century about events in the later third century, describes the sea raiders of the coasts of Britain and Gaul as Saxons acting in conjunction with Franks. This lack of consistency in nomenclature is not so puzzling when we realise that these names represent confederations of peoples and are not necessarily distinct cultural and tribal groupings.

The Roman response was to build chains of coastal forts to act as naval bases along the east and south coasts of Britain and the north coast of Gaul.[12] Portchester Castle in Portsmouth Harbour was among the earliest of these forts to be constructed, probably around the 280s. Despite its presence, successful raids took place on the Sussex coast. It is probably no coincidence that fire destroyed the palace at Fishbourne, the villa at Preston, Brighton, and the native settlement at Park Brow, Sompting, in the last quarter of the third century. Thirteen coin hoards speak of the insecurity in Sussex, and it is possible that the hillfort at Highdown was re-fortified as a refuge centre at this time, or later in the fourth century. The fourth century saw the construction of a new fort in the 'Saxon Shore' defences at Pevensey (*Anderida*), dated by a coin of 330-35, and the addition of projecting bastions to the walls of Chichester. Normally catapults were mounted on these bastions and some form of garrison would be needed to man them. A bronze dolphin-headed buckle may have belonged to a member of such a garrison at the end of the fourth century.

The peace and prosperity of much of the fourth century ended in renewed raiding culminating in a major attack, the 'barbarian conspiracy' of 367. According to Ammianus Marcellinus,[13] the Scots of Ireland, the Picts of Scotland, and the Saxons and Franks on the Continent concerted their raids defeating the Roman armies in Britain. An army under Count Theodosius restored order and reorganised Britain's defences. It was at this time that the garrison at Portchester Castle abandoned the fort and probably transferred to *Clausentum* (Bitterne, Southampton). In the following years, the military needs of more central provinces in the Western Empire took precedence. Armies were led out of Britain in 383 and 407, and we know that in 401 Stilicho was withdrawing troops. After 407, it is probable that no *comitatenses* (field army units) were stationed in Britain and even the *limitanei* (defensive garrison units) were badly denuded.

The official break came in 410, when according to Zosimus,[14] the Emperor Honorius refused to send military aid or appoint governors, and ordered the *civitates* of Britain to organise their own defence. There may have been a brief attempt at oligarchic rule, but according to Procopius,[15] Britain was ruled by usurpers, one of whom is mentioned by Gildas, for the parents of Ambrosius Aurelianus had 'worn the purple'. The accounts of the two visits made by St. Germanus of Auxerre to Britain in 429 and early in the 440s,[17] and the description of St. Patrick's early life,[18] illustrate the degree to which the Roman way of life was preserved in both town and villa. Chichester, like several other *civitas* capitals, was gradually abandoned and decayed slowly. The villas in Sussex were also abandoned, though the rarity of late fourth and early fifth-century coins makes it impossible to state precisely when this happened. The economic basis of trade and industry which supported both town and villa had collapsed, and their days were inevitably numbered.

It was Patrick's mission to the Scots which paved the way for friendly arrangements with Ireland. Around 430 the gravest threat to Britain came from the Picts raiding in ships. According to Gildas, it was for service against the Picts that a 'proud tyrant' hired three shiploads of Saxon mercenaries (about 100 men) and settled them 'in the eastern part of the island'.[19] Nennius's account gives a name to the 'proud tyrant', Vortigern, which is Celtic for 'high king'. The mercenary leader is named Hengest, and we are informed that he and his men were exiles. They were settled on the Isle of Thanet in north-east Kent,[20] though this may represent a later posting after the initial successful campaign against the Picts, who are never again mentioned as a threat to lowland Britain.

The policy of hiring barbarians as mercenaries was not new and it is probable that it was a policy forced on Vortigern by necessity. Germanic peoples had formed an important element of the Roman army at every level from the third century onwards. The significant difference between such regular army Germans and the mercenaries of Hengest and his contemporaries was that the former regarded themselves as Romans and sought to defend the interests of the Empire. Hengest's mercenaries, on the other hand, were military adventurers, who sought wealth and land, and were prepared to turn against their employers if it was to their advantage. Vortigern retained Hengest's services and had reinforcements sent over. The threat to his power now came from enemies within Britain prepared to appeal for Roman military intervention from the Continent, thus explaining Hengest's settlement in Kent guarding the main bridgehead to the Continent. Hengest's force was to betray Vortigern, however, in a rebellion which began a long armed struggle between the British and the Saxons for the control of Britain.

The Angles, Saxons and Jutes on the Continent

The origins of the Germanic settlers of Roman Britain have long been a source of controversy and as with all discussions of the subject, our starting point is Bede's *Ecclesiastical History,* Book 1, Chapter 15. He describes the settlers as:

> the Saxons, the Angles and the Jutes. The people of Kent and the inhabitants of the Isle of Wight are of Jutish origin, and also those opposite the Isle of Wight, that part of the kingdom of Wessex which is today still called the nation of the Jutes. From the Saxon country, that is, the district now known as Old Saxony, came the East Saxons, the South Saxons, and the West Saxons. Besides this from the country of the Angles, that is the land between the kingdoms of the Jutes and the Saxons, which is called Angulus, came the East Angles, the Middle Angles, the Mercians, and all the Northumbrian race . . . as well as the other Anglian tribes.

The fact that we must bear in mind when reading this passage is that Bede is essentially describing the political organisation of the Anglo-Saxons of his own day, and in so doing rationalises the often complex development of the eighth-century kingdoms to give a simple equation. Against this, we must recognise that without Bede's testimony of the Jutish origins of Kent, the Isle of Wight and southern Hampshire, we would under-estimate these districts' connections with Denmark. On the Continent the West German *Land,* or provincial state, of *Niedersachsen* or Lower Saxony, the district of *Angeln* in Schleswig-Holstein, and the Jutland Peninsula preserve the names of these peoples. In archaeological terms, it can be demonstrated that the entire North Sea littoral from the northern Netherlands to southern Scandinavia (southern Norway, southern Sweden and Denmark) contributed settlers to Britain in the fifth and sixth centuries.

Bede was fully aware that in limiting the settlers of Britain to three groups, he had over-simplified. In the turmoil of migration, adventurers of different tribal and racial origins banded together. In Book V, Chapter 9, he listed some of the peoples still living on the Continent in the eighth century who had contributed settlers to Britain. They were the Frisians, who occupied the coastlands of the Netherlands; the Rugii, who within the fifth century moved from the Rhineland to south-west Germany; the Danes, who were migrating south into Jutland in the fifth century; the Huns, who under Attila settled as far west as France; and the Boructarii, who lived in the middle Rhineland and were closely associated with the Franks. All these peoples are acceptable as secondary elements in terms of both the historical and archaeological evidence.

As to the primary settlers, early forms of the cruciform brooch, and pottery vessels which show a marked similarity to pots found in northern Jutland, are succeeded in the later fifth and early sixth centuries by imported square-headed brooches and gold bracteates in the cemeteries of east Kent. The probability that the Hengest of Nennius, Bede and the *Anglo-Saxon Chronicle* is the same man as the Hengest of the *Finnesburgh fragment* associated with the eighth-century Christian poem *Beowulf* would make him a Jute, living in exile, and the leader of a war-band. Asser's *Life of Alfred*[21] recorded that Alfred the Great's mother claimed descent from Stuf and Wihtgar, who were Jutes. The same Stuf and Wihtgar are the first settlers of the Isle of Wight according to the *Anglo-Saxon Chronicle*.[22] Similarly, the Anglian kingdoms contain cemeteries whose brooch forms, notably the cruciform again, and cremation pottery, relate closely to the fifth-century finds in the cemeteries of Schleswig-Holstein and the Danish islands in the Baltic. The Mercian kings also claimed descent from the kings of *Angeln* on the Continent.[23]

The cultural link between the fifth-century Saxon settlement and cemetery finds in the Thames valley, between the Oxford region and the sites at Mucking (Essex) and Northfleet (Kent) at its estuary, and on the coasts of Sussex and Hampshire, and the finds in *Niedersachsen* and the northern Netherlands, are equally clear. The heartland of this Saxon culture was the region between the estuaries of the Weser and the Elbe. German archaeologists[24] have noted the appearance of Anglian pottery forms and decoration from Schleswig-Holstein and their influence on the Saxon pottery of this region in the period prior to the migration. They have termed the resulting fusion of Saxon and Anglian cultural elements, a mixed group culture (*Mischgruppe*). The fifth-century pottery forms of this region are found in Saxon England, whether the small biconical bowls commonly faceted on the carination (*Schalenurne*), or the large urns decorated with incised hanging arches (*stehende Bogen*) and bosses (*Buckelurne*). Brooch forms can be paralleled time and time again, whether of the equal-armed or Luton types not found in Sussex or Hampshire, or the applied and cast saucer brooches, which are developed as the principal brooch form of sixth-century Saxon England.

The region occupied by the Saxons on the Continent is part of the North European plain, of which East Anglia is an isolated extension. Its coastline on the North Sea is extremely low-lying and exposed to marine incursions, particularly in a period of rising sea level as was the case in the late Roman period. The general colonisation of this coastal region, first begun in the seventh or sixth centuries B.C. and renewed at the end of the first century B.C., was a reflection of the shortage of agricultural land. The marshlands of the coastal regions developed their own distinctive settlement type, consisting of wooden houses and outbuildings constructed on artificial mounds known as *terpen* in the Netherlands, and as *Wurten,* and sometimes as *Warften* or *Wierden,* in Germany. The mounds partly result from an accumulation of debris and animal dung in a restricted area, and partly from a deliberate build-up of thick clay layers to provide a building platform above flood level. Some of these terp settlements had to be abandoned in the third century A.D. as a result of rising sea level, but many terp mounds are still occupied by villages today. Their houses and farmyards are still organised in the same radial layout found in their Roman Iron Age predecessors, while the fields surrounding the terp also have a radial organisation.

The main house type found on the Iron Age *terpen* also survives to the present day. It is a long rectangular house with a length at least twice its width. Byres for stalling animals, mainly cattle, take up most of the structure with a small living area at one end. The livestock are stalled at the end of the house which faces the prevailing winds, providing a source of warmth for the partitioned-off living area as the draughts carry the body heat of the animals. The German term for this house type, the 'three-aisled-hall-house', describes its physical structure. The outer walls are fixed on to upright timber posts set in the ground. Within the outer rectangle two parallel rows of posts are set out down the length of the house to support the roof. These provide three internal aisles, the centre being a walkway between the animal stalls on either side. The outbuildings include granaries, which are raised off the ground to keep the stored grain dry, on groups of four or more upright posts. Other outbuildings are rather flimsy wooden sheds and sunken huts (*Grubenhäuser*). The sunken hut is constructed by excavating a sub-rectangular area to provide a lower floor level. A post is set in the middle of the two shorter ends and a roof constructed over the posts. More sophisticated versions can use four or more posts. These sunken huts and sheds seem to have been used for manufacturing purposes rather than for living accommodation.

A typical terp settlement is the partially excavated site of Feddersen Wierde on the Weser estuary to the north of Bremerhaven, Germany. The excavations of 1955–63 are not yet fully published, but the main phases have been described in interim reports.[25] The first settlement belongs late in the first century B.C. and in its early stages consisted of a number of separate farms each occupying its own low mound. It was during the first century A.D. that these coalesced into a developed terp, as the settlement grew to at least 30 houses with a radial plan. In the early second century, a significant development took place on the south-east edge of the settlement. A palisade and ditch were constructed separating a large house from the others. This house dominated this part of the settlement and around it was a concentration of workshop buildings for craftsmen working in wood, leather, antler, and bone. Within the palisade were other houses equipped with stalls, a number of granaries, and a building which has been interpreted as a meeting-hall, the equivalent, perhaps, of a village hall today. By this date there were probably some 50 houses in the settlement, varying in length from 30–10 metres, depending on the number of stalls, and in width from 7–5 metres. The obvious explanation for the palisaded enclosure is that one family had raised itself economically far above the level of its fellows. It is probable that this family continued to provide the chief man of the community by maintaining its economic and social status until the fourth century, and probably right down to the abandonment of the terp around the middle of the fifth century. The late phases of the settlement show no significant change, apart from the addition of bronze and ironworking to the crafts practised in the area of the chief's compound (*Herrenhof*).

The inland region, a lowland area of heaths, moors, bog and meadow, with extensive fertile districts, saw settlements with the same house, granary and hut types. These were not restricted to a confined space as they were on a terp, however, and we do not find the radial plan here. The site at Wijster (also known as Looveen) in the province of Drenthe, Netherlands, is fairly typical.[26] A single farmstead of the second century A.D. marks its earliest settlement. This was successively rebuilt on slightly different sites at least three times. By the beginning of the third century, there were three houses suggesting an extended family hamlet. The hamlet grew substantially during the third century with the houses and outbuildings organised in parallel rows. It is possible to detect a decline early in the fourth century, but after this the settlement grew again and was thoroughly replanned. It was organised into rectangular blocks marked off by palisades with streets between them. This settlement was finally abandoned at some date in the first half of the fifth century.

A question, which at present remains unanswered, is why no structures have yet been found in England equivalent to the three-aisled long houses on the Continent. Sunken huts have been discovered frequently here, and it is likely that some of them were lived in as well as being used as workshops. Rectangular posthole structures have been found at a few sites, such as West Stow (Suffolk),[27] Chalton (Hampshire),[28] and Bishopstone (Sussex).[29] Few of these houses, however, are even as large as the living areas of the Dutch and German long houses. Perhaps the milder climate of southern England made the winter stalling of livestock unnecessary, but the full answer must await the results of future excavation.

Pastoralism played a major part in Saxon farming and cattle were the main domestic animals, forming between one half and two thirds of their livestock. The cattle were small and short-horned. On the coastal marshlands with their treeless pasture land, sheep were the next most important animal. The mixed woodland areas of the riverine marshes and the inland region provided good pasture for pigs, which replaced sheep there as the main secondary element. The grain crops grown were principally barley and oats, while flax, beans, peas and various other vegetables were cultivated. We should not underestimate the technological capacity of the Saxons and other Germanic peoples in the fifth century. Too much attention has been paid to the technical inadequacies of their pottery, which was limited by the Saxons' ignorance of the potter's wheel. We should not forget that pottery vessels only fulfilled a few of their needs for containers and vessels, needs which were perhaps better served by vessels of wood and leather. The ability of Saxons to forge iron weapons and implements, and to cast and decorate gold, silver and bronze ornaments was little inferior to those of the Roman provincial craftsmen, from whom they were always prepared to learn. We must also recognise that trade with the Roman Empire and between Germanic peoples must have formed a source of income for many communities, especially those on the coast. The cultural level of the Saxon communities was far below that of the Romano-British aristocracy, but not very different from that of the Romano-British peasantry.

Saxon burial customs were traditionally based on the burning of the corpse on a pyre and the deposition of the cremated remains in the ground with, or without a pottery container. Cremation urns became increasingly elaborate during the fourth and fifth centuries, and as the jewellery and other objects buried had been distorted often beyond recognition in the process of cremation, cultural analysis has been based principally on pottery forms and decoration. The fourth and fifth centuries also see the increasingly widespread adoption of inhumation as an alternative burial rite there. The unburnt body is instead deposited in a rectangular grave. It has been suggested that inhumation was introduced from Denmark, but it is more probable that it represents the adoption of the late Roman burial practice. Traders and men who had served in the Roman army and later retired to die in their native land, such as the warrior of Liebenau (Germany) Grave I/1957,[30] may well have been responsible for the changed custom. In the Saxon cemeteries of Sussex, as elsewhere, in southern England, the practice of inhumation was more popular than cremation, and it was only in the Anglian regions, that is eastern and north-eastern England, that cremation remained the dominant rite.

The fifth century saw a large-scale abandonment of settlements and cemeteries on the North Sea littoral, whose communities took part in the migration, many apparently sailing to Britain. The pressures of over-population and rising sea level made such a migration inevitable. Many settlements were not to be reoccupied on the Continent until the eighth century, as was the case with Feddersen Wierde.

The fifth century settlement of Sussex

The *Anglo-Saxon Chronicle* contains three entries relevant to the earliest Saxon settlement of Sussex. Under the year 477 it is recorded that Aelle accompanied by three sons, Cymen, Wlencing and Cissa, landed from three ships at a place called *Cymenesora*. British resistance to the landing was broken, leaving some British dead and others fleeing to the safety of a forest called *Andredeslea*. Aelle fought the British again near the bank of a river or stream called *Mearcredesburna* in 485: the victor is not named. Finally, a fort called *Andredesceaster* was captured and its British occupants were all killed by a force commanded by Aelle and Cissa in 491 (or in version F, 490).

Both *Andredesceaster* and *Andredeslea* can be identified with the Saxon Shore fort of *Anderida* at Pevensey and with the forest of the Weald, especially the dense oak forest on the Weald Clay in the neighbourhood of Pevensey. *Cymenesora* is traditionally identified with Selsey Bill. The tradition is not firmly based, however, for it rests essentially on the mention of a place called 'Cumeneshora' in the boundary clause of a charter. The charter's text is preserved in a late copy and purports to represent a gift of an estate on the Selsey peninsula made by Caedwalla, king of the West Saxons to Bishop Wilfrid in 683 (BCS64).[31] Most scholars have agreed that as it stands this document is a forgery. Even those who wish to claim that beneath later distortions lies a genuine charter, must accept that the boundary clause is unacceptable for a seventh-century charter. The addition of an historical place-name to a boundary clause is an obvious trick to make a document appear authentic.

The location of *Cymenesora* at Selsey Bill has not been challenged in the past, because no detailed attempt has previously been made to reconcile the historical and archaeological evidence for the fifth-century settlement in Sussex. There are no finds of Saxon origin from the region of Selsey and Chichester datable earlier than the sixth century. Instead the settlements and cemeteries datable to the fifth century in the *civitas* of the *Regnenses* are at Portchester Castle;[32] and Droxford[33] to the west in Hampshire, and to the east in Sussex at Highdown Hill, Ferring;[34] Malling Hill, South Malling;[35] Rookery Hill, Bishopstone;[36] Alfriston;[37] and Selmeston.[38] The barrow burial finds from Beddingham Hill, Beddingham[39] and a spearhead from a grave at Upper Hamilton Road, Brighton,[40] possibly also date to the fifth century. As long ago as 1913, E. T. Leeds noted that the downland area between the rivers Ouse and Cuckmere contained the densest occupation in terms of early Saxon cemeteries in Sussex.[41] Four cemeteries of certain fifth-century date, and a fifth site possibly belonging to the fifth century, occupy strategic positions there. This area is restricted by the sea to the south and the Wealden forest to the north, as well as by rivers which form its west and east boundaries. A comparison of the distribution maps (Figs. 1 and 2) showing the early Saxon and Roman sites reveals that this same area does not contain a single villa. The only Roman sites known in this area were an early cremation cemetery at Seaford and some peasant farmsteads and hamlets. If any block of land in the *civitas* was dispensable to the villa-estate-owning aristocracy, this was probably it.

Did Aelle launch an invasion of the *civitas* with his small force of perhaps 100 men, or was he granted this land by the Romano-British authorities? The Ouse-Cuckmere settlement certainly has the appearance of a treaty arrangement and the *History of the Britons* of Nennius provides a context for such a treaty settlement in Sussex. Following Hengest's rebellion, we can follow a series of battles fought in Kent between the forces of Vortigern and Hengest both in Nennius[42] and in the *Anglo-Saxon Chronicle*.[43] It seems that neither side was able to obtain a decisive victory, and peace negotiations were begun presumably to arrange a treaty frontier. Vortigern came to meet Hengest accompanied by 300 elders (*seniores*), who may have been representatives from all the *civitates* of Britain. Hengest once again demonstrated his duplicity by having the British delegation murdered with the exception of Vortigern, who at the knife-point ceded Essex, Sussex, and in one version, also Middlesex, to the Saxons. This 'night of the long knives' has an apocryphal ring to it, but may nevertheless contain an element of truth.[44] The cession of Sussex is perhaps confirmed by the name of *Mearcredesburna*. Rivers can be named after individuals, such as 'the river of Mercred', but this is rare. Dr. J. Morris has pointed out that a far more probable translation is 'river of the frontier agreed by treaty'.[45] Both the Ouse and the Cuckmere would fit such a description.

The record of resistance to Aelle's landing need not conflict with the idea of a treaty settlement. Those who were to be dispossessed as a result of this agreement may have decided to contest it, and Aelle may have had to fight for the lands he had been granted. There are three aspects of the *Chronicle's* entries for 477 which suggest that the location of *Cymenesora* was in the Ouse-Cuckmere district, rather than at Selsey. Firstly, it is strange in view of the record of the later capture of Pevensey, that there is no mention of Chichester. In the second place, the flight of the Britons into the Wealden forest makes more sense in the Ouse-Cuckmere district than in the area of Selsey, which is distant from the Weald. Finally, a hostile force based on Pevensey would represent a real threat to the security of the Ouse-Cuckmere region, but not to nearly the same extent for the Selsey district.

We can perhaps see some support for a federate treaty, including grants of land in return for military service, in the evidence of the grave finds from the fifth century cemeteries. The large number of late Roman and fifth-century glass vessels from Highdown, and also the cemeteries at Alfriston and Selmeston, must be noted. There are also numerous pieces of late Roman or insular post-Roman metalwork, notably the brooches and buckles decorated in the Quoit Brooch style at the cemeteries of Highdown, Bishopstone and Alfriston. It is possible that these may represent loot from Romano-British sites, or result from bartering between the Saxons and the British. A perhaps more convincing explanation is that they were gifts and payments in kind to the Saxon grantees made by the Romano-British authorities.

What is the chronology of the fifth-century settlement of Sussex, and can we accept the dates attributed by the *Chronicle* to Aelle's three campaigns? While Dr. J. Morris certainly exaggerated when he claimed that *all* Bede's sources for fifth-century events are known to modern scholars,[46] his argument following C. E. Stevens,[47] that Gildas had misplaced in his narrative his one datable event, and that Bede failed to recognise this, remains convincing. A contemporary Gallic chronicler recorded that in 441–42:

> Britain, which had hitherto suffered various disasters, passed under the control of the Saxons.

This account, written far away in southern Gaul, by 452 at the latest, in all probability records Hengest's rebellion. If we are to fit all the events described by Gildas as coming between the first landing of Saxon mercenaries and this rebellion, we arrive at a date around 430 for the 'coming of the Saxons'. Yet Bede's several attempts to date that event come out around 450, and it is Bede's dating which is followed by the *Anglo-Saxon Chronicle*. Morris has proposed that all fifth-century dates in the *Chronicle* should be corrected by the subtraction of 20 years. On this basis, the entries for 477, 485 and 491 (490) should read *c.* 445, 465 and 470 respectively. There is general agreement that the earliest graves from published cemeteries in Sussex can be dated to around the middle of the fifth century, and certainly there are more fifth-century graves than can be comfortably accommodated in the period 475–500.

Bede makes no attempt to date Aelle's reign, other than to point out that Aelle was the first king to exercise overlordship over the kingdoms south of the Humber, and that the next king to hold such power was Ceawlin of the West Saxons in the sixth century.[49] The *Chronicle* gives a title to this overlordship, naming its holder *bretwalda* (version A), or more properly *brytenwealda*.[50] The question of the extent of Aelle's authority among the Anglo-Saxons in Britain in the second half of the fifth century is virtually impossible to answer. It seems highly improbable that he exercised the powers of later *brytenwealdas* over the rulers of the other emergent Anglo-Saxon kingdoms. Most historians have suggested that he was the most senior of the kings, who in alliance attacked the British in the ill-fated campaign at the end of the fifth century, which saw the decisive defeat of the Anglo-Saxons by Arthur at Mount Badon. According to Gildas, this setback to the Anglo-Saxons resulted in a peace which lasted his lifetime.[51] The suggestion made by Dr. J. N. L. Myres, on the basis of the limited number of pottery vessels from Sussex cemeteries, that Sussex was one of the regions abandoned by the Saxons after Mount Badon, does not bear critical examination.[52] Continued use of the Highdown and Alfriston cemeteries through the first half of the sixth century is demonstrable from metalwork buried there, notably the zoomorphic decorated saucer brooches and the square-headed brooches.

If we accept that Aelle's kingdom was centred on the Ouse-Cuckmere district, where do the cemeteries at Brighton, Highdown and Droxford, and the settlement at Portchester Castle fit in? The evidence of a single spearhead, which, though probably fifth century, might be later, cannot be accepted as firm evidence of a fifth-century settlement at Brighton. The cemetery on Highdown Hill, however, is certainly contemporary with that at Alfriston. It probably represents an isolated community of mercenaries placed on this strategic hilltop within the ramparts of an Iron Age hillfort, which may have been recommissioned in the late Roman period. A settlement there would command views over the entire coastal plain and the sea. The Saxon occupation of Portchester Castle began around the middle of the fifth century. Diagnostic pieces include part of an applied brooch from a sunken hut and an iron strike-a-light and disc brooch from a well, datable to the second half of the fifth or early sixth century. Interestingly, a disc brooch not unlike that from Portchester was also found at *Clausentum* (Bitterne).[53] The Droxford cemetery seems to belong towards the end of the fifth century and may thus be contemporary with the cemetery at Worthy Park, Kingsworthy, just outside Winchester.[54] The historical evidence sees both Portchester and the Meon Valley as part of the West Saxon kingdom. It may well be that the settlement at Portchester was contemporary with, but not under the authority of, Aelle.

Professor Cunliffe has developed the theme of the Ouse-Cuckmere treaty settlement,[55] first proposed by the present author in 1971.[56] He suggested that Portchester Castle and Droxford might represent with Highdown two similar cessions of blocks of territory to the Saxons. Four Romano-British territories are seen, centred on Winchester, Chichester, possibly Hassocks, and Pevensey, with Saxon federate territories sandwiched between them in the Meon Valley and Portchester, the Arun–Adur block, and the Ouse–Cuckmere district. Attractive though this is, it seems over-ambitious to define a block of territory on the basis of a single site at Highdown. Equally, the territory associated with Portchester and Droxford does not have well-defined geographical limits, and there are chronological problems in relating these sites to those of Winchester and its district. Finally, the need to have a late Roman urban or military centre for each of the Romano-British territories requires the elevation of a few scattered sites near Hassocks to the status of a major Roman settlement. Fresh archaeological evidence is therefore needed to justify Cunliffe's thesis.

Sixth-century Sussex

The successful capture of Pevensey of *c.* 470 freed the South Saxons from Romano-British control, and their settlement was able to expand at the expense of the British. Our historical sources desert us for the sixth century, and we do not know the names of the South Saxon kings nor their political and military activities. We can make some guesses, however, from the archaeological record.

A new settlement on Ocklynge Hill, Eastbourne,[57] was made possible by the capture of Pevensey. The majority of grave finds from its earliest cemetery have been lost, but the few written descriptions of them make it probable that it was first occupied in the sixth century. The main direction of colonisation was westward from the Ouse-Cuckmere district across the River Adur to link up with the settlement on Highdown Hill. The cemetery at Saxonbury, Kingston-by-Lewes,[58] and the cemeteries and burials in the area of Brighton and westwards mainly near the coast to Lancing, belong to the sixth and seventh centuries. The kingdom of the South Saxons remained centred on the Ouse-Cuckmere district in the sixth century.

West of the Arun only two objects can be assigned with certainty to the sixth century. They are a small-long brooch, said to have been found at St. Pancras[59] (Plate 1:1), a suburb immediately outside the east gate of Chichester, and a gilt bronze saucer brooch with a seven spiral coil design found unstratified and unassociated at Singleton[60] to the north of Chichester (Plate 1:2). The latter's fittings had been broken off, and a hole drilled through it so that it could be worn as a pendant. A disc decorated with human mask designs and animal figures in Salin Style I from the Chichester district[61] (Plate 1:4), probably belongs to the seventh rather than the sixth century.

The fate of Chichester is unknown, for while it seems to have been abandoned during the fifth century, there is as yet little archaeological evidence for its reoccupation before the ninth century.[62] The name Chichester has been taken to suggest that it may have been named after Cissa, one of Aelle's 'sons', just as Lancing has been thought to derive from Wlencing. The town must increasingly have been more of a fortified refugee camp than an urban centre during the fifth century. With the seizure of villa estates by the Saxons during the later fifth and sixth centuries its function as a shelter to the Romano-British magnates disappeared. By the time the Saxons entered the town, there were probably only a few squatters left in its ruins.

It is often claimed that the Weald was a great barrier behind which the South Saxon kingdom developed in isolation, a view which takes literally Wilfrid's biographer's explanation of the late survival of paganism there. But Roman roads traversed the Weald and some of them were still in working order centuries later. The Saxon fashions in brooch decoration of the Thames valley, which exercised great influence in Sussex in the fifth and sixth centuries, demonstrate that these roads must have formed an important means of external communication. Time and time again, a design popular on applied or saucer brooches in the Upper Thames cemeteries of the Oxford region is to be found also in Surrey, West Kent, or Essex, and also in Sussex. This pattern repeats itself in the great square-headed form; recent excavation of a cemetery at Berinsfield in Oxfordshire[63] produced a brooch of a type hitherto represented only in the Surrey cemeteries of Mitcham[64] and Guildown,[65] and thrice at Alfriston. The sea was apparently a less important means of external contact. The Frankish fashions, which held such an important place in the material culture of east Kent and the Isle of Wight in the sixth century, are only palely reflected in Sussex. Finds such as the perforated spoon from Alfriston Grave 62, the pair of silver gilt bird brooches from High-down Grave 19, and the angon also from Highdown, are relatively rare. They may have reached the South Saxons either directly from France, or indirectly in coastal trade with their Jutish neighbours.

The seventh century and the Christian conversion

The seventh century saw the abandonment of the Sussex cemeteries used in the fifth and sixth centuries. The phenomenon of the double cemetery well known from Leighton Buzzard (Bedfordshire)[66] and Winnall (Hampshire)[67] occurs at Eastbourne. It involves the abandonment of the existing cemetery and the setting up of a new cemetery nearby, which obviously still served the same community. A large cemetery consisting of inhumation graves laid out in neat orderly rows with the graves orientated west-east, stretched along the ridge of Ocklynge Hill. The grave finds mainly consisted of iron knives with a few iron spearheads and buckles. They contrast strongly with the variety of grave finds, including two swords, a bronze-bound bucket, and glass vessels in the earlier cemetery, found on the southern part of the ridge around what is now the Eastbourne College of Further Education.[68] A similar cemetery to that at Eastbourne was partially excavated nearby at Crane Down, Jevington, and has been dated by Miss V. I. Evison[69] to the late seventh or early eighth century. The change of burial place we see at Eastbourne and elsewhere in England in the seventh century was apparently brought about by the Christian missions. In the late cemeteries we see changes of dress fashions with dress pins replacing brooches for fixing women's clothes. At the same time, the men are rarely buried with weapons except for a knife. It may be that the second Eastbourne cemetery antedated the mission of Bishop Wilfrid in the 680s and reflected acceptance as a new fashion of burial practices and dress fashions from already Christian kingdoms such as Kent. The eighth century saw the beginning of churchyard burials in which no grave finds accompany the dead.

A series of inhumation burials, usually only accompanied by a knife, have been found in barrows along the Downs. These were probably seventh century, but there is still little archaeological evidence for occupation of the Selsey and Chichester district in this period. The settlement site at Medmerry Farm[70] and the decorated pot from Pagham churchyard[71] are probably later in date, and a few fragments of goldwork[72] and a Byzantine buckle[73] (Plates 1:3, 5-8) are the only objects which can certainly be attributed to the seventh century. The westward colonisation observed in the sixth century may have continued in the late sixth and seventh centuries into what is now east Hampshire. The cemetery at Snell's Corner, Horndean[74] and the settlement recently excavated at Chalton[75] are on the Downs just over the Hampshire border, but separate from the regions of Portsdown and the Meon Valley, which are known to have been part of the West Saxon kingdom. The striking likeness between a pottery vessel from Horndean and two pots at Highdown suggests this possibility, and the discovery of the cemetery of Chalton may confirm it. The only other archaeological evidence we have to suggest the frontier with the West Saxons is the series of earthworks around Droxfield[76] near the north-west corner of the county boundary with Hampshire.

By the 680s, when the mission of Bishop Wilfrid attracts historical comment, there is no doubt that the region of Selsey and Chichester was the political centre of the kingdom. The king of the South Saxons granted Wilfrid an estate on the Selsey peninsula; on which to build a monastery. Wilfrid's biographer also adds that the estate had belonged to the king himself.[77] Wilfrid was a Northumbrian noble by birth, who enjoyed politics and was not one to shun his obligations to convert the South Saxons through their king. We can presume, then, that a royal hall was not far distant, probably one of the several scattered through the kingdom. The place-name of Kingsham in Donnington parish, south-west of Chichester, is suggestive of a royal manor.[78] Wilfrid's acceptance or choice of Selsey is interesting in that it parallels the position of the early monastery on the island at Lindisfarne in Northumbria. Bede's description of Selsey emphasised the isolation of the peninsula reached across a causeway, while Lindisfarne can only be reached at low tide. While Lindisfarne stands opposite the Bernician royal citadel and capital of Bamburgh, Selsey has a similar relationship to Chichester. It may well be that a royal palace complex, perhaps not dissimilar to that excavated at Yeavering in Northumberland,[79] existed within the walls of Chichester. Dr. D. M. Metcalf has made a case for a sceatta coinage (B.M.C. 3a) being minted at Chichester, probably in the second quarter of the eighth century.

The type has an essentially coastal distribution including two examples found in Sussex (Plate 6). A similar coin exists with the curious inscription R–X CIC in boustrophedon on the reverse, which has been tentatively interpreted as *Rex Cicestriae*[80] (Plate 6). There is as yet no firm documentary or archaeological evidence, however, to support the speculation that Chichester was the capital of the kingdom.

Wilfrid's intention in accepting the estate on Selsey was to found a monastery, but it is by no means certain that he intended this monastery to become a bishop's see. Despite the testimony of his biographer and Bede, Wilfrid should not be regarded as the first bishop of the South Saxons, for he still claimed to hold the see of Northumbria. In general, at least one see was created per kingdom, but, according to Bede,[81] for political reasons, the clergy in Sussex were subject to the bishop of Winchester for many years after Wilfrid's departure in 686. The community at Selsey was finally able to elect a bishop of its own around 705–709. As Roman towns had been chosen almost without exception throughout England, the obvious choice for the see of the South Saxons was Chichester. Inertia within the Selsey monastic community and a pious reverence for St. Wilfrid are the most probable explanations for the see's remaining at Selsey from the early eighth century until the move in 1075 to Chichester.

Bede's account of the gift of the Selsey estate also enables us to glimpse the probable fate of the British under Saxon rule. Wilfrid's first act was to free 250 male and female slaves tied to the estate. Despite the massacres recorded in Aelle's reign, the British peasantry would have remained on their land, much as they did after the Norman Conquest. The Saxons may have lowered their legal status to serfdom or slavery, but there was probably little difference in their material conditions. They farmed for the Saxon instead of the Romano-British landlord. Inter-marriage may well have taken place, and the disc brooch form popular in the later fifth and sixth centuries perhaps indicates this. There are no precursors for the disc brooch in Scandinavia, or Germany, but we can see an origin in the disc brooches of late Iron Age and Roman Britain. The decoration of the disc brooches is often derived from Roman motifs, usually of circle, and circle and dot designs, incised with a compass, or stamped designs, notable a triangle containing three dots. These brooches were worn in pairs on the shoulders by women. Possibly these were British women married to Saxon warriors.

Wilfrid's mission to the South Saxons was not the first contact Aethelwealh, or Aethelwold, king of the South Saxons, and his subjects had with Christianity. It has been suggested that the consecration of a South Saxon called Damianus as bishop of Rochester in the 650s, recorded by Bede,[82] may indicate missionary work in Sussex in the first half of the seventh century. As the only other information we are given concerning Damianus is the time of his death, we cannot assume that he was converted to Christianity, or brought up as a Christian in Sussex. It is more probable that his ecclesiastical training and experience were in the kingdom of Kent. At the time of Wilfrid's mission, a monastery containing five or six monks led by an Irishman, Dicuil (Dicul), existed at Bosham (*Bosenhamm*). Bede does not inform us how long they had been settled there, but condemns the community for its failure to proselytise the faith.[83] Finally, both Bede[84] and the *Anglo-Saxon Chronicle* record Aethelwealh's earlier baptism at which Wulfhere, king of the Mercians stood sponsor. The date of the *Chronicle* entry, 661, is improbable in the light of Bede's statement that this baptism took place 'not long before' Wilfrid's mission of 680–681. The entry for 661 is clearly a conflation of several events, for example placing Wilfrid's mission to the Isle of Wight in 686 in Wulfhere's reign (657–674). Both Bede and the *Chronicle* agree that Wulfhere gave the Isle of Wight to Aethelwealh at his baptism, and Bede adds the province of the Meon Valley (*Meanuarorum provincia*) to this gift. The *Chronicle* credits Aethelwealh with assisting Wulfhere to seize Wight from the West Saxons. Professor C. F. C. Hawkes has pointed out that Wulfhere's campaign, at the end of his reign, culminating in the battle of *Biedanheafele* makes a convincing context for the seizure of West Saxon territory, which accompanied Aethelwealh's baptism.[85] It was immediately after the baptism that Aethelwealh married Eaba, a princess of the Hwicce, a tributary people of the Mercian kingdom.

It should not surprise us if Aethelwealh, baptised at his overlord's request, was half-hearted about the new religion. His behaviour was perhaps not so very different from that of Raewald of the East Anglians who, baptised at Aethelberht of Kent's insistence, placed the Christian altar in his pagan temple beside those of his traditional gods.[86] The king in early Anglo-Saxon society retained a priestly role, and as the history of the East Saxons in the seventh century illustrated on several occasions,[87] in a crisis would tend to turn to the old gods rather than trust in the new religion, when acting on behalf of his people.

The reality of paganism in Sussex is illustrated by an incident which took place in 666 on a voyage prior to Wilfrid's mission here. His ship went aground apparently near Selsey, and Wilfrid's biographer records that the ship was attacked by South Saxons, urged on by a pagan priest, who sought to cast magic spells on the Christians from a high mound.[88] A second example is Bede's reference to mass suicide committed by groups of 40 or 50 men jumping off cliffs, made desperate by the famine which was the result of a three-year drought.[89] It is probable that the suicides represented sacrifices to appease Woden. Rain fell on the day of Wilfrid's mass baptism of the South Saxons and this miracle guaranteed his success.

As we have seen, Wilfrid's biographer exaggerated the isolation of the South Saxon kingdom. His statement that the rocky coast and dense forest protected the kingdom from conquest in the seventh century has an element of poetic licence about it. The *Anglo-Saxon Chronicle* records Ceowulf of the West Saxons fighting the South Saxons in 607. The outcome of his campaign is not mentioned, but it is probable that the South Saxons had to pay tribute and recognise Ceowulf's overlordship. No such ambiguity exists in Wulfhere's relationship to Aethelwealh in the 660s and/or the 670s. Wulfhere was the most powerful Anglo-Saxon ruler of his day. An assessment of the taxation and tribute from the Mercian kingdom and its tributary states, including the kingdoms of Wessex,

Sussex and Kent, as well as Surrey, known as the *Tribal Hidage*,[90] perhaps belongs to his reign. Aethelwealh was well aware that he did not have the power to resist a Mercian attack, and was probably happy to reap the rewards of a loyal tributary to a successful overlord, which at the same time presumably freed him from paying tribute to the West Saxons. The more distant control of a Mercian king in the Midlands must have been preferable to that of the West Saxons. It was not long after Aethelwealh's second baptism by Wilfrid, and certainly before 685, that he was killed by an exiled West Saxon prince Caedwalla.[91] Two South Saxon ealdormen (*duces*), Berthun and Audhun, succeeded in driving Caedwalla's war band out of the kingdom. Their success was short-lived, for Caedwalla became king of the West Saxons and conquered the South Saxons, killing Berthun in the process. Caedwalla's successor, Ine, apparently inherited the subject kingdom of the South Saxons, and Bede notes that the subjection went as far as to place the South Saxon clergy under the bishop of Winchester. Ine's authority did not go unchallenged, however, for in 722 and 725, the *Chronicle* records campaigns against the South Saxons.

The charter and place-name evidence

William of Malmesbury[92] names Aethelwealh's successor as Eadric, but no other source mentions him, and he may have been confused with the Eadric who became king of Kent with South Saxon assistance in 685–86. The next South Saxon king is Nothelm, who granted or confirmed a group of charters at the end of the seventh and the beginning of the eighth century. One of these documents (BCS78) reveals that Nothelm had a contracted form to his name, Nunna, for while the grant was made by Nothelm as king of the South Saxons, the first witness was Nunna, similarly styled king. Nothelm was almost certainly the same man as the Nun (Nunna in versions B and C) recorded in the *Chronicle* as fighting with Ine against the British in 710. In versions A, D and E, he is described as Ine's kinsman (*maege*), which might well imply that he had married a West Saxon princess.

The 17 charters, which purport to record grants of land in the South Saxon kingdom, in the late seventh and eighth centuries, are extremely difficult to interpret.[93] With the exception of one document, they survive in copies made much later with all the dangers entailed in the copyist's misunderstanding of the words and meaning of the original text. Forgery must also be taken into account, and there are many grounds for dismissing the two charters which claim to represent the granting of the Selsey estate to Wilfrid (BCS50 and 64).[94] We are extremely fortunate that one original copy has survived in the Chichester archives of the late-eighth-century charter granted by the ealdorman Oslac, and confirmed by Offa, king of the Mercians (BCS1334). Its authenticity has been demonstrated beyond all reasonable doubt by Dr. P. Chaplais,[95] and it can therefore serve as a model against which we can test these charters. Its text is brief and limits itself to simply naming the two places being granted. No boundaries are given, and indeed in other contemporary copies of seventh- and eighth-century charters in England, the bounds, where given, are limited to a brief mention in Latin of the four points of the compass. The rambling boundary clauses in Old English, which are attached to many of these early Sussex charters, are later additions. They do not necessarily seek to deceive, but we must accept that they represent the estate boundaries of the tenth and eleventh centuries, rather than those of the eighth. They must be used therefore with caution.

A case in point is a grant of 16 hides of land at Stanmer, Lindfield and Burleigh, which despite the corruptions in its text, and the addition of a late boundary clause in Old English, has the appearance of a genuine document (BCS197). The estate is of some interest as it consists of a core of good agricultural land on the Downs at Stanmer, and, if we accept the information of the boundary clause as giving some indication of the eighth-century estate, the rich soils immediately below the downland scarp. It also contains land in the Weald, including swine pastures. Its layout resembles closely the lathe organisation of east Kent, discussed by J. E. A. Jolliffe in his classic study of early medieval agricultural organisation in south-east England.[96] In Kent, the kingdom was divided into districts called lathes, each containing a royal centre (the *villæ regales*). Each lathe contained a cross-section of the different lands available: some ploughland, some pasture, and a share of the wastelands of the Weald, and in each lathe the king owned a share of each type of land. Thus each lathe was an economic and social whole, and its free peasantry contributed to the maintenance of the king. The Stanmer estate stretching north to Burleigh almost on the Surrey border, strongly suggests that the South Saxon kingdom was organised in the same way. Jolliffe strained the evidence somewhat in his attempts to contrast a 'Jutish' or rather Kentish system, with what he saw as the contemporary 'Saxon' system. The problems thus created might well be resolved if, one day, it can be demonstrated that the 'Saxon' system represents later agricultural practice imposed in Sussex on top of the lathe organisation, to a degree not experienced in Kent.

It has already been suggested that the Wealden region of Sussex to the east of Pevensey may have lain outside the jurisdiction of the *civitas*. The total absence of archaeological evidence for its occupation by Anglo-Saxons between the fifth and eighth centuries is remarkable. We know from historical sources and the evidence of place-names that there were people living there by the eighth century. The *Haestingas* are recorded by eight *-ingas* and seven *-inga* place-names within the Rape of Hastings, but outliers are indicated by Hastingford in the parish of Hadlow Down, and Hastingleigh in Kent. The variety of names found in this group contrast with the uniformity of the Ginges and Rodings groups in Essex. Dr. J. McN. Dodgson has suggested that they represent a confederation of folks, in which each constituent folk retained its identity, but the politically dominant folk extended its name to its own focal settlement at Hastings, and over the whole territory and membership of the confederacy.[97] The *Chronicle's* entries for 1011 and 1049 (version D) demonstrate that the identity of the *Haestingas* survived into the eleventh century. The earliest date mentioned for them is preserved by a twelfth-century source attributed to Simeon of Durham. This saw Offa of Mercia conquering the 'people of Hastings' (*Hestingorum gentem*) in 771.[98] It is interesting to note that an extremely corrupt charter text, claiming a date of 772, purports to be a grant by Offa to the bishop of Selsey of an estate near Bexhill (BCS208).

C. T. Chevallier has pointed out that a hitherto unidentified king, who witnessed three charters in the reign of Nothelm (Nunna) as *Wattus rex* (BCS144, 78, and 80) may have ruled the *Haestingas*.[99] Place-names with 'Wat' or 'What' elements do occur in the Hastings region, but are not found in western Sussex. His suggestion that Watt was a sub-king to the South Saxons is plausible. It is when Chevallier goes on to suggest a Frankish origin for the *Haestingas* on the basis of a single place-name, Watten, in north-east France, that his argument becomes less acceptable. It has long been recognised that extensive Saxon settlement took place on the north coast of France, and similarities of place-names need not imply a Frankish origin. A far more plausible explanation is that the folks, who later formed the confederacy of the *Haestingas*, migrated from Kent. If we accept Chevallier's explanation of *Wattus rex*, this migration cannot be later than the seventh century. Kent was the first kingdom to be converted to Christianity at the beginning of the seventh century, and the innovations of the simplified burial rite first appeared there. The total lack of archaeological evidence for the *Haestingas* is less puzzling, if we assume that they were Christian colonists from Kent.

In recent years place-name scholars have reassessed the earliest Old English place-names, notably the *-ingas* formations.[100] If we plot only the oldest forms of *-ingas*, *-ingahām*, and *-wīchām* names on a map, comparison with the archaeological distribution of sites between the fifth and eighth centuries shows them to be on the periphery of the archaeological distribution. In the Selsey peninsula and the coastal plain, they seem to represent seventh-century or later settlement for which no archaeological evidence is at present forthcoming. Thus, the *-ingas* names surrounding Highdown Hill may represent settlements founded after the abandonment of the hilltop site around the beginning of the seventh century. With the exception of the mainly coastal settlements of the *Haestingas*, few of these early forms are found in the Weald. The later forms of *-inga* names are those which record the Wealden settlement. It is clear that the early South Saxons farmed the lands already under cultivation in the Roman period and that, as late as the eighth century, exploitation of the Weald was almost everywhere limited to swine pasturage and timber extraction, with perhaps some iron-working.

Epilogue

The eighth-century charters reveal the names of the South Saxon rulers as Nothelm, Watt, Aethelstan, Aethelberht, Osmund, Oswald, Oslac, Aelhwald, and Ealdwulf. The presence of at least two dynasties has been proposed on the grounds of the predominance of *Aethel-* and *Os-* names. By the 770s Mercian overlordship had been asserted over the whole of southern England, including Sussex, and was maintained by Offa and his immediate successors. Offa went much further than any previous Mercian or West Saxon overlord towards the integration of the tributary kingdoms as provinces of a kingdom of the English. Ealdwulf was perhaps the last South Saxon ruler able to style himself 'king', for in charters of the 780s and 790s (BCS262, 261 and 1334) Ealdwulf and Oslac granted lands as ealdormen (*duces*). Mercian power was shattered by Ecgberht of Wessex's campaigns of 825 and 829.[101] The West Saxon triumph only shortly preceded the Viking invasion which destroyed Northumbria, East Anglia and Mercia. The West Saxon kingdom alone survived the Viking onslaught and under Alfred the Great and his successors re-conquered England. By this time, however, Sussex was a shire of Wessex and had no independent role to play.

ACKNOWLEDGEMENTS

I should like to thank Mrs. Sonia Hawkes and Mr. David Brown for reading and commenting on the manuscript. I also wish to acknowledge my debt to unpublished lectures and discussions with a number of historians in Oxford, including Dr. J. Campbell, Dr. P. Chaplais, Dr. H. Mayr-Harting, Dr. E. Stone, and Mr. P Wormald.

III

SAXON SETTLEMENTS AND BUILDINGS IN SUSSEX[1]

Martin Bell

SUSSEX IS a county of small valley and vale villages which typically comprise only a few dozen old habitations, one or two manor farms and a pond, all clustered around their church. The names of many such settlements are of Saxon origin and it is often assumed that their historic core reflects a settlement plan established early in the Saxon period. A small but growing body of archaeological evidence is a basis from which to test this hypothesis, and to examine the extent to which continuity and change played their part in the development of the Anglo-Saxon settlement pattern.

Archaeological evidence has the advantage of giving us information about the character and exact location of settlements and their component buildings. For the pagan period, in particular, we must rely entirely on archaeological finds together with the place-name evidence. Yet the interpretation which we can put on this archaeological evidence is strictly limited by its quantity and patchy distribution. Seven sites have produced traces of secular buildings, and find spots of pottery and artifacts indicate the locations of another 35 settlements. This is a small number of sites representing a period of some 600 years, when compared, for instance, to 170 finds which point to the location of settlements during the Iron Age, a period of roughly the same duration.[2] We are therefore dependent upon a range of sources which include history, church architecture and place-names. Indeed, the paucity of the archaeological record taken alone becomes even more apparent when compared to these other sources of evidence for the existence of Anglo-Saxon settlements; 337 listed in Domesday Book, 111 mentioned in charters, 157 with names ending in *-ham* and *-ingas* and 26 places with definite surviving pre-Conquest churches. This is not to enumerate all those other places the names of which suggest they were pre-Conquest foundations. From these various sources, with the exception of the last, we have evidence of some 473 settlements in the period between the fifth century and 1086; of those only 7.4 per cent. are represented by archaeological finds.

One explanation is that Saxon settlements must frequently be covered by existing villages which, especially in these enlightened days of conservation areas, are unlikely to produce chance archaeological finds. Of equal significance is the fact that, until recently, we had very little knowledge of the types of pottery in use during this period in Sussex.

The earliest Saxon settlements

In recent years, many of the assumptions upon which our understanding of the Saxon settlement pattern was based have been questioned. It has been demonstrated that the distribution of place-names with the suffix -ingas, as in Ferring or Ovingdean, is inconsistent with the long-held belief that they were the earliest English settlements.[3] Archaeological research has, at the same time, shown that some at least of what we now believe, on archaeological evidence, to be the earliest Saxon settlements are distinguished by a hill top, or at least elevated, location; examples are West Stow, Suffolk; Mucking, Essex; Church Down at Chalton, Hants.; and Rookery Hill at Bishopstone, Sussex. These are failed settlements, the names of which are apparently lost.

Failed settlements imply the habitation of rather marginal land indicating that some of the earliest Saxon settlements may have been fitted into the less desirable areas of a landscape which was still primarily Romano-British. A possible instance is the downland between the rivers Ouse and Cuckmere in Sussex which contained no villa estates, yet here were all of the known fifth-century Anglo-Saxon cemeteries of the county with the exception of Highdown. Martin Welch has suggested that this was a treaty area settled by mercenaries hired in the fifth century to protect Romano-British interests.[4] The excavation of one of these fifth-century cemeteries on Rookery Hill at Bishopstone resulted in the discovery of an associated settlement. The first part of this paper is concerned particularly with that site and with later historically documented developments in its environs.

Rookery Hill, Bishopstone[5]

The site is on Rookery Hill, a spur of chalk downland which rises to 50 metres, runs south and projects as a promontory into the alluvial flats at the mouth of the River Ouse. (Fig. 3). This is a commanding position overlooking the English Channel and the river mouth which would have provided a safe anchorage. The crest of this spur was occupied at various times since the mid-third millennium B.C. In the Iron Age and Romano-British periods a small farming settlement lay within ditched enclosures on the hill top, surrounded by 'Celtic fields' on its sides. Occupation at the end of the Romano-British period is attested by late fourth- or early-fifth-century pottery. This does not, however, provide sufficiently reliable dating evidence to demonstrate whether or not there was a period of desertion prior to the founding of the Anglo-Saxon settlement, an event which, in all probability, occurred about the mid-fifth century A.D.

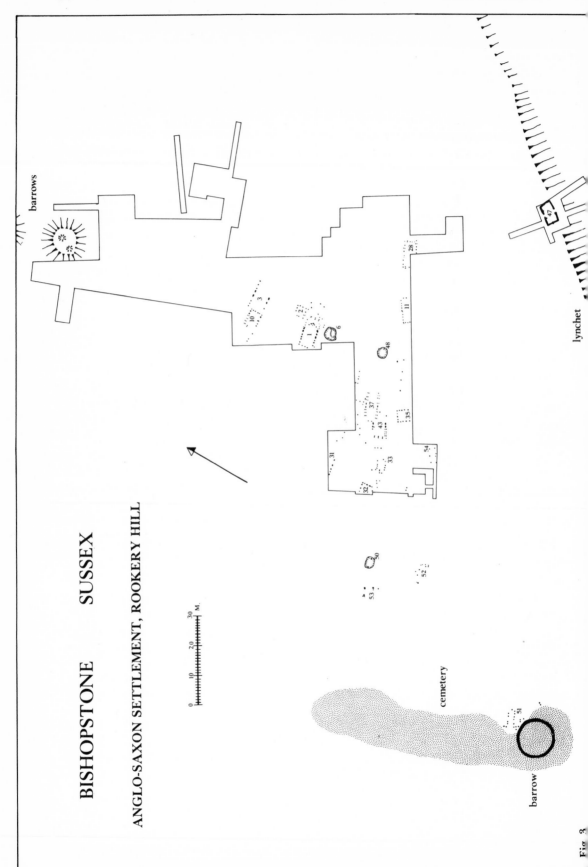

BISHOPSTONE SUSSEX

ANGLO-SAXON SETTLEMENT, ROOKERY HILL

Fig. 3

It is, however, possible to reconstruct some aspects of the landscape within which the Anglo-Saxons chose to settle. Land molluscs show that primary woodland or forest of Neolithic date had, by the Iron Age, been replaced by a short turf flora. The scene when the Saxons arrived must have been of a cleared landscape with fields not long abandoned on the spur sides, and visible traces of the late Romano-British settlement on its summit. Surrounding the promontory on three sides was flooded or marshy land. In situations such as this where a Romano-British site had only recently been deserted we might expect to find continuity of occupation from late Romano-British to early Anglo-Saxon times. Settlements are after all the nodes of a region, the points to which trackways lead, the focus of infield, and a spot at which old timbers, hearthstones and artifacts might be acquired for re-use. Such considerations were probably secondary, however, to the commanding position which the site offered.

The continuity of settlement site is overshadowed by a discontinuity of settlement type. In the Iron Age and Romano-British period the hill was occupied by a small farm, surrounded by its fields, and inhabited perhaps by a single extended family. The Anglo-Saxon site was a large nucleated settlement which partly covered the Romano-British fields, the lynchets of which were utilised as suitable terraces for buildings. The scatter of Anglo-Saxon pottery suggests that the settlement covered at least three hectares (7.4 acres). The one hectare (2.5 acres) excavated between 1967 and 1975 has revealed the sites of 22 buildings, indicating that in the whole settlement there could be up to sixty.

On the west side of the area occupied by buildings a Bronze Age barrow was utilised as the focus of the cemetery, which was excavated by Mr. David Thomson in 1967–8.[6] The cemetery spread out to the north of the barrow forming a shallow crescent, 94m. long by 20m. wide; it comprised 118 burials of which six were cremations and the remainder inhumations. One object from the cemetery has been published; it is a Quoit Brooch Style buckle, which may indicate settlement here as early as the first half of the fifth century.[7] Later Mr. Thomson found the first traces of the settlement, a timber building next to the barrow and a sunken hut, with parts of at least two timber buildings a little uphill and to the north-east of the cemetery. Subsequent excavations[8] further to the north-east have revealed a considerable area of Saxon buildings (Plate 2).

The buildings (Figs. 3 and 4)

The 22 buildings excavated[9] are of four main types, three are sunken huts, 17 are rectangular buildings founded on individual post holes, one is represented by post holes between which are beam slots, and one by eight single large posts. In view of the fact that, until recently, nearly all the Anglo-Saxon buildings known in England were sunken huts, it is instructive to find them greatly outnumbered by post hole buildings at Bishopstone. When taken with similar evidence from other recent excavations it indicates that sunken huts are greatly

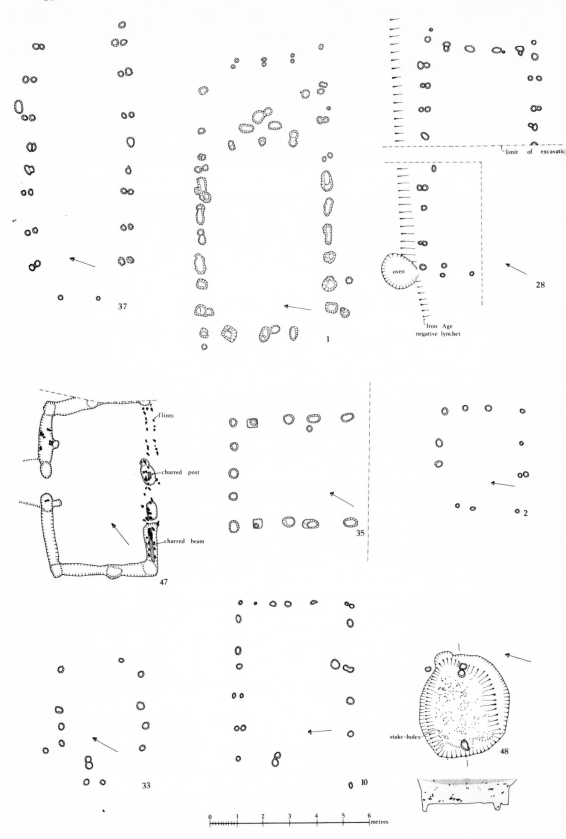

Fig. 4   Anglo-Saxon buildings at Rookery Hill, Bishopstone

over-represented in the archaeological record; they alone are visible in quarry faces and on building sites. This we must bear in mind when we consider the evidence for middle- and late-Saxon settlements in Sussex.

An example of the sunken hut was Structure 48, an oval pit 3.8m. by 3.4m. and 90cm. deep. In the middle of the two shorter sides were large post holes, one of which had been replaced during the life of the building. On the pit floor were 197 small stakeholes, which appeared to have been man-made. No definitely associated post holes were found outside the pit in the vicinity of any of the sunken huts. It is assumed, therefore, that the two post holes took gable principal timbers joined by a ridge piece. A reconstruction of a sunken hut, based in part on one excavated at Bishopstone, has been made at the Weald and Downland Open Air Museum, Singleton (Plate 3). It was based on the assumption that the bottom of the pit was the surface occupied. The gable posts and ridge piece take a thatched tent-like structure with sides that rest directly on the ground. The gable ends are infilled with wattle and daub.

The rectangular post hole buildings were of a wide variety of sizes from large hall-like structures to small square sheds. One of the largest was No. 37 (Plate 4), which was 10m. long by 4m. wide. The side walls were of paired posts bowed out in the centre by about 30cm. Opposing doorways were situated in the middle of the longest walls. The gable walls were only represented by two shallow post holes cut at the west end, none was found at the east end, nor were there any corner posts. The bowed side walls must have resulted in a curved ridge piece known as a hog-backed roof, a shape which was an adaptation to reduce wide stress on a very long building.[10]

Buildings 1, 28 and 3 were of comparable dimensions to the bow-sided building. Structure 1 (Plate 5) was more substantially built than the others and had at least two phases of construction. In its first phase it measured 7m. by 5m. At the centre of the side walls, in a position usually occupied by the doorways, were three massive post holes 40cm. deep, indicating perhaps a two-storey building. In the second phase the length was extended to 10m. and the walls were reconstructed of slighter double posts. Rather less complicated is Structure 28, of which, unfortunately, only three-quarters has been excavated. The side walls were of double posts with an entrance in the north side and probably between two large oval posts at the east end.

Rectangular buildings of similar plan but slightly smaller dimensions were Nos. 43, 11 and 35, of which the latter has been selected for illustration. Just over half of this building appears to have lain in the excavated area. The positions of two opposing doorways were marked by large post holes in the side walls; a small post hole just inside the east doorway probably carried the door itself. In most of the other buildings the doors were in the middle of the longest sides, and if that was the case here then the building measured 4.2m. by approximately 7.5 m. There were three smaller rectangular buildings supported by individual posts, Nos. 10, 33 and 2, which are likely to have functioned as ancillary agricultural buildings. Of these the largest was No. 10, which was 5.6m. long and 4.4m. wide. Opposed entrances were marked by large oval post holes, which in this instance were not centrally placed in the side walls. The building lay end-to-end with a large rectangular structure, No. 3, which had been partly eroded by ploughing.

The least substantial of the buildings was No. 33, identified as a building because opposite posts appear to be paired, but there were no corner posts, and it probably served as a simple shed or pen. No. 2 is a squarish structure which measured 3.6m. by 3m. with a doorway in the middle of the south side. This faces towards the adjoining large rectangular building, No. 1, for which it was perhaps an ancillary structure. One building, No. 47, had vertical posts at intervals with foundation trenches between these. Originally this building was dated to the Romano-British period, on the basis of scraps of pottery from the area.[11] Subsequently, however, buildings constructed in a similar manner have been found at Chalton, Hampshire, indicating that it is more likely to be of Saxon date.[12] Small parts of six other rectangular structures, Nos. 31, 32, 52, 53, 57, and 58 have been uncovered; in addition what was described as a trapezoidal building, No. 51, was found beside the cemetery. This leaves only building No. 54, which consisted of a group of eight large posts. Unfortunately, the few scraps of pottery found mean that we cannot be certain that the building was Saxon, but it was very similar to post-hole groups interpreted as granaries at Flögeln in Lower Saxony.[13]

It will be obvious from this brief résumé of the Bishopstone buildings that they had many architectural features in common. Most were rectangular buildings constructed of numerous small posts, the average diameter of which was between 15cm. and 20 cm. Pairs of posts were frequently employed, and one imagines that between these there was a plank wall. The side walls were more substantially built than the ends, and opposite posts of the two side walls were generally paired, meaning that they were of comparable shape and equidistant from their respective neighbouring posts. The implication was that they were coupled by beams across the building. Most buildings had two entrances in the middle of the longest side, flanked by large oval posts and one inset post on which the door was hung. Corner posts were characteristically weak or absent, and where they were found they were generally slightly outside the angle formed by the adjoining walls (e.g., No. 28). The Bishopstone buildings are well paralleled by those at Chalton in Hampshire and by an increasing number of Anglo-Saxon buildings excavated elsewhere.[14] The ground plan of one of the Chalton buildings has been marked out by posts next to the reconstructed sunken hut at the Weald and Downland Open Air Museum (Plate 3). This gives a rather better idea than any amount of description of the size and plan of this type of building.

The long axis of all the buildings, with the exception of No. 35, was ENE to WNW, giving the impression of an orderly settlement plan. Between buildings were occasional short lines of small post holes, presumably the last vestiges of fences. The only features other than post holes were five hearth pits and a clay oven; large pits, of the types common on prehistoric sites, were absent. Despite the orderly settlement plan there were no clear indications that the buildings had been grouped in functional units. Evidence of this has, however, been found at Chalton,[15] where groups of three buildings were occasionally surrounded by substantial post-built curtilages. The excavators suggested these groupings might represent the hall and ancillary buildings of a ceorl who, as later documents tell us, was the freeholder of one hide. It has further been suggested that the settlement as a whole may be designated a village. Further elucidation of this last point must await definition of the economic and sociological institutions which constitute what we mean by 'village life', and their identification in the archaeological record. Communal cemeteries should perhaps be considered as examples of such institutions especially where, as at Bishopstone, interments of men, women, and children appear to have been made from an immediately adjoining settlement.

The only contexts on the site which produced any quantity of finds, and any environmental and economic evidence, were the sunken huts. Conclusions regarding the economic organisation of the settlement are accordingly somewhat limited. Numerically, the most abundant species of animal was sheep, followed by cattle, pig, horse, domestic goose, domestic fowl, and cat. Fishing was practised, and red deer hunted. Cereals were presumably grown, because there were occasional impressions of barley in the pottery, but no caches of carbonised grain were found and the extent to which arable agriculture was important remains to be established. It may be significant that the settlement was allowed to spread over what must have been a recognisable former field system, but this does not preclude the possibility that fields lower down the slopes were cultivated. Molluscs, collected on the seashore, were an important supplement to the diet, fragments of mussel shell, in particular, being found in almost every Anglo-Saxon post hole. Sheep were probably kept mainly to provide wool for textile production, the major craft activity. No definite examples of loomweights were found, but many other artifacts connected with spinning and weaving were present: spindle whorls, teeth from weaving combs, pin-beaters, and a large netting needle. Spindle whorls and a weaving comb also accompanied burials in the cemetery.

Historical evidence for the settlement pattern in the Bishopstone area

Wooden buildings in the Rookery Hill settlement would probably have required replacement after 30 to 50 years, yet few buildings were reconstructed. They were clearly not all of one phase, Nos. 43 and 37 overlapped, and 1 and 11 had been rebuilt, but the small quantity of pottery and domestic debris suggests that the settlement was not occupied for any very long period of time, probably not after the sixth century. Its successor, as the nodal point for the area, was the present village of Bishopstone. Undoubtedly this was a Saxon foundation; the parish church of St. Andrew is generally thought to be the earliest standing church edifice in Sussex, although it has been variously dated between the seventh and tenth centuries.[16] A small amount of Saxo-Norman pottery has also come from the village.

We might, therefore, assume a simple move from the hill top settlement of the pagan period to the surviving village in the valley below, were it not for some intriguing historical evidence assembled by Dennis Haselgrove. The earliest documentary reference to Bishopstone itself is in Domesday Book, where it appears as an estate of the bishops of Chichester (formerly Selsey). But there is evidence that in the ninth century the estate was called Denton, the name of a nearby village. Disputes over the ownership of this estate are recorded in 801 and 825.[17] The successful claimant, the bishop, maintained that it had been given to his predecessors in the reign of King Offa, that is probably between the late 750s and the late 780s. Both Denton at that time and Bishopstone in Domesday, were assessed at 25 hides. Denton is not mentioned in Domesday, presumably because, as later in the medieval period, it was part of the Bishopstone estate. Possibly therefore, Bishopstone village originated at some time after the acquisition of the estate by the bishop of Selsey in the second half of the eighth century. Had an earlier settlement existed it might be expected to have retained its old name, in common with many other surviving place names of the early Saxon period. Name changes in the Saxon period are not of course unknown, and Professor Sawyer has argued that a permanent name may only have been acquired when a settlement was granted to a body, such as the church, which maintained records.[18] On balance, however, it seems likely that there was an interval between the desertion of Rookery Hill and the foundation of the present village.

What we know of the surrounding settlements is derived from charters and Domesday Book. On the east side of the Ouse valley, where the river alluvium and Chalk Downs meet, there is a string of settlements which were founded by 1086: Bishopstone, Denton, South Heighton, Tarring Neville, Itford, Beddingham and Preston. There is some evidence that Beddingham, a royal estate, was originally fairly sizeable and that from it the smaller estates of Denton/Bishopstone and probably South Heighton were ceded. If so, it is an instance of what Professor Sawyer has called the main development of settlement history in Anglo-Saxon England, the fragmentation of large multiple estates, many of which prove to be of great antiquity.[19] The boundaries of South Heighton are described in a charter of A.D. 957, by which it was granted to the New Minster at Winchester. Fieldwork has demonstrated that the boundaries given are, with minor differences, those of the nineteenth-century parish.[20] Thus, by the tenth century the settlement pattern of this area had achieved a degree of packing and density which led some settlements to assume bounds similar to those of later parishes. Here, and elsewhere in Sussex, they are strip parishes, the catchment of which is distorted by elongation in order that they may combine the resources of river, alluvium and valley edge with the efficient exploitation of the Chalk upland.

Other possible early Saxon settlements in Sussex (Fig. 5a)

This fairly detailed review of the evidence from the Bishopstone area provides us with a body of data against which to examine more fragmentary evidence from other sites. In particular, the excavation has led to the identification of

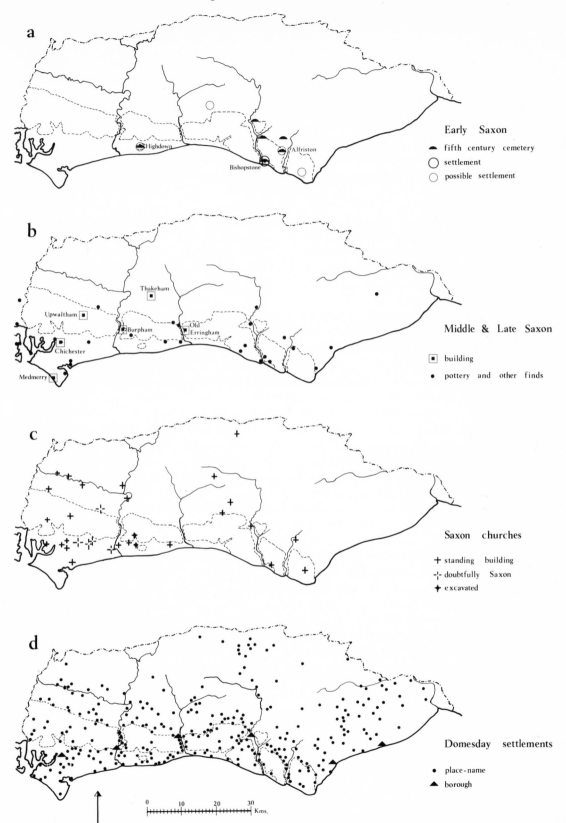

Fig. 5 The distribution of Anglo-Saxon settlement in Sussex

three pottery fabrics in use during the pagan Saxon period. The most predominant, fabric 1, is hard, with a filler of quartz sand; occasionally the surface is ornamented with stamps. Fabric 2 has a predominant filler of sub-angular pieces of multi-coloured flint and traces of plant inclusions. Similar flint grits in fabric 3 are generally larger and the loss of shell or plant inclusions during firing gives it a rather corky appearance; ornament is restricted to simple circular stamps. The first two fabric types have been identified, on the basis of visual inspection, on other sites where they may point to the existence of contemporary settlements. However, without detailed thin section comparison of sherd mineralogy conclusions must remain tentative.

A second result of recent work has been the emergence of what seems to be a close association between pagan Saxon cemeteries and settlements: examples are Bishopstone; Mucking, Essex; and West Stow, Suffolk. It seems possible, therefore, that in the early Saxon period cemeteries were generally established near to the settlements they served. A number of Sussex cemeteries are in geographical situations comparable to Bishopstone and some have produced finds which hint at the existence of a nearby settlement.

Alfriston cemetery is about 45m. O.D., on a spur which runs east from the main Chalk escarpment into the Cuckmere valley, and overlooks the present village of Alfriston just to the south. Bearing in mind that numerous small pottery sherds were found in the graves at Bishopstone, where they are obviously part of a general pot scatter from the settlement, it is interesting to note what may be a parallel situation at Alfriston where 12 graves contained sherds.[21] A similar, rather slight, indication is found at South Malling cemetery where the fill of a grave excavated in 1953 contained a sherd of Type 2 fabric with grass tempering.[22]

The evidence for a settlement associated with the rich Highdown cemetery is rather stronger. The site is on an outlier of the Chalk Downs which rises to 83m. O.D. above the Coastal Plain, and commands a fine view of the English Channel. An Iron Age hillfort took advantage of this position, and within its ramparts was the Saxon cemetery. This was excavated at the end of the last century, but Dr. A. E. Wilson sectioned the Iron Age ramparts in 1939 and 1947.[23] A recent examination of the finds from the 1939 excavation has brought to light a quantity of pottery identical in fabric and vessel form to that found in Anglo-Saxon contexts in the Highdown cemetery and in the Bishopstone settlement. Some of these sherds may of course have been derived from disturbed interments in the cemetery, but most are small abraded sherds from a wide variety of vessels which are best interpreted as broken domestic pottery from a nearby settlement. It is, therefore, necessary to re-examine the post-Iron-Age occupation of Highdown in the light of this evidence. Dr. Wilson identified a late Roman occupation represented by timber buildings and dated by pottery then considered to be third-century. The building was a rectangular structure of double posts. Near it was a second rectangular structure of double posts set in a continuous trench which was dated to the Iron Age. The methods of construction used in both buildings are now known from a variety of

Anglo-Saxon sites, and on this basis alone it is possible that these buildings are of that period. The pottery offers little help with dating, as fourth-century Romano-British and Anglo-Saxon sherds are present in approximately equal proportions. It does seem that three Saxon graves may have post-dated the buildings, but in itself that does not prove they are Romano-British. All that can definitely be said is that pottery sherds from the site indicate that a settlement lies nearby, and the architectural evidence makes an Anglo-Saxon date for the two buildings in Cutting III a possibility. It must, however, be stressed that we know nothing of the homes of the sub-Roman population of fifth-century Sussex, and it remains a possibility that they were of similar construction to those of the intrusive Anglo-Saxon populations.

There is a strong possibility that an important pagan Saxon settlement existed somewhere in the vicinity of Friston, a downland parish between Seaford and Eastbourne. Major Maitland of Friston Place made a collection which, after his death, was given to Barbican House Museum, Lewes, in 1939.[24] Although the material is said to have been found 'near Friston' no exact find spots are recorded. Among the collection are fragments of three annular loomweights, part of a large Saxon cooking pot in a sandy fabric, and three perforated rim lugs[25] of a type which are found on Saxon sites. We have no proof that these finds all came from a single site, nor can we be certain that they are from Friston parish, but it remains an interesting possibility. Two other finds might indicate early settlement sites, a clay loomweight of annular type found in Hurstpierpoint churchyard,[26] and a small group of, possibly Saxon, pottery recovered from Slindon gravel pit.[27]

Evidence for middle- and late-Saxon settlements (Fig. 5b)

A number of the sites discussed so far seem to have been founded during the primary invasion phase and are now deserted. Place-name research does not at present acknowledge any specific type of name as evidence of a settlement of this phase. Indeed the settlements for which we have archaeological evidence appear to have been deserted before the time of the earliest documentary records. Thus their names are lost to us, unless, that is, some are preserved in another way, for example as part of the name of the hundred in which they lie.

The earliest settlements recognisable by place-name evidence are those with the suffix *-ham,* examples being Patcham, Sidlesham and Wepham. *Ham* names are distributed on the periphery of the area occupied by pagan burials, and encroach on what had been the major areas of Romano-British settlement. Dodgson suggests, therefore, that they represent events in the fifth and sixth centuries when immigrant populations represented by the early cemeteries were beginning a process of colonisation.[28] A subsequent stage in the colonisation process is marked by *-ingas* names, like Hastings. These were once considered to be the earliest English settlements, but it has now been demonstrated that they have a distribution quite distinct from that of the fifth- and sixth-century cemeteries.[29] Their distribution spreads into the areas of densest Romano-British occupation, and they belong, therefore, to a time when the whole county had passed into English hands.

Comparison with the archaeological evidence indicates that the colonisation process may, in some cases, have resulted in the desertion of hilltop sites founded in the primary invasion phase. These may often have been superseded by newly-founded settlements in the valleys and vales, many of which are distinguished by the suffixes *-ham* and *-ingas* and survive as villages today. Just such a settlement shift has been documented in the vicinity of Chalton, Hampshire. The earlier settlement, of sixth- and seventh-century date, was on the Downland spur known as Church Down. Professor Cunliffe has suggested that its abandonment led to the foundation of the villages of Chalton, Blendworth and Idsworth in surrounding valleys.[30]

Since, in this later period, we are largely dealing with settlements which have been occupied to this day, it is hardly surprising that the archaeological evidence is rather patchy: six sites with traces of buildings and 31 findspots of pottery and artifacts. During this period pottery dating continues to be a problem; wares were hand-made and seem generally to be of local manufacture with flint, shell and organic temper; occasionally late vessels are ornamented with stamps and strapping. These Sussex wares failed to respond to the stimulus of Continental trade which had such a profound effect on the middle- and late-Saxon pottery of East Anglia. One result of this is that it is seldom possible to distinguish between wares of middle- and late-Saxon date. Wheel-made forms are rare, the earliest known is Portchester Ware from the ninth century onwards found at Fishbourne and Chichester, and on salterns at New Monks Farm, Lancing.[31] Later, in the years around the Conquest, increased Continental trade is evidenced by finds of Pingsdorf pottery from Pevensey, Burlough Castle, and Sompting. Much of this trade, and in particular that in Normandy pottery found in some quantities at Pevensey and also in Lewes, seem to have been stimulated by the Conquest itself.[32]

The existence of Saxon or Saxo-Norman settlements is also suggested by finds of clay loomweights. These are divided into three groups which may be approximately dated: annular, generally pagan in date; intermediate, of seventh- or eighth-century date; and bun-shaped in the period up to the introduction of the horizontal loom in the twelfth century.[33] Neither loomweights nor pottery enable us to draw a firm line at the Norman Conquest. Some of the archaeological evidence discussed here may be post-Conquest, but equally we have so little material of Anglo-Saxon date in Sussex that one suspects some material has been dated too late simply because it can occur in later contexts.

The Downland

Excavations by Eric Holden within and around the Domesday manorial site of Old Erringham, near Shoreham, led to the discovery of traces of middle- and late-Saxon occupation, including a sunken-floored hut.[34] Part of this building had been destroyed before excavation, but it appeared originally to have measured 4.75m. by 3.1m., and about 40cm. deep. There was a large post in the middle of the remaining gable end, and three smaller posts to support the ridge pole. It has obviously been a weaving hut, and scattered on the pit floor were about 75 baked clay loomweights, mostly of intermediate type. Other finds included a fine caterpillar brooch of eighth-century type, pottery, spindle whorls, querns, and a bone needle. The artifacts indicate a date range for the building at some time within the latter part of the middle- and late-Saxon periods. The reconstruction of a sunken hut at the Weald and Downland Museum (Plate 2) is partly based on the Old Erringham building and contains a reconstruction of the loom. Trial excavations in the surrounding area did not succeed in revealing the sites of any other buildings. Further evidence of Saxon occupation was, however, preserved in a buried soil below a defensive ringwork associated with the Domesday manor; this included two coins of Ethelred II, *c.* 1000 A.D., and more loomweight fragments.

A site which may perhaps have been rather similar to Old Erringham was destroyed when a barn was built at Telscombe in 1964. Two loomweights and two pottery fragments were all that remained for archaeological examination, but it is recorded that other pieces were originally found.[35] We have documentary evidence for a late Saxon settlement at Telscombe in a charter of 966 A.D., by which King Edgar gave Telscombe, with a church and 10 hides of land, to the New Minster at Winchester.[36] It is interesting that such an isolated Downland site was occupied by the tenth century. Nearby in a dry valley at Saltdean builders have recently brought to light a few fragments of Saxo-Norman pottery and a piece of fired clay which could be part of a loomweight.[37] Only about 500m. north of this site Saxon burials were found in 1950, inserted into the edge of a 'Celtic' field system.[38] There is, however, no documentary record of Saxon or Medieval settlement in the Saltdean valley, and one imagines that this windswept spot may eventually have been deserted in favour of the nucleated settlement of the parish of Rottingdean.

The now much shrunken village of Upwaltham, on a dry valley routeway between Chichester and the Petworth area, has also produced evidence of Saxo-Norman occupation. A roadside ditch dug in 1961 cut across a depression in the solid chalk which seems likely to have been another sunken hut. It was 11.7m. long by 0.6m. deep, filled with dark soil. Standing vertically in this was a large storage jar elaborately decorated with strapping. From the same area was another sherd and some bones.[39] A settlement at Waltham in Boxgrove hundred is recorded in Domesday Book.

Possibly the most complete sequence of Anglo-Saxon occupation on the downland has been uncovered as the result of building work on the Upperton ridge at Eastbourne. Near the ridge crest, in the area of St. Annes Road, was a sixth-century cemetery. About 300m. north is the site of Kitcheners Furlong where six bun-shaped loomweights were found by H. M. Whitley in a rubbish pit.[40] Some 500m. south of the cemetery is Enys Road where a 'scoop in the chalk' was discovered which contained a pot decorated with applied strapping and pieces of several bun-shaped loomweights.[41] It is tempting to conclude that associated with the pagan cemetery was a settlement which was occupied into the late-Saxon period. This site may eventually have been abandoned in favour of the site of Medieval (East)Bourne on an adjoining ridge to the south.

The only example, in a later Saxon context, of timber buildings of the types which predominated at Bishopstone and Chalton are from within the Saxon *burh* at Burpham.[42] This was a promontory fort which projects into the alluvium of the Arun and was strongly fortified by an earth rampart on the north side. A rescue excavation in a small area just inside the entrance produced a complex of postholes, representing several phases in the life of a rectangular building. Nearby were two pits which contained tenth- or early-eleventh-century pottery. The interior of the *burh* is deserted today, but this small excavation demonstrated clearly that it contained a Saxon settlement which presumably later moved outside to the present site of Burpham village. The other Downland burh, at Lewes, has also produced evidence of late-Saxon occupation. Excavations in North Street and the Naval Prison revealed a series of cess pits containing interesting groups of Saxo-Norman pottery and bun-shaped loomweights.[43]

Stray finds of Saxo-Norman pottery at Denton, Bishopstone, Bramber Castle and Castle Hill, Newhaven, presumably point to the existence of settlements of some kind, the first two of which are, as we have seen, known from documentary sources.[44]

Combining this evidence with what we have from other sources it appears that by the end of the Saxon period the downland had achieved a high density of settlement. This was at its densest, as Domesday shows, in the river valleys with their diverse resources. Settlements extended into the dry valleys, the potential of which was more limited, but which it was necessary to occupy in order to achieve the fullest exploitation of this geographical area. In addition to the dry valley settlements attested by archaeological traces, there are others represented by churches like Upper Barpham, where a church exhibiting three phases of pre-Conquest work was uncovered by excavations that also produced a few scraps of pottery from the presumed settlement,[45] others such as Jevington, with its fine standing Saxon church and sculpture, and Ovingdean, Stanmer and Balmer which are recorded in Domesday Book.

The Coastal Plain

This is an area rich in Saxon place-names and churches, heavily occupied at the time of Domesday (Fig. 3d). Part of a settlement at Medmerry Farm, Selsey, was exposed by coastal erosion in 1934.[46] Finds were made along 140m. of cliff and the settlement seems to have been of some size. Five 'living floors', which were probably sunken huts, are recorded, and from these, a pit and two 'shell middens', came quantities of animal bones, bun-shaped loomweights and middle to late Saxon pottery. If anything of the site remains it is potentially a very important one since wattles and woodwork were preserved by a high water table.

Equally promising is the village of Pagham where recent rescue excavations at Becket's Barn uncovered a cobbled path, overlain by a midden deposit which in turn was cut into three ditches.[47] Pottery from the midden is consistent with a middle-Saxon date, *c.* 650–800 A.D., and charcoal from one of the ditches gave a radiocarbon date of 820±60 A.D. (Har–1085). Sixty metres north-west of the site is Pagham church where a pot of sixth- or seventh-century date was found with parts of two other vessels in the churchyard.[48] Fragments of bone adhered to the pot indicating that it may have served as a cinerary urn. The suggestion, which without further burials should not be regarded as proven, is that a pagan cemetery on the site was succeeded by a Christian graveyard and church.

On the opposite side of Pagham harbour at Church Norton is an anomalous earthwork which seems designed to cut off the area of the church from the land. Excavations have produced coarse pot sherds of possible late-Saxon date, and a very fine ornamented strap-end, divided into four compartments, each of which is ornamented by a nude human figure. These finds pre-date the earthwork which the excavator argues was a defence of the Armada period.[49]

A number of sites in the Saxon *burh* of Chichester have produced late-Saxon and Saxo-Norman pottery and loomweights. An account of one building is published, a wattle and daub hut found at East Pallant House in 1950.[50] It was recognisable as a concentration of burnt daub and charcoal, which was, however, so badly disturbed by later features that it is impossible to ascertain the type of building represented. Indications of other possible settlements on the Coastal Plain are finds of Saxo-Norman pottery from Nyetimber (Pagham), and near Aldingbourne church.[51]

The Weald

Wealden places mentioned in Domesday concentrate at the foot of the Chalk downs escarpment, largely on the Lower Greensand belt and in the West Rother valley. A similar pattern is reflected in the distribution of pre-Conquest churches (Figs. 5 c, d). Domesday Book does not, however, provide an accurate impression of settlement in the Weald, where estates were often assessed with their parent settlements on the downland and Coastal Plain, and are thus not individually mentioned. However, the Domesday map probably does reflect a Saxon pattern which was considerably less dense than in the area to the south. This does not completely explain the sparse distribution of archaeological evidence which is, in part, a reflection of the lack of field-work and excavation. The only building for which we have evidence is the probable site of a sunken hut recorded on the Lower Greensand at Thakeham, near Pulborough, by the Curwens in 1934.[52] It was visible in a section cut whilst making a swimming pool, as a pit of diameter 4m. and depth of 0.76m. The finds included fragments of a soft brown hand-made pottery dated between the sixth and eighth centuries A.D.

Excavations at Steyning, which documentary evidence shows was a Saxon town and port with a mint, have revealed occupation from the tenth century in St. Cuthman's field opposite the church.[53] Possibly pagan Saxon burials found below a cottage 30m. from the church indicate that this is a settlement with an early foundation.[54] A somewhat similar situation is found at Selmeston on the ridge of Lower Greensand, east of Lewes. Within the historic village, and only 230m. north of the church, is a rich pagan Saxon cemetery.[55] The possibility that this settlement has been continuously occupied from the fifth century is strengthened by finds of later-Saxon material from the village.[56] A sandpit 140m. east of the church has produced extensive chance finds from all archaeological periods showing that the ridge hereabouts was a favoured settlement site since the Mesolithic period. Saxon finds from the sandpit include two intermediate type loomweights and one bun-shaped example, and sherds of late-Saxon pottery, some of which are recorded as coming from a hearth.

An assemblage of Saxo-Norman pottery found within the Roman fort of Pevensey is generally considered to be of post-Conquest date,[57] the assumption being that the site was deserted between its sacking by Aelle in 491 and the arrival of William, who constructed 'a very strong rampart' within the still-surviving Roman walls after his landing in 1066. Recently, a continuous sequence of Saxon occupation has been found in the shore-fort of Portchester[58] and it seems at least plausible that some of the crude flint-tempered pottery found at Pevensey may represent pre-Conquest occupation. Pevensey lies on a low ridge of Lower Greensand that projects into the surrounding levels, and at the end of which is the Roman fort. The present settlement is on the ridge outside the east entrance to the fort. Its early importance is emphasised by the possession of a mint in the Saxon period and by its status as a Domesday borough. Several sites on the ridge have been excavated and have failed to reveal any traces of occupation earlier than the twelfth century,[59] suggesting perhaps that earlier occupation was either within the Roman fort or in a fairly small area just outside the gate. Further finds which may point to Wealden settlements are Saxo-Norman sherds from the Durhamford valley, near Battle, a fragment of a cooking jar found near Bignor villa, and two bun-shaped loomweights from Banks Farm, Barcombe.[60]

Conclusion

A tendency in the past has been to regard the Saxon settlement pattern as a static entity, in the belief that primary colonists of the invasion period established the nucleated villages with *-ingas* names that survive today. Place-name research has now shown that these were not the earliest settlements, and the archaeological evidence indicates that the Saxon settlement pattern underwent considerable change and evolution. Some of the earliest settlements, such as Bishopstone and Highdown, are on hilltop sites, which were deserted during the early-Saxon period. These sites may not, however, be typical of the early settlements; others which have been continuously occupied since are less likely to be available for archaeological excavation. Evidence from these settlements is likely to be confined to chance discoveries during building operations. In a few cases, these do seem to hint at pagan origins for surviving villages. Examples are Pagham, Selmeston, and possibly Steyning where pagan burials have been found near the present church. Conversely, there is evidence of short-lived settlements like Medmerry, founded and deserted in the mid- to late-Saxon period. In some cases, villages may have shifted their position or changed their overall morphology whilst retaining an old name. Specific instances are Pevensey, Burpham, possibly (East)Bourne, and the deserted medieval village of Hangleton. Here extensive excavations failed to find any trace of the settlement of 44 villeins and bordars recorded in the Domesday survey, indicating that the village had changed its position during the thirteenth century.[61] What emerges is a settlement pattern with some stable components, but in which, at any one time, some settlements were in the process of dispersing in order to colonise parts of a newly-conquered or cleared landscape, just as, in other areas, settlements were becoming nucleated to exploit better the economic resources which those areas offered.

With the abandonment of our concept of the Anglo-Saxon settlement pattern as static the full potential of archaeological research in the period may now begin to be realised. The need is for field-work and excavation in and around the sites of chance finds and villages which documentary records and place-names suggest are of Saxon origin. Detailed work is badly needed in specific limited areas, such as parishes or hundreds, where the range of evidence from archaeology, history and environmental studies can be viewed against the common backcloth of the landscape. These areas, if documented in detail, will provide the foundations for broader theory building. In this process excavation has a crucial role; only by excavation will we be able to determine the plan and the size of Saxon settlements and decide whether the vills listed in Domesday Book were, generally speaking, villages of the type which Sussex people know so well.

IV

PLACE-NAMES IN SUSSEX: THE MATERIAL FOR A NEW LOOK

John McNeil Dodgson

NOT THE LEAST obvious result of the South Saxon invasion of Britain is the English toponymy of Sussex. The purpose of this essay is the provision of a grid-referenced list of those place-names which, according to the latest theories of English place-name studies, might seem to be important, and whose distribution might seem significant, in the history of the English settlement in Sussex. It attempts very little in conclusion: but it opens the way to a new analysis of place-name material for comparison with the different facts of history, geography and archaeology—a comparison which the local geographer, historian and archaeologist is best qualified to make.

The apparatus

We know of this toponymy only from those place-names which fell within the purview of *The Place-Names of Sussex* (two parts), English Place-Name Society, Vols. 6 and 7 (Cambridge 1929–30), a range limited by the list of principal manors, villages and hamlets known of for dates before 1500, by the accident of gazetteering in and from the 6in. and 1in. Ordnance Survey Maps, by the limited availability of ancient record for perusal in 1925–1930, and by the degree of perception required by the name-study techniques of those days. The apparatus does not include a systematic survey of field-names and names of minor local features, ancient and modern, such as would nowadays replace pp. 558-64 of Part 2 of the English Place-Name Society's *Sussex* with hundreds of pages of list and etymology.

In the years since publication, the English Place-Name Society's *Sussex* volumes have been overtaken by new thinking. So it is necessary to review the apparatus for the study of Sussex place-names. The English Place-Name Society's volumes on Sussex represent the state of knowledge in 1930. This work (PNSx) is a dangerous tool, unless handled carefully with up-to-date annotations. An important reference-work behind it was E. Ekwall, *English Place-names in -ing*

(Lund 1923); this (PN-ing[1]) was partially out-dated by a second edition (PN-ing,[2] Lund 1962) which to some degree defied, and to some degree attempted to come to terms with, the English Place-Name Society's discoveries. PN-ing[2] itself needs serious moderation by reference to A. H. Smith 'Place-names and the Anglo-Saxon Settlement', *Proceedings of the British Academy*, 42 (1956), 67–88 and to his *English Place-Name Elements*, Part 1, s.vv. *-ing, -ingas*. The etymological elements in PNSx refer to *Chief Elements in English Place-Names*, ed. A. Mawer (E.P-N. Soc., Vol. 1, Part 2, Cambridge 1924), which has been superseded by A. H. Smith, *English Place-Name Elements, Parts 1 and 2*, E.P-N. Soc., Vols 25 and 26 (Cambridge 1956), and the addenda thereto which have appeared in subsequent E.P-N. Soc. volumes and in JEPN (*Journal of the English Place-Name Society*), 1 (1969), *et. seq.* Serious users of the Sussex volumes have to use these additional references. They ought, moreover, to peruse the 'Addenda and Corrigenda' section of E.P-N. Soc., Vols. 8–50, for the numerous and important modifications to Vols. 6 and 7 (*Sussex*) which have become necessary as time has passed. Out-dating has also overtaken the essay by P. A. Nicklin and E. G. Godfrey-Faussett, 'On the distribution of place-names in Sussex', *Sussex Archaeological Collections*, 76 (1935), 213–21, and other work deriving from the researches of 40 years ago. The time draws near for a fundamental revision of the E.P-N. Soc. volumes. It will probably become necessary for the *Sussex* and *Surrey* volumes (E.P-N. Soc. 6, 7, 11) to be revised while the E.P-N. Soc. volumes for *Kent* are being put together. The significance of the place-names of South-East England is not to be discerned properly unless we can see the sweep of things across the whole peninsula. Research for the *Kent* volumes involves more and more revaluations of the *Sussex* and *Surrey* ones (not yet comparable, though, with those which have to be aimed at J. K. Wallenberg's two valuable, difficult-to-use, learned, traps-for-the-unwary, books, *Kentish Place-Names* (Uppsala, 1931), and *The Place-Names of Kent* (Uppsala, 1934). The most important further revisions which the *Sussex* reader has to make, will be discerned in the following articles:—

(i) H. C. Darby, 'Place-Names and the geography of the past', in A. Brown and P. Foote (eds.) *Early English and Norse Studies presented to Hugh Smith in honour of his sixtieth birthday* (London 1963), pp. 6–18; (EENS).

(ii) Margaret Gelling, 'The element *hamm* in English place-names: a topographical investigation', *Namn och Bygd*, 48 (1960), pp. 140–62 (NoB).

(iii) K. I. Sandred, *English Place-Names in Stead* (Uppsala 1963). (Sandred.)

(iv) Margaret Gelling, 'English place-names derived from the compound *wicham*', *Medieval Archaeology*, 11 (1967), pp. 87–104. (MA).

(v) Margaret Gelling, 'The chronology of English place-names', in T. Rowley (ed.), *Anglo-Saxon Settlement and Landscape* (*British Archaeological Reports*, 6, Oxford 1974), pp. 93–101 (BAR).

(vi) J. McN. Dodgson, 'The significance of the distribution of the English place-name in *-ingas, -inga-* in South-East England', *MA*, 10 (1966), pp. 1–29.

(vii) J. McN. Dodgson, 'The *-ing-* in English place-names like Birmingham and Altrincham', *Beiträge zur Namenforschung,* 2 (1967), pp. 221–45; (BNF).

(viii) J. McN. Dodgson, 'Various forms of Old English *-ing* in English place-names', *BNF,* 2 (1967), pp. 325–96.

(ix) J. McN. Dodgson, 'Various English place-name formations containing Old English *-ing',BNF,* 3 (1968), pp. 141–89.

(x) J. McN. Dodgson, 'Place-Names for *ham,* distinguished from *hamm* names, in relation to the settlement of Kent, Surrey and Sussex', *Anglo-Saxon England,* 2, ed. P. Clemoes (Cambridge 1973), 1–50. (ASE).

(xi) B. H. Cox, 'The significance of the distribution of English place-names in *ham* in the Midlands and East Anglia', *Journal of the English Place-Name Society,* 5 (1973), 15–73. (JEPN).

(xii) Gillian Fellows Jensen, 'English Place-Names such as Doddington and Donnington', *Sydsvenska Ortnamnssällskapets Arsskrift,* 1974, 26–65. (SOA).

In these studies, investigation is made into the nature and occurrence of place-names in Old English *denn* 'a woodland pasture' and *fald* 'a fold, a pen for animals' and also the element *hyrst* 'wooded hill', in the Weald (Darby EENS); *leah* 'a wood, a glade, a clearing in a wood' and *tun* 'an enclosure, a farmstead, an estate, a village', in the Midlands (Gelling BAR); the various manifestations of the OE noun-forming suffix *-ing* (*-ingas* nom. pl., *-inga-* gen. pl., *-ing* nom. sg., *-inğ* nom. sg. toponymic, *-ing-* sg. in compound forms) in English place-names in general and in the south-eastern counties (Dodgson, MA, 10, BNF, 2–3, Fellows-Jensen, SOA); *ham* 'a village, a manor, a homestead; a principal village', and *hamm* a river-meadow, an enclosure, a paddock' (Gelling NoB, MA 11, Dodgson, ASE, Cox, JEPN, 5). The whole series presents a revision of the hypotheses upon which the analysis of place-names in *The Place-Names of Sussex* was based. In the last 15 years, the interpretation of English place-names has been violently re-directed.

The interpretation of Sussex place-names

It was formerly supposed, following nineteenth-century hypotheses of Leo and Kemble, as codified by Ekwall (PN-ing[1]) that the Anglo-Saxons immigrated into a virtually uninhabited country in tribal expeditions (each group under a leader whose name his followers took, whether descendants, dependants, or merely associates) which sailed up the best available rivers as far as their ships would take them, or made their way inland along the river-valleys (in much the same way as the European migrants and colonists of the eighteenth and nine-teenth centuries explored and settled the 'empty' lands in North America and South Africa and Australia) and took up whatever land suited their needs and was convenient for taking, in ignorance of, and in despite of, any native population.

This pattern of things will not do. Roman Britannia may have been in a rather run-down state in the fifth century, but it would seem to have been full of Britons, with a lot of fairly good roads, and towns, villages, villas, and a fair notion of civilised life, so there is no historical need to envisage the wild invader blundering through forest, field, and fen towards the promised land. The immigrating English could more easily travel by road. As to the land-taking, it is doubtful whether there was that much no-man's land in south-east England, for the casual taking-up of these supposed cross-country orienteers: the original Anglo-Saxons ought to be seen as licensed immigrants coming in under government contract and scheme to do a particular soldiering job, for which they were quartered in specified garrison districts. After the revolution, of course, things would be different. After the massacre at Anderida there would be a nascent Sussex; until then there would be a district of Britain with an immigrant problem in the making and on the move.

The archaeologist and the historian having begun to see and to point out a different order of possibilities, the problem of the discontinuity between place-name evidence and that of archaeology became urgent. J. N. L. Myres reviewed in *Antiquity* 10 the first edition of the Ordnance Survey *Map of Britain in the Dark Ages* in which O. G. S. Crawford drew a comparison between Ekwall's evidence of *-ingas* place-names (the supposed memorials of the immigrating tribes) and the archaeological evidence of the earliest pagan-burial-making English. The distribution patterns do not conform as they should. In MA 10 the present author suggested that the disjunction of the spatial distribution of *-ingas* place-names and Anglo-Saxon pagan-burials was due to the disjunction of their distribution in time. I set up a model which enabled us to see the *-ingas* place-names as belonging to a later phase of development in English society than that which produced and used the pagan cemeteries. This hypothesis continues to be tested. It still waits for the rigorous application of a full 'nearest-neighbour' analysis (by whatever polygonal [or polyhedral?] structure might best serve for the comparison of non-static disparates across a time-scale!) so that the type can be related to a recognisable context. So far, the author has only seen Sarah Kirk, 'A distribution pattern: *-ingas* in Kent', JEPN 4 (1972), 37–59. For the time being, it is taken that the place-name in *-ingas* belongs to a phase of early Anglo-Saxon history that follows upon the immigration—to some juncture in the long colonisation which commenced when the English expanded out of their original reservations, out of the earliest pagan-burial districts.

The removal of the inhibitions by which the *-ingas* theory had constrained our investigations—the *-ingas* place-name had been an incubus; it *had* to be fitted into the earliest stratum of record, the very beginning of English history in its district, even in the teeth of known facts which indicated otherwise—enabled other hypotheses to be tried. It now appears that place-names in *ham* have a better right to our reverence, if the sort of distribution-analysis which has hitherto been used will stand further pressure. Certainly, the present author's observations on the south-east counties, and Dr. Cox's on the Midland counties, indicate the possibility that place-names in OE *ham* lie rather more significantly near to areas of Roman or early English archaeology than do *-ingas* place-names. As a result of Cox's work, we now see a chronological stratification in the order *-ham, -ingham, -ingas,* a complete inversion of the previous model. Furthermore, since it is now laudable to take an objective view of place-names, more attention is being paid to relationships between different types of place-names. Dr. Gelling's pioneering work on the Midland *leah/tun* relationship deserves careful attention by Sussex historians. Place-names containing these elements could belong to the earliest stratum of English nomenclature in the colonisation of the district.

It is doubtful whether the study of place-names will ever enable us to recapture the fourth- or fifth-century English names of the settlements into which the immigrant *foederati* were directed; our place-names are memorials of the English *take-over* of Britain, a more political and lasting process than the mere transport-and-billeting routine of immigration. But we need to recognise that this new aspect of the subject requires a different sort of scrutiny. The present author attempted the re-orientation in 'The English Arrival in Cheshire', *Transactions of the Historic Society of Lancashire and Cheshire* 119 (1967) 1–37, but we have not evolved the sort of notation for describing a place-name which we shall need if we are to extend our analysis properly; a notation which comprehends the archaeological, manorial, archival, etymological and typological matrices in which a place-name exists—all we can do at this moment is to identify the etymological elements and the simpler orders of composition, which ignore the graduations of etymological value and the more subtle modes of internal relationship between the parts of a compound. This essay is obliged to be unsatisfactory because this branch of science has not yet evolved a language in which its findings and its hypotheses can be exactly stated and precisely measured and tested.

The English place-names of Sussex

However, I think it a good thing to put to the heirs and inheritors of the South Saxons the problems which await us in the reading of their place-names —some one or two may set to work, and bring forward the next brick for the pyramid, if we leave enough straws in the wind. Let us see what can be divined at this juncture from the place-names of Sussex. It is remarkable how completely English this nomenclature is. The characteristic evidences, of the co-existence of an English and a British community, which are signalled by place-names in OE *wealh* (genitive plural *weala*) 'a foreigner, a serf, a Briton', and by place-names which have a British Celtic element as basis (other than, say, river-names. and loan-words such as *camp, funta, ceaster,* 'field, spring, fortified city') are not frequent in Sussex. Walton PNSx 59 (SU 815045 in Bosham) with perhaps the nearby Critchfield PNSx 58, and Wallhurst PNSx 211 (TQ 223237 in Cowfold) are all. Whereas, in Surrey there are two Waltons, and Wallington, Walworth, Caterham (perhaps), Chertsey, Crooksbury, Limpsfield, and Penge; in Kent, two Waltons, and Walmer, Wallinghurst, Chevening, Chattenden, Chatham, Rochester,

Eccles, Faversham, Lympne, Reculver, Richborough, Dover, and Thanet, and the unidentified *Cæt hærst, Weliscinge,* and *Penny crych.*

The contrast leads to an inference that the British-speaking inhabitants of the Sussex region were quite suddenly and completely overwhelmed by the English cultural and linguistic medium. The English domination of the British population of what became Sussex seems to have been achieved suddenly because there would appear not to have been enough time and occasion for that continuing common contact as equals or as recognised parties in trade and society which enables and makes necessary the borrowing of words and names from one language into the other; the lack of British place-names in Sussex indicates a lack of noticeable or considerable British natives quite soon after the Saxon onset.

In a geographical area which has not in the last 1500 years been subjected to repeated immigration by populations speaking different languages, we lack in Sussex place-names the 'stratification' of names by language and custom. We cannot work out the significance of the English place-names by comparison with, say, Welsh, Norwegian, Norman French, or Danish place-names, as we do in other counties farther to the north or to the west, where speakers of Celtic or Scandinavian vernaculars have lived alongside the English. In Sussex, we have to look for a model of the stratification of the range of place-names of English origin found in the county, and perhaps in the country at large, which seems likely to offer the most sensible correlation of place-names with history, geography and archaeology. From such a correlation we might see what aspects of the fortunes of Aelle's descendants the place-names commemorate. Before that can be done, however, we have to identify the preponderant types of place-names in Sussex, and discover the factors which control their distribution.

The occurrence of place-names

The distribution-patterns of place-names types are formed in time and space; that is to say, there is a geographical distribution, of the sort which appears on a map, and a temporal distribution whereby the prevalence of a particular type of place-name varies as time goes on. The distribution-maps prepared for place-name studies are usually summaries presenting both a present-day and a past situation. We ought to look at place-name evidences with regard to the time factor. It is impossible to be sure of the survival of ancient documents, there are many different dates of first record; some place-names are recorded in early Anglo-Saxon charters, or by Domesday Book; others not until quite modern times. An ancient place may be obscure and unnoticed for centuries; a new farm may get into lawsuits straightaway. Many English place-names not recorded before the thirteenth century must be pre-Norman formations. There is nothing at all in the average English *-ington* type of place-name to prevent it belonging to the sixth or seventh centuries, yet the majority of such place-names are not recorded in documents before the thirteenth century. On the other hand by

1300 the names of the principal setlements in England have all been written
down and by 1500 most of the more obscure and insignificant ones also; this
is the result of administration and record.

In order to see what the medieval settlement of Sussex amounted to, we
should need to spend a deal of time searching Ancient Deeds, etc., for the names
of all places, however unimportant the places, even the field-names, recorded
by 1500. In order to see what the settlement of early Medieval Sussex looked
like, we need to restrict our examination to the place-names on record by 1300.
Out of these, it is useful to distinguish the names of places which were already
'important', or valuable, enough to feature in record before 1100—i.e., in Anglo-
Saxon Charters and Domesday Book. So we obtain one list of names which
serves to give us a view of the earliest manorial centres; and another list of names
of other places which gradually emerge into independence, by name, in the
records after 1100. Of course, we are not sure that we thereby catch *all* the
examples of a place-name type that were used by the inhabitants of Sussex
down to 1300 or 1100 either; nevertheless we have a fair representation of
the frequency and spread of the item. We must remember that Domesday Book
does not name every place that existed in 1085 or 1066, and it is quite obvious
that many places which first emerge by name in the thirteenth-century record
must have been in existence, with a place-name, by 1086.

So, the Appendix to this article lists the names of (a) places whose names are
on record by 1100 or which are medieval parish-church villages, (b) other places
which emerge into record by 1300.

The types of place name in Sussex

The place-names of Sussex fall into three kinds of toponymic formation:
folk-names, nature-names, and habitation-names. Folk-name toponyms are
the names of communities, extended to the place where they live or to a
place in some way associated—perhaps, better, identified—with them. Nature-
name toponyms denote places identified by relation (usually adverbial,
with prepositions *at, by, in,* locative inflection, and so forth; often tacit)
to the natural feature or features of the site or its environment. Habitation-
name toponyms are those which contain an element which denotes a building
or dwelling-place or a human activity or a work-site. They will also fall into
the historical categories already mentioned—in part accidental, in part
historical, in part political—according to whether the place-name happened,
by politics and geography (i.e., rateable value!), to be worth recording in a
pre-1066 document, or in Domesday Book, or to be capable of sustaining
a parish priest, or to be recorded by, say, 1300. By this date one may suppose
that most pre-Norman settlements had eventually been caught up and sorted
out by church, state and landlord, inheritance, tenure, dowry, felony, bank-
ruptcy, and taxation, with the charters, deeds, writs, lawsuits, and enrolments
which ensue.

Folk-names

The most frequent types of place-name in Sussex appear in our lists. Among the folk-names, the *-ingas* ('followers of-, dependents of-, descendants of-') type is fairly numerous: see List A. The distribution is illustrated and discussed in MA 10. What is interesting about these place-names is the obvious antiquity and status of the places they denote. There are 38 *-ingas* place-names in Sussex recorded before 1100, 28 of these places are parochial, and only seven *-ingas* place-names belong to non-parochial, 'post-Domesday Book' places. They lie in south Sussex along the edges of the Downs; they appear to belong to districts settled when the English were just expanding out of their first immigration-areas. I do not think the *-ingas* place-name necessarily belongs to that era, but the places so denoted could well do so. Earliness of colonisation would confer seniority on such settlements—and the *-ingas* label a mark of antiquity, and with it a recognition of the evolution and conservation of a more complex inheritance, and customs more ancient, than those governing other, more recent, places. In fact, I consider it possible that the *-ingas* formula might often have over-ridden a true place-name; the present author cites a number of instances where this occurs in his BNF articles.

Nature-names

Among the nature-names, the best represented elements recorded by 1300 are shown: *leah** 'forest glade or clearing', *hyrst** 'wooded hill', *cumb** 'valley', *feld** 'open country', *eg** 'water-meadow, marsh, island', *denu** 'valley', *burna** '(intermittent) stream', *ford** 'ford', *hrycg** 'ridge', *ora** 'river-bank, hill-side', *welle** 'spring', *halh* 'nook, corner, recess, projection', *wudu* 'wood', *hyll* 'hill', *dun** 'Down, upland area', *mere** 'pool, lake'. Elements such as *halh, wudu, hyll* and *broc* 'marshy meadow' figure quite rarely as parish-names or in pre-1100 records, but show up in the 1100–1300 category. For analysis in List B I have taken the most numerous, marked with an asterisk. Among the nature-names, these must be considered the most prevalent types in Sussex.

Habitative-names

The habitative element is represented by *tun* (and its compounds *leactun, burh-tun, ham-tun, tun-steall*—the latter (Tunstall TQ 723212) my only concession to first-element position), *wic* 'dairy-farm, industrial or trading settlement' (and *berewic* 'dependent farm; granary-farm'), *worð* 'private enclosure, curtilage, *ham* 'principal settlement, manorial centre', *gesell* 'herdsmen's buildings', and *fald* 'a fold, a paddock'. It is very remarkable indeed that the most numerous class here is that in *tun* 'farmstead; farmyard, enclosure or stockade; village', the other elements in this list are not comparable in frequency of occurrence. The element *ham* makes a poor showing—but this is problematic, for there are many place-names in the county with the spelling *-ham* in their ancient and their modern forms, which could be derived from either *ham* or *hamm*. This problem leads to the category of place-name in List D. Here I have analysed out place-names in *hamm* (or *ham*), *stede* 'site of, place', and *denn*. These are place-names which, of themselves, taken lexically, fall between the classifications habitative and natural. For example, a *hamm* may be any or many of a range of things—a natural feature or a man-made paddock; a *stede* can only be defined when final in a compound, where the first element denotes the function; a *denn* is a natural-feature, a forest retreat, put to a pastoral use; *denn* and *hamm* place-names usually connote a human activity—animal husbandry, etc., at suitable sites—and it is difficult to know what meaning out of a possible range the elements have at a particular time. It will be observed that the *hamm* type of place-name is about as frequent in Sussex as the *tun* type.

The distribution of typical Sussex place-names

Now, given this repertoire of the most numerously represented settlement-names, we find that the typology to some extent reflects the geography of the county. The most salient facts are as follows. The distribution of place-names in *tun* is bounded to the north by the western river Rother and the Roman road (Margary 140) Pulborough-Keymer-Barcombe along the scarp-foot vale. It is not a type of name used during the colonisation of the Weald. The distribution of *tun* names behind Hastings, shows a few places so named scattered about the high ground on the watershed above Pevensey Marshes; but the impressive feature is the picture of the Chalk-downs edged by *-tun* place-names.

In the same configuration as the *tuns* we find the *-ingas* names: again, these occur, almost without exception, in proximity to the edges of the Downs. The elements *wic* and *worð* are not thus restricted: they show a random occurrence, although the latter tends to be rather more frequent in the Weald than in the downland. The distribution of the few place-names which are allowed for *ham* generally follow that for *tun* and *-ingas*.

We would expect the elements denoting woodland and forest to appear more frequently in the Weald area. The element *leah* appears almost entirely within the Weald forest areas—a few exceptions appear in the old common forest-land in the Manhood, south of Chichester. With *leah* in the nearly exclusively off-Downs distribution come the elements *hyrst* and *feld*. The distribution of these two elements requires analysis by a different skill from mine. They correspond to characteristics of geomorphology and vegetation. This is the sort of problem indicated by Darby in EENS. Place-names in *-hurst* are numerous in north-west Sussex, in the hilly district bounded by Rother and Arun, and they appear in a scatter along the central ridge of the Weald running north-west from Hastings. The *feld* names appear to be distributed at random: but behind each there must be some controlling factor which produces lighter woodland or an open country at one place rather than another. This is for ecology, not philology.

Also in the Weald occur the place-names in *fald*, *denn*, and *gesell*. As was remarked by Darby in EENS (and indeed it was observed by the editors of the

E.P-N. Soc. when the *Surrey* and *Sussex* volumes were done), the *fald* place-names are strongly clustered in north-west Sussex—part of a great group which extends into Surrey. Darby contrasts this set of *fald* names in Sussex and Surrey, on the Weald claylands, with a group of distinctive place-names at the other end of the county, the type from OE *denn*. The distribution of this element shows a scatter of a dozen or so in mid-Sussex, generally east of the river Adur and its head-waters, and a close cluster in north-east Sussex about the head-waters of the eastern river Rother. This is part of a larger distribution in East Surrey and in Kent. There is another such distribution-pattern in this end of the Weald, of the element *gesell*; again it is an east Sussex pattern—towards the Kent border and the eastern Rother, with one or two in the central upland behind Hastings and one outlier at the head-waters of the river Ouse.

To these elements we must add the apparently ubiquitous *hamm*, inasmuch as as it is rather rare in the Downs, fairly frequent along all the main river-valleys as would be expected, and very common indeed all over the levels of Pevensey, Brede and the eastern Rother. In these two last, the distribution is part of a larger one extending into Kent—there is an ecology and geomorphology in the old estuaries of Rother and Lympne which produces a characteristic site: it is curious that this district has never come to be called The Hams!

The starting-point

Now it would be tedious to spend further time in describing to the reader the distributions which he can bring out of the Appendix, given an ordnance map and some tracing paper. The point, which is very important and quite simple, but still needs all this qualification and presentation, is that the place-names of Sussex looked at from the new viewpoint offered by recent work, and analysed out into the Appendix to this article, give us a model of English settlement nomenclature as controlled by geography and history. We have observed the geographical factors of Chalk down, Weald Clay, sandstone ridge, and so forth, causing sharp typological divisions. Obviously, different types of farming and subsistence, different organisations of society and ownership, different conditions of ground and requirement, beget different structures and lay-outs. There may have been a great architectural difference between a *fald* and a *denn*: or it may have been a question of use, not structure. These matters arise from geographical conditions and cultural tradition.

But the time factor bears on the distribution. We know from tradition that the South Saxon take-over of this part of Britain would have developed late in the fifth century, to be interrupted when Aelle's ascendancy was arrested by British resurgence. The impression of English place-names on the scene would be confirmed by the end of the sixth century, after the English recovery; but the process must have begun as soon as Sussex became Aelle's for the taking, the last local British power broken. It is possible to see the distribution of *-ingas* and *-tun* place-names, which coincides with the main area in which Roman archaeological evidences are discovered, describing the first inheritance of the new, English, masters, from which they set out to colonise the Weald through *fald* and *denn* and *gesell,* at *hyrst* and *hamm* and *leah* and *feld* and *hrycg.* Sussex place-names report to us the typology of English toponymics in a situation polarised in space between downland and forest, and in time and culture between Britain and England. Until regions like this, where a marked controlling geography and a known historical date-span are given, are scrutinised with an open mind, we shall not be able to use place-names properly. Of course, what is true for Sussex may not be true of Hampshire, or Kent, or Yorkshire. The place-names of Sussex have only to be typical of Sussex, but it is this typicality which will establish them in the typology of English place-names at large.

APPENDIX: TYPICAL SUSSEX PLACE-NAMES

This Appendix consists of four sections: *A.* Folk-names in OE *-ingas; B.* Nature names; *C.* Habitation-names; *D.* Place-names between nature-names and habitation-names. The material is sorted into two categories: (*a*) places whose names are on record by 1100 or which are medieval parish centres; (*b*) other places which emerge into record by 1300. The entry in the name-list is arranged as follows: the place-name, followed by brackets containing the name of the parish in which the place lies or lay—this item is omitted when the head-name is that of a parish; next the National Grid reference; next the bibliographical reference and a summary etymology; and the date at which the p-n. first comes to light if not by 1100 A.D. The order of the place-names is not alphabetical, but follows the west-to-east order of the E.P-N. Soc. *Sussex* volumes, so that the typological distribution may be emphasised rather than the individual etymologies.

A: Sussex place-names in OE *-ingas* on record before 1300.

(*a*) As names of medieval parishes, or of places recorded by 1100.

COCKING, SU 879176, PN Sx 16, MA *10* 23.

IPING, SU 852230, PN Sx 22, MA *10* 23.

WOOLBEDING, SU 873227, PN Sx 31, MA *10* 23.

DIDLING, SU 838185, PN Sx 34, MA *10* 23; 12th century.

HARTING, SU 785195, etc., PN Sx 35, MA *10* 23.

OVING, SU 901050, PN Sx 75, MA *10* 23, BNF *2* 366, 384.

WITTERING, East and West, SZ 796972, 779985, PN Sx 87, MA *10* 23.

GLATTING (Sutton), SU 971141, PN Sx. 120, MA *10* 23.

CLIMPING, TQ 002025, PN Sx. 138, MA. *10* 23.

PEPPERING (Burpham), TQ 035093, PN Sx *167, MA* 10 23. This p-n. shows an alternation of spellings from *-ingas, -ing, -ingtun,* i.e., an alternation of plural and singular, compounded and uncompounded forms of *-ing* suffix place-name.

FERRING, TQ 095025, PN Sx 167, MA *10* 23.

GORING, TQ 105023, PN Sx 168, MA *10* 23.

POLING, TQ 047047, PN Sx 171, MA *10* 23; 12th century.

WEST TARRING (Broadwater), TQ 132040, PN Sx 194, MA *10* 23.

WORTHING (Broadwater), TQ 150029, PN Sx 194, MA *10* 23.

LANCING, TQ 185055, PN Sx 199, MA *10* 23.

SOMPTING, TQ 160051, PN Sx 201, MA *10* 23.

LOWER and UPPER BEEDING, TQ 220274, 195105, PN Sx. 203, 205.

BIDLINGTON or MAUDLIN or MAUDLYN (Bramber), TQ 179103, PN Sx 223, 224, MA *10* 23, BNF *2* 355, *3* 163. In MA I describe this p-n. as ambiguous between an *-inga-* gen. pl. formation and an *-ing* singular. In BNF I analyse further, showing alternation of a plural folk-name in *-ingas* and a composition on either *-inga* (gen. pl.) or *-inge* (locative of *-ing* singular), or *-ing* (singular, uninflected).

STEYNING, TQ 175113, PN Sx 234, MA *10* 23.

PATCHING,TQ 088065, PN Sx 248, MA *10* 23.

FULKING, TQ 247114, PN Sx 284, MA *10* 23.

PERCHING, TQ 244114, PN Sx 285, MA *10* 23, PN-ing² 838–9.

POYNINGS, TQ 264120, PN Sx 286, MA *10* 23.

DITCHLING, TQ 325153, PN Sx 300, MA *10* 23.

MEECHING, TQ 443012, PN Sx 323, MA *10* 23.

HARPINGDEN (lost, Piddinghoe), PN Sx 325, MA *10* 35.

TARRING NEVILLE, TQ 444038, PN Sx 339, MA *10* 23.

FLETCHING, TQ 428235, PN Sx 345, MA *10* 23.

MALLING, TQ 415110, PN Sx 354, MA *10* 23.

PEELINGS (Westham), TQ 617049, PN Sx 448, MA *10* 23.

RENCHING (Westham), TQ 629039, PN Sx 448, MA *10* 23.

BRIGHTLING, TQ 683210, PN Sx 471, MA *10* 23.

WARTLING, TQ 656092, PN Sx 483, MA *10* 23.

GILLINGE (lost, Crowhurst), PN Sx 502, MA *10* 23.

WILTING (Hollington), TQ 780110, PN Sx 504, MA *10* 23; ASE *2* 33.

Wilting is an example of the alternation of simplex and compounded forms of an *-ingas* plural folk-name.

GUESTLING, TQ 855145, PN Sx 508, MA *10* 23.

HASTINGS, TQ 815095, PN Sx 534, MA *10* 23.

(*b*) As names not recorded before 1100, and not parish names.

ASHLING (Funtington), SU 800083, PN Sx, 60 MA *10* 23; 1185.

LIPPERING (Birdham), SZ 814999, PN Sx 81, MA *10* 23, 12th century.

CHYNGTON (Seaford), TV 504987, PN Sx 364, EPN Soc. XI, xli, MA *10* 32, BNF *2* 355; 1180.

BIRLING (East Dean), TV 557969, PN Sx 417, MA *10* 23; 1210.

FILCHING (Jevington), TQ 569029, PN Sx 422, MA *10* 23; 1288.

COODEN DOWN (Bexhill), TQ 714075, PN Sx. 491, MA *10* 23; 12th century.

GENSING (Hastings), TQ 815105, PN Sx 535 and vi, MA *10* 23; 12th century.

B: Sussex place-names of the nature-name type (whose final el. denotes a natural feature) recorded before 1300.

The 16 most frequent final elements in this type are listed. The numbers show the total, the number of parish names, the number recorded by 1100, the number which came to light between 1100 and 1300. The elements are: *leah* (77, 14, 24, 53), *hyrst* (70, 10, 13, 57), *cumb* (27. 5, 9, 18), *feld* (26, 16, 16, 10), *eg* (22, 5, 11, 11), *denu* (22, 7, 12, 10), *burna* (20, 7, 10, 10), *ford* (18, 5, 6, 12), *hrycg* (14, 0, 2, 12), *ora* (13, 3, 8, 5), *welle* (10, 0, 4, 6), *halh* (9, 1, 0, 9), *wudu* (9, 0, 1, 8), *hyll* (8, 1, 1, 7), *dun* (8, 5, 6, 2), *mere* (12, 7, 9, 3). Thereafter *broc*, *beorg* and *graf* 7x, *bece* and *horn* 6x, *hlinc*, *hoh*, *stan* and *hese* 5x; but note: *halh*, *wudu*, *hyll*, *broc* appear in only one or two instances each as parish names or ante-1100: but in several in the post-1100 list, similar to *hrycg* or *welle*.

B.1. leah. (*a*) As a parish-name, or recorded by 1100.

EARNLEY, SZ 815969, PN Sx 82; first el. OE *earn* 'eagle'.

HIGHLEIGH (Sidlesham), SZ 844982, PN Sx 86; first el. supposed *heah* 'high', but I suspect that the form has been met-analysed from OE *hygel-eg* 'hillock meadow, hillock island', which would be more relevant to the site.

SOMERLEY (Wittering), SZ 817985, PN Sx 89; first el. *sumor* 'summer'.

AMBERLEY, TQ 028132, PN' Sx 146; first el. a personal-name.

APSLEY (Thakeham), TQ 119195, PN Sx 181; *æspe* 'aspen-tree'.

SHIPLEY, TQ 145218, PN Sx 188; *sceap* 'sheep'.

TRULEIGH (Edburton), TQ 225115, PN Sx 207; first el. probably *þruh* 'a conduit, a drain'.

WANTLEY (Henfield), TQ 215163, PN Sx 219; pers. n.

WOOLFLYS (Henfield), TQ 225172, PN Sx 219; *wulf* 'a wolf'.

MORLEY (Woodmancote), TQ 235175, PN Sx 221; *mor* 'a marsh'.

ARDINGLY, TQ 347295, PN Sx 251; pers. n.

CRAWLEY, TQ 268365, PN Sx 261; *crawe* 'a crow'.

WEST HOATHLY, TQ 360320, PN Sx 270; *hæð*, *hað*, 'heath'.

CHIDDINGLY (West Hoathly), TQ 360340, PN Sx 271; *-ingas* folk-name; cf. Chiddingly Sx 398 *infra*.

BURLEIGH (Worth), TQ 354372, PN Sx 280; *burh* 'manor house; fortification'.

CHAILEY, TQ 390190, PN Sx 296; *ceacga* 'broom, gorse, brushwood'.

FAIRLIGHT (East Grinstead), TQ 410388, PN Sx 332; *fearn* 'bracken'.

HADLOW DOWN, TQ 530240, PN Sx 395; pers. n.; 1254.

CHIDDINGLY, TQ 543143, PN Sx 398, MA. *10* 24; *-ingas* folk-name; cf. Chiddingly Sx 271 *supra*.

EAST HOATHLY, TQ 520161, PN Sx 400; *hað* 'heath'; 1287.

BOWLEY (lost, Hailsham), TQ 5909, PN Sx 436; pers. n.

HELLINGLY, TQ 580123, PN Sx 438, MA *10* 24; *-ingas* folk-name.

GLYNLEIGH (Westham), TQ 604067, PN Sx 446; *glind* 'fence, enclosure'.

WHILIGH (Ticehurst), TQ 656313, PN Sx 454; *wig* '(heathen) shrine or temple'; cf. Whyly Sx 401 *infa*).

ROWLEY (Ticehurst), TQ 678315, PN Sx 453; pers. n.

BEXHILL, TQ 7407, PN Sx 489; *byxe* 'box-tree'.

CORTESLEY (lost in Hollington), TQ 790110, PN Sx 503; pers. n.

FAIRLIGHT, TQ 860119, Pn Sx 507; *fearn* 'bracken'; 1176.

BECKLEY, TQ 842237, PN Sx 526; pers. n.

RAMESLIE (Rye), TQ 920200, PN Sx 536 and vii, PN Sx vi-vii; ? *ramm* 'a ram'.

B.1. leah. (*b*) As the name of a place first recorded 1100–1300 and not a parish-name.

HENLEY (Fernhurst), SU 895258, PN Sx 19; *hund* 'a hound'; 1296.

MARLEY (Fernhurst), SU 882310, PN Sx 20; unidentified; 1296.

WARDLEY (Iping), SU 845277, PN Sx 23, pers. n.; 1279.

RIPSLEY (Trotton), SU 826292, PN Sx 45; *rispe* 'shrub, brushwood'; 1265.

DOWNLEY (West Dean), SU 863143, PN Sx 49; *dun* 'upland tract, hill country'. 1271.

BOWLEY (North Mundham), SZ 885998, PN Sx 73; pers. n.; 1296.

EGLEY (lost, in Oving), SU 9005, PN Sx 76; pers. n.; 1296.

TOPLEIGH (Ambersham), SU 920180, PN Sx 99; pers. n., or *topp* 'top (of a hill, etc.)'; 1249.

SHILLINGLEE (Kirdford), SU 965325, PN Sx 106, EPN Soc. IX 503, MA *10* 24, BNF *3* 154, 178; OE *scil(l)ing* 'a parting, a division, a dividing or separating'; 1279.

LEE (in Fittleworth), TQ 0019; (location not ascertained), PN Sx 127; simplex; 1206.

GORINGLEE (Thakeham), TQ 113223, PN Sx 181, 195n, EPN Soc. IX x, MA *10* 24, also J. K. Wallenberg, *Kentish Place-Names* (Uppsala), 238–241; *-ingas* folk-name; 1242, perhaps 934 also.

LYWOOD (Ardingly), TQ 3419; (location not ascertained), PN Sx 253; simplex; 1271.

SHELLEY (Crawley), TQ 249315, PN Sx 261; *scylf* 'shelf, hill slope'; 1279.

HANLYE (Cuckfield), TQ 3024, PN Sx 262; *heald* 'sloping'; 1296.

BENTLY or BENTLEY (Cuckfield), TQ 314278, PN Sx 262; *beonet* 'bent-grass'; 1312.

EDGERLEY (Hurstpierpoint), TQ 2716, PN Sx 275; pers. n.; 1296.

OCKLEY (Keymer), TQ 316164, PN Sx 277; *ac* 'oaktree'; 1296.

CUTTINGLYE (Worth), TQ 350390, PN Sx 281, MA *10* 24; -*ingas* folk-name; 1244.

HAILEY (Westmeston), TQ 347150, PN Sx 305; *(ge)hæg* 'enclosure'; 1272.

BOTLEY (East Grinstead), TQ 3938, PN Sx 331; pers. n.; 1296.

HAIRLEY (East Grinstead), TQ 365364, PN Sx 332; *heald* 'slope'; 1272.

LUDLAY (Selmeston), TQ 523075, PN Sx 338; pers. n.; 1287.

NUTLEY (Maresfield), TQ 442277, PN Sx 350; *hnutu* 'nut-tree'; 1249.

THE LAY (Beddingham), TQ 447069, PN Sx 359; simplex; 1212.

CORSLEY (Withyham), TQ 4935, PN Sx 371; not known. 1285.

HOADLEY'S (Withyham), TQ 4935, PN Sx 372; *haδ* 'heath'; 1287.

HENLEY (Frant), TQ 610344, PN Sx 375; *heah* 'high'; 1288.

RAMSLYE (Frant), TQ 5935, PN Sx 375; pers. n. or *hræfn* 'raven'; 1262.

RENDLIE (Rotherfield), TQ 5530, PN Sx 379; *rymde* 'cleared, emptied'; 1288.

BLETCHINGLEY (Rotherfield), TQ 575301, PN Sx 377; *ingas* folk-name; 1262.

HORLEIGH (Mayfield), TQ 5626, PN Sx 382; *horh* 'filth'; 1288.

HAMLY (Chiddingly), TQ 556136, PN Sx 399; pers. n.; 12th century.

WHYLY (East Hoathly), TQ 516169, PN Sx 401; *wig* '(heathen) temple or shrine'; 1246.

DUNLY (Waldron), TQ 5419, PN Sx 406; *dun* 'upland tract, hill'; 13.

TURFLEIGH (lost, Willingdon), TQ 5802, PN Sx 425; *turf* 'turf, peat'; 13.

NUTLEY (Hellingly), TQ 5812, PN Sx 441; *neat* 'neat, calf'; 1285.

PASHLEY (Ticehurst), TQ 706290, PN Sx 453; pers. n.; 1230.

HOADLEY (Ticehurst), TQ 657279, PN Sx 452; *haδ* , *hæδ* 'heath'; 1285.

MARKLY (Heathfield), TQ 586226, PN Sx 465; *mearc* 'boundary'; 1202.

CRALLE (Warbleton), TQ 608160, PN Sx 469; *crawe* 'a crow'; 1288.

KINGSLEY (Warbleton), TQ 6117, PN Sx 469; pers. n. ?; 1296.

TILLEY (Wartling), TQ 6509, PN Sx 484; *tun* 'a village, a farm'; 1288.

FRECKLEY (Catsfield), TQ 7213, PN Sx 485; pers. n.; 13.

HENLEY'S (Catsfield), TQ 7312, PN Sx 486; *heah* 'high'; 1288.

BRAMSES (Bexhill), TQ 7407, PN Sx 490; pers. n.; 13.

COODEN DOWN (Bexhill), TQ 714075, PN Sx 491 n1; -*ingas* folk-name: 12.

SIDLEY (Bexhill), TQ 7409, PN Sx 494; *sid* 'wide'; 1279.

PETLEY (Battle), TQ 7616, PN Sx 499; *pytt* 'a pit'; 12.

WATTLEHILL (Ewhurst), TQ 781218, PN Sx 521; *hwæte* 'wheat'; 1180.

GOATLEY (Northiam), TQ 8324, PN Sx 523; *gat* 'a goat'; 1210.

LUDLEY (Beckley), TQ 8520, PN Sx 528; pers. n.; 13.

FLACKLEY (Peasmarsh), TQ 880233, PN Sx 532; pers. n.; 12.

MARLEY (Peasmarsh), TQ 8821, PN Sx 532; *(ge)mære* 'boundary'; 1275.

B.2. hyrst (a)

FERNHURST, SU 897285, PN Sx 19; *fearn* 'bracken'; 1195.

MIDHURST, SU 887215, PN Sx 27; *mid* 'middle'; 12th century.

CHITHURST, SU 843230, PN Sx 33; pers. n.

IDEHURST (Kirdford), TQ 033249; PN Sx 105; *hyd* 'a hide of land'.

MADEHURST, SU 986102, PN Sx 129; *mæδel* 'a speech'; 12th century.

BILLINGSHURST, TQ 085257, PN Sx 147, BNF 2 329, 3144, 163; **bil(l)ing* 'a hill'; 1202.

WARMINGHURST, TQ 117169, PN Sx 182; -*ing* singular formation, perhaps of the -*ing*

variety discussed in BNF; the el. *hyrst* probably replaces *ersc* 'stubble' in this p.n.; the name is first recorded 1188.

ASHURST, TQ 176163, PN Sx 183; *æsc* 'ash-trees', *æscett* 'ash wood, ash copse'; 1248.

EWHURST (Shermanbury), TQ 2118, PN Sx 213; *iw* 'yew-tree'.

NUTHURST, TQ 1926, PN Sx 231; *hnutu* 'nut-tree'; 1228.

HURSTPIERPOINT, TQ 279164, PN Sx 274; simplex.

BROCKHURST (East Grinstead), TQ 408375, PN Sx 331; *brocc* 'a badger'.

WADHURST, TQ 640319, PN Sx 385; pers. n.; 1253.

SALEHURST, TQ 749243, PN Sx 457; *sealh* 'willow'.

PENHURST, TQ 695165, PN Sx 476; pers. n.

HERSTMONCEUX, TQ 643103, PN Sx 479; simplex.

CROWHURST, TQ 757124, PN Sx 502, EPN Soc. XIV, li and 127; *croh* 'a corner', as also in Crowham in Westfield Sx 505.

EWHURST, TQ 795245, PN Sx 518; *iw* 'a yew tree'.

HURST (Sedlescombe), TQ 788190, PN Sx 526; simplex.

BELLHURST (Beckley), TQ 869258, PN Sx 527; the first el. in this and Bellhurst Sx 456 (see *infra*), is probably OE *bel* 'a bonfire, a beacon, a pyre'.

IBBANHYRSTE (not identified, ? near Bexhill), Sawyer 108 (BCS 208), date 772 (13); a gavel-land of Bexhill manor; first el. a pers. n.

B.2. hyrst. (b).

HOLLIST (Easebourne), SU 8824, PN Sx 19; *hol* '(in a) hollow'; 1296.

SLATHURST (Stedham), SU 8622, PN. Sx 30; *sliete* 'mud'; 1296.

HAWKHURST (Kirdford), TQ 025231, PN Sx 105; *hafoc* 'a hawk'; 1288.

LANGHURST (Kirdford), TQ 985259, PN Sx 106; *lang* 'long'; 1230.

OAKHURST (Kirdford), TQ 0126, PN Sx 106; *ac* 'oak-tree': 13th century.

SLIFEHURST (Kirdford), TQ 005277, PN Sx 107; *slifu* 'slippery place'; 1199.

TODHURST (Kirdford), TQ 0126; PN Sx 108; first el. not identified; 1271.

WEPHURST (Kirdford), TQ 025289, PN Sx 108; pers. n.; 1230.

BROCKHURST (Lurgashall), SU 925275, PN Sx 111; *broc* 'meadow, marshland'; 1279.

CHILLINGHURST (Lurgashall), SU 9327, PN Sx 112; pers. n.; final el. alternates with *ersc* 'stubble'; 1288.

PARKHURST (Lurgashall), SU 9327, PN Sx 112; *pearroc* 'enclosure, paddock'; 1279.

ROUNDHURST (Lurgashall), SU 928305, PN Sx 112; *rymde* 'cleared'; 1296.

PARKHURST (Tillington), SU 950246, PN Sx 122; *pearroc* 'enclosure, paddock'; 1296.

KIMBERS (Tillington), SU 9621, PN Sx. 122; first el. unidentified; 1288.

BRINKHURST (Wisborough), TQ 0525, PN Sx 131; pers. n.; 1296.

AMBLEHURST (Wisborough), TQ 0428, PN Sx 131; pers. n.; 1195.

DOUNHURST or DUNHURST (Wisborough), TQ 035279, PN Sx 132; *dun* 'upland, hill'; 1244.

HURST (Wisborough), TQ 043292, PN Sx 133; simplex; 1279.

TODHURST (Walberton), SU 973046, PN Sx 144; Pers. n.; 1279.

WEYHURST (Rudgwick), TQ 0733, PN Sx 158; *weg* 'a road'; 13th century.

PINKHURST (Slinfold), TQ 131307, PN Sx 160; pers. n.; 13th century.

BLAKEHURST (Warningcamp), TQ 046067, PN Sx 174; *blæc* 'black, dark'; 1263.

SHARPENHURST (Itchingfield), TQ 137276, PN Sx 177; *scearp* 'pointed, steep'; 13th century.

LACKENHURST (Shipley), TQ 1421, PN Sx 189; pers. n.; 1285.

WALLHURST (Cowfold), TQ 223237, PN Sx 211; *wealh* 'foreigner, serf, Briton'; 1279.

BISHOP'S PLACE (Albourne), TQ 263157, PN Sx 215; *bisceop* 'bishop'; 1262.

WAKEHURST (Ardingly), TQ 3331, PN Sx 254; pers. n.; 1206.

TILLINGHURST (Ardingly), TQ 338308, PN Sx 254, MA *10* 24; *-ingas* folk-name; 1296.

SPITHURST (Barcombe), TQ 427175, PN Sx 313–4; first el. not identified; 1296.

TABLEHURST (Forest Row), TQ 429353, PN Sx 329; first el. not identified; 1200.

ASHURSTWOOD (Forest Row), TQ 4235, PN Sx 327; *æsc* 'an ash tree'; 1169.

TILKHURST (East Grinstead), TQ 368371, PN Sx 333; *telga* 'a branch, a twig'; 1285.

BROADHURST (Horsted Keynes), TQ 3828, PN Sx 337; *brad* 'wide'; 12th century.

BADHURST (lost, Lindfield), TQ 3425, PN Sx 340; pers. n.; 1200.

LANDHURST (Hartfield), TQ 4735, PN Sx 368; *lane* 'a lane'; 1107.

FAULKNER'S (Hartfield), TQ 4735, PN Sx 367; pers. n.; 1199.

BUCKHURST (Withyham), TQ 490350, PN Sx 370; *boc* 'beech-tree'; 1199.

ISENHURST (Mayfield), TQ 565231, PN Sx 382; *isen* 'iron': 1279.

CHITTINGHURST (Walhurst), TQ 615290, PN Sx 386; singluar *-ing* formation upon unidentified basis; 1296.

HORSELUNGES (Hellingly), TQ 578119, PN Sx 440, simplex; 1317.

RAMSHURST (lost, Hellingly), TQ 5812, PN Sx 441; *ramm* 'a ram'; 1284.

WINKENHURST (Hellingly), TQ 583145, PN Sx 442; a p.n. in *tun*; 1296.

BRICKLEHURST (Ticehurst), TQ 658292, PN Sx 451; pers. n.; 1279.

BAREHURST (Ticehurst), TQ 667266, PN Sx 451; *bære* 'woodland pasture'; 12th century.

TICEHURST, TQ 688300, PN Sx 450; *ticcen* 'a kid'; 1248.

BELLHURST (Etchingham), TQ 7228, PN Sx 456; *bel* 'bonfier, beacon, pyre'; 1260.

BERNHURST (Salehurst), TQ 7424, PN Sx 458; first el. not ascertained; 1230.

CROWHURST (Burwash), TQ 683263, PN Sx 461; *crawe* 'crow'; 1170.

MILKHURST (Heathfield), TQ 5920, PN Sx 465; *meoluc* 'milk'; 1279.

BROADHURST (Heathfield), TQ 628253, PN Sx 464; *brede* 'stretch, expanse, of land'; 1215.

BATHURST (Warbleton), TQ 6217, PN Sx 469; pers. n.; 1121.

CROWHURST (Mountfield), TQ 728190, PN Sx 475; *crawe*; 1296.

AGMERHURST (Ashburnham), TQ 702144, PN Sx 477; pers. n.; 1209.

CHILTHURST (Herstmonceux), TQ 650130, PN Sx 480; *cild* 'a male heir, a young (noble)man': e.13.

MAPLEHURST (Ore), TQ 805135, PN Sx 505; *mapel* 'maple tree'; 1296.

UPPER SNAILHAM (Icklesham), TQ 859170, PN Sx 510; *grafa* 'a grove'; 1296.

LINTHURST (Icklesham), TQ 8816, PN Sx 512; *lind* 'lime-tree'; 1220.

B.3. cumb. (a).

SHEEP COMBE (Findon), TQ 135065, PN Sx 198; *sceap* 'sheep'.

COOMBES, TQ 190081, PN Sx 224; simplex.

BALCOMBE, TQ 309308, PN Sx 255; pers. n.

SADDLESCOMBE (Newtimber), TQ 272114, Pn Sx 286; *sadol* 'saddle, col'.

PYECOMBE, TQ 285129, PN Sx 287; *pie* 'midge, gnat'.

MOULSECOOMBE (Patcham), TQ 329068, PN Sx 294; pers. n.

ASHCOMBE, TQ 377095, PN Sx 320; pers. n.

HALCOMBE (Piddinghoe), TQ 420029, PN Sx 324; *horh* 'dirt'.

TELSCOMBE, TQ 405034, PN Sx 326; pers. n.

SEDLESCOMBE, TQ 780180, PN Sx 524; *setl* 'seat, residence'.

B.3. cumb. (b).

PATCHESCUMBE (lost, Heyshott), SU 8918, EPN Soc. XVI, xxxv, PN Sx 249; pers. n.; 1230.

MALECOMB (East Dean), SU 922139, PN Sx 47; pers. n.; 1200.

BRINSCOMBE (lost, Singleton), SU 8713, PN Sx 53; pers. n.; 1295.

MOLECOMB (Westhampnett), SU 895100, PN Sx 78; ME *molle* 'a mole'.

HORN COMBE (West Hoathly), TQ 347305, PN Sx 272; *horn* 'a projection, a promontory'; 1279.

DENCOMBE (Slaugham), TQ 272306, PN Sx 277; pers. n.; 12th century.

VARNCOMBE (Pyecombe), TQ 276101, PN Sx 288; *fearn* 'bracken'; 1279.

COOMBE (Hamsey), TQ 393124, PN Sx 315; simplex; 1296.

RANSCOMBE (South Malling), TQ 439086, PN Sx 355; *ramm* 'ram'; 1291.

COOMBE (West Firle), TQ 4707, PN Sx 361; simplex; 12th century.

COMBE (Wadhurst), TQ 6228, PN Sx 386, simplex; 1197.

MOTCOMBE (Eastbourne), TV 6099, PN Sx 431; *gemot* 'moot, meeting'; 1219.

GOTHAM (Bexhill), TQ 709090, PN Sx 492; first el. not ascertained; 13th century.

CARCOMBE (Whatlington), TQ 7618, PN Sx 501; *catt* '(wild) cat'; 12th century.

CHITCOMBE (Brede), TQ 8218, PN Sx 515; pers. n.; 1220.

WATCOMBE (Beckley), TQ 851223, PN Sx 528; pers. n.; 1248.

B.4. feld. (a).

ITCHINGFIELD, TQ 131289, PN Sx 176, MA *10* 24; *-ingas* folk-name; 1222.

IFIELD, TQ 247376, PN Sx 207; *ig, iw* 'yew-tree'.

HENFIELD, TQ 212162, PN Sx 215; *heah* 'high'.

CUCKFIELD, TQ 303245, PN Sx 261; *cucu,* 'cuckoo'.

BENEFELD (lost, Twineham), TQ 2419, PN Sx 279; *beonet* 'bent-grass'.

WIVELSFIELD, TQ 338207, PN Sx 305; *wifel* 'a weevil', or a pers. n.

LINDFIELD, TQ 349259, PN Sx 340; *lind* 'lime-tree'.

HENFIELD (Lindfield), TQ 3624, PN Sx 342; *heah* 'high'.

SHEFFIELD (Fletching), TQ 4124, PN Sx 347; *sceap* 'sheep'.

MARESFIELD, TQ 465140, PN Sx 349; *mersc* 'a marsh'; 1234.

Note that Maresfield is identified with *Mesewelle* DB fol. 22b in the *Domesday geography of England* etc., but the names are not identical. DB *Mesewelle* would be the antecedent form of a place-name exactly like Miswell(s) in Worth, in Buttinghill Hd., see B.11 *welle. (a). infra.* A note

on PN Sx 381 reports an attempt to identify *Mesewelle* DB with Mayfield, TQ 585270, in Loxfield Camden Hd., by supposing the rather bizarre palæographic reduction of a form *Megevelle.*

HARTFIELD, TQ 479357, PN Sx 365; *heorot* 'hart, stag'.

ROTHERFIELD, TQ 557297, PN Sx 376; *hryð er* 'cattle'.

MAYFIELD, TQ 585270, PN Sx 381, *mægþe* 'mayweed'; see note on Maresfield *supra*; 12th century.

FRAMFIELD, TQ 495203, PN Sx 392; pers. n.

ISFIELD, TQ 4417, PN Sx 396; pers. n.; 1215.

UCKFIELD, TQ 472215, PN Sx 396; pers. n.; 1220.

HEATHFIELD, TQ 598203, PN Sx 463; *hæð* 'heath'; 12th century.

CATSFIELD, TQ 729134, PN Sx 485; pers. n. or *catt* 'cat'.

NINFIELD, TQ 705124, PN Sx 487; *niwenumen* 'newly taken in'.

NETHERFIELD (Battle), TQ 706188, PN Sx 498; *næddre* 'adder'.

WESTFIELD, TQ 809153, PN Sx 505; west 'west' or *weste* 'waste'?

B.4. feld. (b).

WATERSFIELD (Coldwaltham), TQ 015158, PN Sx 126; *wæter* 'water (a stream, etc.)'; 1226.

CHATFIELDS (Bolney), TQ 2622, PN Sx 257; pers. n.; 1279.

SELSFIELD (West Hoathly), TQ 348342, PN Sx 272; *sele* 'a hall'; 1279.

BENFIELD (Hangleton), TQ 2607, PN Sx 289; *beonet* 'bent grass'; 1296.

LOVEL (Chailey), TQ 3919, PN Sx 297; *hlot* 'allotment'; 1288.

FRESHFIELD (Horsted Keynes), TQ 3825, PN Sx 337; *fersc* 'fresh, clean'; 1296.

AMBERSTONE (Hailsham), TQ 595112, PN Sx 435; pers. n.; 1180.

PERRYFIELD (Brightling), TQ 6821, PN Sx 472; *pyrige* 'pear-tree'; 1229.

MAXFIELD (Guestling), TQ 834153, PN Sx 509; *meox* 'dung'; 12th century.

STREETFIELD (Ewhurst), TQ 7820, PN Sx 520; *stræt* 'street, Roman road, paved road'; 1230.

B.5. eg. (a).

WEST THORNEY, SU 769024, PN Sx 62; *þorn* 'thorntree'.

LIDSEY (Aldingbourne), Su 939030, PN Sx 63; pers. n.

MEDMERRY (Selsey), SZ 841934, PN Sx 83; *medeme* 'medium'.

SELSEY, SZ 8593, PN Sx 82; *seolh* 'a seal'.

THORNEY (Wittering), SZ 8096, PN Sx 89;

þorn 'thorntree'.

SHRIPNEY (Bersted), SU 930020, PN Sx 91; first el. not ascertained.

BOLNEY, TQ 262227, PN Sx 257; pers. n.; 1263.

HORSEY (Eastbourne), HORSE EYE (Pevensey), TQ 626084, PN Sx 430, 444; *hors* 'a horse'.

PEVENSEY, TQ 648048, PN Sx 443; pers. n.
LANGNEY (Westham), TQ 630020, PN Sx 447; *lang* 'long'.

RYE, TQ 9220, PN Sx 536; simplex; 12th century.

B.5. eg. (b).

HONEY (West Grinstead), TQ 1720, PN Sx 187; *hol* '(in a) hollow'; 1279.
DANNY (Hurstpierpoint), TQ 2716, PN Sx 274; not ascertained; 1296.
RISE (Southover), TQ 415089 and 423082, PN Sx 322; simplex; 1237.
HYDNEYE (Willingdon), TQ 5802, PN Sx 424; pers. n.; 1200.
ST. ANTHONY'S (Eastbourne), TQ 629014, PN Sx 433; pers. n.; 1249.
MANXEY (Pevensey), TQ 640070, PN Sx 445; pers. n.; 1200.
CHILLEY (Pevensey), TQ 636061, PN Sx 444; pers. n.; 13th century?
RICKNEY (Westham), TQ 625069, PN Sx 449; pers. n.; 1291.
NORTHEYE (Bexhill), about TQ 689063, PN Sx 493; *norð* 'north'; 1188.
SOUTHEYE (Bexhill), TQ 677056, PN Sx 494; *suð* 'south'; 1203.
GLASSEYE (Beckley), TQ 835215, PN Sx 527; not ascertained; 1189.

B.6. denu 'a valley'. (a).

EAST DEAN, SU 905130, PN Sx 47, xlv; *æþ eling* 'prince'.
WEST DEAN, SU 861127, PN Sx 41, xlv; *æþ eling* 'prince'.
EGDEAN, SU 998200, PN Sx 101; pers. n.; 1279.
PANGDEAN (Pyecombe), TQ 293117, PN Sx 288; pers. n.
WITHDEAN (Patcham), TQ 3007, PN Sx 294; pers. n.
RADYNDEN (lost, Preston), TQ 3006, PN Sx 295, Sawyer, 43, Forsberg 63–4; simplex.
STANDEAN (Ditchling and Pyecombe), TQ 3111, PN Sx 302; *stan* 'stone, rock'.
BEVENDEAN (Falmer), TQ 350063, PN Sx 308; pers. n.
OVINGDEAN, TQ 355038, PN Sx 311, MA *10* 24, BNF, *2* 366, 383, *3* 150. The prototheme is a sg. *-ing* suffix formation.

in genitive singular and locative singular inflexion, perhaps alternating with a gen. pl. from an *-ingas* folk-name, based on an OE pers. n. Cf. Rottingdean *infra*.
ROTTINGDEAN, TQ 369026, PN Sx 311, MA *10* 24. In MA *10* the prototheme is analysed as the gen. pl. of an *-ingas* folk-name based on an OE pers. n. But the spellings in *inge-. -ing-, inges-* indicate that this p.n. ought to be considered the same type as Ovingdean *supra*—an *-ing* singular formation in uninflected, locative and genitive inflexion—and it ought to have been discussed at BNF *loc. cit.*
BALSDEAN (Rottingdean), TQ 378059, PN Sx 312; pers. n.
EASTDEAN, TV 557977, PN Sx 417; simplex.
WESTDEAN, TV 525996, PN Sx 419; simplex.

B.6. denu. 'a valley'. (b).

ADSDEAN (Westbourne), SU 794094, PN Sx 55; pers. n.; 1194.
DEAN (Tillington), SU 950221, PN Sx 124; simplex; 13th century.
MARRINGDEAN (Billingshurst), TQ 0825, PN Sx 149; p.n.; 1288.
PYTHINGDEAN (Pulborough), TQ 038205, PN Sx 154; *-ing* sg. formation; 1279.
COBDEN (Sullington), TQ 100109, PN Sx 179; pers. n.; 1256.
HIGHDEN (Washington), TQ 112114, PN Sx 242; *heah* 'high'; 1288.
BRAMBLEDEN (lost, Shoreham-by-Sea), TQ 2105, PN Sx 247; *bremel* 'bramble'; 1100.
HOUNDEAN (Lewes), TQ 396098, PN Sx 320; *hund* 'hound', or pers. n.; 1230.
DEANS (Piddinghoe), TQ 427037, PN Sx 324; simplex; 1279.
PEAKDEAN (Eastdean), TV 559987, PN Sx 418; *peac* 'hill'; 1198.

B.7. *burna* 'a stream; a seasonal or intermittent stream'. (*a*).

EASEBOURNE, SU 895225, PN Sx 16.
WESTBOURNE, SU 755073, PN Sx 55.
ALDINGBOURNE, SU 923055, PN Sx 62.
FISHBOURNE, OLD and NEW (anciently part of Bosham), SU 836045, PN Sx 58, 70.
NUTBOURNE (Pulborough), TQ 075189, PN Sx 154.

ALBOURNE, TQ 257162, PN Sx 215.
WINTERBOURNE (Lewes), TQ 380090, PN Sx 321.
EASTBOURNE, TV 605995, PN Sx 426.
BOURNE (Salehurst), TQ 752255, PN Sx 458.
ASHBURNHAM, TQ 688146, PN Sx 477, ASE 2 24.

B.7. *burna* (*b*).

NUTBOURNE (Westbourne), SU 777055, PN Sx 56; 12th century.
EBERNOE (Kirdford), SU 973280, PN Sx 104; 1262.
HASLINGBOURNE (Petworth), SU 982203, PN Sx 116, MA *10* 24; 13th century. It is not clear whether this place-name contains as first element an *-inga-* genitive plural folk-name formation or an *-ing* singular noun, or an *-ing* singular place-name, i.e., *Hæslinga-burna* 'bourne of the folk who live at a hazelwood', or *Hæslinge-burna* 'the bourne at-, -related to-, -known as-, *Hæslinge* (i.e., at *Hæsling*, place where hazels grow)' alternating with *Hæsling-burna* 'the bourne (which is-, -called)

Hæsling (thing connected with hazel(s), hazel-tree or wood)'.
LIMBOURNE (Fittleworth), location not indicated, PN Sx 127; 1288.
SWANBOURNE (South Stoke), TQ 015080, PN Sx 143: 1273.
HAYBOURNE (Pulborough), location not indicated, PN Sx 153; 1262.
HAWKSBOURNE (Horsham), location not known, PN Sx 227; 1242.
WAPSBOURNE (Chailey), TQ 399234, PN Sx 298; 1197.
GLYNDEBOURNE (Glynde), TQ 452107, PN Sx 353; 1288.
WENBONS (Wadhurst), TQ 6329, PN Sx 387; 1271.

B.8. *ford* 'a ford', *fyrde* 'a fording-place'. (*a*).

TREYFORD, SU 825185, PN Sx 43; *treow* 'a tree'.
DUMPFORD (Trotton), SU 830219, PN Sx 33, 44; unidentified.
KIRDFORD, TQ 017265, PN Sx 102; pers. n.; 1228.

FORD, TQ 003037, PN Sx 141; simplex; 1194.
ITFORD (Beddingham), TQ 434055, PN Sx 358; pers. n.
SEAFORD, TV 483990, PN Sx 363; *sæ* 'the sea'.

B.8. *ford, fyrde*. (*b*).

DURFORD (Rogate), SU 778233, PN Sx 39; *deor* 'an animal'; 12th century.
RATFORD (Petworth), SU 9721, PN Sx 119; *hreod* 'a reed (bed)'; 1249.
AVISFORD (Walberton), SU 975065, PN Sx 136, 143; pers. n.; 1253.
SLAUGHTERFORD (Itchingfield), TQ 1328, PN Sx 177; *slohtre* 'a slough, a muddy place'; 1276.
WORTLEFORD (Cuckfield and Hurstpierpoint), TQ 2821, PN Sx 266; pers. n.; 1291.
KEYSFORD (Lindfield), TQ 3425, PN Sx 342; pers. n.; 1296.

LUXFORD (Crowborough), TQ 525315, PN Sx 373; pers. n.; 1279.
HASTINGFORD (Hadlow Down), TQ 522258, PN Sx 395, MA *10* 24; *-ingas* folk-name; 1279.
CHILVER (Arlington), TQ 535068, PN Sx 409; *ceosol* 'gravel, shingle'; 1252.
LUNDSFORD (Etchingham), TQ 716256, PN Sx 456; pers. n.; 1170.
BATSFORD (Warbleton), TQ 6018, PN Sx 469; pers. n.; 1100.
BLACKFORD (Herstmonceux), TQ 609144, PN Sx 482; *blæc* 'black, dark-coloured'; 1272.

B.9. *hrycg.* (*a*).

HAWKRIDGE (Hellingly), TQ 555115, PN Sx 440, MA *10* 24; -*ingas* folk-name.

HRIGGE (? near Bexhill), TQ 7407, PN Sx 489, Sawyer 108; simplex.

B.9. *hrycg.* (*b*).

BRANTRIDGE (Balcombe), TQ 287302, PN Sx 255; *brant* 'steep'; 1292.

TICKERIDGE (West Hoathly), TQ 3632, PN Sx 273; *teag* 'paddock'; 1296.

CAVERIDGE (Barcombe), TQ 4114, PN Sx 313; pers. n.; 12th century.

DALLINGRIDGE (Forest Row), TQ 430360, PN Sx 328, MA *10* 24; -*ingas* folk-name; 1271.

RIGG (Fletching), TQ 4223, PN Sx 346; simplex; 1202.

GILLRIDGE (Withyham), TQ 517328, PN Sx 371; *gold* 'golden'; 1285.

ERIDGE (Frant), TQ 5734, PN Sx 374;

earn 'eagle'; 1203.

EUEREGGE (Frant), TQ 5935, PN Sx 374, note; *iw* 'yewtree'; 1296.

CLEARHEDGE (Waldron), TQ 5419, PN Sx 406; *clæfre* 'clover'; 1288.

IRIDGE (Salehurst), TQ 735269, PN Sx 459; *iw* 'yew'; 1248.

FAIR RIDGE (Salehurst), TQ 7424, PN Sx 458; *fearn* 'bracken'; 1210.

FRONTRIDGE (Burwash), TQ 6724, PN Sx 462; *funta* 'spring'; 1248.

WIVELRIDGE (lost, Peasmarsh), TQ 8821, PN Sx 532; *wifel* 'a weevil', or pers. n.; 1248.

B.10. *ora.* (*a*).

WEST ITCHENOR, SU 799007, PN Sx 82; pers. n.

BOGNOR, SZ 935990, PN Sx 92; pers. n.

HONER (Pagham), SZ 875983, PN Sx 94; *holh* 'hollow'.

LT. BOGNOR (Fittleworth), TQ 005205, PN Sx 126; pers. n.; 1248.

WARNINGORE (Chailey), TQ 374137, PN Sx 298; -*ing* suffix formation.

SIDNOR (lost, Selmeston), TQ 5107, PN Sx 339; *sid* 'wide'.

TUGMORE (Hartfield), TQ 4735, PN Sx 369; pers. n.

CUDNOR (Westham), TQ 6304, PN Sx 446; pers. n.

ORE, TQ 835114, PN. Sx 504; simplex; 1121.

B.10. *ora.* (*b*).

KEYNOR (Sidlesham), SZ 849976, PN Sx 86; *cu* 'cow'; 1187.

ROWNER (Pulborough), TQ 072269, PN Sx 154; *ruh* 'rough'; 1261.

SANDORE (lost, Seaford), TV 4899, PN Sx

364; *sand* 'sand'; 1275;

HODORE (Hartfield), TQ 4735, PN Sx 367; *haˠ* 'heath'; 1274.

KITCHENOUR (Beckley), TQ 869240, PN Sx 527; pers. n.; 12th century.

B. 11. *welle.* (*a*).

STONELAND (West Hoathly), TQ 350330, PN Sx 272; -*ingas* folk-name.

MISWELLS (Worth), TQ 338363, PN Sx 282; *meos* 'moss'. See note on Maresfield *B.4. feld.* (*a*) *supra*.

SHOYSWELL (Etchingham), TQ 692275, PN Sx 450, 457; first el. not identified.

FRANKWELL (Ashburham), TQ 669145, PN Sx 478; pers. n.

B.11. *welle.* (*b*).

BUTTLESWELL (lost, Rogate), SU 8023, PN Sx 39; pers. n.; 1278.

BLACKWELL (Kirdford), TQ 0126, PN Sx 108; *blæc* 'black, dark'; 1296.

COLWELL (Wivelsfield), TQ 3320, PN Sx 306; *col* 'cool, cold'; 1296.

DUDDLESWELL (Maresfield), TQ 469277, PN Sx 350; pers. n.; 1295.

FLIMWELL (Ticehurst), TQ 715312, PN Sx 452; *fliema* 'a fugitive'; 1210.

DUDWELL (Burwash), TQ 676238, PN Sx 461; pers. n.; 1200.

B.12. mere. (a).

LINCHMERE, SU 869309, PN Sx 24; *hlinc* 'hill, ridge'; 1186.

TANGMERE, SU 901062, PN Sx 97; *tang* 'fork'.

ELMER (Middleton), SU 985002, PN Sx 142; *æl* 'an eel'.

KEYMER, TQ 315153, PN Sx 276; *cu* 'cow'.

BALMER (Falmer), TQ 358099, PN Sx 308;

burg ' a fortified place'.

FALMER, TQ 355087, PN Sx 308; *fealu* 'dark, fallow'.

STANMER, TQ 3409, PN Sx 312; *stan* 'stone, stony'.

RINGMER, TQ 445125, PN Sx 355; *hring* 'a ring, a circle, circular'; 1275.

UDIMORE, TQ 865190, PN Sx 516; pers. n.

B.12. mere. (b).

BATCHMERE'S (Birdham), SZ 8299986, PN Sx 80; pers. n.; 1296.

CODMORE (Pulborough), TQ 049202, PN Sx 153; pers. n.; 1288.

HAREMERE (Etchingham), TQ 7226, PN Sx 456; *har* 'venerable, on a boundary'; 12th century.

B.13. dun. (a).

MARDEN, SU 7914, PN Sx 51; *mære* 'boundary'.

SLINDON, SU 9608, PN Sx 96; *slinu* 'slope'.

FERNDEN (Ambersham), SU 899309; EPN Soc. XVI, xxxvi. PN Sx 97; *fearn* 'bracken'.

FINDON, TQ 116085, PN Sx 197; *fin* 'heap'.

ANNINGTON, TQ 190095, PN Sx 222, MA *10* 24; pers. n.

WILLINGDON, TQ 589025, PN. Sx 424; pers. n.

B.13. dun. (b).

ECCLESDEN (Angmering), TQ 089044, PN Sx 165; pers. n.; 1176.

DOWNASH (Hailsham), TQ 600078, PN Sx 436; simplex; 1240.

C. Sussex place-names formed from habitative elements, recorded before 1300.

C.1. tun 'farmstead, enclosure, farmyard, village'. *(a).*

BEPTON, SU 855183, PN Sx 15; pers. n., *-ing-*.

BUDDINGTON (Easebourne), SU 883225, PN Sx 17; pers. n., *-ing.*

TROTTON, SU 835225, PN Sx 44; OE **træding* 'path, stepping stones'.

BINDERTON, SU 849108, PN Sx 46; pers. n., *-ing-*.

PRESTON (Binderton), SU 854111, PN Sx 46; *preost* 'a priest'.

COMPTON, SU 778148, PN Sx 47; *cumb* 'valley'.

LAVANT, SU 8608, PN Sx 50; river-name.

MIDLAVANT, SU 8508, PN Sx 50; river-name.

RACTON, SU 776094, PN Sx 52; pers. n.

LORDINGTON (Racton), SU 781098, PN Sx 52; pers. n., *-ing.*

SINGLETON, SU 877132, PN. Sx 53; *sengel* 'brushwood'.

STOUGHTON, SU 800115, PN Sx 54; *stocc* 'tree-stock'.

FUNTINGTON, SU 800083, PN Sx 60, SOA 47; *-ing* suffix formation on *funta* 'a spring'; 12th century.

STRETTINGTON (Boxgrove), SU 893072, PN Sx 68; *stræt* 'Roman road'.

EASTHAMPNETT (Boxgrove), SU 920066, PN Sx 67; *heah* 'high'.

DONNINGTON, SU 8502, PN 69; pers. n.

MERSTON, SU 894032, PN Sx 72; *mersc* 'marsh'.

RUNCTON (North Mundham), SU 885023 PN Sx 74; pers. n., *-ing-*.

WESTHAMPNETT, SU 880061, PN Sx 78; *heah* 'high'.

ALMODINGTON, SZ 827977, PN Sx 85. pers. n., *ing-*; 1166.

CHARLTON (lost, Pagham), SZ 8897, PN Sx 93, *ceorl* 'peasant'.

BARLAVINGTON, SU 972159, PN Sx 100; pers. n., *-ing-*.

BURTON, SU 968173, PN Sx 100; pers. n.

DUNCTON, SU 961174, PN Sx 101; pers. n., *-ing-*.

WOOLAVINGTON or WEST and EAST LAVINGTON, SU 943163, PN Sx 109; pers. n., *-ing-*.

SUTTON, SU 978156, PN Sx 120; *suð* 'south(ern)'.

TILLINGTON, SU 963217, PN Sx 121; pers. n., *-ing-*.

HOUGHTON, TQ 019115, PN Sx 128; *hoh* 'spur, promontory, hill'.

MIDDLETON, SU 977003, PN Sx 142; *middel* 'middle'.

TORTINGTON, TQ 003049, PN Sx 143; pers. n., *-ing-*.

WALBERTON, SU 972057, PN Sx 143; pers. n.

YAPTON, SU 982034, PN Sx 144; pers. n., *-ing-*.

STORRINGTON, TQ 085142, PN Sx 161; *storc* 'stork'.

ANGMERING, SU 067043, PN Sx 163, MA 10 23; *-ingas* folk-name.

HANGLETON (Ferring), TQ 089035, PN Sx 168; *hangra* 'wood on a hill'; 13th century.

TODDINGTON (Lyminster), TQ 033035, PN Sx 171, SOA 43; pers. n. or *tot* 'look-out', *-ing-*.

EAST PRESTON, TQ 070015, PN Sx 172; *preost* 'priest'.

RUSTINGTON, TQ 050023, PN Sx 172, SOA 45; pers. n. or *rust* 'rusty coloured', *-ing-*; 12th century.

WEST CHILTINGTON, TQ 089183; PN Sx 174, SOA 33, DEPN; pers. n. or *cilte* 'hill', *-ing-*.

SULLINGTON, TQ 099130, PN Sx 179, SOA 46; **syling*, an *-ing* sg. formation on OE *sol* 'mire', *syle* 'mud'.

ASHINGTON, TQ 128158, PN Sx 183, MA 10 24; *-ingas* folk-name.

DURRINGTON, TQ 118053, PN Sx 195, SOA 50; pers. n. or *deor* 'animal', *-ing-*.

OFFINGTON (Durrington), TQ 135050, PN Sx 196; pers. n., *-ing-*.

DANKTON (Sompting), TQ 165080, PN Sx 202; *denu*, *-ing-*.

HORTON (Upper Beeding), TQ 1910, PN Sx 205; *horh* 'dirt'.

TOTTINGTON (Upper Beeding), TQ 215115, PN Sx 206, SOA 44, pers. n. or *tot* 'look-out', *-ing-*.

EDBURTON, TQ 233115, PN Sx 206; pers. n.; 12th century.

EATONS (Henfield), TQ 187162, PN Sx 217; *ea* 'river'.

BIDLINGTON or MAUDLIN (Bramber), TQ 179103, PN Sx 223–4, MA 10 23, BNF 2 335, 3 163; *-ingas-* folk-name or *-ing* sg.

WASHINGTON, TQ 122130, PN Sx 240, MA 10 24; *-ingas* folk-name.

CHANCTON (Washington), TQ 1313, PN Sx 242; first el. not identified.

WISTON, TQ 1512, PN Sx 243; pers. n.

BUDDINGTON (Wiston), TQ 162123, PN Sx 244, MA 10 24; *-ingas* folk-name.

BUNCTON (Wiston), TQ 145138; PN Sx 244, MA 10 24; *-ingas* folk-name.

KINGSTON-BY-SEA, TQ 235053, PN Sx 245; *cyning* 'king'.

CLAYTON, TQ 298139, PN Sx 259; *clæg* 'clay'.

ALDRINGTON, TQ 275050, PN Sx 288, MA 10 24, BNF, 2 360, 3 158; pers. n.; *-ing-*.

HANGLETON, TQ 267073, PN Sx 289; *hangra* 'wood on a hill'.

WEST BLATCHINGTON, TQ 275072, PN Sx 290, SOA 55; pers. n. or *blæc* 'black, dark', *-ing-*.

BRIGHTON, TQ 310040, PN Sx 291; pers. n.

PRESTON, TQ 305065, PN Sx 295; *preost* 'priest'.

WOOTTON (East Chiltington), TQ 379151, PN Sx 300; *wudu* 'a wood'.

EAST CHILTINGTON, TQ 369151, PN Sx 299, SOA 33; pers. n. or *cilte* 'hill', *-ing-*.

PLUMPTON, TQ 356136, PN Sx 303; *plume* 'plum-tree'.

MIDDLETON (Westmeston), TQ 345140, PN Sx 305; *middel* 'middle'.

WESTMESTON, TQ 339136, PN Sx 304; *westmæst* 'most westerly'.

KINGSTON (near LEWES), TQ 392082, PN Sx 310; *cyning* 'king'.

ALLINGTON, TQ 385135, PN Sx 321; pers. n., *-ing-*.

SELMESTON, TQ 510070, PN Sx 338; pers. n.

SHERRINGTON (Selmeston), TQ 505075, PN Sx 338, SOA 57; pers. n. or *scir* 'bright', *-ing-*.

PRESTON (Beddingham), TQ 458076, PN Sx 358; *preost* 'priest'.

HEIGHTON (West Firle), TQ 479074, PN Sx 361; *heah* 'high'; 1139.

COMPTON (West Firle), TQ 483063, PN Sx 360; *cumb* 'valley'.

CHARLESTON (West Firle), TQ 490069, PN Sx 360; *cearloc* 'charlock'.

SOUTH HEIGHTON, TQ 4500028, PN Sx 363; *heah* 'high'.

EAST BLATCHINGTON, TV 483998, PN Sx 362, SOA 55; pers. n. or *blæc* 'black, dark', *-ing-*; 1169.

BISHOPSTONE, TQ 472009, PN Sx 365; *biscop* 'bishop'.

DENTON, TQ 455025, PN Sx 365; *denu* 'valley'.

CHALVINGTON, TQ 519094, PN Sx 398, SOA 49; pers. n. or *cealf*, *-ing-*.

ECKINGTON (Ripe), TQ 513098, PN Sx 404; an *-ing* suffix formation.

ARLINGTON, TQ 544074, PN Sx 408; pers. n., *-ing-*.

WOOTTON (Folkington), TQ 565053, PN Sx 412; *wudu*, *-ing-*.

FOLKINGTON, TQ 559038, PN Sx 411; pers. n., *-ing-*.

LITLINGTON, TQ 523019, PN Sx 412; pers. n., *-ing-*; 1191;

WILMINGTON, TQ 545045, PN Sx 412; pers. n., *-ing-*.

ALCISTON, TQ 505055, PN Sx 414; pers. n.

TILTON (Alciston), TQ 495067, PN Sx 414; pers. n.

ALFRISTON, TQ 520030, PN Sx 415; pers. n.

WINTON (Alfriston), TQ 520038, PN Sx 416, MA *10* 24; pers. n., *-ing-*.

LULLINGTON, TQ 525025, PN Sx 417, SOA 41; pers. n. or *lulle* 'slope, valley', *-ing-*.

CHARLSTON (Westdean), TQ 520007, PN Sx 419; *ceorl* 'peasant'.

FRISTON, TV 551982, PN Sx 420; pers. n.; 1200.

BECHINTON (lost, Friston), TV 5599, PN Sx 420. pers. n., *-ing-*.

JEVINGTON, TQ 561015, PN Sx 421, MA *10* 24; *-ingas* folk-name.

RATTON (Willingdon), TQ 587015, PN Sx 425; pers. n.

CHOLLINGTON (lost, Eastbourne), TU 6099, PN Sx 428; pers. n., *-ing-*.

BEVERINGTON (lost, Eastbourne), TV 6099, PN Sx 427, MA *10* 24; *-ingas* folk-name.

YEVERINGTON (lost, Eastbourne), TQ 6100, PN Sx 434, MA *10* 24; *-ingas* folk-name.

BULLINGTON (Bexhill), TQ 765087, PN Sx 491; pers. n., *-ing-*.

HOLLINGTON, TQ 795119, PN Sx 503; *-ingas* folk-name.

WHATLINGTON, TQ 760184, PN Sx 500, MA *10* 24; *ingas* folk-name.

DALLINGTON, TQ 657190, PN Sx 473; pers. n., *-ing-*.

WARBLETON, TQ 608182, PN Sx 468; pers. n., *-ing-*.

C.1. tun. (b).

WOLVERSTONE (Cocking), SU 874156, PN Sx 16; pers. n.; 1261.

UPPERTON (Harting), SU 789210, PN Sx 37; *uppe* 'up, higher'; 1180.

CHARLTON (Singleton), SU 887127, PN Sx 54; *ceorl* 'peasant'; 1271.

WALDERTON (Stoughton), SU 790106, PN Sx 55; pers. n.; 1167.

WALTON (Bosham), SU 815045, PN Sx 59; *wealh* 'foreigner, serf, Briton'; 1227.

KIPSON (Hunston), SU 858009, PN Sx 71; pers. n.; 1187.

DRAYTON (Oving), SU 882047, PN Sx 76; *dræg* 'a drag, a dray'; *c.* 1200.

WESTERTON (Westhampnett), SU 895073, PN Sx 79; *westerra* comp. 'more westerly', but perhaps an archaic adj. *wester* 'western' as in Westerham K.; 12th century.

EASTON (Sidlesham), SZ 832969, PN Sx 86; *east* 'east'.

NUNNINGTON (Wittering), SZ 789987, PN Sx 88; pers. n., *-ing-*; 14th century.

RIDLINGTON (Duncton), SU 954177, PN Sx 101; pers. n., *-ing-*; 1261.

UPPERTON (Tillington), SU 957227, PN Sx 124; *upper* 'higher up': 1191.

ATHERINGTON (Climping), TQ 005008, PN Sx 139; pers. n., *-ing-*; 1203.

ANCTON (Felpham), SU 9800, PN Sx 140; pers. n.; 1279.

SOUTH EATON (Billingshurst), TQ 047237, PN Sx 148; *ea* 'river'; 1249.

HURSTON (Storrington), TQ 073160, PN Sx 162; *hyrst* 'wooded hill'; 1287.

WEST PRESTON (Rustington), TQ 063023, PN Sx 173, 169–170 note; *preost* 'priest'; 1230.

OLD CLAYTON (Sullington), TQ 109138, PN Sx 179; *clæg* 'clay'; 1296.

SALVINGTON (Durrington), TQ 128052, PN Sx 197; pers. n. -*ing*-; 1249.

BLACKSTONE (Woodmancote), TQ 239160, PN Sx 221; pers. n.,-*ing*-; 1262.

CHARLTON (Steyning), TQ 168118, PN Sx 237; *ceorl* 'peasant'; 1279.

MIDDLETON (Chailey), TQ 3919, PN Sx 297; *middel* 'middle': 1288.

STANTONS (East Chiltington), TQ 371149, PN Sx 300; *stan* 'stone, rock'; 1288.

NOVINGTON (Westmeston), TQ 368141, PN Sx 305; pers. n., -*ing*- ; 1261.

RUSTON (Fletching), TQ 443230, PN Sx 346; *rysc* 'rush'; 1289.

NORLINGTON (Ringmer), TQ 446132, PN Sx 356; -*ing* suffix formation upon *norð* 'north'; 1248.

ASHTON (Ringmer), TQ 461121, PN Sx 355; *æsc* 'ash tree'; 1150.

PRESTON (West Firle), TQ 463078, PN Sx 362; *preost* 'a priest'; 1121.

SUTTON (Seaford), TV 493997, PN Sx 364; *suð* 'south(ern)'; 12th century.

NORTON (Bishopstone), TQ 471018, PN Sx 365; *norð* 'north'; 13th century.

CHYNGTON (Seaford), TU 504987, PN Sx 364, MA *10* 32, BNF *2* 355; -*ingas* folk-name and sg. -*ing* formation.

MILTON (Arlington), TQ 526037, PN Sx 409; *middel* 'middle'; 12th century.

UPPERTON (Eastbourne), TV 6099, PN Sx 433; *uppe* 'high up', *upper* comparative; 1176.

WERLINGTON (Hellingly), about TQ 579119, PN Sx 442; pers. n., -*ing*-; 1274.

WINKENHURST (Hellingly), TQ 583145, PN Sx 442; not identified; 1296.

DITTONS (Westham). TQ 603046, PN Sx 446; *dic* 'ditch'; 1292.

COLLINGTON (Ticehurst), TQ 6830, PN Sx 451; pers. n.; 13th century.

BANTONY (Salehurst), TQ 740247, PN Sx 458; ? *bean* 'bean'; 1288.

BECKINGTON (Heathfield), TQ 5920, PN Sx 464; pers. n. -*ing*-; 1250.

SAPPERTON (Heathfield), TQ 593193, PN Sx 466; pers. n.; 1210.

RUNTINGTON (Heathfield), TQ 582193, PN Sx 466, SOA 54; pers. n. or *hrunta* 'tree-stump', -*ing*-; 1139.

EATENDEN (Mountfield), TQ 735185, PN Sx 475; pers. n., -*ing*-; 12th century.

TILTON (Catsfield), TQ 719129, PN Sx 486; pers. n.; 13th century.

BIRCHINGTON (Bexhill), TQ 719077, PN Sx 490; -*ing* suffix formation on *birce* 'birch tree'; 1278.

COLLINGTON (Bexhill), TQ 725075, PN Sx 491, SOA 36; pers. n. or *coll* 'hill', -*ing*-; 12th century.

HURCHINGTON (Bexhill), TQ 7407, PN Sx 492; pers. n., -*ing*-; 1263.

NEATENDEN (Westfield), TQ 8015, PN Sx 506; *neoð era* 'lower, nether'; 1120.

PATTLETON'S (Westfield), TQ 823162, PN Sx 506; -*ingas* folk-name; 1215.

EDGINGTON (Ewhurst), TQ 7924, PN Sx 519; -*ingas* place-name; 1197.

HEIGHTON (lost, Beckley), TQ 8423, PN Sx 527; *heah* 'high'; 1248.

C.1.1. leactun. (a).

LAUGHTON, TQ 503132, PN Sx 402; simplex.

C.1.2. burh-tun. (a).

WESTBURTON (lost, Friston), TV 5497; PN Sx 421; *west* 'west'.

BROUGHTON (Jevington), TQ 565035, PN SX 422; simplex.

C.1.2. burh-tun. (b).

WEST BURTON (Bury), SU 997137, PN Sx 125; *west* 'west'; 1230.

NORBELTON (lost, Hellingly), TQ 5812, PN Sx 441; *norð* 'north'; 1287.

C.1.3. ham-tun. (a).

LITTLEHAMPTON, TQ 030020, PN Sx 169, ASE *2* 34; simplex.

C.1.4. tun-steall. (*b*).

TUNSTALL (Mountsfield), TQ 723212, PN Sx 476; simplex. 1190.

C.2. wic. 'dairy farm. industrial settlement, trade centre'. (*a*).

RUMBOLDSWHYKE (Chichester), SU 865042, PN Sx 13, 14; simplex.

TERWICK, SU 820240, PN Sx 42; *tord* 'a turd, dung'; 1271.

STRUDGWICK (Kirdford), TQ 0126), PN Sx 107; *strod* 'marsh'.

RUDGWICK, TQ 091342, PN Sx 156; *hyrcg* 'ridge'; 1210.

LYDWICKE (Slinfold), TQ 106296, PN Sx 160; *hlið* 'a slope'.

WICK, TQ 025032, PN Sx 171; simplex; 1261.

SOUTHWICK, TQ 239054, PN Sx 248; *suð* 'south'.

HAZELWICK (Worth), TQ 3036, PN Sx 281; *hæsel* 'hazel-tree'.

NEWICK, TQ 422208, PN Sx 316; *niwe* 'new'; 12th century.

SMITHWICK (Southover), TQ 420095, PN Sx 322; *smi ð* 'a smith'.

ORLESWICK (lost, Piddinghoe), TQ 4303, PN Sx 325; pers. n.

C.2. wic (*b*).

WICK WOOD (Chithurst), SU 8423, PN Sx 34; simplex; 1286.

SHOPWYKE (Oving), SU 888050, PN Sx 76; *sceap* 'sheep'; 12th century.

ALDWICK (Pagham), SZ 912987, PN Sx 93; *ald* 'old'; 1235.

DRUNGEWICK (Wisborough), TQ 061307, PN Sx 131; a sg. *-ing* formation on a pers. n.; 1279.

LYNWICK (Rudgwick), TQ 075339, PN Sx 157, MA *10* 24, BNF *2* 368, *3* 146; *lind* 'lime-tree'; 1279.

HOWICK (Rudgwick), TQ 080316, PN Sx 157; *hoh* 'spur, promontory'; 1166.

THORNWICK (lost, Storrington), TQ 0814, PN Sx 162; *þorn* 'thorn-tree'; 1269.

BARPHAM WEEK (lost, Angmering), say SU 069087; PN Sx 165; place-name Barpham; 1255.

WHITENWICK (West Grinstead), TQ 1720, PN Sx 187; pers. n., *-ing-*; 1296.

HALEWICK (Sompting), TQ 1605, PN Sx 202; simplex; 1273.

GREATWICK (Cowfold), TQ 211209, PN Sx 210; *grafet* ' a grove': 1288.

SEDGEWICK (Nuthurst), TQ 180270, PN Sx 231; *secg* 'sedge, rush'; 1222.

TRUBWEEK (lost in Haywards Heath, formerly Cuckfield), say TQ 3323, PN Sx 269; pers. n.; 1166.

OLD HO. or FELDWYCKS (lost, Haywards heath, formerly Cuckfield), say TQ 3323, PN Sx 273; *feld* 'an open space'; 1296.

WICK (Hove), TQ 2805, Pn Sx 293; *hearra* 'higher'; 13th century.

EASTWICK (Patcham), TQ 317095, PN Sx 294; *east* 'east'.

WICK (Rottingdean), TQ 357060, PN Sx 312; simplex; 1296.

GOTWICK (Forest Row), TQ 418395, PN Sx 328; *gat* 'a goat'; 1279.

GODDENWICK (Lindfield), TQ 362281, PN Sx 341, MA *10* 24; *-ingas* folk-name; 1261.

HOLYWYCH (Hartfield), TQ 484402, PN Sx 367; *hol* 'in a hollow'; 1229.

HONEYWICK (Chiddingly), TQ 5414, PN Sx 399; *hunig* 'honey'; 1285.

ENGLEWICK (Wilmington), TQ 550041, PN Sx 413; *endleofan* 'eleven'; 1279.

UPWICK (Eastbourne), TV 6099, PN Sx 434; *uppe* 'up, higher'; 1296.

NORTHWICK (Eastbourne), TV 6099, PN Sx 432; *norð* 'north'; 1121.

NEWICK (Heathfield), TQ 595228, PN Sx 466; *niwe* 'new'; 1121.

C.2.1. berewic. (*a*).

BERWICK, TQ 518050, PN Sx 411; simplex.

C.3. worð 'enclosure, curtilage; private estate'. (*a*).

LODSWORTH, SU 926232, PN Sx 26; pers. n.

COLWORTH (Oving), SU 915027, PN Sx 75. pers. n.

PETWORTH, SU 9721, PN Sx 114; pers. n.

FITTLEWORTH, TQ 009193, PN Sx 126; pers. n.

HAYWARDS HEATH (Cuckfield), TQ 3323, PN Sx 268; *hege* 'hedge' or *heg* 'hay'; 1261.

WORTH, TQ 302363, PN Sx 280; simplex.

ATLINGWORTH (Portslade), TQ 254089, MA *10* 24, PN Sx 290; *ingas* folk-name; 11th century.

WORTH (Lt. Horsted), TQ 461182, PN Sx 349; simplex.

ETCHINGWOOD (Buxted), TQ 505222, PN Sx 390, MA *10* 24; *-ingas* folk-name.

KEYWORTH (Bexhill), TQ 7407, PN Sx 492, v; pers. n.

C.3. *worð*. (*b*).

WONWORTH (lost, Graffham), SU 9217, PN Sx 21; pers. n.; 1271.

ALDSWORTH (Westbourne), SU 766086, PN Sx 56; pers. n.; 1271.

DENSWORTH (Funtington), SU 8307, PN Sx 61; pers. n.; 1261.

WORTH (lost, Boxgrove), SU 9007, PN Sx 68; simplex; 12th century.

GUMBER (Slindon), SU 961118, PN Sx 97; pers. n.; 1261.

BYWORTH (Petworth), SU 980209, PN Sx 116; pers. n.: 1279.

HESWORTH (Fittleworth), TQ 005192, PN Sx 127; pers. n.; 1296.

ABINGWORTH (Sullington), TQ 103165, PN Sx 180; *-ingas* folk-name; 1296.

SMITHERS (Shipley), TQ 1421, PN Sx 191; *smeðe* 'level, smooth': 1220.

CHESWORTH (Horsham), TQ 175295, PN Sx 226; pers. n.; 1280.

SUGWORTH (Cuckfield), TQ 3024, PN Sx 265; pers. n.; 1279.

PIDDINGWORTH (Ditchling), TQ 329109, PN Sx 302, MA *10* 24; *-ingas* folk-name; 1200.

PIPPINGFORD (Maresfield), TQ 440306, PN Sx 350; pers. n., *-ing-*; 1352.

COTCHFORD (Hartfield), TQ 475344, PN Sx 366; first el. obscure; 1265.

BEVINGFORD (Buxted), TQ 484248, MA *10* 24, PN Sx 390; and *-ing* formation on a pers. n.; 1296.

POSSINGWORTH (Waldron), TQ 535205, PN Sx 407; *-ingas* folk-name; 12th century.

TEDDARD'S (Jevington), TQ 5601, PN Sx 423; pers. n.; 1189.

NETTLESWORTH (Heathfield), TQ 597188, PN Sx 465; 1202.

TOTTINGWORTH (Heathfield), TQ 614218, PN Sx 467; pers. n., *-ing-*; 1248.

C.4. *ham*. See D *infra*.

C.5 *gesell* 'herdsmen's buildings; a herding camp or out-station'. (*a*).

BUXSHALLS (Lindfield), TQ 352272, PN Sx 340; *boc* 'beech'.

DRIGSELL (Salehurst), TQ 747230, PN Sx 458; *dryhten* 'lord'.

C.5. *gesell*. (*b*).

BOARZELL (Ticehurst), TQ 723292, PN Sx 451; *bar* 'boar'; 1123.

WIGSELL (Salehurst), TQ 760274, PN Sx 459; not identified; 1166.

BUGSELL (Salehurst), TQ 727241, PN Sx 458; *boc* 'beech'; 1260.

WOODSELL (Dallington), TQ 6519, PN Sx 474; *wudu* 'a wood'; 1288.

BEMZELLS (Herstmonceux), TQ 6410, PN Sx 480; *beam* 'a tree'; 1296.

BREADSELL (Battle), TQ 7415, PN Sx 496; *bred* 'a plank'; 1189.

FOXHOLE (Battle), TQ 7415, PN Sx 497; pers. n.; 1296.

YORKSHIRE WOOD (Ewhurst), TQ 7924, PN Sx 521; pers. n.; 1184.

C.6. *falod*. (*a*).

SLINFOLD, TQ 118315, PN Sx 159; *slinu* 'hollow, slope'; 1165.

COWFOLD, TQ 213227, PN Sx 209; *cu* 'cow'; 1255.

C.6. falod. (b).

BARKFOLD (Kirdford), TQ 028265; PN Sx
103; pers. n.; 1279.

CHILSFOLD (Kirdford), TQ 0126, PN Sx
103; pers. n; 1271.

CRAWFOLD (Kirdford), TQ 000261, PN Sx
103; *crawe* 'a crow'; 1310.

FRITHFOLD (Kirdford), SU 986295, PN Sx
104; *fyrhð* 'a wood'); 1280.

HYFFOLD (Kirdford), TQ 0126, PN Sxc 105;
hyd 'a hide of land'; 1296.

LINFOLD (Kirdford), TQ 022259, PN Sx
106; *lind* 'lime-tree'; 1239.

IFOLD (Kirdford), TQ 025318, PN Sx 106;
eg 'meadow'; 1296.

DIDDLESFOLD (Lurgashall), SU 940298, PN
Sx 112; pers. n.; 1156.

RAMSFOLD (Lurgashall), SU 9327, PN Sx
112; *ramm* 'a ram'; 1279.

WINDFALLWOOD (Lurgashall), SU 927278,
PN Sx 113; inidentified; 1296.

BUCKFOLD (Petworth), SU 9721, PN Sx
115; *boc* 'beech-tree'; 12th century.

PETSALLS (Petworth), SU 9721, PN Sx 118;
pytt 'a pit'; 1280.

HARSFOLD (Wisborough), TQ 050248; PN
Sx 133; unidentified; 1279.

HEADFOLDSWOOD   (Wisborough),   TQ
035306, PN Sx 133; pers. n., *-ing-*; 1296.

GRAININGFOLD (Billingshurst), TQ 102283,
PN Sx 148, MA *10* 24; pers. n., *-ing-*;
1220.

HADFOLD (Billingshurst), TQ 079235, PN
Sx 148; pers. n.; 1279.

KINGSFOLD (Billingshurst), TQ 089242, PN
Sx 149; *cyning* 'king'; 1279.

TEDFOLD (Billingshurst), TQ 083268, PN Sx
150; pers. n.; 1296.

REDFOLD (Pulborough), TQ 074200, PN Sx
154; *(ge)ryd(d)* 'cleared land'; 1296.

CLEMSFOLD (Slinfold), TQ 1131, PN Sx
159; pers. n.; 1288.

WOLDRINGFOLD (Cowfold), TQ 208247,
PN Sx 211; pers. n., *-ing-*; 1325.

DARWELL (Mountfield), TQ 709205, PN Sx
475; *doer* 'animal'; 1294.

HEMINGFOLD (Battle), TQ 774149, PN Sx
497; pers. n.; 1121.

D.

Sussex place-names based on elements which of themselves fall between the habitative and the natural; i.e., a *hamm* may be a natural feature or a man-made paddock; a *stede* is conditioned by the first element of the compound name; a *denn* is a natural-feature put to a particular use. In such names, it is not so much the *meaning* of the element as the significance of the mode of its use or the significance of the way it is compounded, that gives significance to the place-name.

D.1.1. hamm, considered with ham.

Consideration of place-names in this list is based on the work published in ASE *2*: comparison will show that a few reconsiderations have been made. It is sometimes very difficult to decide on the question whether a place-name ending in the spelling *-ham* comes from OE *ham* or OE *hamm*. In ASE *2* I identified p.ns. with *hamm*, *hamme* and *hame* spellings, or plural inflexions, as derived from OE *hamm*. I then typified the sites of such places (following on from Gelling in NoB 48), see ASE *2* 6–7:

hamm 1.   'a land in a river-bend'.

hamm 2a.   'a promontory of dry land into marsh or water';
  b.   'a promontory into lower land even without marsh or water' perhaps hence 'land on a hill-spur'.

hamm 3.   'a river-meadow'—an extension fron sense 1.

hamm 4.   'dry ground in a marsh', from 1, 2 and 3.

hamm 5a.   'a cultivated plot in marginal land';
  b.   'an enclosed plot, a close'.

hamm **6a.**   'a piece of valley-bottom land hemmed in by higher ground, especially at a place where the valley broadens for a space, as at a confluence'.
  b.   'a piece of land in a bay of higher ground'.

hamm 7.   'land on a shelf over a river' (the sort of site occupied by Barkham PN Sx 345, Offham Pn Sx 316).

I suggested in ASE 2 that other place-names spelt only *ham* (i.e., with no characteristic *hamm* spellings), but occupying similar sites, might also be considered *hamm* names. Names of places which are ancient manors or villages, and which have no marked *hamm* site-characteristic as well as no characteristic *hamm* spelling or inflexion, are considered to be *ham* names on account of their status.

This consideration of status depends upon a tradition—that *ham* is a naming-element in the names of 'more important' places, that places with names in *ham* are usually more 'important' than places with names in *hamm*. Yet, consider the *hamm* in *Hamwic* (Southampton). The fact of the matter is, that in Sussex place-names the two forms *ham* and *hamm* seem to have fallen together quite early—late OE and early ME spelling confuse them. Many a *ham* in Anglo-Saxon Sussex must have lain in a site which was a *hamm*: many a settlement founded in and named after a *hamm* must have become somebody's *ham*. This would explain the confusion in forms: it might point to the importance of *site* characteristic as an indicator of the significance of a name-form.

D.1.2. Sussex place-names from OE *hamm*. *indicates that *hamm* spellings are recorded; † indicates that *ham* is a strong possibility.

(*a*) mentioned before 1100, or appearing as the name of a parochial village.

TODHAM (Cocking), SU 904208, PN Sx 18, ASE 2 46; a *hamm* 3 on R. Rother; first el. either a pers. n. or OE *tade* 'a toad'.

STEDHAM, SU 864226, PN Sx 29, ASE 2 46; a *hamme* 1 on R. Rother: cf. Horsham *infra*.

*BOSHAM, SU 803038, PN Sx 55, ASE 2 25, NoB 48 147 a *hamm* 2, 4, 5.

CHIDHAM, SU 793039, PN Sx 59, ASE 2 42, NoB 48; a *hamm* 2a on a peninsula in Chichester harbour.

APPLEDRAM (formerly in Bosham), SU 840032, PN Sx 65, ASE 2 48; a *hamm* 3-5 an apple-orchard.

†KINGSHAM (Donnington), SU 857037, PN Sx 69 ASE 2 50; this place is of secondary status in the parish and would seem therefore to be a *hamm* rather than *ham*; but neither spellings nor topography are conclusive and *ham* is a possible basis.

EARTHAM, SU 939093, PN Sx 70, ASE 2 49, a *hamm* 6b.

†MUNDHAM, NORTH, SU 875022 and **SOUTH,** SU 877005 PN Sx 72, ASE 2 33. In ASE 2 this was analysed as a *ham* name with a pers. n. as first el., on account of the place's status as a parish and an ancient manor. But I now question whether this is so certain; this could be a *hamm* name, for these reasons: there is an inflected form —*hame* (⥽ OE *hamme*); second, the formula *se northra Mundan ham, other*

Mundan ham 680 for 685 (10) BCS 50, Sawyer 230, could be read as 'the more northerly *Mundan-hamm*, the second *Mundhan-hamm*', i.e., two places called 'Munda's *hamm*' or two *hamms* named from the one man; third, the situation of these two places between Bremere Rife and Pagham Rife (near, and similar, to that of Saltham and Crimsham) would suit *hamm* in any of aspects 1-5, especially 3 and 4.

BIRDHAM, SU 823002, PN Sx 80, ASE 2 41; *hamm* 2a, 3, 4, 5b.

BABSHAM (Bersted), SU 915015, PN Sx 91, ASE 2 33; *hamm* 4 or 5a.

PAGHAM, SZ 883975, PN Sx 92, ASE 2 27; *hamm* 2-5.

*WAERMUNDES HAMM (Pagham), SU 948015 approx., PN Sx 93 note; *hamm* 3-5.

CRIMSHAM (Pagham), SZ 897009, PN Sx 94, ASE 2 49; *hamm* 3-5.

AMBERSHAM, SU 915207, PN Sx 97, EPN Soc. XVI, xxxvi, ASE 2 41; the site of South Ambersham SU 916207 is a *hamm* 1 by R. Rother.

STOPHAM, TQ 025185, PN Sx 120, EPN 2 46; a *hamm* 1 and 3 by R. Arun and R. Rother.

*GRITTENHAM (Tillington), SU 9422215, PN Sx 122, a *hamm* 3 or 5 by R. Rother.

HARDHAM, TQ 039175, PN Sx 128, MA 10 24, BNF 3 170, ASE 2 49-50; a *hamm* 1 by R. Arun.

BARNHAM, SU 960040, PN Sx 137, ASE *2* 41, *hamm* 2a, 3, 4.

*ILSHAM (lost in the sea), TQ 0200, PN Sx 139, ASE *2* 26; 1212.

*FELPHAM, SQ 949998, PN Sx 140, ASE *2* 25, *hamm* 2, 4, 5.

OFFHAM (South Stoke), TQ 026087, PN Sx 142, ASE *2* 33; a *hamm* 1 by R. Arun.

BILSHAM (Yapton), SU 970020, PN Sx 145, ASE, *2* 49; a *hamm* 3 or 4 near Rye-bank Rife.

GREATHAM, TQ 044160, PN Sx 151, Ase *2* 49; a *hamm* 1 or 3 by R. Arun.

PARHAM, TQ 060140, PN Sx 152, ASE *2* 33; *hamm* 5b, a perry orchard.

RACKHAM, TQ 050136, PN Sx 156; a *hamm* 2a site, but *ham* 5b is possible, too, a rick-yard; 1166.

*HAM (Angmering), TQ 057037, PN Sx 165; *hamm* 3-5;

SAKEHAM (Shermanbury), TQ 223190, PN Sx 213, ASE *2* 46; a *hamm* 3 by R. Adur.

APPLESHAM (Coombes), TQ 195072, PN Sx 224, ASE *2* 48; a *hamm* 2b, near R. Adur, but *ham* 5b would also make sense, an apple-orchard.

†HORSHAM, TQ 170305, PN Sx 225, ASE *2* 50; *hamm* as final el. would give good sense —'horse paddock, horse meadow' from OE *hors*—and would give a place-name comparable with that of the adjacent parish Warnham PN Sx 238 (*infra*), from OE *wræna*, 'stallions' *hamm*' and with the p.n. Stedham PN Sx 29 (*supra*), from OE *steda* and *stod*, 'stud *hamm*'—the *hamm* in these being either topographical or type 5b. Other horse-keeping or breeding establishments seem to have been commemorated by the place-names Horsted Heynes Sx 336 and Little Horsted Sx 348 (See *D.3.* (*a*)). The site of Horsham may have been a *hamm* 3 near R. Arun, but this is not clear. However, the place is a parish and recorded early (tenth century) so *ham* is a possible basis for the name.

WARNHAM, TQ 159335, first recorded 1166, PN Sx 238, ASE *2* 46-7; Ekwall in DEPN and Studies 2 68 suggests *hamm* 3 or 4, but *hamm* 5b 'paddock' would do, cf. Horsham *supra*.

(OLD) ERRINGHAM (Old Shoreham), TQ 205077, PN Sx 246, MA *10* 23, BNF *2* 352, 357 note, *3* 146, 171-2, ASE *2* 43; a *hamm* 1 by R. Adur.

SLAUGHAM, TQ 257280; PN Sx 277; site a *hamm* 2b between two streams but *hamm* 5b would give good sense, with OE *slah*— 'sloe garden'.

*HAMSEY, TQ 414121, PN Sx 315, a *hamm* 1 by R. Ouse.

OFFHAM (Hamsey), TQ 400121, PN Sx 316; the first el. is OE *woh* 'crooked', and the editors of PN Sx suppose the 'crooked *hamm*' refers to the great bend of R. Ouse under Offham village. But Offham is on the bluff side of the river-bend, and there is no flat in Offham at this place, so the reference is elsewhere. Offham lies under the north end of Offham Hill on a shelf over the bluff west bank of R. Ouse at the opening of a crooked valley running west into the downs at 395120. The *woh-hamm* would be this valley: a *hamm* 6a or 7.

*BARKHAM (Fletching), TQ 438216, PN Sx 345, DEPN, ASE *2* 24 (where the site characteristics of *hamm* 7 are described in explanation of this p.n. and Blackham Sx 370, *infra*); a *hamm* 7 or 6.

*BEDDINGHAM, TQ 445079, PN Sx 357, MA *10* 24, ASE, *2* 24; a *hamm* 2a.

*BLACKHAM (Withyham), TQ 500378, PN Sx 370, ASE *2* 24; *hamm* 2 or 7; cf. Barkham *supra*.

*WITHYHAM, TQ 493355, Sx 370, ASE *2* 28; there is a *hamm* 2b, but the name probably originated at the *hamm* 3, 6a (493360) as the first el. is *wiþig* 'willow'. A lost place-name *Wythiham* is noted PN Sx 370, in which the *hamm* would be 1 or 3-5.

*STOCKINGHAM (lost, Laughton), TQ 5012, PN Sx 402, MA *10* 24, ASE *2* 28; site not known, type of *hamm* not determined, probably *hamm* 5; note that the proto-theme may be a singular place-name in -*ing*, *inge*, *Stoccinge*, not a plural folk-name, *Stoccingas*, or the two may alternate, the basis being OE *stocking* 'place full of tree-stumps'.

†SESSINGHAM (Arlington), TQ 540083, PN Sx 410, MA *10* 23, ASE, *2* 50; site a *hamm* 2a, 3, 4, near Cuckmere River, Claverham Sx 409 (*infra*) and Michelham Sx 409 (*infra*), but the p.n. looks like an -*ingaham* type.

CLAVERHAM (Arlington), TQ 536090 and 532092, PN Sx 409, ASE *2* 42: site a *hamm* 3 or 5, 'water-meadow or river-meadow where clover grows; clover field'.

*ERSHAM (Hailsham), say TQ 5908), PN Sx 436; site not known, perhaps a *hamm* 5 as the first el. is a pers. n.

*HANKHAM (Westham), TQ 620055, PN Sx 447, ASE *2* 26; *hamm* 4.

*WESTHAM, TQ 638045, PN Sx 446, ASE *2* 28; *hamm* 2b, 4; 1222.

*ETCHINGHAM, TQ 711261, PN Sx 455, MA *10* 24, ASE *2* 25; *hamm* 2, 3 and 6; 1158.

†BURGHAM (Etchingham), TQ 702279, PN Sx 456, ASE *2* 49. Since the place was a DB manor, it might appear to have a *ham* name. But the site is a *hamm* 3 by the little R. Linden, near to Kitchingham. Also, like Burpham Sx 166 *infra*, D.1.3. 1. (a), there may be a *hamm* 5 sense, 'fortification enclosure'.

*BROOMHAM (Catsfield), TQ 720137, PN Sx 485, ASE *2* 25; topographically a *hamm* 2 or 7, but the first el. *brom* 'broom' also suggests *hamm* 5a, b.

*WHYDOWN (Bexhill), TQ 707095, PN Sx 494; formerly *Swynhamme* 'pig *hamm*', a *hamm* 5 but also a *hamm* 2.

WORSHAM (Bexhill), TQ 754091, PN Sx 494, ASE *2* 25 s.n. Filsham; site resembles those of Pebsham Sx 493, Filsham Sx 504, see *infra*; *hamm* 2, 3, 6.

*UCKHAM (Battle), TQ 752163, PN Sx 499, ASE *2* 28; a *hamm* 2b.

FOXHAM (lost, Crowhurst), TQ 7512, PN Sx 502, ASE *2* 44; an outlier from the manor of Bexhill, perhaps a *hamm* 5a.

*FILSHAM (Hollington), TQ 783095, PN Sx 504, ASE *2* 25; *hamm* 2, 3, 6a;

*ICKLESHAM, TQ 880165, PN Sx 510, ASE *2* 26; *hamm* 2, 3 or 7; note that the prototheme shows that alternation between personal-name and gen. sg. of an -*ing* singular place-name which is discussed in BNF *3* 141–156 esp. 149 s.n. Muggleswick.

*BODIAM, TQ 782255, PN Sx 518, ASE *2* 25, BNF *3* 171; original site perhaps 785260, a *hamm* 2 between Kent Ditch and R. Rother.

*NORTHIAM, TQ 829245, **HIGHAM** (Northiam), TQ 820249, PN Sx 522, 523, ASE *2* 27; these are, in fact, originally the same name for the same place, *Northiam* simply a form distinguished from *Higham* Sx 538 (at Winchelsea). The first el. could be *heah* 'high', but more likely *ig., iw* 'yew-tree'; perhaps *hamm* 5, but the site TQ 820249 could be classed as *hamm* 2b or 7.

HIGHAM (Northiam), see prec.

*GLOSSHAMS (Beckley), TQ 859215, PN Sx 527, vi, presumably a *hamm* 5.

*KITCHENHAM(Peasmarsh), TQ 883250, PN Sx 532, ASE *2* 26; a *hamm* 2a by the Rother Levels.

*LEASAM (Rye Foreign),   TQ 909215, PN Sx 537, ASE *2* 26; a *hamm* 2 by a tributary of R. Tillingham.

*HIGHAM (Winchelsea), TQ 901176, PN Sx 538, ASE *2* 26; the first el. may be *eg* 'island' or *ig, iw* 'yew tree'; the site is a *hamm* 1–2, but *hamm* 5 is possible; cf. Higham (Northiam) *supra*.

D.1.2. (*b*). Sussex place-names from *hamm*, not of parochial villages and not recorded before 1100.

PITSHAM (Cocking), SU 878194, PN Sx 16, ASE *2* 45; presumably a *hamm* 5; 1327.

KINGSHAM (Chithurst), SU 836250–255, PN Sx 33, ASE *2* 44; *hamm* 1 and 3; 1285.

WENHAM (Rogate), SU 789236, PN Sx 41, ASE *2* 47, *hamm* 3 by R. Rother; 1195.

WAKEHAM (Terwick), SU 819229, PN Sx 43; a *hamm* 3 by R. Rother; 1279.

BROADHAM (Singleton), SU 888146; PN Sx 54, ASE *2* 42; hamm 6a or 5; 1279.

RATHAM (Funtington), SU 812063, PN Sx 61, ASE *2* 45; *hamm* 3 or 5; 1279.

SALTHAM (North Mundham), SU 889013, PN Sx 75, ASE *2* 46; *hamm* 2, 4, 5; 1272.

GREATHAM and **LITTLEHAM** (Sidlesham),

SZ 837950, 838044, PN Sx 86, and
OAKHURST FM, Sx 842962, all lie within *Hamme* 1271, 1380, a district bounded by Broad Rife, a *hamm* 1, 2a, 3, 4.

*HAM (Tangmere), SU 9006, PN Sx 97; type of *hamm* not known; 1222.

BLEATHAM (Egdean), SU 997197, PN Sx 101, ASE *2* 41–2; *hamm* 2a. b; 1121.

FLEXHAM (Egdean), TQ 0022, PN Sx 102, ASE *2* 44; the name refers to the ground occupying the triangle between converging streams and valleys at 005215, a *hamm* 2 or 3; a *fleax-hamm* might be a waterside place, or even an enclosure (*hamme*), for the growing of flax; 1278.

BITTLESHAM (Kirdford), SU 970282, PN Sx 103, ASE *2* 41; *hamm* 1, 2b, 5b.

ALVERSHAM (East Lavington), SU 9517, PN Sx 110, ASE *2* 41; perhaps a *hamm* 5a; 1229.

KILSHAM or KELSHAM (Petworth), SU 966196, PN Sx 117, ASE *2* 44; a *hamm* 1 by R. Rother; 13th century.

ELKHAM (Petworth), SU 994256, PN Sx 116, ASE 2 43; *hamm* 2b; 1242.

COLLUMN (Sutton), location not ascertained, PN Sx 120; 1288; this is as likely to be a *hamm* of some sort, as a *ham.*

SHOPHAM (Sutton), SU 984185, PN Sx 121, ASE *2* 46; a *hamm* 3 on R. Rother; 1279.

PALLINGHAM (Wisborough), TQ 044224, PN Sx 134, MA *10* 23, ASE *2* 45; a *hamm 1* on R. Arun; 1233.

*MALHAM (Wisborough), TQ 062287, PN Sx 134, ASE *2* 27; *hamm* 3, 6a, 7; 1230.

FLANSHAM (Felpham), SU 9600012, PN Sx 140, ASE *2* 44; *hamm* 4; 1220.

*HAMS (Yapton), SU 962025, PN Sx 145, *hamm* 3, 4 near Ryebank Rife near Flansham; 12th century.

WASHINGHAM (Greatham), TQ 049157, PN Sx 151, MA *10* 24, ASE *2* 47; *hamm* 1, 3 and 4 by R. Arun; 1296.

DEDISHAM (Slinfold), TQ 112327, PN Sx 159, ASE *2* 43; *hamm* 3 by R. Arun; 1257.

BARPHAM (Angmering), LOWER, TQ 071092, UPPER, 067089, PN Sx 164, ASE *2* 41; 1121 Lower Barpham is at a *hamm* 6a. Both Barphams would also have been outlying paddocks of the manor of Angmering—*hamm* 5.

CALCETTO (Lyminster), TQ 023047, PN Sx 171; perhaps *hamm* 2-4; 1151.

*HAM (Durrington), PN Sx 196; perhaps *hamm* 5 as PN Sx, but the site is a *hamm* 3-4; 1257.

*WYNDHAM (Shermanbury), TQ 235194, PN Sx 213, ASE *2* 28; a *hamm* 3 by R. Adur and a tributary.

STREATHAM or STRETHAM (Henfield), TQ 201137, PN Sx 219; a *hamm* 3-4 by R. Adur and on a Roman road; 1200.

†OREHAM (Henfield), TQ 223135, PN Sx 218; 1170. To be precise Oreham Manor 225135, LIttle Oreham 224138, Oreham Common 225141. In ASE *2* 33 I took this place-name for a *ham* type. But I am not now so sure; the site could be a *hamm* 2b, 5 or 7 on a two-contour ridge between streams.

NUTHAM (Horsham), TQ 163254, PN Sx 228, ASE *2* 45; first el. *hnutu* 'nut-tree' might suggest a woodland enclosure, *hamm* 5, but a *hamm* 3 is also possible; 1261.

STAMMERHAM (Rusper), TQ 2037, PN Sx 233; probably a *hamm* 5; 1255.

NEWHAM (Steyning), TQ 1711, PN Sx 238; probably a *hamm* 5; 1267.

*BINEHAM (Chailey), TQ 388199, PN Sx 297, ASE *2* 24; *hamm* 3; 1296.

*RUTTINGHAM (Fletching), TQ 445247, PN Sx 347, MA *10* 24, ASE *2* 28; 1200; *hamm* 2b or 5a.

*DALEHAM (Fletching), TQ 4223, PN Sx 346, ASE *2* 25; location not ascertained, probably *hamm* 5 or 6a; 1202.

COLEHAM (Fletching), TQ 406240, PN Sx 346, ASE *2* 43; a *hamm* 1 and 3 by R. Ouse; 1296.

*CHALKHAM (South Malling), TQ 422126, PN Sx 354, MA *10* 23, ASE *2* 42. *hamm* 3; 1340, so really the limit of this survey, but it has an OE prototheme *scealcing*-, < *scealc* 'servant, soldier', which must mark the name as pre-Conquest.

*STONEHAM (South Malling), TQ 422119, PN Sx 355, ASE *2* 28; a *hamm* 1 and 3 on R. Ouse; 1279.

SOUTHERHAM (South Malling), TQ 425094, PN Sx 355; *hamm* 5, 6 or 7, compare Middleham *infra*; 1262.

*HAM (Ringmer), TQ 439132, PN Sx 357; a *hamm* 2; 1296.

*WELLINGHAM (Ringmer), TQ 430133; UPPER W. 435137, PN Sx 357, MA *10* 24, BNF *3* 156, ASE *2* 28; a *hamm* 1 by R. Ouse; 1100.

MIDDLEHAM (Ringmer), TQ 445120, PN Sx 356, ASE *2* 44-5; compare Southerham *supra*; *hamm* 5, 6 or 7; 1248.

ASHAM (Beddingham), TQ 440062, PN Sx 358, ASE *2* 41; first el. may be OE *assa* 'an ass', whence 'ass paddock' (*hamm* 5), but the place is in a valley, so *hamm* 6 is also possible; early 12th century.

*FINCHAM (Hartfield), TQ 463337, PN Sx 367, ASE *2* 44; *hamm* 2b, 5 or 6; 1295.

*HAM (Withyham), TQ 513372, PN Sx 372; *hamm* 2a-3; 1265.

BAYHAM (Frant), TQ 649363, PN Sx 374, ASE *2* 20, *hamm* 3 or 6; 1228.

*BIVELHAM or BIBLEHAM (Mayfield), TQ 631263, PN Sx 382, ASE *2* 24; *hamm* 2; 12th cent.

NEWNHAM (Buxted), TQ 492288, PN Sx 391, ASE *2* 45; *hamm* 2b or 5a; 1266.

PECKHAM (Framfield), TQ 494168, PN Sx 393, ASE *2* 45; *peace-hamm* would suggest *hamm* 5 'paddock on a hill', but the site is also at the top end of a side-valley opening on to a tributary of R. Ouse, and could be a *hamm* 6 or 7; 1298.

*BUCKHAM (Isfield), TQ 449200 to 450204, PN Sx 396 ASE *2* 25; *hamm* 2 or 5; 1215.

*BROOMHAM (Laughton and Ripe), TQ 524127, 525124, PN Sx 403; site 524217 is a *hamm* 3; but the formation *Broomham* (*brom-ham*) recurs at Sx 468, 485, 509, and we may have a *hamm* 5a, 'enclosure among the broom', i.e., out on the heath; 1287.

BRAILSHAM (Waldron), TQ 561196, BN Sx 406, ASE *2* 42; site near a *hamm* 1 but it could be a *hamm* 2 or 5 since the place lies on a narrow ridge between two streams. If the first el. is as DEPN says, OE *brægels* 'burial place', the place-name could be either 'enclosure near a barrow' or 'enclosure for burials'; 1230.

MICHELHAM (Arlington), TQ 558093, PN Sx 409, ASE *2* 44, 48; a *hamm* 1 by Cuckmere River; the place-name seems analogous with Mitcham and Mickleham, Surrey, PN Sr 51, 81; 1219.

CLAPHAM (Litlington), TQ 525014, PN Sx 412; *hamm* 6; 1224.

*PUSLINGHAM or PUZZLINGHAM (Eastbourne), TV 6199, PN Sx 432, ASE *2* 28; type of *hamm* not known; 1277.

OTHAM (Hailsham), TQ 587057, PN Sx 437, ASE *2* 45; probably a low-lying *hamm* 4-5; 1154.

LAMPHAM (Pevensey), TQ 655073, PN Sx 445; *hamm* 3, 4, 5b; 13th century.

KITCHINGHAM or KETCHINGHAM (Etchingham), TQ 706278. PN Sx 456, ASE *2* 44; *hamm* 3 or 6a; 1242.

*HAM (Burwash), TQ 6724, PN Sx 463; type not known. 1279.

*BROOMHAM (Heathfield), TQ 604242, PN Sx 468; presumably a *hamm* 5a, cf. Broomham Sx 403, 485, 509, 1296.

WILLINGFORD (Brightling), TQ 656225, PN Sx 473; *hamm* 3; 1241.

*GLOTTENHAM (Mountfield), TQ 725222, PN Sx 475, MA *10* 24, ASE *2* 26; *hamm* 2: 1164.

*KITCHENHAM (Ashburnham), TQ 681131, PN Sx 478, ASE *2* 26; *hamm* 2; 13th cent.

*WILSON'S (Ashburnham), TQ 672132, PN Sx 479, ASE *2* 28; first el. could be OE **wil* 'trap, snare' (EPN *2* 265), second el. *hamm* 5b; 1296.

CHILSHAM (Herstmonceux), TQ 635135, PN Sx 480, ASE *2* 42; 1261.

NUNNINGHAM (Herstmonceux), TQ 639132, PN Sx 481, MA *10* 23, ASE *2* 45; *hamm* 2a; 1296.

COURT HOREHAM (Herstmonceux), TQ 609151, PN Sx 481; probably *hamm* 5; 1296.

BOREHAM (Wartling), TQ 665113, PN Sx 483, ASE *2* 49; *hamm* 2 or 5; 12th century.

PEBSHAM (Bexhill), TQ 765089, PN Sx 493, ASE *2* 25, 45; *hamm* 2b, also 3 and 6; 12th century.

TELHAM (Battle), TQ 759139, PN Sx 499; Telham Hill may have been the site of a *hamm* 2; 12th century.

*CROWHAM (Westfield), TQ 817169, PN Sx 505, ASE *2* 43; *hamm* 2 or 7; 1210

DOLEHAM (Westfield), TQ 832167, PN Sx 505, ASE *2* 43, 27; *hamm* 2; 1199.

*MARSHAM (Fairlight), TQ 878128, PN Sx 508, ASE *2* 44; *hamm* 2; 1279.

*LIDHAM (Guestling), TQ 839116. PN Sx 509, ASE *2* 27; *hamm* 2; PN Sx sites first record from 1220; but Lidham, near the boundary of the Hundreds of Guestling and Baldslow, may be the identity of *Iuet* 1086 DB fols. 19b, 20, assuming *Iuet* < *Luet* < *Hlyde* < *hlyda* 'shelf'; in that case, we could also hazard *hamm* 6 or 7.

*NEPSAMS (Fairlight), no location, PN Sx 2, v, ASE *2* 45; the plural indicates *hamm* 5; 1296.

BROOMHAM (Guestling), TQ 852152, PN Sx 509, ASE *2* 42; perhaps *hamm* 2, probably *hamm* 5, compare Broomham Sx 403, 468, 485; 1220.

PICKHAM (Guestling), TQ 867149, PN Sx 509, ASE *2* 45; *hamm* 2; 1220.

*LOWER SNAILHAM (Guestling), TQ 852172, PN Sx 510, ASE *2* 28; *hamm* 2; 1201.

WICKHAM (Icklesham), TQ 898165, PN Sx 512, ASE *2* 26 s.n. Higham, 34, 47, and see note to Higham Sx 538; not a *wic-ham* but a *wic-hamm*, a *hamm* 2; 1200.

BILLINGHAM (Udimore), TQ 864195; PN Sx 517, ASE *2* 41; the first el. OE **bil(l)ing* 'promontory', suggests *hamm* 2; 1401.

*LONEHAM (Udimore), TQ 893192, PN Sx 517, ASE *2* 27; perhaps a *hamm* 5a; 1288.

*OCKHAM (Ewhurst), TQ 784249, PN Sx 520, ASE *2* 27; *hamm* 2; 1205.

*PADGHAM (Ewhurst), TQ 804250, PN Sx 520, BNF, *3* 171, ASE *2* 27; *hamm* 2b; 1200.

*UDIAM (Ewhurst), TQ 773242, PN Sx 520, BNF *3* 171, ASE *2* 46; *hamm* 2 or 3; 1180.

CRAINHAM (Ewhurst), TQ 772238, PN Sx 522, ASE *2* 43; *hamm* 2b or 6; 1207.

BARHAM (Northiam), TQ 8224, location not ascertained, PN Sx 522, ASE *2* 24; *hamm* 5a or b; 1296.

DURHAMFORD (Sedlescombe), TQ 772189, PN Sx 525, ASE *2* 43; probably a *deor-fald* 'a pen for animals', cf. Dorfold, Cheshire; 1296.

METHERSHAM (Beckley), TQ 863268, PN Sx 528, Nob *48* 159; *hamm* 2, 4; first el. OE *mæðere* 'mower'; 1185.

*PELSHAM (Peasmarsh), TQ 877207, PN Sx 532, ASE *2* 27; *hamm* 2b, 5, 7; 1200.

*TILLINGHAM (Peasmarsh), TQ 887204, PN Sx 532, MA *10* 23, ASE *2* 27, 46; *hamm* 2; 1296.

D.1.3.1. Sussex place-names in *-ham* more likely from OE *ham*, but † indicates the possibility of a *hamm* site-characteristic.

(*a*) Appearing as the name of a parish, or on record before 1100.

GRAFFHAM, SU 927170, PN Sx 21, ASE *2* 33.

†SELHAM, SU 935207, PN Sx 28, ASE *2* 33; this might be a promontory *hamm* 2.

†KINGSHAM, PN Sx 69, see *hamm* list *supra*, *D.1.2.* (*a*).

†MUNDHAM, PN Sx 72, see *hamm* list *supra*, *D.1.2.* (*a*).

UP WALTHAM, SU 943137, PN Sx 77, ASE *2* 33; 'manor or village in the forest', like Coldwaltham *infra*; on these, see note on Albursham, *infra*, and, recently, R. M. Huggins, 'The Significance of the place-name *Wealdham*', MA *19* (1975), 198–201, esp. 200, 201.

SIDLESHAM, SZ 855990, PN Sx 85, ASE *2* 34; also a *ham-stede* type.

BRACKLESHAM (Wittering), SZ 805965, PN Sx 87, ASE *2* 34; also a *ham-stede* type.

COLDWALTHAM, TQ 023165, PN Sx 126, ASE *2* 33; see notes on Up Waltham *supra*, Albursham *infra*.

COOTHAM (Storrington), TQ 075145, PN Sx 162, ASE *2* 33.

†WEPHAM (Burpham), TQ 043085, PN Sx 167, ASE *2* 33; this site needs reconsideration, for *hamm* 2a or 7.

†BURPHAM, TQ 039089, PN Sx 166, ASE *2* 33; the site requires reconsideration, for *hamm* 1–3, or for *burh-hamm* 'fortification

enclosure', *hamm* 5, cf. Burgham PN Sx 456, *supra*, *D.1.2.* (*a*).

NYETIMBER (West Chiltington), TQ 0817, PN Sx 175.

THAKEHAM, TQ 110173, PN Sx 180, ASE *2* 33.

CLAPHAM, TQ 093063, PN Sx 195, ASE *2* 33.

†MUNTHAM (Findon), TQ 111097, PN Sx 198, ASE *2* 33; this site needs reconsideration, for *hamm* 6.

COKEHAM (Sompting), UPPER, TQ 173055, LOWER, TQ 172043, PN Sx 201, ASE *2* 33.

†HORSHAM, PN Sx 225, see *hamm* list *supra*, *D.1.2.* (*a*).

OLD SHOREHAM, TQ 208060, PN Sx 246, ASE *2* 33.

†PATCHAM, TQ 302091, PN Sx 293, ASE *2* 33; this site needs reconsideration, for *hamm* 6.

†SESSINGHAM, PN Sx 410, see *hamm* list *supra*, *D.1.2.* (*a*).

HAILSHAM, TQ 592095, PN Sx 435, ASE *2* 33.

†BURGHAM, PN Sx 456, see *hamm* list *supra*, *D.1.2.* (*a*).

WILTING (Hollington), TQ 780110, PN Sx 504, MA *10* 23, ASE *2* 33.

D.1.3.1. (*b*). Recorded after 1100.

CAKEHAM (Wittering), SZ 784975, PN Sx 88, ASE *2* 33; 1226.

†BEDHAM (Fittleworth), TQ 017218, PN Sx 126, ASE *2* 49. the site may be a *hamm*

6; 1245.

†ALBURSHAM (lost, Waldron), TQ 3419, PN Sx 405, ASE *2* 41; 1230; as there are no *hamm* spellings or inflexions, and the

site is not identified, this place-name is analysed as a *ham* type, with a personal-name as prototheme. However, the place is not on record until 1230, and it is subject to Waldron, the parish village and DB manor. The territory of Waldron already contains Brailsham (PN Sx 406, *supra*, *D.1.2. [b]*), and one might conjecture that Waldron, 'house in the forest', would be, as Coldwaltham and Up Waltham (*D.1.3.1.* (*a*)), a settlement projected into the Weald from somewhere not in the Weald—these names would otherwise be pointless (see reference to MA *19* 198–201 under Up Waltham *supra*); then, Albursham and Brailsham might be two of its woodland or upland outlying *hamms*, only emerging into independent legal record in the 13th century.

MAGHAM (Hailsham), TQ 608113, PN Sx 437, ASE *2* 33; 13th century.

D.1.3.2. Sussex place-names in *wic-ham* recorded before 1300.

(*a*) Recorded by 1100.

WYCKHAM (Steyning), TQ 190133, PN Sx 237, MA *11* 92, ASE *2* 34; as it happens, the site is a *hamm* 1, 2a or 4, but no *hamm* spellings have been observed.

WICKHAM (Hurstpierpoint and Clayton), TQ 291167 and 296164, PN Sx 275, MA *11* 92, ASE *2* 34.

D.2. Sussex place-names in *ham-stede* recorded before 1300.

(*a*) Occurring as a parish-name or before 1100.

SIDLESHAM, occasional early alternative to *ham*, see *D.1.3.1.* (*a*).

BRACKLESHAM, occasional early alternative to *ham*, see *D.1.3.1.* (*a*).

BERSTED, NORTH, SU 9201, **SOUTH**, SU 9300, PN Sx 90, ASE *2* 34, Sandred 251.

(*b*) Recorded after 1100.

HEMPSTEAD (Framfield), TQ 487216, PN Sx 393, ASE *2* 34, Sandred 256, 12th century.

HEMPSTEAD (Arlington), TQ 574102, PN Sx 409, 440, ASE *2* 34, Sandred 255, 256; 1202.

D.3. Sussex place-names in *stede*.

(*a*) Appearing as parish-names, or recorded before 1100.

ELSTED, SU 816196, PN Sx 34, Sandred 254.

BINSTED, SU 9806, PN Sx 138, Sandred 253.

WEST GRINSTEAD, TQ 170207, PN Sx 184, Sandred 255; 1230.

EAST GRINSTEAD, TQ 396380, PN Sx 331, Sandred 254; 12th century.

HORSTED KEYNES, TQ 383287, PN Sx 336, Sandred 257; firsl el. *hors* 'a horse'; cf. Little Horsted *infra*, see notes on Horsham at *D.1.2.* (*a*).

WALSTEAD (Lindfield), TQ 357244, PN Sx 343, Sandred 258.

LITTLE HORSTED, TQ 470183, PN Sx 348, Sandred 256; cf. Horsted Keynes *supra*.

BUXTED, TQ 485228, PN Sx 389, Sandred 253.

(*b*) Not recorded before 1100.

MINSTED (Stedham), SU 856208, PN Sx 30, Sandred 257.

PRINSTED (Westbourne), SU 765053, PN Sx 56, Sandred 257.

HICKSTEAD (Twineham), TQ 267201, PN Sx 279, Sandred 256.

WORSTED'S (East Grinstead), TQ 408378, PN Sx 334, Sandred 259, EPN *2* 271.

CROCKSTEAD (Framfield), TQ 493178, PN Sx 393, Sandred 254.

D.4. Sussex place-names in *denn.*

(*a*) Appearing as parish-names, or recorded by 1100.

HAZELDEN (East Grinstead), TQ 3938, PN Sx 332; *hæsel* 'hazel-tree'.

HENDON (lost, Hellingly), TQ 5812, PN Sx 440; *heah* 'high'.

IDEN, TQ 915237, PN Sx 530; *iw* 'yew-tree'.

PLAYDEN, TQ 919216, PN Sx 533; *plega* 'sport, game, mating of animals'.

(*b*) Not recorded by 1100.

GOSDENSHEATH (Ambersham), SU 9120, PN Sx 98; *gos* 'goose'; 1249.

PENDEAN (West Lavington), SU 890200, PN Sx 110; pers. n.; 1296.

HEBERDEN (lost, Madehurst), SU 9810, PN Sx 130; pers. n.; 1279.

? SELDEN (Patching), TQ 076064, PN Sx 166, EPNS VIII, liii; pers. n.; originally *denn* but thereafter *denn* and *denu* alternate, i.e., it is a *denn* in a *denu* 'valley'; 1271.

SUMMERSDEANE (Edburton), TQ 233093, PN Sx 207; *sumor* 'summertime'; *denn,* but in a *denu* 'valley'; 1296.

OAKENDEAN (Cowfold), TQ 226226, PN Sx 210, MA *10* 24; *-ingas* folk-name; 1279.

THORNDEAN (Cuckfield), TQ 270257, PN Sx 265; *þorn* 'thorn-tree(s)'; 1288.

HAMMINGDEN (West Hoathly), PN Sx 271; pers. n., *-ing-*; 1296.

DEANHOUSE (Hurstpierpoint), TQ 284203, PN Sx 274; simplex; 1296.

VARNDEAN (Patcham), TQ 3009, PN Sx 294; *fearn* 'bracken'; 1296.

HACKENDEN (East Grinstead), TQ 3938, PN Sx 332; pers. n.; 1300.

DANEHILL (formerly part of Fletching), TQ 402275; PN Sx 335; simplex. 1279.

PEGDEN (Lindfield), TQ 378239, PN Sx 342; pers. n.; 1296.

PLUMMERDEN (Lindfield), TQ 365262, PN Sx 342; ME *plumere* (plumber, i.e., lead-worker'; 1296.

BIRCHDEN (Withyham), TQ 535365, PN Sx 370; *bircen* 'growing with birch trees'; 1203.

RUMSDEN (Rotherfield), TQ 530276, PN Sx 379; *rum* 'spacious'; 1295.

BAINDEN (Mayfield), TQ 596263, PN Sx 381; pers. n.; 1296.

SHARNDEN (Mayfield), TQ 603283, PN Sx 383; *scearn* 'dung'; 13th century.

FLATTENDEN (Wadhurst), TQ 638283; PN Sx 386; pers. n.; 1279.

BROOMDEN (Ticehurst), TQ 6730, PN Sx 451; pers. n., *-ing-*; 1272.

COTTENDEN (Ticehurst), TQ 675284, PN Sx 452, MA *10* 24; *-ingas* folk-name; 1180.

HAMMERDEN (Ticehurst), TQ 661271, PN Sx 452; *hamer* 'a hammer (forge)'; 1279.

MAPLESDEN (Ticehurst), TQ 653287, PN Sx 453; *mapel* 'maple-tree'; 1190.

RINGDEN (Ticehurst), TQ 6830, PN Sx 453; *hring* 'circular, ring-fenced'; 1271.

WITHERENDEN (Ticehurst), TQ 653270, PN Sx 454; pers. n., *-ing*; 1180.

ROUNDEN (Brightling), TQ 675215, PN Sx 472; *ruh* 'rough'; 1197.

HASELDEN (Dallington), TQ 675191, PN Sx 474; *hæsel* 'hazel-tree'; 1200.

BRIGDEN (Ashburnham), TQ 666155, PN Sx 478; pers. n.; 1279.

STUDDING'S (Herstmonceux), TQ 6214; PN Sx 481; *stod* 'stud (of horses)'; 1296.

COWDEN (Wartling), TQ 657132, PN Sx 483; *cu* 'cow'; 13th century.

DINGLESDEN (Peasmarsh), TQ 867206, PN Sx 531; *þengel* 'prince'; 1279.

V

THE SUSSEX MINTS AND THEIR MONEYERS

Ian Stewart

Introduction

ON 21 DECEMBER, 1866, four days before the Christmas which marked the eighth centenary of the coronation of William the Conqueror, there was unearthed at Chancton Farm, three miles from Storrington, a great hoard of coins from the reigns of Edward the Confessor and Harold II, doubtless hidden at the onset of the Norman invader. Its original owner was unable to recover his treasure. Perhaps he perished in the battle, was dispossessed, or had to flee; and it is probably no coincidence that of the relatively few recorded finds of coins from this period two more ending with coins of Harold Godwinson have come from Sussex, one in 1789 at Oving, near Chichester, and the other seven years later at Offham, two miles north of Lewes.[1]

Eleventh-century coinage consisted solely of silver pennies. A very few halfpennies had been struck in the mid-tenth century, but except briefly under Henry I (only a single specimen has survived) they were not coined again before Edward I's time. The only other departure from the norm was the very occasional striking of pieces in gold from regular penny dies, presumably for special presentation or ceremonial use. One of the extremely rare extant examples, of Ethelred's *Helmet* type, was found at Hellingly, only 10 miles east of Lewes where it was struck.[2]

Most types of the late Anglo-Saxon and Norman coinage were minted at 50 or 60, or even more, of the principal towns in the country, and it is not therefore surprising that the Conquest hoards from Sussex have made coins from local mints amongst the most plentiful to have survived from the mid-eleventh century. Had large hoards been recovered in the south of England from the period of the Viking invasions nearly two centuries earlier, they would have supplied no material for our purpose, since in Sussex, as in most other counties of southern England it is most unlikely that any mint was established before the tenth century. Up to that time mints were few and rarely named on their coins. At

89

one time or another in the eighth and ninth centuries there had certainly been mints at Canterbury, Rochester, London, and York, and in Wessex and East Anglia. Alfred and Edward the Elder seem to have planned a West Saxon coinage from mints at Winchester, Gloucester, Bath and Exeter. Not, however, until Athelstan inherited with his conquests a number of mints which had come into being in the Danelaw, can English coinage clearly be seen to have been reorganised on a regional basis. Part of Athelstan's administrative policy was to increase the number of mints and to situate them not only in the traditional centres, but also in the new *burhs* which he and his father had founded. More than 30 mints, including Lewes and Chichester, are named on Athelstan's coins, but the majority are nevertheless without mint name, and although the practice was in part revived by Eadwig only a very small proportion of the coinage struck between 939 and the reform late in Edgar's reign carries a mint name.

Edgar transformed the English coinage. The type was standardised throughout the country, and his penny bore on the reverse not only the name of the moneyer responsible for its issue, as almost all English coins had done since Offa's day, but also (usually in an abbreviated form) that of its mint. For the first time in the history of English coinage we thus have positive evidence of how many separate mints were operating throughout the country. They numbered over 30 before Edgar's death, and, like Athelstan's, included Chichester and Lewes. By the reign of Ethelred II more than 60 were active at one time or another and some others of these had possibly operated under Edgar or Edward the Martyr without their coins having survived. It is to the following century and a half, during which the coin-types were frequently changed and a network of mints throughout the country was needed to facilitate local re-minting, that Sussex coinage largely belongs (Fig. 6).

In the next four sections various aspects of Sussex coinage are considered in a national context—the scope of the surviving material, the re-coinage system with its frequent changes of type, the activity of the mints and the functions of their moneyers. These are followed by a detailed analysis of the Sussex mints and moneyers period by period. At least one coin of each Sussex mint is illustrated on the plate accompanying this paper, and the figured coins, ranging from Edward the Elder to Stephen, have been selected where practicable to include previously unrecorded or unillustrated examples.[3]

The material

Our knowledge of Anglo-Saxon mints, being almost entirely derived from the coins themselves, depends upon the number and size of the hoards recovered from each period and area. This is of course partly a matter of chance, but it is heavily influenced by the political and military circumstances of the time. Coins were regularly hidden or buried for safety, but in times of peace and social continuity they were normally recovered. Only in times of disturbance and hostilities were they lost on any scale. For example, few hoards have been discovered in southern England dating from the early and middle years of the tenth century but from the subsequent Danegeld period enormous quantities of coins of Ethelred II have been unearthed in Scandinavia. The flow of English coins across the North Sea continued with the *Heregeld* throughout the reign of Cnut, though it dwindled in the 1040s. With a paucity of hoards from England also until the Conquest, surviving material for the first half of the reign of Edward the Confessor is much less complete than that of his later years, although some Sussex coins can be identified as deriving from incompletely recorded hoards of the 1040s and 1050s, including one found in 1843 at Milton Street,[4] a hamlet six miles north-east of Eastbourne.

The contents of the Oving and Offham hoards are unknown in any detail, and unfortunately the published list of coins from Chancton Farm is of little use as a guide to the numbers of each mint and moneyer, since of more than 1,700 coins examined (out of a larger total) only about 700 are recorded, these being merely the varieties retained by the British Museum. A more complete record does, however, exist of the great hoard found in 1876 at Sedlescombe, only three miles from Battle.[5] Although it lacked coins of Harold II and the last issue of Edward, the cause of its non-recovery, even though not the occasion of its assembly or deposit, may well have lain in the events of 1066 which culminated in the Norman victory nearby. In Table A are set out the numbers of each of the four types from the four Sussex mints and from the three mints

TABLE A

Contents of the Sedlescombe Hoard

Types	18	19	20	21	Total
Mints	Helmet	Sovereign	Hammer Cross	Facing Bust	
Sussex					
Chichester	0	2	14	0	16
Hastings	36	54	454	143	687
Lewes	3	6	36	1	46
Steyning	0	0	1	0	1
Largest contributors elsewhere					
London	18	6	26	2	52
Romney	1	4	7	34	46
Winchester	8	4	43	0	55
All others	59	38	133	3	233
Total	125	114	714	183	1,136

outside the county with the largest numbers. The local weighting of this hoard is very marked, only Canterbury and Exeter otherwise contributing more than 20 coins in all and London being rivalled not only by Winchester, but even by the minor neighbouring mint of Romney. The Hastings figures suggest that coins of earlier types could survive in the close vicinity of their mint in spite of subsequent re-coinages. Also, the figures of type 21 from Hastings and Romney show that at the start of a new issue, as is to have been expected, only locally re-minted coins were available.[6]

After the Conquest we are much less fully provided with either coins or information. An early hoard from Walbrook in the City of London was primarily composed of pre-Conquest coins and is useful for being without a Sussex bias.[7] Then there is a hoard from Scaldwell (Northants.)[8] of the Conqueror's fifth issue, followed by the huge hoard from Beauworth (Hants.) composed almost entirely of the *Paxs* issue (*BMC* type VIII of William I).[9] Thereafter, apart from an early William II hoard of about 300 coins from Tamworth,[10] there is no detailed hoard evidence of any size available until the end of Henry I's reign, represented most fully in the recent Lincoln find,[11] followed by the Civil War hoards of the Stephen period.[12] More reliance thus has to be placed on individual hoards for the Norman coinage and their fewness means that there are many gaps and imbalances in our knowledge, particularly for the early twelfth century.

The pattern of finds is reflected in the modern distribution of the material. Saxon coins up to the 1040s are predominantly to be found in Scandinavian national collections, primarily at Stockholm and Copenhagen, but also at Oslo and Helsinki. The systematic collection in Stockholm, compiled eclectically from nineteenth century Swedish hoards, was admirably catalogued by Hildebrand,[13] but much has been found since; while all the English coins in Copenhagen have recently been illustrated in a series of *Sylloge* volumes.[14] The British Museum collection is also an important general repository for this period, while for coins of Edward, Harold, and the Norman kings it is pre-eminent; its holdings of Anglo-Saxon coins were catalogued by Keary, and of Norman coins by Brooke,[15] though hoards of the late Norman period and a determined policy of acquisition in the late Anglo-Saxon series from the dispersal of great private collections and other sources have greatly enriched the national collection since the catalogues were published. Other good series of accessible material are the university collections at Cambridge (Fitzwilliam), Glasgow (Hunterian), and Oxford (Ashmolean), all of which have been published in recent *Sylloge* volumes.[16]

The most important specialist collections of Sussex coins were those formed by J. H. Daniels, a local dealer, now in the Brighton Museum, and by Horace King, author of *The Coins of the Sussex Mints*, an extensively illustrated catalogue containing full lists of readings and varieties of all the Sussex coins known to him after many years of research.[17] The present paper is intended to complement King's by supplying a commentary on the activities of the Sussex mints and the moneyers who worked them; it does not attempt to deal with numismatic detail except where relevant to this wider theme. When technical study of the coins is carried to a further stage it will be greatly facilitated by

TABLE B

Numbers of Coins of all Mints, all Sussex Mints and Selected Regional Mints in Various Hoards and Other Sources

	Ethelred II Hildebrand		1016–42 Hildebrand		Edward the Confessor Hildebrand		Walbrook		William I Beauworth, Paxs		Henry I South Coast hoard—XIV		Lincoln hoard—all types		Watford hoard		Stephen, type I Prestwich hoard	
		%		%		%		%		%		%		%		%		%
All Mints	4,346		5,130		800		2,198*		6,439		353		744		593*		831	
All Sussex	120	2.8	113	2.2	16	2.0	42	1.9	444	6.9	15	4.2	29	3.9	20	3.4	25	3.0
Canterbury	130	3.0	109	2.1	28	3.5	81	3.7	285	4.4	6	1.7	18	2.4	17	2.9	25	3.0
Exeter	166	3.8	98	1.9	9	1.1	39	1.8	180	2.8	4	1.1	4	0.5	9	1.5	7	0.8
Lincoln	400	9.2	531	10.4	114	14.3	190	8.6	171	2.7	2	0.6	71	9.5	9	1.5	125	15.0
London	1,003	23.1	1,318	25.7	196	24.5	458	20.8	792	12.3	54	15.3	166	22.3	96	16.2	77	9.3
Norwich	110	2.5	129	2.5	21	2.6	151	6.9	236	3.7	10	2.8	23	3.1	24	4.0	52	6.3
Stamford	148	3.4	216	4.2	39	4.9	61	2.8	51	0.8	8	2.3	10	1.3	2	0.3	12	1.4
Thetford	151	3.5	141	2.7	26	3.3	212	9.6	123	1.9	13	3.7	24	3.2	10	1.7	13	1.6
Winchester	315	7.2	277	5.4	36	4.5	129	5.9	1,587	24.6	30	8.5	38	5.1	47	7.9	28	3.4
York	406	9.3	539	10.5	77	9.6	75	3.4	84	1.3	9	2.5	30	4.0	13	2.2	64	7.7

*Note: Large numbers of 'illegible' specimens have been excluded from the 'All Mints' totals for the Walbrook and Watford hoards.

the munificence of Mr. King who donated to the British Museum every specimen from his cabinet which was not already there represented by a coin from the same pair of dies; this has enriched the national collection by no less than 200 coins, mostly of Sussex mints and many of outstanding rarity and interest.

For a recent metrological study, Petersson traced some 40,000 coins from Edgar's reform to the Conquest.[18] Perhaps Sussex mints contributed between 1,000 and 2,000 of these, since listed material suggests that Sussex coins normally amounted to about two or three per cent. of the national currency, and the Conquest hoards from Sussex have clearly distorted their survival rate. As a guide to the natural proportions in currency, and so implicitly of mint output, the totals of several hoards should, where practicable, be combined. Unfortunately this is not always possible, but worthwhile attempts can be made at several points in the series to assess the proportion of the total English coinage produced collectively by Sussex mints, and to some extent by each individually.

Table B gives selected data on important individual mints throughout the country (not always the largest, but the most consistent over the period) with a global figure for Sussex. Figures for the separate Sussex mints are discussed below, period by period. For Ethelred II it is sufficient to take the totals listed by Hildebrand. Since the prosperous south often attracted Viking raids, Sussex coins may be over-represented, but there is no way of adjusting accurately for this. The same probably applies to the 25 years of Danish rule, the reigns of Cnut and his sons, whose coins have been aggregated in Table B, again from Hildebrand's lists. Only Edward's early types reached Scandinavia in number, but Hildebrand's totals, albeit small, are still probably indicative; for the later types only the Walbrook hoard is large enough to be of value, in spite of its East Anglian bias.

Unfortunately the one sizeable late eleventh-century hoard, Beauworth, is heavily weighted in favour of surrounding mints, mainly Winchester, but also Wilton, Salisbury and Chichester; and the Scaldwell hoard is too small for useful comparison. For late Henry I the Lincoln figures (biassed to Lincoln and Northampton) may be set beside those of a south coast hoard,[19] all but four recorded coins from which were of type XIV. For the Stephen period the totals from Watford[20] and the recent Prestwich hoard (dominated by the Chester mint) give a geographical mix. These various figures give no more than a general indication of the relative output of different mints, but they are our only means of achieving even this.

Types and Issues

Late in the ninth century the stylised royal portrait, previously a usual feature of the coinage in the Mercian and West Saxon periods, was discontinued. Perhaps under the influence of the aniconic design of Islamic coinage which was increasingly finding its way to northern Europe, a plain epigraphic type came to be adopted for the bulk of English coinage. The typical English penny of Alfred and his successors had the name and title of the king in a circular inscription on the obverse, with a small cross in the centre of an otherwise plain field, and on the reverse the name of the moneyer in two lines often with ornaments such as crosses or pellets or trefoils above, below and in between. Some issues had a circular inscription on the reverse also, but portraits, except in parts of the Danelaw area, only rarely occur during the first three-quarters of the tenth century.

The reform late in Edgar's reign constitutes one of the major watersheds in the history of British coinage. From this time onwards for centuries, English coins were to carry the king's portrait, or at least a face or bust, accompanied by such symbols of kingship as a crown and sceptre, the only exception to this being an abortive type late in the reign of Ethelred II which depicted the *Agnus Dei.*

Edgar's *Reform* type, a simple design with a small cross in the centre of an otherwise plain reverse, was continued unchanged through the short reign of Edward the Martyr, but under Ethelred II it was soon replaced and the period between then and the Civil War of Stephen's reign, which destroyed the system,[21] saw a succession of no less than 52 separate issues, each of distinctive type.[22]

There are many variations in the way in which the king is depicted: one issue of Edward the Confessor shows not the usual head and shoulders portrait but a full-length enthroned figure, while another has a facing bust. Pre-Conquest portraits are otherwise in profile, and usually accompanied by a sceptre. The head is sometimes crowned or helmeted, but often bare or adorned merely by a diadem in the Roman fashion. Indeed many of the portraits on Anglo-Saxon coins were based on late Roman prototypes, a conscious form of archaism which may have been encouraged by the discovery of coin hoards from the late Roman period.

Reverse types consist usually of some form of cross, or cruciform device, partly as a religious symbol, but also to enable pennies to be cut into halves and quarters for use as small change. Sometimes the cross extends to the edge of the coin, thus dividing the inscription into four segments and calling for abbreviation and ligation of letters. Other notable types are that of Ethelred II's first new issue, the *Manus Dei,* or Hand of Providence, the inscription PAX (a forlorn hope) written across the field on coins of Harold II and the birds which occur on the reverse on the sovereign type of Edward the Confessor. The Conquest did not have a dramatic effect on the appearance of English coinage, although facing heads soon outnumber profiles and the sceptre is sometimes, no doubt meaningfully, replaced by a sword. From the 1090s the standard of workmanship deteriorated and many of the coins of Henry I and Stephen are very badly struck, although the dies themselves continued usually to be well engraved.

Five major type changes took place during Ethelred's reign, three under Cnut, two under Harold I, one in Harthacnut's sole reign, 10 under Edward the Confessor, one for the few months of Harold II, 13 under the two Norman Williams, and 15 under Henry I. Whether or not such type changes were part of Edgar's original plan, they clearly soon became an established feature of the coinage. Periodic changes of type, involving at least a partial re-minting of earlier issues, can be paralleled in other parts of Europe during the feudal period. Besides keeping the coinage up-to-date and in good order, the real purpose of this system of *renovatio* (or *mutatio*) *monetae,* as it was called, seems to have been to raise revenue for the issuer. Partly this would have derived from charges for minting and the issue of new dies, but it also enabled the weight of the coins to be manipulated. We can only guess at how this worked in detail, but the observed pattern in the late tenth and early eleventh centuries is that earlier coins of any issue are usually heavier than later ones, although there is at least one issue, the fifth of the Confessor (type 17), during which a sharp and substantial increase in the weight took place. Under the Conqueror the weight seems to have been stabilised. Perhaps in order to compensate for the loss of potential profit from weight adjustments, there was levied in the Norman period a charge on the moneyers at the beginning of each issue; most mints were farmed and this charge enabled the king to benefit from the extra profits made on re-minting in the period immediately following a change of type. A Domesday entry under Sussex is representative: *In burgo de Lewes cum moneta renovatur dat XX solidos unusquisque monetarius.*[23]

The dating of the coinage in the *renovatio* period presents problems. The average length of each issue up to the death of Cnut must have been about six years and from then on about two or three. In its early stages, until after Ethelred's *Hand* type, the system seems to have been in an experimental stage. Later it settled down to greater regularity, but although there are some historical indicators suggesting issues of approximately six years' duration from the later years of Ethelred until more frequent changes were introduced in the 1030s, we have no means of knowing whether the administration of the time, often no doubt dislocated by emergency and unrest, attempted to work to a system of *renovationes* at fixed intervals or, if it did, how successful it proved in practice. There are certainly grounds for believing that some Anglo-Saxon types (e.g., type 5, Ethelred's *Helmet*) did not run for as long as others (e.g., type 6, *Last Small Cross*), and uneven length of types is also probable in the Norman period. On the basis of the survival of earlier types in later hoards and of typological variation it seems, for example, that *BMC* type V of William I and types VII and X of Henry I were abnormally plentiful and struck probably over a longer period than the respective types which followed them.[24] Unfortunately the likelihood that issues were of variable duration means that we cannot easily estimate exact dates for them, although simple interpolation, based on the number of types and the years of each reign, will usually give at least an approximate chronology.

The mints

In the sections on each period the importance of individual mints is considered in the light of the relative quantities of their surviving coins and the number of moneyers named upon them. As noted above, local bias in hoards can seriously

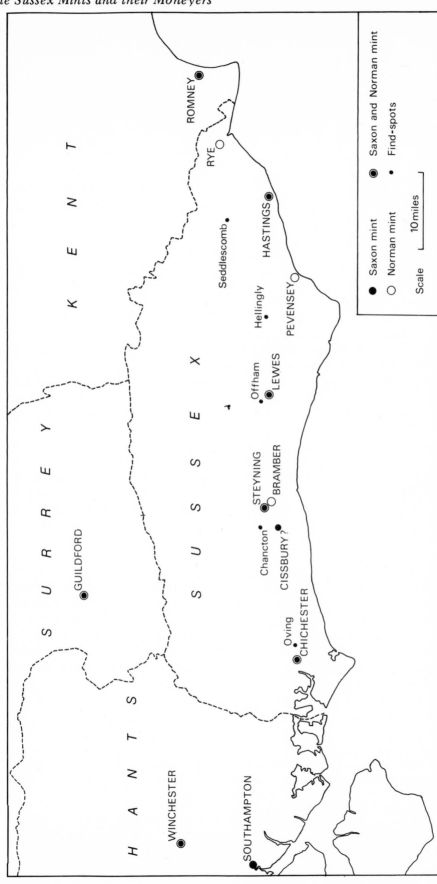

Fig. 6 Mints in and near Sussex and findspots of Sussex coins

distort proportions, and this may be even more pronounced in the case of single mints than of counties or regions as a whole; nevertheless, at various points in the series the contents of hoards are at least indicative of the standing of one mint or another.[25] Even though we often have little means of knowing how complete our information is about the number of moneyers who were active in each type, at most periods the number recorded is, subject to some qualifications discussed below, a guide to the level of activity of their mint, and these numbers are tabulated for each mint and type.

On the basis of such information we may conjecture, often rather imprecisely, what were the patterns of mint activity and output. In doing so, we are apt to use a kind of numismatic shorthand language—to speak, for example, of the Lewes mint, or to say that the Hastings mint was active throughout the eleventh century. This implies that a mint was an institutional part of a *burh,* an establishment with a physical existence and a continuous function. It may be true of a few places, such as London or Winchester, that at this period they contained a workshop or workshops, located in the same position for many years, and occupied in the more or less uninterrupted production of coin. But elsewhere minting can have been only an intermittent feature of town life, much of it concentrated in the early months after a change of type, and thereafter conducted as and when required to meet commercial, fiscal or other needs. In a *burh* of some standing like Lewes, mint operations might have been for regular periods or at frequent intervals, with regard to seasons and trade and markets. In smaller places, such as Steyning (and in the Norman period perhaps at many of the larger also), they can only have been occasional.[26] That this was so is a necessary inference from the limited number of dies used—where the coins have survived in adequate numbers, this can be estimated with reasonable accuracy. Often the number in any one type is far too small to have been used for daily or even weekly coin production over a period of two or three years. Really, we should be stricter in our terminology and for many purposes speak not of mints but, like Sir Frank Stenton, of minting-places, a term which begs no questions about the permanence, status or activity of the factories in which coins were made.

Although minting itself was so effectively decentralised during the *renovatio* period, each mint had to work at least broadly within national policy with regard to changes of type and weight. Standardisation was also assisted by the distribution of dies which were at times cut centrally for the whole country (as, with few exceptions, was the case in the Norman period), but at others[27] appear to have been made at regional centres for neighbouring mints. Some variations of the basic type do occur—Lewes coins of types 7 and 18 exist with the bust facing the wrong way—but they are rare and modest departures from the norm.[28] Occasionally the need for a die may have been met by a local workman, as appears to have been the case with an unusual obverse of type 20 at Steyning.[29] The transfer of dies between mints may sometimes have been prompted by economy, but the die-links between *Sithesteburh* and Chichester in type 7, and between Guildford and Chichester in the post-Conquest *Paxs* type could each have occurred as a result of temporary or permanent closure of a very small mint.

TABLE C

Activity of Sussex Mints by Reign

	Edward the Elder	Athelstan	Edmund	Edred	Edwig	Edgar	Edward the Martyr	Ethelred II	Cnut	Harold I	Harthacnut	Edward the Confessor	Harold II	William I	William II	Henry I	Stephen	Henry II	Richard I	John
Chichester	M	X	(M)	(M)	(M)	X		X	X	X	X	X	X	X	X	X	X			X
Lewes		X	M	M	(M)	X	X	X	X	X	X	X	X	X	X	X	X	X		
Hastings		G					X	X	X	X	X	X	X	X	X	X	X			
Sithesteburh								X	X											
Steyning									X	X	10	X	X	X	X					
Pevensey														X	X	X	X			
Rye																	X			
Bramber																	X.			

Key:

X	Coins recorded of mint for reign.
M	Coins recorded with name of moneyer known for this mint in another reign.
(M)	As M, but identity of moneyer very doubtful.
G	Reference to mint in Code of Grately.
10	Coins of Harthacnut known only of type 10 (Jewel Cross issue of joint reign with Harold, 1035-7).

Table C sets out the reigns of which coins are known of each Sussex mint. First come the *burhs* established early in the tenth century at Chichester and Lewes, which continued to be the most consistent throughout the eleventh and into the twelfth century. Lewes, the prime mint at almost all stages, alone contributed to the new coinage introduced by Henry II in 1158 though of this issue, which ran until 1180, the few coins that can be attributed to Lewes belong to its middle or later years. Coins were again struck at Chichester briefly in John's re-coinage of 1205, when the bishop was granted the privilege of minting; he had one die of his own and farmed two others from the king. These were the last coins to be struck in Sussex, where none of the towns enjoyed sufficient commercial importance to qualify for a mint during the subsequent re-coinages of the later middle ages.

Mostly the mint names on the coins are straightforward. Chichester begins as *Cissan* (or *Cyssan*) *Civi(tas)* under Athelstan, with *Cis(s)e Ci* under Edgar; an occasional early form such as *Cisan* or *Ciscae* occurs under Ethelred, with *Cyse* once later. Ethelred's coins normally, however, have forms based on *Cisecest* (with odd variants *Ciscesere, Cicstere*, etc.); some are without the first *s* (*Cicestr*), and these become commoner under Cnut. By 1035 the *s* is lost and forms akin to Domesday's *Cicestre*, with variants like *Ciceas, Cicst*, etc., then occur throughout, with the exception of *Cisi* (if correctly of this mint)[30] on one early coin of Henry I.

Lewes was one of the few *urbes* of Athelstan's coinage (*Lae Urb*); thereafter the normal forms are *Laewe* or *Laeve*, sometimes without *a*; odd variants include *Lawa, Leawe, Laeew, Laewve, Laewwe, Laewenen, Laehwea, Laehwge* and (perhaps) under Henry II, *Lewies* and *Levas*.[31] Because of unclear readings beginning LA or LE, Lewes coins have sometimes been misattributed to other mints.[32]

It is doubtful whether Hastings, in spite of Athelstan's decree, had a mint before the Danegeld period, when the forms *Aes* and *Aest* are presumably to be associated with the same mint as the more usual *Haesting*. Early in the twelfth century, and sometimes before, the *e* is dropped, but otherwise variation is limited to the occasional loss of the aspirate, of *a* (*Hest-*), or of other letters (*Aestic, Haetin, Hst, Haesn, Estnc*). *Haesd* and *Haesthin* also occur; and *Haestien* in the second half of the Confessor's reign. Two dies of type 17 have a different form, *Hestinpor(t)*. After a modest start, Hastings was a steady, and sometimes a prolific mint, as when its output, on the evidence of surviving coins, temporarily surpassed that of Lewes under Cnut.

The next mint to be opened, towards the end of Ethelred's reign (type 6), was at a place described on its coins as *Sithmes-* or *Sithesteb(urh)*. The obverse die-link with Chichester suggests a Sussex location and a linguistically plausible identification has been proposed with Cissbury, the Iron Age fort, which is called Sissabury on early maps.[33] The use of a hill-fort as a retreat in a time of Danish attacks can be paralleled in the emergency mint of Cadbury, transferred from Ilchester in type 6. *Sith(m)est* means latest, or last, and the name given to this new *burh* perhaps supports the idea that it was situated where there had not previously been an Anglo-Saxon settlement.[34] After the establishment of the

Danish dynasty in England under Cnut, the mint was re-located at Steyning, a few miles to the north, where it continued to contribute on a small scale to most, perhaps all, of the issues up to the end of the reign of William II. The name is found as *Staen-* or *Stenige* throughout, with the former dying out soon after the Conquest. When a mint was again needed in this neighbourhood, at the end of Stephen's reign, the Norman castle of Bramber[35] was preferred to the little Saxon town.

Although several new mints were opened under the Confessor, including Hythe and Sandwich in Kent, none was added in Sussex. The castle of Pevensey, built by the Normans close to the spot where William had landed, was one of the very few new minting-places of the Conqueror's reign; its modest and probably very occasional, contributions to the coinage are recorded intermittently until the end of the Norman period. The mint signature is *Pefnese, Pfns, Pene* or *Peven.*

The reign of Henry I saw or confirmed the closure of a number of Anglo-Saxon mints, Steyning and nearby Guildford included. Stephen, however, opened a number of new ones in south-eastern England when other parts of the country were lost to him. One of these was at Rye, which is known of three types of Stephen, including the first.[36] Its coins were once attributed to Castle Rising, another new mint of the reign, but there can be no doubt that they were struck at Rye, which thus presumably qualifies as Domesday's unnamed *novus burgus* in east Sussex; the mint signature, *Rie(e),* occurs on a disproportionately large number of coins of type II from the Linton hoard (found only 22 miles from Rye), while the moneyer's name Rawulf is corroborated by entries in Henry II's Pipe Rolls.

Moneyers

Of all the known names of pre-Conquest inhabitants of Sussex more are those of moneyers than of any other category of person. This is due partly to the durability of coins compared with other kinds of document, and partly to the fact that like printed books, but unlike manuscripts, they were produced in large numbers of identical copies. Moneyers' names are thus a major source of evidence for philologists, not infrequently supplying name-forms otherwise unrecorded (e.g., Sexbyrht of Lewes). Also, they often provide a greater variety of spelling than manuscripts since die-sinkers seem to have been inclined to indulge in a certain amount of phonetic license: a remarkable example of this is provided by the range of forms at Hastings and Lewes in the early eleventh century which all seem to denote a single moneyer—Lefa, Leffa, Leofa, Leoffa, Leva, Levifa, Liefa, Lyefea, Lyva. This is one of the few cases at the period of hypochoristic shortened names, which only occur in the south; another is Cynna of Chichester.[37] It also illustrates the degree of vowel interchange in the late tenth and early eleventh centuries, a period of marked phonological development as can often be observed on the coinage (e.g., the change from Aethelm to Aegelm at Chichester).

The moneyers of the Sussex mints in the Anglo-Saxon period mostly had pure West Saxon names. The foreign element in southern England is chiefly Germanic, for example Godefryd, Godeman and Theodgar at Lewes; but the Norse name Onlaf also occurs at this mint (a rare occurrence in the south), and later there is a Northman. The Norman Conquest does not seem greatly to have disturbed the tenure of office of late Saxon moneyers, and two-thirds of those who struck for Harold II continued to work for William. Until after 1100 the list of names is indistinguishable in content from the pre-Conquest period, mostly Old English, with occasional Germanic or Scandinavian items. Under Henry I foreign names began to appear, such as Boneface at Hastings, but it is not until the Stephen period that we find Norman names as plentiful as English, with Willems at Lewes and Bramber, Hervei and Hunfrei at Lewes, Rawulf at Rye, Rodbert at Hastings, and so on throughout the country. Not all of them, of course, need represent Frenchmen, since English families were probably beginning to follow new fashions in name-giving.

Little is known in detail about the status and function of moneyers although the indications are that they belonged to the official, or mercantile, class. Only occasionally can they be identified, before the period of Pipe Rolls, with historical persons known from other sources. There is a good case for seeing a number of personal identities between the late Saxon moneyers of Lincoln and the lawmen of the city in 1066 as recorded in Domesday,[38] and the Winchester Survey contains many references to persons who can be equated with pre-Conquest moneyers.[39] A rare name can sometimes alert one to the possibility of a documentary reference to a man who acted as a moneyer, such as the Celtic Maeglsothen, who was granted land in Staffordshire in 956 and seems likely to have been the moneyer named on Chester coins of Edgar and Edward the Martyr as Maelsuthan.[40] For all the Wulfrics and Leofwines such associations cannot, of course, be made because the names are too common, but some of them no doubt have left other historical traces.

It has long been realised that Anglo-Saxon moneyers must sometimes have held office at more than one mint. Recent work on the Devon mints has suggested that the practice may have been more widespread and frequent than has hitherto been supposed.[41] Identity of name does not, of course, establish identity of person, and in the case of common names their occurrence at neighbouring mints may be accidental. But the cumulative evidence of the West Country mints is overwhelming, and the repeated occurrence of identical names at groups of two or more mints in the region cannot be explained either by localisation of the names themselves or, in many cases, by their general commonness. In various cases, from different parts of the country, supposed identities have been corroborated by obverse die-links between the mints involved, as in the case of *Sithesteburh* and Chichester. Often the run of types involved for a moneyer at different mints suggests the transfer of activity, sometimes repeated, from one mint to another, like that of Lyva from Hastings to Lewes, or of Eadnoth from Chichester to Winchester and back again. In a very few cases, including a Winchester name at Lewes in type 6 and a London one at *Sithesteburh* in type 7, there are even grounds for supposing that a moneyer may occasionally have struck coins at a mint other than that named on his die.

As yet little systematic work has been done in assessing how the interchange of moneyers between mints varies from one area or period to another, and so the Sussex evidence is of some importance. It suggests that considerable changes took place in the inter-relationship of mints. Under Ethelred and Cnut, for example, a number of moneyers appear to have divided their activities between Winchester and Chichester, and others between Lewes and Hastings or Winchester.[42] In Edward the Confessor's reign two moneyers seem to have had responsibilities shared between Lewes and Chichester, another at the same mints plus Hastings, and a fourth at Hastings, Chichester and Steyning. In the Norman period, when generally fewer moneyers were operative, there is only one possible interchange between mints within the county before the time of Stephen. But there is also a case of one name running in parallel in consecutive types at both Pevensey and the nearby Kentish mint of Sandwich in the late eleventh century, which is the more remarkable in that most of the few observed interchanges of moneyer under William I and II involve permanent removals from one place to another (e.g., Seword who transferred from Exeter to Barnstaple, or Cild whose mint went with him from Bedwyn to Marlborough).

In the sections below, individual cases of possible moneyer identities are discussed. Some of them are very doubtful. For example, the name Wulfnoth occurs at Winchester under Ethelred and Cnut, at Chichester in Cnut's first type, and at Hastings in his last. All these, or any two of them, could represent an identity, but without other evidence none can be regarded as more than a possibility. It is also impossible to establish with reasonable confidence whether one name at a mint represents a single moneyer if the span of time is very long or if there is an interruption. Thus a Dunninc is recorded at Hastings intermittently from the sixth type of Edward the Confessor to type XI of Henry I, a span of 60 years or more. There are various breaks, notably between William II type II and Henry I type VII. But even if we assume Henry's Dunninc to be another man (a relative perhaps, for the name is rare), the remaining period still exceeds 30 years; another change may have taken place during that time, but the missing types are all rare and the possibility is that we have an unusually long-serving moneyer. A similar problem is posed by the name Godwine at Chichester in the second half of the eleventh century. In the earlier period, where the material is more complete, a gap of more than one type is often likely to indicate separate moneyers of the same name.

The number of moneyers recorded for a mint in any type is a useful but not uncomplicated indicator of its importance. It is not to be assumed that all the moneyers named were operating simultaneously, and sometimes, no doubt, if one man's tenure was very brief, an office may have changed hands more than once during the currency of a single type, especially those with long periods of issue under Ethelred and Cnut. Over a period of time such distortions even out and it is often possible to guess at the normal complement of moneyers at a mint. This in turn is a fairly reliable guide to its relative importance and scale of operations compared with other mints, often more reliable, in fact, than the numbers of their surviving coins, which can be heavily distorted by local hoards like Chancton and Sedlescombe. Numbers of moneyers are not, however, a very safe guide to the varying importance of the same mint, unless fundamental changes in mint organisation (about which we still know very little) are taken into account, such as the distinct trend to fewer but more prolific moneyers in the mid-eleventh century. Equally, it seems likely that some moneyers had a more limited function than others—for example, surviving coins suggest that Aegelm's output at Chichester under Cnut may have been consistently greater than that of Leofric. We do not know to what extent moneyers worked either simultaneously in separate *officinæ* or alternately in each other's. The degree of obverse die-linking between moneyers sometimes suggests more of the latter than we have supposed; and in that case, their shifts of duty may have been of unequal duration or frequency. Sometimes extra moneyers seem to have been needed under special circumstances for limited, perhaps single, occasions. Four of the Lewes moneyers of Edward the Confessor are recorded only in the one type of which, within his career, no coins are known of the prolific moneyer Oswold; was he perhaps then absent or indisposed? Clearly, moneyers who divided their time between different mints were likely to have contributed less at each of them than the permanent officers, but again, too little of the evidence has yet been analysed to permit conclusions to be drawn.

The early period

Section 14 of the Code of Laws issued by Athelstan[43] at Grateley, which provided that there was to be 'one coinage over all the king's dominion, and no-one is to mint money except in a *burh*', stipulated the number of moneyers who were to operate at each mint. At Canterbury there were to be seven, four for the king, two for the bishop, and one for the abbot. At Rochester three, two for the king and one for the bishop. At London there were to be eight, at Winchester six, at Lewes two, at Hastings one, another at Chichester, at Southampton two, at Wareham two, at Dorchester one, at Exeter two, at Shaftesbury two, and in the other *burhs* one each. It is notable that this list, though relating to southern England, should nominate as many as three mints in Sussex, although Hastings is one of the two named in it of which no surviving coins of the period have been identified.

Lewes, with two moneyers to one each at Chichester and Hastings, must have been rated a greater mint than the others, for a time at least, under Athelstan, and Lewes-signed coins of this reign are known with two names, Wilebald and Eadric. Wilebald's two mint-signed coins are of the type with on each side a small cross in the centre of a plain field and the legend in circumscription;[44] this type is dated by Blunt to *c.* 928–33 at southern mints. The only other known coins of the period with this name are of the type without mint signature but with the moneyer's name in two horizontal lines on the reverse (dated *c.* 925–8);[45] since one of the two recorded specimens is certainly of southern style, these coins

TABLE D

Sussex Moneyers of the Early Period

	Edward the Elder	Athelstan			Edmund	Edred	Edwy	Edgar		
	Two-line	I Two-line	V Cross	VIII Crowned Bust	Two-line	Two-line	Two-line	I Two-line	III Cross	VI Reform
Chichester										
Iohan	(X)	(X)	X							
Cynsige									X	X
Flodwin									X	X
Sideman					(?)		(?)	(?)		X
Lewes										
Wilebald	(X)	(X)	X							
Eadric				X	(X)	(X)				
Sexbyrht										X
Theodgar										X
Goldstan										X

Key:

X   Mint-signed coins.

(X)   Coins probably of same moneyer but without mint name.

(?)   Same or similar name occurs, but identity very doubtful.

may also be attributed, provisionally, to Lewes. There is no evidence that Eadric
worked concurrently with Wilebald, since his unique coin of Athelstan is of the
crowned bust type,[46] which Blunt dates to *c.* 933–8 in the south, and the only
other two coins with the same name are of later issue. One of these is of Edmund,
the other of Eadred, and being both of southern style they could well represent
later stages in the career of Athelstan's second Lewes moneyer.[47] No coins
of Edward the Elder are recorded with either of these names, and the mint
at Lewes may have owed its origin to Athelstan. Although three moneyers are
found striking at Lewes in the *Reform* type of Edgar, none of their names occurs
on earlier issues of that king or his predecessors, and so we have no means of
identifying what coins, if any, may have been struck there after Eadric's period
of office.

Chichester's three known mint-signed coins of Athelstan are all of the 'cross'
type and by the moneyer Iohan.[48] The same name occurs on relatively plentiful
coins of southern style of Athelstan's two-line type[49] and there is no reason why
they should not all be attributed to Chichester except that this implies the mint
may have been more prolific than would perhaps have been expected. There were
coins of Edward the Elder in the Vatican hoard with the name Iohan[50] and they
are stylistically close to Athelstan's, suggesting the possibility of an earlier date
for the opening of a mint in Chichester.

Iohan's name is not found in later reigns[51] and we must therefore look to
Edgar's *Reform* type for clues towards the possibility of attributing any
intervening issues to Chichester. Here there are three Chichester moneyers striking
—Cynsige, Flodwin, and Sideman. Of these, the first two names are also known
in Edgar's cross type, and neither is recorded for any other mint in the reign.
Flodwin's coins of this type[52] have a C at the end of the reverse inscription,
presumably the initial letter of the mint name, but the unique example of
Cynsige is unfortunately fragmentary and reads only —A (CISA perhaps).[53]
The name Sideman is known in Edgar's last type also at Rochester and (in
the form Sedeman) at York. It does not occur in the previous (cross) type,
but coins with the same, or a comparable, name exist in some numbers of the
two-line type from Edmund to Edgar, and there is a southern flavour about
some of these coins. It is not therefore impossible that amongst them could be
coins of Chichester's Sideman, but the gap in the middle of Edgar's reign
(especially when compared with the relative plentifulness of the name in Edgar's
two-line type) argues against this.[54]

As can be seen from Table D, we are left with a very sketchy picture of Sussex
minting before the 970s. Although there is every reason to think that mints in
Chichester and Lewes were active during much of the period from Athelstan to
Edgar, and in Chichester perhaps from Edward the Elder, for these mints—as
for most others in the mid-tenth century—positive evidence is largely lacking.
Whether Hastings ever produced coins for Athelstan or his successors we cannot
tell; its apparent absence from the scene after Edgar's reform until the Danegeld
period, and its very minor role at the outset even then, does not help to make a
case for its having been a minting-place in previous years.

Ethelred II

No coins of Edward the Martyr or of Ethelred II's very rare *First Small Cross* type, which was merely a short-lived continuation of his two predecessors' coinage, are known of Chichester; since none of the three moneyers who struck Edgar's *Reform* type there reappears in Ethelred's reign, it seems possible that no minting took place at Chichester in the later 970s. At Lewes the picture is different: all three of the *Reform* moneyers are recorded for Edward's reign (see No. 6 of Plate) or Ethelred's *Hand* type or both. Curiously, none of them is yet known in the *First Small Cross* type, in which a new name, Herebyrht, occurs.

The six main types of Ethelred's coinage (with their Hildebrand labels) are:

1.	*First Small Cross*	(A)	4.	*Long Cross*	(D)
2.	*Hand*	(B)	5.	*Helmet*	(E)
3.	*Crux*	(C)	6.	*Last Small Cross*	(A)

Of these, only *Hand* shows significant variety. *First Hand* (Hild. B1) has a diademed head and no sceptre, *Second Hand* (B2) has a cross pommée sceptre and a slightly more elaborate reverse, while *Benediction Hand* (B3) has a cross pattée sceptre, no diadem and the *Manus Dei* with two fingers clasped, but without other ornament on the reverse. These three variants constitute the only case in the late Anglo-Saxon coinage of significant variation of a basic type, and it has been proposed that *First* and *Second Hand* may each have been main issues. There are different views about this—*Second Hand* is lacking from some important northern mints, and the variation of design could be no more than an experimental feature of the new system in what was only the second type since Edgar's reform. One of the very few known mules between the two main varieties of *Hand* (B2/ B1) was struck by Theodgar of Lewes. *Benediction Hand,* which shows an increase in weight, is very rare and it is notable that it is the earliest known type of three out of the four Sussex moneyers who struck it.

All Sussex coins of Ethelred before type 3 (*Crux*) are very rare. The increase in moneyers and mint output marks the start of the Danegeld period, with heavy coinage at Lewes and Chichester in the 990s and towards the end of Ethelred's troubled reign, when the mint of *Sithesteburh* was added. Type 5 (*Helmet*) is the least plentiful of Ethelred's later issues; a decline in output, or a shorter period of issue, is suggested by the absence of recorded examples by some moneyers (Leofnoth and Godefrith of Lewes and.Aelfwine of Chichester) who were active in earlier and later issues, although others (such as Leofwine, author of the gold penny of this type) may have been abnormally productive.

Several cases have been noted by King of Sussex coins of the *Helmet* and *Last Small Cross* types with additional marks on the reverse. In one case there is an A in the field, but usually the marks are pellets, in twos or threes.[55] Die-duplicate specimens struck before and after the addition of pellets are known from one Lewes die of the *Helmet* type and one Hastings and three Lewes dies of *Last Small Cross*. It has been suggested that such marks may have been designed to indicate a change of weight standard.[56]

Table E shows the number of moneyers' names found in each type from Edgar's reform to the end of Ethelred's reign.[57] Lewes was undoubtedly the major Sussex mint of this period, with steady support from Chichester once it resumed activities in the *Hand* type. Hastings coins of Ethelred are of considerable rarity and are not recorded earlier than *Second Hand. Sithesteburh,* the fourth mint, appears only in the last type of reign. The relative size of the contributions of each of the four mints can be seen from the number of coins recorded by Hildebrand and in the Copenhagen *Sylloge,* as set out in Table F.

It is not easy to estimate how many moneyers may have been operating at each of the Sussex mints at any one time. Lewes seems to have had three moneyers from late Edgar to early Ethelred, and seven (or more) at the end of the reign, with a gradual increase in the interim. Chichester's three under Edgar were hardly, if at all, increased under Ethelred, while Hastings probably had a single moneyer at times and only sometimes two. Neither of the two *Sithesteburh* names continues under Cnut, so they might have been operating either together or in succession.

In Table G are shown the names of moneyers which occur under Ethelred at more than one of the mints of Sussex plus Winchester. Most of the Lewes moneyers seem to have been confined to that mint. Three of them, however, have names also found at Hastings, and of these there can be little doubt that at least the name Lyva, found nowhere else, represents a single person. He seems to have moved from Hastings to Lewes during type 5. A different pattern is presented by the name Aelfwerd which appears first in type 6 at both mints, lasting until type 9 at Lewes and type 12 at Hastings; this is not such a rare name but the parallel occurrence is striking. Also to be noted is that the single type of the Lewes Wulfstan immediately follows the single type of Wulfstan at Hastings, while the same name occurs at Winchester under Edward the Martyr and in *First Hand.* This raises the question whether under Ethelred, as later, there may have been some movement of moneyers between Winchester and the more distant Sussex mints. Other possible cases are those of Godman, or Godeman, a name which switches from Winchester to Lewes in type 6, and (though less likely because there is a gap in the common *Long Cross* issue) of Eadsige, found at Winchester up to type 3 and at Hastings from type 5.

The most remarkable association between Winchester and Lewes at this period, however, is contained in a chain of die-links in type 6 involving 10 reverse dies in the names of five different moneyers.[58] Four of these are of Lewes— Aelfwerd (three dies), Godeferth (four dies), Leofnoth (one die), and Liofwine (one die)—but the fifth reads SIRIC ON PINCST. Only three coins in all are recorded of Siric, and each is from a separate observe die otherwise found only with a Lewes name. It is apparent from these associations that Siric's one known reverse was part of the stock of dies in use not at Winchester, but at Lewes. This appears to be one of the extremely rare cases where medieval coins can be shown with reasonable certainty not to have been struck at the mint named on them, although how Siric's coins came to be struck at Lewes rather than Winchester, and what his function was there, is, of course, a mystery.

TABLES E and F

Sussex Moneyers and Coins of Types 1-6

Table E: Numbers of moneyers by type and mint.

Types	1 Small Cross			Ethelred II 2 Hand			3	4	5	6	Total Ethelred II
	Edgar	Edward	Ethelred	First	Second	Benediction	Crux	Long Cross	Helmet	Last Small Cross	
Chichester	3			2	2	2	5	5	2	4	9
Hastings					1		2	1	2	2	6
Lewes	3	2	1	4	3	2	6	6	3	9	18
Sithesteburh										2	2

Table F: Number of coins listed by Hildebrand and in Copenhagen.

	Edgar	Edward	Ethelred	First	Second	Benediction	Crux	Long Cross	Helmet	Last Small Cross	Total
Chichester	1			2	2	1	10	10	6	5	37
Hastings					1		2	4	7	4	18
Lewes	1	1	1	9	2	0	16	21	8	40	99
Sithesteburh										2	2

TABLE G

Names of Ethelred Moneyers occurring at more than one of the Mints in Sussex, plus Winchester

Types	2 Hand			3	4	5	6	Later
	First	Second	Benediction	Crux	Long Cross	Helmet	Last Small Cross	
Aelfwerd							HL	HL
Aelfwine			C	C	C		C	LW
Aethestan	W	W		WC	C			
Cynna				C	W	W		W
Eadnoth		C	C	WC	C			
God(e)man				W	W	W	WL	L
Heawulf	C			CW	W	C		
Lyva					H	HL	L	L
Wulfstan	W	H		L				
Wunstan		C		W				

More extraordinary still is the case of the name Leofwine in type 6. This prolific London moneyer is involved in three obverse die-links with other mints, one of them *Sithesteburh,* where the same name appears as a moneyer in type 7. The other two mints are the unlocated *Gothaburh* (probably in South West England, in view of common moneyers' names and another die-link with Exeter) and Stamford.[59] In these cases Leofwine's reverse dies appear to have stylistic affinities more with the other mints than with London; it therefore seems unlikely that the coins were struck at London, in spite of their mint-signatures. If that is so, Leofwine must have been no ordinary moneyer but one who undertook special assignments sometimes far afield, including perhaps assistance at the opening of the new mint at *Sithesteburh.*

No less than six of Chichester's nine Ethelred moneyers have names found also at Winchester, and in most of these cases identity is very possible. Cynna is a name common to these two mints alone, Chichester in type 3, Winchester thereafter. Wunstan (or Wynstan) appears to have made an earlier move in the same direction, but Aethelstan in the opposite. Two other moneyers may have gone to Winchester and then returned. Eadnoth is recorded at Chichester both before and after the *Crux* issue (type 3), but only in that type itself from a single pair of dies of the late *Transitional Crux* variety with a curly-headed portrait. It can hardly be a coincidence, then, that the only Winchester coins with this name are of the *Crux* type proper. Similarly, Heawulf's career at Chichester is broken in *Long Cross* (type 4), but this rare name is found at Winchester·just at that point (types 3–4). The occurrence of an Aelfwine at Chichester in Ethelred's later types and at Lewes and Winchester in the next type (7) under Cnut is to be noted, but it is a common name.

Imitations of Anglo-Saxon coins struck in Scandinavia and Ireland in the Danegeld period, beginning with the *Crux* type, often cause problems. A 'Sussex' example is a *Long Cross* coin with a reverse purporting to be by Aethelm of Chichester, but which (unlike some others) is not deceptive it has Ethelred's name replaced on the obverse by that of the Dublin king Sihtric.[60]

The Danish Kings

No coins are known, and probably none were struck, for Edmund Ironside (1016) whose death after a brief reign removed the last obstacle to the conquest of England by Cnut of Denmark. Under Cnut the coinage system of Ethelred with its lengthy issues seems to have been continued, but between his death in 1035 and the accession of Edward the Confessor in 1042 three separate types were issued. The first of these (type 10), with a *Jewel Cross* on the reverse, was issued in the names of both Harold I and his half-brother, Harthacnut, but their nominal joint rule ended in 1037; then, or soon after, a new type (11), with fleurs-de-lys, sometimes degenerated to trefoils, in the angles of a long cross on the reverse, was introduced in Harold's name alone and this was still in issue at the time of his death in 1040. The sole reign of Harthacnut (1040-2) marked by a type (12) depicting the king in profile and showing, unusually, his arm across the bust, holding his sceptre.

Coins of types 7–9, the three issues of Cnut, *Quatrefoil* (Hildebrand E), *Helmet* (G), and *Short Cross* (H), are all quite plentiful of the three main Sussex mints. The output of the fourth mint, at *Sithesteburh* in types 6–7 and at Steyning thenceforth, was very limited. All the coins of type 10 (see No. 9 of Plate) are rare, particularly those in the name of Harthacnut which are mostly—and exclusively at the Sussex mints except for Lewes—of a distinctive design with the bust to right instead of left.[61] Type 11 (*Fleur-de-lys*) is the least rare of the Harold-Harthacnut period, but type 12 (*Arm-and-Sceptre*) is one of the rarest of all eleventh-century types, only Lewes of the Sussex mints having contributed significantly to its issue, while no coin of Steyning and only one of Chichester is recorded. It is a curious feature of type 12 that the king's name on the majority of the coins appears not as *Harthacnut* but as *Cnut*[62]—in fact King listed only one Sussex coin, by Edwerd of Lewes, with the full name.

A considerable change took place at this period in the relative importance of the three principal mints, to judge by surviving specimens (see Table J). After a minor role up to type 7, Hastings seems suddenly to have become the most prolific mint in the county for three issues and to have more than held its own for second place with Chichester thereafter. From the numbers of moneyers recorded in each type (Table H) there does not appear to have been a fixed complement at each mint. Their number declined, along with the volume of coinage, during Cnut's reign, and further in the 1040s, although the rarity of the later coins may mean that other names only await discovery.

There are some names that have found their way into the list of Sussex moneyers at this period for which the evidence is doubtful or mistaken. A Liofsi of Lewes has long been accepted on the evidence of a *Quatrefoil* coin of Cnut listed by Hildebrand, apparently confirmed by two die-duplicates of the next type recorded by King.[63] The former, however, is a blundered coin of Bedford misread,[64] while the *Helmet* coins have the curious mint-reading LAEPVDE. Stylistically these belong to a group mainly associated with Lincoln, and although it is unrealistic to attribute them to Lewes, the identity of the mint of *Laewude* remains a mystery.[65] Onlaf of Lewes, undoubted under Ethelred, was recorded for Cnut by King on the basis of a *Quatrefoil* coin from the Lübeck hoard, with a retrograde inscription on the reverse; this and another coin of the same type with the name Onlaf (not retrograde), may, as described in the Copenhagen *Sylloge*, be imitations.[66] The Leofwine coin attributed to Hastings[67] is more probably of Southampton, while the two of Brihtnoth should be transferred respectively to Winchester and Malmesbury.[68]

Although some of the possible cases of mint interchanges by moneyers in this period are doubtful or complicated, there are at least a few which are strong probabilities and these provide clearer evidence of movements between Winchester and the more distant Sussex mints (Table K). Most striking is the case of Alfred, a name found at Hastings in type 9 and at both Winchester and Hastings in the *Jewel Cross* issue (type 10) with right-facing bust in Harthacnut's

TABLES H and J

Sussex Moneyers and Coins of the Danish Kings

Table H: Numbers of moneyers by type and mint.

Types	Cnut			Harold & Har-thacnut	Harold I	Hartha-cnut	Total
	7	8	9	10	11	12	
	Quatrefoil	Pointed Helmet	Short Cross	Jewel Cross	Fleur-de-lys	Arm-and-Sceptre	
Chichester	6	3	4	3	4	1	9
Hastings	3	3	5	5	3	2	12
Lewes	11	5	3	4	4	3	16
Sithesteburh	1						1
Steyning		1	2	1	1	0	2

Table J: Numbers of coins listed by Hildebrand and in Copenhagen.

Chichester	19	11	12	3	6	1	52
Hastings	8	31	25	8	6	3	81
Lewes	26	20	17	7	6	11	87
Sithesteburh	1						1
Steyning		4	7	0	3	0	14

TABLE K

Names of Moneyers occurring at more than one of the Mints of Sussex, plus Winchester, under the Danish Kings

	Ethel-red II	7	8	9	10		11	12	Edward
					Hartha-cnut	Harold I			
Aelfric				C		CW	C		
Aelfweard	HL	HL	HL	HL		HW	H	H	
Aelfwine	C	WL							
Alfred				H	HW				
Brihtnoth	W	WC							
Eadwine	W	W	L	L		LH	LW	L	L
Edwerd		LW	W		L	L	L	L	L
Goda			W	W			C		
Godric				W			C		
Leofwine	LW	LWCS	WC	C	C		W	H	H
Lifinc							HW	W	W
Widia*			S	S*	*	W*	W	W*	W*
Wulfnoth	W	WC	W	WH					

*Winchester coins known with names Godwine Widia.
Note: S denotes *Sithesteburh* in type 7, Steyning in types 8–9.

name; this is an extremely rare variety[69] and the occurrence in it at the two mints of a name otherwise unrecorded in this area and period can scarcely be a coincidence.

Equally decisive is the case of Widia (or Wydia, Wudia, etc.), the first Steyning moneyer, whose name occurs elsewhere only at Winchester. After two types (8 and 9) at Steyning under Cnut, the name is found at Winchester from type 10 onwards into the reign of Edward. Further, from type 9, there is a parallel series with the two names Godwine Widia at Winchester. At this period the names Godwine Cas, Godwine Ceoca and plain Godwine are also found there. It has been suggested on the analogy of coins of Edgar with double names that the Godwine Widia coins represent joint issues of two moneyers.[70]

Of the Winchester–Chichester links, the simplest is probably that of Aelfric, a name briefly found at Winchester in the middle of his three known types of Chichester. It is also worth noting that there are two late Cnut moneyers of Winchester, Goda and Godric, whose names both appear a little later at Chichester in a single issue (type 11).

Curiously enough, although there are eight other cases of names shared between Winchester and Sussex mints, of which no less than five involve more than one of the latter, there are no observed cases of two Sussex mints at this period sharing a name which does not, at least at some stage within its span, occur at Winchester too. Thus Aelfweard, after a long parallel run at Lewes and Hastings, is found at Winchester in one type only, immediately after he ceases at Lewes. Aelfwine, prominent at Chichester under Ethelred, occurs not only at Lewes in the first issue of Cnut (type 7) but also at Winchester, of which there is but a single coin recorded with his name, reflecting what was presumably a very short-lived period of office there. Brihtnoth and Wulfnoth, both Ethelred moneyers of Winchester continuing under Cnut, each occur briefly at Chichester in type 7 (Brihtnoth's last type), and Wulfnoth at Hastings also in type 9 (his last issue at Winchester).

More difficulty surrounds the two names Eadwine and Leofwine. Eadwine, a long-running name at Lewes (types 8–19), is found in type 10 at Hastings and type 11 at Winchester, but there was also an earlier run of the name at Winchester ending in type 7, just before it begins at Lewes. Which, if any, of the other occurrences of this name may relate to the Lewes moneyer we cannot tell, but it is a modest problem in comparison with the complex picture presented by the name Leofwine. This runs from type 2 to type 7 at Lewes, from type 5 to type 8 at Winchester, and from type 7 to type 10 at Chichester, with an appearance at *Sithesteburh* in type 7 only; thereafter, the name is again found at Winchester (type 11) before a run at Hastings beginning in type 12. There is an obverse die-link between Chichester and *Sithesteburh* (where Leofwine was the only moneyer in type 7, and which Leofwine of London seems to have visited in type 6), which suggests that at these two mints the same Leofwine was involved but whether any of the other instances of this common name are related is impossible to say.

Finally there are two Winchester names which occur also at a single Sussex mint: Edwerd at Lewes, and Lifinc at Hastings. On the basis of known coins of

Lewes alone, Edwerd's lengthy career would have seemed to have been interrupted after a single issue (type 7); but the occurrence of the same name in
types 7 and 8 at Winchester may in part explain the gap. Lifinc, on the other
hand was basically a Winchester name, beginning in type 11, but in that issue
alone it is also found at Hastings.

Edward the Confessor

Ten main types were struck in the 24 years of Edward's reign and another
in Harold II's. They are:

13.	*Pacx*	(D)	18.	*Helmet*	(F)
14.	*Radiate*	(A)	19.	*Sovereign*	(H)
15.	*Trefoil–Quadrilateral*	(C)	20.	*Hammer Cross*	(G)
16.	*Small Flan*	(B)	21.	*Facing Bust*	(Ac)
17.	*Expanding Cross*	(E)	22.	*Pyramids*	(I)

and 23, Harold's *Pax*. The first five of Edward's types show a clean-shaven bust,
diademed in the Roman fashion, as had been the pattern since the last issue of
Cnut; but on the last five types this is replaced by a more naturalistic, bearded
portrait.

A view of the relative importance of the Sussex mints is more difficult to
obtain for the mid-eleventh century than previously since the Scandinavian
material fades and only the Walbrook hoard lacks the heavy local bias of
Sedlescombe (Hastings) and Chancton (Steyning). The distorting effect of
these hoards can be illustrated by the contrast between the rarity of Hastings
coins of type 22 (only modestly represented at Chancton of this mint and absent
from Sedlescombe) and the commonness of types 18 to 21. Nevertheless, the
Walbrook figures only cover the later types and show how erratic a small sample
may be (see Table M), while for the earlier types the total number of coins
recorded by King (Table L) is probably a better guide than the scanty Scandinavian figures, at least up to type 17, when Hastings first benefits from the
contents of Sedlescombe. The best guide, therefore, is probably the number of
moneyers operating (Table N).

Lewes remained much the largest of the Sussex mints at this period. Fifteen
moneyers are named in all, but the normal complement seems to have been no
more than three or four. Only five moneyers are known of more than two types,
while no less than seven occur in a single issue only (mostly in types 15 and 16,
when additional activity at the mint must for some reason have been needed).

Hastings continued the position which it had reached in the 1030s as second
of the county mints, and provides as clear an example as can be found to demonstrate a consistent complement of moneyers, each new name being matched
by the departure of an old one in the same or in the immediately preceding issue.
Thus Brid and Leofwine, both of whom had been in office before Edward's
reign, operated together until type 17, after which Leofwine is found no more,
but two new names, lifting the team to three, appear. Of these, Dunninc

TABLE L

Numbers of Sussex Coins of Early Types of Edward the Confessor recorded by King

Type	13 Pacx	14 Radiate	15 Trefoil	16 Small Flan	17 Expanding Cross
Chichester		1	4	2	7
Hastings	3	6	6	2	14
Lewes	3	5	10	13	13
Steyning..	2	3	1	1	8

TABLE M

Sussex Coins of Edward the Confessor in the Walbrook Hoard

Type	15 Trefoil	16 Small Flan	17 Expdg. Cross	18 Helmet	19 Sovereign	20 Hammer Cross	21 Facing Bust	22 Pyramids
Chichester	1		5		1	11		
Hastings		1	1	1	1	3	1	
Lewes			3		1	2	2	
Steyning..				2	2	3		1

TABLE N

Numbers of Sussex Moneyers recorded in each Type of Edward the Confessor and Harold II

Type	13 Pacx	14 Radiate	15 Trefoil	16 Small Flan	17 Expdg. Cross	18 Helmet	19 Sovereign	20 Hammer Cross	21 Facing Bust	22 Pyramids	23 Harold-Pax	Total
Chichester		1	3	1	1	3	3	3	2	2	2	5
Hastings	2	2	2	1	2	3	3	4	3	2	3	6
Lewes	2	2	6	7	5	4	4	4	3	3	3	15
Steyning..	2	1	1	1	2	1	1	1	1	1	1	4

continues beyond the Conquest, but Wulfric is known only for three issues, types 18[71] to 20. Brid's career also closed with type 20, but two new names follow them, Theodred being first found in type 20, and Colswegen in type 21. Even in this tidy pattern there are two lacunae neither of which is necessarily to be explained by the accident of non-survival: Leofwine is not known in type 16, while Dunninc is missing in type 22. Leofwine's possible absence for one type might be explained by the occurrence of the same name in that type and the next at Lewes. Dunninc's could represent a temporary reversion to a complement of two, in which case he would need to have been quickly reinstated (or followed by a namesake) since all three names are found under Harold, when a coinage in the new king's name was wanted quickly for political reasons, and all three continued under William I. Although the Conquest did not generally cause the replacement of moneyers, it is apparently without parallel at any other English mint for a whole team to have survived throughout 1066.

Although Chichester had quite an active mint in Edward's middle and later years, it appears to have been largely inoperative in the late 1030s and early 1040s. No coins are known from it of types 11 or 13, and only one specimen each of type 12 and of type 14 is recorded. Thereafter two or sometimes three moneyers are found in most types, but every name can be matched elsewhere in Sussex or at Winchester.

For much of this period Steyning had a one-moneyer establishment, although a second name, Wulfget, appears in one type (17) during Wulfric's career, just as in the Norman period Lifsi does during Thurbern's. Frithewine continues from Harold's reign for three types under Edward (the absence of the rare type 12 may be accidental), after which he was replaced by Wulfric, a name found also on a coin of type 13 (*Pacx*). The thought that *Pacx* should be the last type of Frithewine and the first of Wulfric, if Steyning had been strictly a one-moneyer mint, led King to argue for a different sequence for Edward's early types, but the cumulative evidence of moneyer continuity at other mints precludes this.[72] It seems that occasionally, under special circumstances, the sole moneyer may either have been provided with a colleague or have needed a temporary replacement.

The only names which occur both at Chichester and Winchester are Aelfwine and Godric; the former, particularly, is too common at this period to carry any positive likelihood of personal identity.[73] Several moneyers, however, appear to have been involved with more than one Sussex mint (Table O). First, Leofwine: the name runs from type 12 to type 15 at Hastings, is found at Chichester only in type 15,[74] at Lewes in types 16 and 17, and then reverts in type 17 to Hastings, a curiously coincidental sequence if they were four separate moneyers. Then Leofnoth: both Chichester and Lewes have a moneyer of this name, and both in a single issue, type 15. Next, Wulfric: the name occurs at three Sussex mints, Steyning in types 13 and 16–19, Hastings in types 18–20, and Chichester in types 18–22. Finally, Godwine: types 17–23 are represented at Lewes, and types 18–20 and 23 (No. 12 of Plate) at Chichester. Although these names, too, are quite common, the patterns of types and the concentration in the area are

TABLE O

Names of Moneyers occurring at more than one of the Mints in Sussex, plus Winchester under Edward the Confessor

Types			13	14	15	16	17	18	19	20	21	22	23
			Earlier	Pacx	Radiate	Trefoil	Small Flan	Expdg. Cross	Helmet	Sovereign	Hammer Cross	Facing Bust	Pyramids	Harold-Pax
Aelfwine	..	..		W	(C?)	C	C	CW	CW	CW	CW	CW	CW	CW
Godric	..	..			W	WC	W							
Godwine	..	..						L	LC	LC	LC	L	L	LC
Leofnoth	..	..				LC								
Leofwine	..	..	H	H	H	HC	L	LH						
Wulfric	..	..		S			S	S	SHC	SHC	HC	C	C	

highly suggestive,[75] and most if not all of these instances seem to me to be likely to involve the movement of moneyers. Parallel occurrence of names at two or more neighbouring mints over a period of time has been noticed elsewhere in this reign[76] and perhaps reflects an administrative change in the function of moneyers or the organisation of minting.

William I and II

Thirteen separate types occur.with the name William. Of these Brooke in the *British Museum Catalogue* assigned the first eight to the Conqueror and the last five to Rufus, but this division between the reigns is not beyond question.[77] Since the early Norman coinage is a direct continuation of the late Saxon, the numeration of types can conveniently be extended from the pre-Conquest series down to 1100 (after which there is doubt about the sequence of types). The 13 issues, with their *BMC* numbers and Brooke's descriptive labels are:

Type No.	Label	BMC	
24	*Profile* [left] *–Cross fleury*	William I, type I	
25	*Bonnet*		II
26	*Canopy*		III
27	*Two Sceptres*		IV
28	*Two Stars*		V
29	*Sword*		VI
30	*Profile* [right] *–Cross and Trefoils*		VII
31	*Paxs*		VIII
32	*Profile [and Sword]*	William II, type I	
33	*Cross in Quatrefoil*		II
34	*Cross voided*		III
35	*Cross pattee and fleury*		IV
36	*Cross fleury and piles*		V

TABLE P

Numbers of Sussex Moneyers Recorded in each Type of William I and II

BMC notation Types	William I								William II					Total
	I	II	III	IV	V	VI	VII	VIII	I	II	III	IV	V	
	24	25	26	27	28	29	30	31	32	33	34	35	36	
Chichester	1		1	1	2	2	1	2	2	3	2	2	1	3
Hastings	3	1			1			2	1	3	3	3	2	7
Lewes		1	1	3	2	1	1	3	2	3	3	1	2	6
Pevensey					1			1	1	1	1			1
Steyning		1			1	1		1		1	2		1	3

TABLE Q

Numbers of Sussex Coins of each Type of William I and II recorded by King (and of Type 31 in the Beauworth Hoard)

Types	24	25	26	27	28	29	30	31		32	33	34	35	36
								King	Beauworth					
Chichester			1	1	7	4	2	46	(242)	4	6	2	2	1
Hastings	8	1		1	2			19	(72)	2	8	5	4	2
Lewes		1	1	4	3	1	1	26	(77)	3	6	5	1	4
Pevensey					1			3	(7)	1	1	1	1	
Steyning		1				1		16	(46)		2	3		1

All four pre-Conquest mints in Sussex struck coins for the two Williams, though Steyning apparently lost its mint about 1100 since no coins of it are known after the last issue of Rufus. However, the Conqueror added a new mint at Pevensey, the earliest known coin of which is of his fifth issue (type 28).

Sussex coins of type 31 (*Paxs*), particularly those of Chichester, have survived in abnormally large numbers as a result of their local advantage in the hoard from Beauworth in Hampshire. In the absence of other large hoards buried in the later eleventh century, all other issues of William I, except types 25 and 28, and all of William II are distinctly rare. Consequently our knowledge of the types struck by each moneyer is probably much more deficient than for the later Saxon period, and there are gaps in the tables for many moneyers who may have had continuous careers: Oswold of Lewes, Dermon of Steyning, Dunninc of Hastings, and Aelfheh of Pevensey are cases in point. Table P gives the numbers of moneyers recorded in each type,[78] and in Table Q are shown the numbers of coins recorded by King (with the Beauworth *Paxs* totals for comparison). The only moneyer additional to those listed by King is Edwine of Lewes, represented by a single coin of type 34 recently discovered in a parcel from the 1871 Shillington find, which reads (L?)IE and seems likely to be of this mint; if so, it is notable that Chichester's Edwine is known up to type 33, and an identity between the two would be possible.

None of the mints is yet recorded in all eight types attributed by Brooke to William I, but we cannot tell whether this too is due entirely to the accident of discovery or in part to interruption of mint activity. For example, while the lack of Steyning coins of types 24, 26 and 27 may be due to the non-survival of small issues, the absence of Lewes in the first post-Conquest issue (type 24) could indicate temporary closure. In type 24 all three late Saxon moneyers of Hastings (see No. 13 of Plate) are found, and a new moneyer at Chichester, while of the next three types King records a total of no more than four coins from Hastings, Chichester and Steyning together; Lewes, on the other hand, has left surviving coins of each of these three types, so the omission of type 24 is the more remarkable. Otherwise Lewes seems to have retained its position as the largest of the Sussex mints. Hastings is unknown of the four rarest types of William I, but Chichester, relatively, enhanced its position in this reign. Under William II these three are amongst the least rare of the smaller English mints. Coins of Steyning are (except for type 31) very rare, and of Pevensey extremely rare in these two reigns.

It is difficult on the evidence of the surviving material to establish with any confidence what the complement of moneyers may have been at each mint. Thus Lewes could be thought to have had a quota of three moneyers from type 27, with Brihtmaer replacing Oswold, and Edwine and then Aelfwine following Aelfric. There are three moneyers in Henry I's first issue to confirm the pattern, but there are many gaps, and, if Aelfric in type 27 was an abnormal addition, a complement of two moneyers could be postulated for much of the period with Aelfric replacing Oswold in type 31 (of which the latter's coins are the least plentiful of the three moneyers), to be succeeded in type 33 or 34 by

Brihtmaer. Immediately after the Conquest Hastings retained its three Saxon moneyers and three seems also to have been its complement in the 1090s; but Dunninc could have been the sole moneyer in the 1070s, joined later by Cipinc, then Godric, and finally succeeded by Diorman (a relative of the earlier Steyning moneyer, perhaps) or Sperlinc.

At Chichester Bruman may have been sole moneyer in the early post-Conquest issues, with Godwine, Edwine and Godwine again as a colleague thereafter. Except for an apparent duplication in type 34, Steyning continued to be, as it had been before the Conquest, a one-moneyer mint under normal circumstances. So clearly was Pevensey, which for a time at least shared its moneyer Aelfheh with Sandwich (where he is known in types 31 and 32); this name occurs only at these two places in the Norman period and so an identity is beyond reasonable doubt.

Henry I

Fifteen separate types were issued in the thirty-five year reign of Henry I, but behind a pattern superficially similar to that of the eleventh century fundamental changes were taking place. The quality of the coinage declined both aesthetically and intrinsically. Coins of the early types were relatively well produced, but the dies themselves were inferior, whilst in the middle period, although dies of some types were quite artistically designed and executed, the standard of striking was often very poor. The evenly-struck and well-rounded penny which had been a feature of Anglo-Saxon currency now disappeared, with momentary exceptions in the re-coinages of 1180 and 1205, for more than a century. Recent analysis has revealed that surviving examples of the coinage of Henry's middle years, though often deficient in weight, were not much debased;[79] but there was clearly concern at the time about forgery and mal-practice by the moneyers, which was voiced by the chroniclers, and is evidenced by the invariable (and so presumably official) nicking of the edge of the coins of the middle types, as a check against plating. Two major inquisitions were held into the state of the coinage and the conduct of the moneyers, one in 1108 and the other (at Winchester) before Christmas, 1124.

Henry's last three types show evidence of attempts to improve the weight and workmanship of the coinage, though the latter with only partial success. By the end of the reign both die-making and striking had again deteriorated, and with the improvisations and emergencies of the 1140s English coinage sank to what was probably the lowest technical level it ever reached.

Unfortunately only two substantial Henry I hoards have been recovered, both from near the end of the reign; and where his coins are found in hoards from the civil war period they are usually of the last type. Only coins of his last two issues (BMC types XIV and XV) are therefore at all plentiful. With two exceptions (BMC types VII and X), all the other types are very rare, some being known today from no more than a dozen or two specimens in all. The material is so limited—more so than from any other period of English coinage after the early ninth century—that of two issues (BMC types V and VIII) no coin from Sussex has been traced at all, while of some others (BMC types II, III, VI and IX) they are recorded of only one mint in the county.

With so few specimens to work on, and these often partly illegible through poor striking, our knowledge of the coinage of Henry I, during which the *renovatio* system itself appears to have come under increasing strain, is tantalisingly incomplete. Even the sequence of the middle issues is uncertain and that of Brooke's BMC type numbers may not be correct. Until new hoards provide us with adequate evidence of the relationship of the various types to each other in currency and of the careers of individual moneyers, the proper order cannot be established with any confidence. Professor Dolley has suggested that BMC types X and XI should be transposed and Miss Archibald that type IX may have followed immediately after types V and VI, and other rearrangements may need to be made.[80]

In the present state of knowledge any sensible attempt to date Henry's middle types is therefore precluded. Even if their sequence was established there are indications of more variable duration than was perhaps normal in earlier reigns. It may be that a premature type change or an extended replacement issue would have followed an inquisition, or that other changes in administration or control may have been prompted thereby. One fundamental change, which seems generally to have escaped published comment in this connection, was a drastic reduction in the number of mints at the end of the reign. The highly localised process of re-minting, which had been the basis of *renovatio* since Ethelred's day, must have been modified, since in some counties such as Sussex and Wiltshire, which did not boast a commercially substantial township, every single mint was closed. It could be that this was a delayed consequence of the Winchester inquisition and was accompanied by or arose out of a lengthening of the period of issue.

In Table R are given the numbers of specimens of each mint and type as recorded by King and as contained in the Lincoln and Bournemouth hoards. These figures not only give a fair idea of the patchiness and inadequacy of the surviving material, but also show how misleading it can be. For example, before the find at Lincoln, it might have been wondered whether a mint was operating at all in Lewes between BMC types II and XII; and yet Lincoln produced at least eight Lewes coins of type X against only five of Hastings, though three of the latter mint were already known. This is a clear warning against drawing any but the simplest and most limited conclusions from so small a sample of the total coinage.

All three late-eleventh-century moneyers of Lewes are known in the first issue of Henry I, and each of the three of Hastings is known in one of his first four issues. At Lewes only one of them, Winraed, is known to have continued beyond the first type, perhaps for some time, since it is just possible that a fragment of type X from Lincoln, reading only WIN(R?-), should be attributed to this moneyer and mint (though, if so, the time span means there must have been more than one Lewes moneyer of the name in the Norman period). Sperlinc

TABLE R

Numbers of Sussex Coins of Henry I recorded by King and in the Lincoln and Bournemouth Hoards

BMC types	I	II	III	IV	V	VI	VII	VIII	IX	X	XI	XII	XIII	XIV	Total
Chichester				1		1	1			1		2	2+1	6+3(10)	14+4
Hastings	1		1				3+1			3+5	1			2+9 (3)	11+15
Lewes	5			1			+1			+8		1	+1	5+2 (2)	12+12
Pevensey									1					1	2+0

Key: 1—one coin listed by King; +1—one coin in Lincoln hoard; (1)—one coin in Bournemouth hoard.

TABLE S

Numbers of Moneyers recorded at Sussex Mints in each Type of Henry I

	I	II	III	IV	V	VI	VII	VIII	IX	X	XI	XII	XIII	XIV	Total
Chichester ..						1	1			1	1	1	2	2	3
Hastings ..				1			2			5	1			3	8
Lewes ..			1				1			3		1	1	2	7
Pevensey ..									1					1	1

of Hastings is known intermittently from the reign of Rufus to type X of Henry I. Otherwise the Sussex moneyers of Henry's middle types were new, though Dunninc of Hastings carried a traditional name.

It could be argued that Lewes and Hastings each normally had a complement of three moneyers from before 1100 until the civil war, on the evidence of Henry I's early types and type XIV, and of Stephen type I. This would, however, require assumptions about more than one change of office at Hastings during type X and perhaps one in the same type at Lewes. Chichester seems to have had two moneyers working together late in the reign; it is the only Sussex mint recorded in all issues from BMC type X to type XIV, but evidence for its earlier activity is extremely tenuous.[81] Pevensey's output was probably very small, so it is a curious chance that has preserved a coin of this mint alone from Sussex in BMC type IX. In Table S are set out the numbers of moneyers known in each type of Henry I, but again it must be emphasised how defective the information may be even for those types of which a number of specimens have survived, and how unpredictable newly-discovered entries may be. Thus the 18 separate Sussex moneyer/type combinations in the Lincoln hoard duplicated eight items already known, gave six new types for known moneyers (one of them only from Stephen's reign) and added four names of moneyers previously unknown, but the distribution of these categories between mints is haphazard.[82]

Two Sussex moneyers are named in the sole surviving Pipe Roll of Henry I (1129/30).[83] Under Chichester, Brand accounted for £20, of which he paid £4 and owed the rest, *'ne esset disfactus cum aliis monetariis'*—a reference presumably to a fine in lieu of the mutilation which was administered extensively, according to the chroniclers, to moneyers found guilty of malpractice at the Winchester inquisition, and one which can be paralleled at other mints. Brand's coins are of the middle and late types of the reign, confirming that he performed his office both before and after that date. The other reference is to Boneface of Hastings, not described as the moneyer but almost certainly so in view of the rarity of this name for a layman. Someone (the text is defective) was paying fees for a writ of right to the land of Boneface his relative. The natural interpretation of this would be that he was then dead, and if this was so it is a fact of numismatic significance. Boneface is known of BMC types X and XIV; in the latter type he appears to have been the most prolific of the Sussex moneyers.[84] So, if he died in or before 1129/30, type XIV must have been in issue rather earlier than has usually been supposed, and it would be possible to regard only the last three types of the reign, which form a stylistically related group of better weight, as belonging to the period after the inquisition.[85]

The Stephen period

After Henry I's death, changes in the coinage system began to take place rapidly. Like Harold II, Stephen seems to have been anxious to fortify a precarious claim to the throne by an early mintage of coins in his own name, and for this many of the old local mints were revived—Chichester, Hastings, and Lewes among them. Eight or nine Sussex moneyers are named on Stephen's type I, but only two of them have the same names as are found in type XIV of Henry I, which suggests that the mints may have been closed for some time. Government administration was soon threatened by disturbances in the north and moves towards the civil war which during the 1140s deprived Stephen for many years of control of much of the country. The first of his four main coin-types (with a crowned bust in profile to the right, with a sceptre) accordingly remained unchanged for perhaps 10 years or more, sometimes imitated, adapted or varied by supporters and adversaries alike at mints beyond his direct influence. A good number of coin hoards must have been lost as a result of these hostilities of the early and middle 1140s and the recovery of several of these has provided us with considerable quantites of coins of the first half of the Stephen period.[86]

Only in East Anglia and the south-east did a regular royal coinage persist. Eventually and perhaps not before the later 1140s, two new types appeared in this part of the country, the order of which is confirmed by the existence of two very important mules from Sussex mints. The earlier type, with a nearly facing bust (BMC type II), is known mainly from a hoard found at Linton, near Maidstone, in which Sussex coins were, relatively speaking, well represented; the only known mule of certainly official workmanship between types I and II is a coin of Rye. There appears to be no recorded English hoard provenance for the (consequently very rare) later type (BMC VI) which has a bust in profile to the left; its position in the series is indicated by a unique type VI/VII mule, struck at Hastings. Although these two types were not—and could not have been—national issues, they may perhaps represent an attempt to revert to a *renovatio* system. With one or two possible exceptions in type II,[87] their mints are concentrated in south-eastern England and include places such as Castle Rising (near King's Lynn) and Rye, of which no coins are known of any other reign.

There are no baronial or irregular coins of the Sussex mints since they remained, with the possible exception of Chichester, within Stephen's control. The only direct evidence of the disturbances is that one coin is known of Chichester and another by Sawine of Hastings which have been struck from partially defaced obverse dies.[88] The usual explanation of such coins, which exist from a number of scattered mints, is that they represent a rejection of Stephen's royal authority, but many of them are from loyalist mints (like Hastings) and Miss Archibald has suggested that the more modest forms of defacement, often not more than a scratch or two (as on the two Sussex coins), could have arisen from recalling into use dies that had been cancelled as due for replacement by dies of a new type which the war prevented from being promulgated.

The final issue of Stephen's reign (BMC type VII), which closely resembles type II except for having small lis instead of mullets in the quarters of the reverse cross, was struck at mints throughout the country.[89] It must have followed the Treaty of Wallingford in 1153, whereby Stephen finally regained control of the Angevin west and the dissident north, and was probably designed to replace the mixture of royal, Angevin, baronial and counterfeit money which had come into circulation during the war years. As well as the revival of many mints which had been inoperative or in unofficial hands in the interim, new ones appeared in a number of unexpected places which made only this one brief contribution to English coinage, such as Chippenham (?), Hedon (near Hull), and Bramber. Many of the coins of BMC type VII may have been struck after Stephen's death, since Henry II did not introduce his own coinage until 1158; when he did, all vestiges of the late Anglo-Saxon monetary system disappeared, for the type remained unchanged until 1180 and his grandfather's policy of concentrating the coinage in the larger boroughs and of closing local mints was resumed and intensified.

When Stephen re-opened the Sussex mints, Lewes and Hastings were to continue throughout all four main types, but coins of Chichester, which was reduced to a single moneyer (though apparently a prolific one), are not known after type I. Its closure, which, like that of Winchester and all Stephen's mints to the west, may have taken place because of loss of royal control, was compensated in the east of the county by the revival of Pevensey mint and the opening of a new one at Rye (see No. 16 of Plate), both perhaps late in type I. The Rye moneyer was Rawulf, who moved to work at Canterbury under Henry II and who as Radulfus de Ria is stated in the Pipe Roll of 1176/7, when certain Canterbury moneyers were heavily amerced or fined, to have owed with his wife the enormous sum of 1,000 marks, of which 100 marks were paid and £600 left owing.[90]

No coin of the third issue (BMC type VI) is known with the mint name of either Rye or Pevensey, although it is possible, even likely, that they may have struck it, since each is known to have issued both of the less rare second and fourth types (BMC II and VII). The Pevensey moneyer at this time was Alwine, but a new name, Felipe, also occurs in type VII.[91] The evidence for Pevensey in Stephen type I consists of a single and only partially legible coin from the South Kyme hoard: it reads HERV—EV, and would naturally be attributed to Lewes, where the moneyer, Hervei, probably the same man, is well attested in the type, except for the fact that in the view of many who have examined it closely the letter before EV is certainly not an L, but might be a P.[92]

The last of the Sussex mints, Bramber, is known only in type VII, but with no less than three moneyers, Orgar, Rodbert, and Willem. This is an extraordinary number for such a short-lived mint in a place of no great importance and must be due to special circumstances unrelated to the normal need for a network of local mints in a re-coinage. The attribution itself is based on the identification of Orgar (see No. 17 of Plate) with a moneyer of this by no means common name who appears in the Pipe Roll of 1160/1 as having settled a debt to the crown by payment of £1 to the knights of Pevensey. Within the area, the mint-signature BRAN can hardly be associated with anywhere other than the ancient borough of Bramber, with its Norman castle.[93]

TABLE T

Numbers of Moneyers at Sussex Mints in Main Types of Stephen

	I	II	VI	VII	Total
Bramber				3	3
Chichester	1				1
Hastings	3	2	1	1	4
Lewes	3	2	1	1	5
Pevensey	1(?)	1		2	3
Rye	1	1		1	1

The name Rodbert also occurs at Hastings and elsewhere. Certainly there is general evidence again in the Stephen period of moneyers transferring from one mint to another or of holding office at more than once place. It is particularly noticeable in East Anglia, beginning with Ode of Thetford who started his career with a brief appearance at Bury St. Edmunds in type XIV of Henry I. The occurrences in the south-east of Rodbert therefore need to be considered from this point of view; even though it is not a rare moneyer's name, it is noteworthy both that it occurs at only one mint elsewhere in the country in Stephen's type I (Shrewsbury), and that it is the only name at either London or Canterbury of which coins are recorded of all four main types of the reign. The mints and types of which it is found are set out in Table U. One remarkable fact about the name is that in type VI it accounts for nearly half of the two dozen or so recorded specimens, including all those (at least six) of Castle Rising; such dominance of one moneyer's name in a single type is without parallel,[94] and it seems quite possible that in type VI at least the four Rodberts (that is, including the Hastings mule) were one and the same, an implication which would then extend to types II and VII. If so this Rodbert, whoever he was, must have had some very unusual function.

TABLE U

Mints of the Stephen Period with a Moneyer Rodbert

	Henry I	Stephen				
		I	II	VI	VI/VII	VII
Bramber						X
Canterbury	XV	X	X	X		X
Hastings	XIV	X	X		X	X
London		X	X	X		X
Rising			X	X		

Conclusions

Sussex in the tenth and eleventh centuries (as ever since) was without a great city or an international port. Yet its towns were more substantial than, say, the remote and tiny local *burhs* of West Wessex, and from its situation close to, but not generally within, the most active areas of English medieval commerce and culture it derived a continuous and respectable prosperity which is exactly reflected in the steady but unexceptional activity of its mints. The coinage of Sussex thus exemplifies, in low relief, the nature and development of the late Anglo-Saxon monetary system, our growing knowledge of which has done so much recently to enhance the reputation of pre-Conquest government in England. The first moves towards a nationally organised but locally operated coinage were made in step with the unification of England by Athelstan and his successors, and standardisation was finally achieved by Edgar. In spite of the Viking raids, and perhaps partly because of the resultant Danegeld, repeated re-coinages were executed throughout the kingdom until a more or less regular system of withdrawal and re-minting became established. Perpetuated and refined by the Danish dynasty and adjusted by the Normans, it nevertheless continued with many of its fundamental characteristics intact, until economic pressures and dynastic war finally undermined what was perhaps the most enduring legacy of Anglo-Saxon administration.

But as new research repeatedly emphasises, we are still only at an early stage in our progress towards an adequate understanding of how the system really worked. A study of this kind is therefore apt to raise more questions than it answers. We can note what information it provides about the relative size of mint output and how it varied; but we cannot tell why Hastings became so much more important as a mint under Cnut, why Lewes had to call on extra moneyers *c.* 1050, or suffered a brief eclipse immediately after the Conquest. Perhaps one day such shreds of evidence will help to illustrate, confirm or extend what is known from other sources. Meanwhile we struggle to interpret them.

Our problem is not that numismatics are difficult to reconcile with the evidence of archaeology and history, but that in detail they overlap so little. In the coins we have a form of evidence that is more continuous and pervasive than any other, which derives from an important but otherwise largely undocumented aspect of government, was operated locally under central control and was a basic factor in the economic, the commercial and probably the fiscal life of the community. But before we can assess what the coins tell us about Anglo-Saxon Sussex, we need to know how the activities of Sussex mints and moneyers are to be compared with those elsewhere. As yet we are ill-equipped to make such a comparison in any detail. There do exist some studies of individual mints, and one of Lincoln has shown how much can be learned when analysis is made of every recorded die; but for whole counties or regions, in which a number of considerable mints were in operation concurrently over a long period, nothing comparable seems yet to have been attempted.

The present survey is therefore in many ways something of an experimental exercise. It reveals at once inadequacies of material, knowledge and understanding.

Yet it does demonstrate the nature of the information obtainable from comparative study about the behaviour and relationships of mints and moneyers. It illustrates, in particular, that the interchange of moneyers between neighbouring mints was of much more normal occurrence than has until recently been supposed and that a major regional mint, in this case Winchester, exchanged personnel regularly with the lesser establishments in its area. The wider consideration of such features must wait until they can be tested against the evidence of other counties, but at least the implications of the Sussex material suggest lines of enquiry which might profitably be pursued elsewhere.

*   *   *   *   *   *

APPENDIX

Tables of known types struck by Sussex moneyers from Edgar to Stephen:

TABLE I

Ethelred II

	1 Small Cross				2 Hand			3	4	5	6		Notes
Type	Edgar earlier	Edgar	Edward	Æthelred	1st	2nd	Ben.	Crux	Long Cross	Helmet	Last Small Cross	Later types	
Chichester													
Cynsige	III	X											
Flodwin	III	X											
Sideman	?	X											
Heawulf					X			X		X			Rare name
Æthelm					X			X	X	X		X	Also Winchester
Eadnoth						X		X					Also Winchester
Wunstan						X	X						(King 'Dunstan'.) Also Winchester
Ælfwine							X	X	X		X		(Includes Aelfwi). Also Winchester and Lewes in type 7
AEthestan								X	X				Also Winchester
Cynna									X		X		Name only here and at Winchester
Dunstan											X		
Leofric											X	X	
Hastings													
Wulfstan						X		X					Also Lewes and Winchester
Ælfred								?					
(Ælwine ?)								X					Bruun lot 135 unverified
Eadstan									X				
Lyva									X	X			Also Lewes
Eadsige									X	X	X	X	Also Lewes
Ælfwerd											X	X	Also Lewes

TABLE I—*continued*

Ethelred II

Type	1 Small Cross				2 Hand		3	4	5	6		Notes
	Edgar earlier	Edgar	Edward	Æthelred	1st	2nd Ben.	Crux	Long Cross	Helmet	Last Small Cross	Later types	
Lewes												
Sexbyrht		X										
Theodgar		X	X									Unique name
Goldstan			X		X	M						M-mule 2nd/1st Hand only
Herebyrht				X	X							
Leofstan					X			X				
Leofwine						X	X	X	X	X		Two moneyers
Oswold						X	X	X	X	X	X	Gold penny of type 5
AElfnoth							X					
Wulfstan							X					Also Winchester and Hastings
AElfgar							X	X				
Leofnoth							X	X		X	X	
Merewine								X	X			
Godefrith										X	X	
Leva									X	X	X	Also Hastings. Many spellings
Godwig										X	X	Also Hastings
AElfwerd										X	X	Also Winchester
Godeman										X	X	
Onlaf										X	?	? Leofwine
? Wine												
Sithesteburh												
Ciolnoth										X		
Godwine										X		See No. 7 of Plate

TABLE II

Type	Ethelred	7 Quatrefoil (Cnut)	8 Pointed Helmet (Cnut)	9 Short Cross	10 Jewel Cross (Harthacnut)	10 Jewel Cross (Harold)	11 Fleur-de-Lis (Harold I)	12 Arm-and-Sceptre (Cnut)	12 Arm-and-Sceptre (Harthacnut)	Edward	Notes
Chichester											
Aegelm	X	X	X	X							Also AEthelm
Leofric	X	X	X	X	X	X	X	X			Also Winchester
Brihtnoth		X									K. 60b (reads CICI)
Liofwerd		X									Also Hastings and Winchester
Wulfnoth		X	X	X							Also Lewes, *Sithesteburh* and Winchester. Includes Leofwi.
Leofwine					X						
Aelfric				X		X	X				Also Winchester
Goda							X				K. 85 ('Godric?'). Also Winchester.
Godric							X				Also Winchester
Hastings											
Eadsige	X		X								Also Etsige
Aelfwerd	X	X	X	X	X	X	X	X			Also Lewes and Winchester. Add Hild. 1307 ('Leicester')
Elst		X	X								
Aelsige		X		X							Also Aegelsige
Eadnoth				X							
Wulfnoth				X							Also Chichester and Winchester
Brid					X	X	X			X	
Cinewni						X					Cinewine?
Edwine					X	X					Also Lewes and Winchester
Alfred				X							Type 9, K. 52 ('Aelfweard'). Also Winchester.
Lifinc							X				Also Winchester
Leofwine								X		X	Also Winchester

TABLE II—*continued*

Type	Ethelred	Cnut — 7 Quatrefoil	Cnut — 8 Pointed Helmet	Cnut — 9 Short Cross	Harold I — 10 Jewel Cross, Harthacnut	Harold I — 10 Jewel Cross, Harold	Harold I — 11 Fleur-de-Lis	Harold I — 12 Arm-and-Sceptre, Cnut	Harold I — 12 Arm-and-Sceptre, Harthacnut	Harold I — 12 Arm-and-Sceptre, Edward	Notes
Lewes											
Godeman	X	X									Hild. 1280 (type 9) is Canterbury
Leofnoth	X	X									
Leofwine	X	X									Also Chichester, *Sithesteburh* and Winchester
Godwi	X	X	X								K. 150a (Hild. 1339, 'Leicester') Type 7 includes bust rt.
Leofa	X	X	X	X							Also Hastings and Winchester
AElfweard	X	X	X	X							
Godefrith	X	X		X							
AElfwine		X									Also Winchester and (Ethelred) Chichester
Ealdred		X									
Wulfeh		X									K. 149b (Stockholm); Sotheby, 24 June 1970, lot 63.
Edwerd		X			X	X	X	X		X	Also Winchester.
Collini			X				X	X	X		
Eadwine			X	X	X	X	X	X		X	Also Hastings and Winchester
Wulfric					X	X	X				
Northman					X	X	X	X		X	
Godwine											
Sithesteburh											
Leofwine		X									Also Chichester (die-linked), Lewes and Winchester
Steyning											
Widia			X	X			X				Also Winchester (and as Godwine Widia)
Frithewine				X	X					X	For type 9, see No. 8 of Plate

TABLE III

| | | Edward the Confessor | | | | | | | | | | Harold | | |
Types	Earlier types	13 Pax	14 Radiate	15 Trefoil-Quadrilateral	16 Small Flan	17 Expanding Cross	18 Helmet	19 Sovereign	20 Hammer Cross	21 Facing Bust	22 Pyramids	23 Harold II Pax	Later types	Notes
Chichester														
Ælfwine				X	X	X	X	X	X	X	X	X		Also Winchester
Leofnoth				X										Also Lewes
Leofwine				X			X	X	X					Also Hastings and Lewes
Godwine							X	X	X	X	X	X		Also Lewes
Wulfric														Also Hastings and Steyning
——ne			X											
Hastings														
Leofwine	X	X	X	X		X	X	X	X					Also Chichester and Lewes
Brid	X	X	X	X	X	X	X	X	X					
Wulfric							X	X	X					Also Chichester and Steyning
Dunninc										X	X	X	X	
Theodred										X	X	X	X	
Colswegen										X		X	X	

TABLE III—*continued*

Types		Edward the Confessor											Harold		
	Earlier types	13	14	15	16	17	18	19	20	21	22	23	Later types	Notes
		Pacx	Radiate	Trefoil-Quadrilateral	Small Flan	Expanding Cross	Helmet	Sovereign	Hammer Cross	Facing Bust	Pyramids	Harold II Pax		
Lewes														
Northman	X	X												
Edwine	X	X	X	X	X		X	X	X	X	X	X	X	Type 18 includes bust left
Oswold			X	X		X	X	X						
Edwerd				X	X	X	X	X						
Godric				X										Also Winchester
Leofnoth				X										Also Chichester
Osmund				X	X									
Leofwine					X	X								Also Chichester and Hastings. Type 17 British Mus. (No. 11 of Plate)
Dirinc					X									
Eadwig					X									
Leofman					X									
Aelfsie														
Godwine						X	X	X	X	X	X	X		Also Chichester
Leofweard									X	X	X	X		
Wulfwine									X					
Steyning														
Frithewine	X	X	X				X	X						
Wulfric		X	X		X	X		X						Also Hastings and Chichester
Wulfget				X		X	X							
Diorman							X		X	X	X	X	X	Type 20 includes local die

TABLE IV

Types	Harold II	I	II	III	IV	V	VI	VII	VIII	I	II	III	IV	V	Henry I	Notes
BMC notation		24	25	26	27	28	29	30	31	32	33	34	35	36		
				William I								William II				
Chichester																
Bruman		X		X	X	X	X	X	X	X	X	X	X		X	34, Lockett 1022
Godwine						X	X				X	?	X	X		28, see *SCBI* York 1210
Edwine						(?)			X	X	X					
Hastings																
Colswegen	X	X														
Theodred	X		X													
Dunninc	X														(X)	No. 13 of Plate
Cipinc						X			X		X					
Godric										X	X	X	X	X	X	
Diorman											X	X	X	X	X	
Sperlinc												X	X		X	
Lewes																
Oswold	X		X					X	X	X	X	X	X		X	32, Drabble 613
Winraed				X	X		X		X	X	X					
AElfric					X				X		X					
Brihtmaer												X				
Edwine												X		X		Shillington find; also Chichester?
AElfwine														X	X	
Pevensey																
AElfheh									X	X	X	X				For type 34, see No. 14 of Plate; also Sandwich
Steyning																
Dermon	X		X			X										
Thurbern							X		X		X	X		X		
Lifsi												X				

TABLE V

	William II	Henry I														Stephen	Notes
		I	II	III	IV	V	VI	VII	VIII	IX	X	XI	XII	XIII	XIV		
Chichester																	
Colbrand					X												
Brand							X	X									
Godwine											X	X	X	X	X	X	XI *SCBI* Stockholm 283-4
Hastings																	
Dorman	X	X															
Godric	X			X													
Sperlinc	X				X		X	X		X	X						IV Coins & Antiquities Ltd. list
Dunninc					X		X	X				X			X		XIV Lincoln No. 5, 1970
Ailmer										X	X						Lincoln
Wulnot										X	X						Lincoln
Boneface											X				X		
Rodbert											X				X	X	X Lincoln
Lewes																	
AElfwine	X	X															
Brihtmaer	X	X															
Winraed	X	X	X														X Lincoln fragment (?)
Alfward								X			(?)						
Ordmer											X						Lincoln
Edmund											X		X		X		X Lincoln
Oswold											X			X	X		X, XIII Lincoln; for XIII see No. 15 of Plate
Pevensey																	
A(..)red										X							

TABLE VI

	Henry I	Stephen						Henry II	Notes
		I	I/II	II	VI	VI/VII	VII		
Bramber									
Orgar							X	X	No. 17 of Plate
Rodbert							X	X	*BNJ* XXXVI, 90. Also Hastings
Willem							X	X	
Chichester									
Godwine	X	X							One with defaced die (Prestwich)
Hastings									
Rodbert	X	X		X		X	X		VI/VII, *BNJ* XXXVI, 90. Also Bramber
Sawine		X							One with defaced die (*BNJ* XXXVII, 59)
Wenstan		X		X					*Num. Chron.* 1922, 53 (probably Hastings)
Aldred					X				
Lewes									
Hervei		X							
Willem		X							
Osebern		X		X					I, *BMC* 49 confirmed by Prestwich
AElmar				X					
Hunfrei					X		X		
Pevensey									
Herv(..)?	?								*Num. Chron.* 1922, 58 (mint doubtful)
Alwine				X			X		
Felipe							X		
Rye									
Rawulf	X	X	X	X			X		I, *BNJ* XXII, 332 (see No. 16 of Plate); I/II, *BNJ* XXXV, 48; VII, *BNJ* XXX, 188.

VI

THE SOUTH SAXON *ANDREDESWEALD*

Peter Brandon

Introduction

THE MOST STRIKING feature of the South Saxon landscape must have been the immense wild country which spread across the Wealds of Kent, Surrey and Sussex between the inward-facing North and South Downs and the present mouth of the Eastern Rother as far west as Privet, near Petersfield. The evolution of this primeval forest of the Weald into the complete landscape we know today is paradoxically one of the best known and also one of the least understood of all the processes contributing to the general drama of English achievement. Once visualised as a widespread and apparently impervious barrier of forest which still defied human penetration as late as the sixteenth century, it is now becoming hard to escape the conclusion that the Weald as a scene of human existence had undergone a long and complex series of land clearances and abandonments over many previous centuries. The story of this development has the further interest that it offers one of the clearest examples in Britain of the struggle between man and a continuously receding, uncultivated waste, illustrating in microcosm the task of opening the wilderness which stands to the credit of a type of backwoodsman, irresistibly recalling the similar picture of the American West. The forest dwellers were so engrossed in herding and clearing that settlements were left to build themselves. Their houses originated as primitive seasonal shelters long before they became permanent homesteads. Not until population increased and migrated did those who held summer houses for pasturing their herds convert them into permanent farms. Contemporaneously, those sharing rights on woodland commons successfully establish claims to encroach upon them. Setting a date to these new beginnings is the obscurest question in the Weald's history. Older even than sites of present buildings is the intricate network of droveways, many of which remain as lanes to this day, which were the roads along which cattle and swine passed to and from their feeding grounds in the distant Weald and the parent farms on the woodland margins. Some of these at least are probably Roman 'iron ways' used to bring out iron and they doubtless served a droving function as far back as the

138

prehistoric Iron Age. So much we once thought of as newly Saxon now recedes further and further into pre-history.

This essay attempts to discover something of the historical character of the Weald and examines inter-acting aspects of the forest economy of the South Saxons and the process of settlement. The span of time reviewed stretches from the migration of Aelle's war-band from across the North Sea until the end of the eleventh century. This is more than six obscure, though formative, centuries, during which generations of Saxons wrested a living from the grudging soils with a single-minded absorption. In judging the achievement of the age, no appreciable light is yet thrown by archaeology on the subjects for discussion and the information in the Saxon annals is meagre. Our best hope of understanding the Saxon and his fields is by means of topographical studies drawing upon the nature of the soil, and place-names in conjunction with Saxon charters.[1]

This approach involves the crossing of several academic disciplines and the bringing together of material from specialist works. This has its dangers and difficulties, but it is the only approach likely to resolve many of the perplexities with which the beginnings of English society are still surrounded. The author's greatest debt is owed to the various scholars of the *English Place-Name Society* whose derivations of Sussex place-names have been so extensively used in this essay.[2] As Professor H. C. Darby, in an illuminating essay on 'Place-names and the geography of the past' has written, 'the full bearing of such information upon the history and forms of settlement has yet to be investigated'.[3] This essay is an attempt to make a more comprehensive use of what little material is available.

Contemporary sources of information tell us little about the Saxon Weald. The annalists of the *Anglo-Saxon Chronicle* mention it in connection with military events on four occasions. The first entry is under 477, the traditional year of Aelle's landing, when he and his sons are said to have driven the Britons to flight into 'the wood which is called *Andredesleah'.[4] Under 755(7) is the celebrated story of the assassination of the unjust Sigeberht, ex-king of Wessex, who was driven into the Weald by his deposer Cynewulf and was eventually stabbed to death by a swineherd. This annal helps to define the western boundary of the Weald and the mention of the swineherd is the earliest hint of the great importance attached by the Saxons to the use of distant forest pastures in stock-raising.[5]

Under 892(3) is a valuable record which is worth quotation:

> [The great Danish army] . . . came up into the estuary of the Lympne with 250 ships. That estuary is in East Kent at the east end of that great wood (*se micla wudu*) which we called *Andred*. The wood is from east to west 120 miles long, or longer, and 30 miles broad. The river of which we spoke comes out of the Weald. They rowed their ships up the river as far as the Weald, four miles from the outer part of the estuary, and there they stormed the fortress. Inside that fortification there were a few peasants camping and it was only half-made.[6]

To understand this annal we must reconstruct the geography of the local shorelines which have greatly changed since the embanking of Romney Marsh. It has been plausibly suggested that the 'estuary of the Lympne' and the river

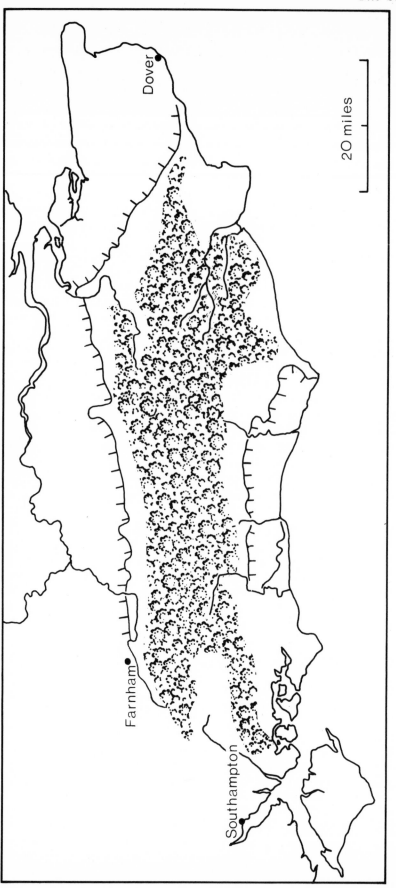

Fig. 7 *Andredesweald*, after Guest

which 'comes out of the Weald' must refer to the Eastern Rother before it assumed its present course to Rye. The original course of the river probably followed the line of the disused Military Canal. The partially-built fort is said to have been near the site of Rye, which does not appear to have originated as a harbour before the eleventh century. There is the strong possibility that the half-built fortress could be *Eorpburnam,* one of the Burghal Hidage *burhs.*

In his estimation of the dimensions of the Weald the annalist was accurate as to its breadth, but exaggerated its true length by some 30 miles. This curious blend of knowledge and ignorance is a valuable clue for the agrarian historian. The familiarity with the distance between the Surrey Downs and the coast points to early intercourse across the impenetrable Weald by means of Roman roads and the remarkably dense system of droving routes still traceable on the ground. By contrast, there were no very obvious lines of communication across the length of the Weald, so this remained untravelled and thus immeasurable. Even in the thirteenth century guides were needed to conduct distinguished strangers from Kent into the Weald of Sussex.[7]

The final entry in the *Anglo-Saxon Chronicle* which is of present concern is the mention under 1011 in connection with the continued harassment of south-east England by the Danes, of the *Haestingas,*[8] the people of east Sussex in the hinterland of Hastings who were apparently still living in semi-independence. These people have the distinction of being among the first Saxons to have made any significant inroads into the Weald and their individuality is commemorated to this day by a distinctive place-name nomenclature.

This literary record does little to advance our knowledge of the physical environment of the Weald and the long-drawn-out process of Saxon settlement. Other literary sources are little more helpful. The most valuable is Eddius's *Life of Bishop Wilfrid,* written *c.* 700, which refers to the Weald as *'desertum Ondred'* and describes Sussex, in the earliest topographical description which has come down to us, as a land 'which has resisted attack by the other [Anglo-Saxon] kingdoms owing to its many hills and the thickness of its woods' (*que pro rupium multitudine et silvarum densitate*).[9] In this phrase the writer conveys a sense of a Sussex ringed round with a wild 'no-man's land', the strategically protective and settlement-delimiting wood which was so effective a barrier against the enemies of the South Saxons and which even today lends an air of seclusion to the deeper Weald.

The physical environment of the Weald

The first to map the probable distribution of the natural woodland that bore the name of *Andred* in the sixth century was Edwin Guest.[10] The basis of his map, originally published in 1849 and again in 1883 without amendment, is unstated, but it is evidently geological, the edge of the dense woodland being marked by the southern termination of the Weald Clay formation. A feature of Guest's reconstruction is the large-scale forest clearance in the hinterland of the Roman *Anderida* (Pevensey) which is unsubstantiated by any documentary source. A re-drawn version of Guest's pioneer map was used by John Richard Green in his highly popular works *The Making of England* and *A Short History of the English People* and Green was probably the earliest English writer to appreciate the stature of the Saxon achievement in taming the wilderness depicted by Guest[11] (Fig. 7). In the 1920s the matter was approached afresh by H. A. Wilcox whose maps of early woodland published in 1933[12] were influenced by Sir A. G. Tansley's studies of past vegetation. Her work appears to have strongly influenced O. G. S. Crawford of the Ordnance Survey who applied a woodland symbol to the Second Edition of the Dark Age map in 1935. Both authorities distinguished the more open woodland characteristic of the Lower Greensand formation and the sandier tracts of the High Weald from the dense woodland likely to have been supported by the Weald Clay. Wilcox also drew attention to the very varied woodland cover which could be expected from the variegated lithology of the High Weald, though her maps were on too small a scale to allow for this. In broad terms, Wilcox distinguished three major vegetation types in the Weald: the thick and almost impenetrable mixed oak woodland on the Weald Clay and the Wadhurst Clay; the lightly wooded, perhaps scrubby, ridges in the High Weald; and the heathy type of woodland on the sandy outcrops.

Wilcox's work was concluded before the publication in 1929–30 of the English Place-Name Society's *The Place-Names of Sussex*[13] and this provided new evidence on which to base answers to questions about the primitive vegetation of the Weald. Professor Darby showed in 1963 how descriptive names surviving after the features they had described have disappeared help in the reconstruction of the primitive landscape. This place-name evidence corroborates remarkably well the independently-conceived work of Wilcox. The distribution of names in *-feld* 'open land'; *-leah* 'woodland, glade or clearing'; *haep* or *hap*, heath; *fearn*, bracken; *-denn*, 'woodland swine pasture'; *hyrst*, 'wooded hill'; and the like, provide cumulative evidence that trees began to thin out on the ridges of the High Weald, yielding probably only a sparse cover on their summits and that on sandier tracts clumps of trees and bushes probably stood above a continuous cover of bracken, or more rarely grass. Clearly, no more than any medieval forest, was the Saxon Weald an unrelieved woodland.

Moreover, although the place-names of the Weald overwhelmingly perpetuate the former existence of woodland, the considerable number of early 'open land' names in localities which on geological grounds one would have expected natural woodland is striking. Examples are Fairlight, in East Grinstead, 'the bracken clearing'; Lindfield, 'open land by the lime trees'; Wivelsfield, 'Wivel's open land'; Henfield (two instances), 'at the high open land'; Hartfield, 'open land where harts graze'; East and West Hoathly (from *hap*, heath).

To this list should be added the other 'open-land' place-names recorded in the earliest Saxon charters, such as *baere leah*, 'the pig clearing', *Citangaleahge*, 'clearing of Cita's people', the unidentified *hafocungaleahge* mentioned in a charter of *c.* 765–771 and relating to places in or near West Hoathly.[14] Two other early names deserve notice. Sheffield and Shipley are Saxon place-names embodying the name sheep (O.E. *sceap*). The location of the 'sheep-clearing' names is not on the more windswept and presumably more open ridges of the High Weald as might have been expected, but in the Low Weald, where the natural woodland is assumed to have been more dense. As sheep nibble the leaves of herbaceous plants, their Saxon presence must be regarded as implying considerably early forest clearance. Sheep were not raised in pioneer districts without great difficulty: wolves were common, and winter feed was scarce. The names seem to imply that these places had evolved from their earliest stages of development into rudimentary farmland. It is perhaps not coincidental that both Shipley and Sheffield emerge as small independent manors in Domesday where six villeins and two ploughs were at work at the former and as many as 14 peasants and eight ploughs at the latter. In this development we appear to have confirmation that the earlier sheep runs had come to be worked more intensively as farms, and that their precocious development was due to early grazing which gave them a 'head-start'.

We should also take into account other early place-names embodying the names of domestic animals. Goats give names to two places recorded in Saxon charters (*Gotwick* in Rusper and *Gatham,* a lost place in Durrington). Bearing in mind that place-names are denotive as well as connotive, these 'goat' names probably indicate places specialising in goat breeding or in some way remarkable for having goats. The goat thrives in a pioneering situation. It is hardier and more domesticated than sheep, is less worried by adversaries, and produces milk over a longer period. It needs little attention because it feeds on whatever foliage and bark comes its way. It is evidently to the goat, that great ravager of woods, that we can attribute some of the clearing of the Wealden woodland.

A number of other South Saxon place-names offer definite evidence of change in vegetation. Several names compounded with hazel, such as Hazelwick in Worth, and Hazelhurst in Ticehurst, presumably record hazel's vigorous growth and abundance of fruit when this shrub is stimulated by the clearance of overshadowing trees such as oak, ash and beech. Hazel would also have formed a pioneer woodland phase when land was abandoned. One swine pasture of Annington, mentioned in 946, that of *Fernthe* (wild country covered by bracken) suggests that total deforestation had locally occurred. It is at this point that consideration needs to be given to the consequences for forest pasture by the practice of cattle and swine grazing. Cattle have an inclination to attack woody plants, especially when grass is scarce, and, as they consolidated ground by trampling, grass would have grown at the expense of woodland. The pig's effect on woodland is less clear. S. R. J. Woodell has recently argued that rooting pigs may have encouraged forest regeneration by stamping seeds into the soil and by aerating it and destroying vermin and insects which would have eaten tree seedlings. This opinion is confirmed by that of nineteenth-century foresters who also considered that wild pigs did much less damage than other game. It is commonly stated that the widespread practice of *wood pannage,* that is the feeding of pigs off fallen acorns and beech nuts, etc., would have thinned woodland.[15] This is erroneous; by its very nature pannage probably did little,

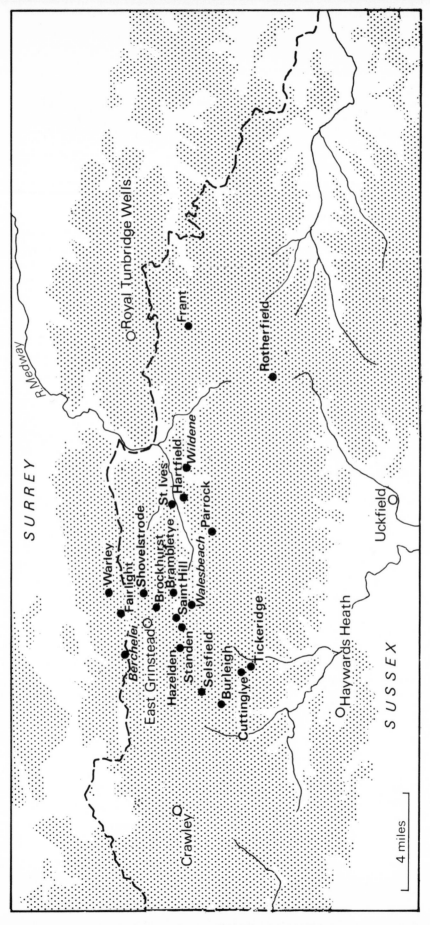

Fig. 8 Early Saxon settlements around Ashdown Forest

if any, damage to the forest. The pig, then, cannot be regarded as a major agency in the clearing of the once all-covering forest of the Weald. The felling of timber for fuel and building was probably a more important cause in the slow but persistent deforestation. The scale of cutting is indicated by the annual rent payable in wood which half-cleared lands at *Healdeleia* (Hurley or Hairley farm in East Grinstead) owed Lewes Priory in *c.* 1103 (and to Ripe manor previously), namely four freshly-made carts, 200 boards of beech, and 40 cartloads of logs.[16]

These and many other examples testify to a considerable thinning of the woodlands, even so early as the eighth and ninth centuries. We must presumably imagine the originally dense Wealden woodland cover being progressively opened out into a parkland appearance by the effects of grazing and felling, so greatly facilitating the subsequent settlement. It is quite conceivable that by 450 A.D. appreciable areas on the Wealden margins, e.g., in Laughton, East Hoathly, Henfield, and Lindfield, had been cleared by the Romano-British villa economy and peasant grazing and were supporting not dense forest but more open secondary woodland scrub or heath. Until recently the South Saxons were conceived as working on a *tabula rasa* and the ecological effect of any previous occupation of the Weald was little considered. Archaeological investigations still continuing by C. F. Tebbutt and others have now yielded evidence of much more Roman and prehistoric activity than had hitherto been supposed. We must not necessarily assume that the land the South Saxons discovered in the Weald was wholly new.

The Saxon forest economy

Our knowledge of the daily life and settlement of the Saxon turns largely upon the interpretation of the evidence afforded by place-names. Such is the distinctiveness and importance of Sussex place-names that they have engaged the attention of several writers in a variety of contexts, but they have not been fully considered as witnesses to the forest farming of the Saxons and the evolution of their Wealden settlements. Particularly significant are the place-names embodying the names of domestic animals. In the absence of any literary or archaeological evidence, they can be brought into service to give some information as to the various species of livestock kept by the Saxons in the Weald and the relative proportions of the surviving names for each animal may reasonably be expected to throw some light on the composition of their flocks and herds. Confining attention to place-names recorded before the end of the eleventh century, the pig is represented to an overwhelming degree (over 60 names), the horse (probably wild) takes a poor second place (five names), cattle are represented four times, and the subservience of sheep and goats is indicated by their last position, each with only two names.[17] A similar investigation of place-names recorded in *The Place-Names of Sussex* and bearing the names of domestic animals first recorded between 1100 and 1350 brings out some significant changes in the rankings as compared with the earlier period. 'Pig' names again preponderate, though less strongly than earlier; 'cattle' names rise comfortably to second place (13 names); sheep and goats are represented by six names each and there are no proven 'horse' names at all. These changes in the composition of the livestock in the Weald over a combined period of more than five centuries appear to reflect faithfully the gradual extirpation of timber and undergrowth and the extending acreage under farmland. Caution is needed in the handling of evidence of this kind because some of the place-names not recorded until the later period may have originated earlier, but despite its crudity the investigation appears to reflect a changing relationship between people of Saxon stock and their forest land which is not discoverable by other means.

Returning to consider the Saxon use of the Weald, it is plain from the frequency of early names that today end in *-den*, O.E. *-denn*, 'a woodland pasture', or include the element O.E. *baer(e)*, of similar meaning, or the archaic elements *(ge)sell* and *scydd*, which will be considered later, that the mixed oak forest of the Weald of Sussex was early developed by Saxons as an immense larder providing rich sustenance for herds of rooting swine which furnished excellent bacon. The sight of well-stuffed swine being driven homewards back to the ancestral villages near the coast in late autumn must have been a familiar one. The grand scale of woodland pig-rearing in the late eleventh century is corroborated by the large swine renders recorded in Domesday as paid by peasants to their respective lords. These renders imply tenants' herds of 500, and even exceptionally as large as 1,500–2,000, to which totals the demesne herd need to be added.

Cattle are probably under-represented in Sussex place-names because they would have contentedly browsed the dense foliage in the swine pastures, but the supposition that amongst the South Saxons the pig was the most important source of meat supply seems amply supported by the preponderance of surviving 'pig' names. Only four 'cattle' names can definitely be assigned to the period before 1066. These are Rotherfield 'open land for cattle' in the east Sussex High Weald, and Rotherbridge, the name of a hundred in West Sussex, both compounded with O.E. *hryther*, cattle; Keymer, 'the cow's mere', and Cowfold. The name of Rotherfield was probably bestowed by cattle-drovers from the manor of East Blachington, near Seaford, who held land in the parish of Rotherfield and who would have brought their animals back to lower ground in the 'home' village in autumn. All the coastal communities probably sent up cattle with swine to the detached swine pastures in this way.

Horse rearing must have been especially developed on the margins of the large wastes known after the Norman Conquest as Ashdown and St. Leonard's Forests, for in these districts we find places named after pastures for horses which later became the site of villages. Whether the Saxon herds of horses were indigenous or introduced is a question which will perhaps never be answered, but it seems clear that the life of the horse-breeder with his pony-'drifts' and way of life now only associated with Dartmoor and similar isolated places, must have been an important one in the heart of the Saxon Weald.

With his wealth largely bound up in flocks and herds it is not to be wondered at that Saxon herders lived in constant fear of the wolf. The harassment by this animal is reflected in several names such as *wulfpyte* in the Stanmer Saxon charter (*c.* 765–771, A.D.), an early snare (O.E. wulf-pyte) identified with the site of Woolpack farm in Sheffield, the *wulfa biorh* (wolves' hill), mentioned in the Durrington charter, *c.* 934, Woolfly in Henfield (Overlie in Domesday), and Woolborough farm in Ashington.

It will have been noted that the place-names considered are older than the villages themselves. This is usual in the Weald of Sussex where the site chosen for a human habitation generally had already a well-known name as a pasture. A number of 'pasture' names embody the names of trees which yielded valuable fodder. The lime (linden) tree is notably well represented in Sussex place-names. Branches of the lime were cut by early people as cattle fodder and the sites of places such as Lindfield, 'open pasture by the lime trees', had probably been especially attractive to seasonal herders before a permanent village was set up there.

The great antiquity of some of the Wealden place-name elements testifies that the South Saxons were driving herds from the coastal areas up to parcels of land specially denominated as common swine pastures from an early date. Sir Allen Mawer, the place-name scholar, wrote on the conclusion of his work on Sussex place-names '. . . the place-name evidence suggests that the settlements of the Wealden area took place at a quite early date . . . the South Saxons soon made their way right into the heart of it'.[19] His comment was prompted by the discovery that a patch of water-meadow in Horsham bearing the name of Horn Brook had earlier forms including *Horningebrok*. This made it almost certain that the *-ingas* group of South Saxons called *Honingas* in Washington (who also gave their name to *Horningacumb*) must also have held common forest pasture in Horsham from the early days of the English invasion. A well-known example of the same kind is recorded in the Saxon charter for *Derantun* (Durrington) in 934 which mentions a swine-pasture called *garungaleah,* which is identical, at least in name form, with Goringlee in Thakeham and Goring which adjoins Durrington.[20] A third example which will be cited is the mention in a charter of 953 relating to Felpham, near Bognor, of swine pastures 'in the common forest pasture which is called *Palinga schittas'.*[21] These pastures are identified with the present Limbo farm in Petworth and *Palinga* with the *-ingas* form of Poling, a village not far from Felpham, so that *Palinga schittas* probably means 'the swine-cotes of the people of Poling'.

Apart from these place-names which preserve survivals of the old folk-names from the pre-migration period, two very early place-names which appear to tell us something about the activity of the first Saxon farmers in the Weald are the elements *glind* and *saenget*. *Glind* is not found anywhere in England outside east Sussex, where it testifies to the early conquest of the area and the isolating effect of wooded hills and marsh. The word is thought to derive from one used in the continental homeland meaning 'enclosure made with boards'. The name takes us back, therefore, to the first laying-out and fencing of land in the newly-colonised districts. Bexhill, Peasmarsh and Westham each have a name with this element and it is also preserved in the place-name of Glynde, near Lewes.[22]

Saenget, also a rare English element, is identical with *sengel* names in the woodland districts of Westphalia and is held to mean 'burnt clearing'. The word seems to occur in Singleton, mentioned in a charter of the eighth century, and in the old name of Cowdray Park, called *La Sengle* as late as the thirteenth century. Deep in the heart of the Weald we encounter the element at two other places bordering Ashdown Forest—Saint Hill and St. Ives. This element seems to confirm that the practice of burning the forest for cultivation was an established custom amongst the first invaders of the wilderness.[23]

Place-name elements recording some of the earliest cultivation sites in the Weald are O.E. *etisc,* 'a cornfield' (possibly unenclosed), and *ersc* a later form with the meaning of ploughed field or stubble. The first element is an extremely archaic word-form which is represented on the continent in the *esch* names of Westphalia, Oldenburg and Holland, but it quickly dropped out of use with the Anglo-Saxons in England and is found in very few places in England outside the extreme south-eastern corner of Sussex, where in Icklesham and surrounding parishes it is preserved in such 'exe' names as Cleeve Axe and Platnix. This is some of the most favoured farmland of the *Haestingas* and was evidently settled from a very early date in the Saxon conquest. Ekwall regards there 'exe' names as being the main characteristic of the place nomenclature of the Hastings district.[24] The *ersc* form in Sussex is also mainly confined to the eastern part. Ticehurst has a sprinkling of these names: Hazelhurst, 'earsh land grown over with hazels', is mentioned in 1018 and Battenhurst, 'Beta's earsh', first mentioned *c.*1200, bears a Saxon personal name. Burwash, 'the *burh* with ploughed land' is also of this variety, and there are several more of an undoubtedly early date.

The use of the *ersc* instead of a word denoting an enclosure may be significant for it may preserve a primitive phase of shifting agriculture in the Weald preceding a stage of fixed fields. This hypothesis is buttressed by the name Hazelhurst and also by the lost name of *Birchen ersh* in Cowfold, meaning 'earsh land grown over with birch trees'. A recurrent theme in the history of the Wealden landscape has been the temporary cultivation of land which was subsequently taken over again by the force of nature in the form of scrub or forest until its reclamation was once more attempted when the tide of settlement turned again. Names like Hazelhurst and *Birchen ersh* appear to be hinting at this transience. We may be able to link these *etisc* and *ersc* names with the *saenget* names previously mentioned, and postulate a stage when early South Saxons were burning and felling patches of the forest and moving on to fresh woodland as crop yields fell off. This is pure conjecture at present, but scientific archaeology may ultimately penetrate the obscurity and light up the facts about Saxon farming before the increasing pressure of population required permanently cleared and ring-fenced farms. The Saxon place-names are constant reminders against the over-simplification of issues which are really complex.

The evolution of Wealden settlement

It has already been remarked that most Wealden place-names are older than the villages and towns that bear them. It is also apparent that many Wealden settlements, including the minor settlements of the farms, evolved from a stage of temporarily-occupied huts and shelters associated with seasonal pastoral farming before they were permanently occupied by farmers who cultivated the land within ring-fenced fields. This evolution is one of the most distinctive characteristics of the settlement history of the Weald. The evidence for these successive stages of settlement is greater than for the change-over from one utilisation to the other. One must again eagerly await the future discoveries of archaeologists. Particularly valuable in this connection are place-names which include the element O.E. *(ge)sell,* meaning a group of shelters for animals, herdsmen's huts, or both. The prefix *ge* has a collective function. This term *gesell* is one of the very archaic ones in the Sussex place-name nomenclature which appears to have early gone out of use, so that it takes us back to the stage when man was erecting his first buildings in the Wealden landscape. Ekwall distinguishes 12 of these names in the Weald of Sussex. They are mostly in eastern Sussex and are chiefly drawn from Saxon charters. The first element of some of these place-names denotes the material used in the construction of the huts. Thus Breadsell in Battle is derived from O.E. *Bredgesell (a),* 'huts made of planks'. Others denote a situation or the name of the animals' houses: Bremzells in Herstmonceux (O.E. *Beamgesell*) means a shelter built of logs or one sited by a beam serving as a bridge, and Boarzell in Ticehurst is derived from O.E. *Bar(a)-gesell* meaning 'herdsmen's camp where the boars stand'. Occasionally the first element contains a personal name. Drigsell in Salehurst is compounded with the very early word O.E. *Drihten,* lord, which must have fallen out of use soon after the Saxon invasion of Sussex because it is extremely rare in English place-names. It is possible that several later name forms conceal *-gesell* terminations, but already by the thirteenth century the Saxon suffix was so little understood that it was pronounced 'hull' and confused with 'hill'.[25]

Most of the *-gesell* sites eventually developed from these primitive collections of wooden huts into fully-fledged farmsteads. The farms bearing *-gesell* names thus have an exceptionally long and interesting history, and are often larger than the average size for their district. The scientific work of archaeologists will eventually do much to solve the appearance of the herders' huts and the *gesell* sites may one day yield pottery and other archaeological material. It is not yet known whether they were settlements protected by earthworks of banks and ditches or simply scattered over a hillside or along lonely stream banks in the manner of the simple seasonally-occupied huts still existing in the mountain districts of Europe.

To help fill out the picture further, more shed-dwellers herding swine are attested by the place-names derived from O.E *scydd,* shed, which in modern names is usually rendered as 'shot' or 'shott'.[26] Gunshot Common in Wisborough Green, Bowshots farm in West Grinstead, and Limbo farm in Petworth, at or near the site of *Palinga schittas,* are examples of this type. Bowshots is compounded with *burh* and *scydd* and this probably denotes an enclosure for the huts and the growing of summer crops.

The *scydd* names occur in west Sussex. In the Adur basin of central Sussex are a number of names in *-wick* (O.E. *wic*) given to swine-pastures in the Stanmer, Annington, Durrington and Washington charters (765–963 A.D.).[27] These tend to occur between the *-fold* names to the west and *-den* names on the east. Again and again, the study of early Sussex place-names leads to the conclusion that the first settlers in the Weald had each their own local vocabularies and this seems to imply that they had been semi-independent groups from their first landing in Sussex, and that they tended to live in the Weald in relative isolation from each other for several generations. As J. H. Round remarked, the 'distribution of Sussex place-names is in favour of vertical, not lateral progress, of separate settlements up the rivers'.[28] Most of the *-wick* names are now borne by farms. 'Wick' has several meanings including 'dwelling-place', 'dairy farm', 'camp', 'trade or industrial settlement', and 'dependent farm'. Since the charter names in *-wic* are of forest pastures the last meaning is probably the sense required and Ekwall has suggested that the state of dependence conveyed by the meaning 'dependent farm' is probably 'abode' or 'quarters' more especially 'temporary abode (quarters)' . . . A *wic* was probably at first generally a temporary shelter for cattle or for herdsmen or for fishermen or woodcutters or the like, especially an outlying one, where animals were kept or some activity was carried on during part of the year.[29] Ekwall's definition of *-wic* best seems to fit the Sussex context and this suggested origin puts it in the same category as the *(ge)sell* and *scydd* names previously discussed and also those in *-denn* (forest pasture, especially for swine) commonly found in East Sussex.

In the upper Ouse valley another local place-name makes an appearance, the second element "stye' in such names as Bursteye and Pipstye in Ardingly, Casteye in Balcombe, and Ansty and Pilstye in Cuckfield. These farms are of almost certain early Saxon origin, for they occupy some of the best sites on the lower slopes of the valley. The editors of *The Place-Names of Sussex* were inclined to derive the 'stye' element from O.E. *stig*, a path, a word which appears to have been mainly used in the sense of a narrow, ascending trail. Later work on place-names has shown that it is very difficult to distinguish *stig* from O.E. *stigu, stig*, meaning a stye or pen.[30] Bearing in mind the ubiquity of forest swine-pastures in the Weald this is the most likely derivation for the central Sussex 'styles', especially as the gentle topography of the upper Ouse valley seems to rule out steeply-rising trails. If this supposition is correct we have yet another element which preserves the link between a site of sheds and temporary huts used as swinecotes and the eventual building of a permanent farm on the site.

Very characteristic of the West Sussex Low Weald, and also of the adjoining part of Surrey, are the sites of Saxon or early Norman churches and their attendant farmsteads bearing the suffix *-fold* (O.E. *falod*). These folds are found on the edge of dry land in the Arun valley and elsewhere are invariably situated upon low swells of better drained soil of a lighter texture and browner colour (and hence more fertile) than those variegating the surface of the Low Weald

Plate 1: 1. Small-long brooch, St. Pancras, Chichester (British Museum), see page 27; 2. Saucer brooch, Singleton (Chichester Museum), see page 27; 3. Syrakus type buckle, The Broyle, Chichester (reproduced with permission from *Antiquaries' Journal*, vol. IV, 1924, p. 50), see page 29; 4. Disc mount, Chichester district (British Museum), see page 27; 5. Gold fragment, Selsey (Ashmolean Museum), see page 29; 6. Gold fragment, Selsey (British Museum), see page 29; 7. Runic inscription on a gold bar, Selsey (British Museum), see page 29; 8. Silver bar set with gold cloisonné cells, Selsey (British Museum), see page 29.

Plate 2: Aerial view of the Anglo-Saxon Settlement on Rookery Hill, Bishopstone, during excavations. The cemetery was between the second and third rows of bungalows in the background. (*Photo*: S. Adams)

Plate 3: Weald and Downland Open Air Museum, Singleton. Background, reconstructed sunken hut based on examples from Old Erringham and Bishopstone. Foreground, rectangular building based on one at Chalton, Hants. (*Photo*: Weald and Downland Open Air Museum)

Plate 4: Bishopstone. Rectangular Building no. 1, with Sunken Hut no. 6 to its left. (*Photo*: B. Westley)

Plate 5: Bishopstone. Bow-sided Building no. 37, with Iron Age post-holes in the foreground. (*Photo*: B. Westley)

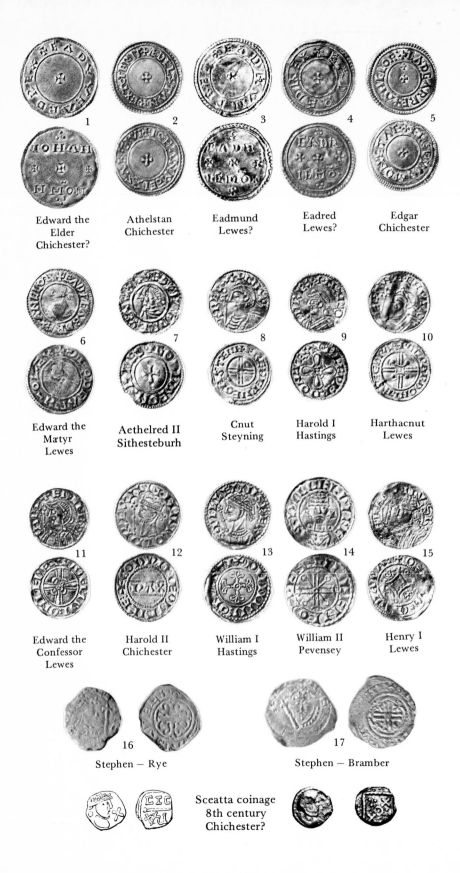

1	2	3	4	5
Edward the Elder Chichester?	Athelstan Chichester	Eadmund Lewes?	Eadred Lewes?	Edgar Chichester
6	7	8	9	10
Edward the Martyr Lewes	Aethelred II Sithesteburh	Cnut Steyning	Harold I Hastings	Harthacnut Lewes
11	12	13	14	15
Edward the Confessor Lewes	Harold II Chichester	William I Hastings	William II Pevensey	Henry I Lewes

16

Stephen — Rye

17

Stephen — Bramber

Sceatta coinage
8th century
Chichester?

Plate 6: Coins of the Sussex Mints.

generally. There is no better living witness to the earliest farming sites selected by the first woodlanders than these *fold* sites. The first to perceive that the essence of the Low Weald scene were these fertile rises (presumably supporting dense wood in their virgin state, and hence more covered in vegetable mould than the more marshy, low-lying lands interspersed between them) was William Marshall, the eighteenth-century agricultural writer, whose careful observation of the landscape led him to conclude that the 'fertile rising grounds' were 'probably cultivated long before the rest was cleared, being in the first stage of society . . . groups of huts in wide spreading woods . . .'[31] These *fold* names help to recall the ancient forest landscape and the earliest graziers for the word denotes staking off a pasture-ground and cattle (or swine) pen. The very general use of the suffix suggests that the Wealdsmen who pitched their *folds* in openings in the woods were originally herders of animals rather than farmers. Such people would have felt insecure without defences to protect their herds: as John Ruskin remarked, 'the sweetest word which men learned in the pastures of the wilderness is "fold"'.[32] The probability is that the *fold* names were given to pastures or shelters for animals by the men who farmed on coastal manors and seasonally herded animals to and from the outlying grazings by the network of drovers' roads which still lace together the parent centres to the backwoods sites. Many such pastures or shelters appear to have subsequently developed into homesteads (commonly moated) or villages, thus making the *folds* correspond to the other place-name elements we have been discussing.

The existence of many *folds* on the Weald Clay formation by the tenth century is confirmed by their mention in the Ambersham, Durrington and Washington charters (934–963 A.D.)[33] and that swine, and probably cattle and other animals as well, were penned is clear from the use of the word *fold* in the charter to denominate a swine-pasture. Their actual origin is probably very much older, perhaps reaching back to the early years of the English conquest, or even beyond. Their restricted distribution straddling the Sussex-Surrey border inevitably invites speculation as to the location of the parent villages responsible for the hiving-off of men and animals into the forest. Are we to envisage two distinctly different groups of Saxons, one from the Sussex coast, and the other from mid-Surrey hewing their way towards each other and meeting along the line of a later-drawn common boundary between the two shires? Or do the *folds* commemorate the summer swinecotes of one dominant group?

The balance of probability is towards the second suggestion and as the Saxon population on the Sussex coastal plain and along the edge of the South Downs is likely to have been much greater than along the more restricted ribbons of fertility in Surrey, this points to a Sussex origin. The artificiality of the present boundary between the two counties is also suggestive. Surrey names such as Pallinghurst in Cranleigh, which appears to come from the same word root as Poling, near Felpham, and Pinkhurst, Barfold, High Billinghurst, and Rumbeams, all of which have almost identical namesakes across the border in Sussex, may indicate that *-ingas* groups of South Saxons had spread freely across the whole width of the Low Weald before the present boundary between the two counties was demarcated. Perhaps it is not too fanciful to conjecture that the *folds* now in Surrey were some of the fruits of Aelle's bretwaldaship.

When the generality of *folds* passed under more direct human sway as permanently inhabited places, is as obscure as the similar evolution of the east Sussex *-dens*. From the Saxon charters there are a few clues. The Ambersham charter lists four *folds* lying on the land boundary of the estate; two bear personal names which implies that their owners permanently resided there. The Washington charter of 947[34] appears to tell us something as to the process by which a once common swine-pasture developed into a *fold* held by such individuals. Two *folds* mentioned are called *ridan* and *hunreding* in a late copy. Both words probably contain the O.E element *(ge)ryd* and *denn*, 'cleared swine pasture'. The two *folds* mentioned in the Durrington charter of 934 are called *byring* (perhaps 'place at or with a byre') and *faesten* (fortress) and these names also seem to imply permanent occupation.[35] The Domesday evidence which can be brought to bear on the problem is discussed below.

The *feld* names bring us back to east Sussex. P. A. Nicklin and E. G. Godfrey Faussett published a distribution map of this element in their essay on Sussex place-names in 1935.[36] They did not differentiate between the original use of the name *feld*, meaning 'open land' from the later Middle English use of the term to denote a cultivated field. The latter term occurs frequently in west Sussex manorial accounts of the thirteenth century onwards, but it needs to be eliminated from the present discussion. The use of the earlier meaning draws us to the three eastern rapes, that is to part of Sussex dominated by the *Haestingas*. We have already noted how the element *feld* tends to occur on the higher, bleaker ridges of the High Weald. The question now arises as to what light they thrown on social organisation and settlement evolution. Dr. Margaret Gelling has recently suggested that when *feld* was in living use in the language of Berkshire the term may have been used for belts of common pasture of a heathy type.[37] This attractive idea is certainly worth considering in a Sussex context. Implicit in her suggestion is that the villages which eventually developed on the *felds*, such as Cuckfield, Heathfield, Mayfield, and the like, were later in origin than surrounding farms once inter-commoning their livestock on sites subsequently becoming villages. One of the Sussex *feld* names is compounded with a term which seems to indicate just such a secondary phase of evolving settlement. The name of Ninfield, near Hastings, is thought to mean 'at the newly reclaimed feld' (*[aet] niwnumenanfelda*),[38] which seems to imply land-breaking for cultivation by a community previously settled in the district. Heathfield is possibly another example of a secondary settlement. Its name, compounded with *-feld* and *haeð*, heath, signifies a stretch of once uncultivated open land. We know from thirteenth-century records that Heathfield was an outlier of waste belonging to the manors of Laughton and Bishopstone and that it was then still being colonised. Lindfield, Rotherfield and Sheffield, whose names have been discussed, also appear to have a similar origin. Yet another example is the 'little heath' (*lytean haeðfeld*) mentioned in the Bexhill charter of 772,[39] the first recorded of the Sussex *felds*, which can be identified with the present Barnhorne Woods.

On general grounds, too, we may favour the Gelling hypothesis. The present author has argued that medieval evidence suggests that the course of settlement in the High Weald was for the densely wooded narrow valleys (ghylls) to be colonised before peasants moved upwards on to the more exposed and wilder ridges in the period of rising pressure on land and increased trade in the century before the Black Death in 1348. The example of the evolution of Rotherfield is treated *supra*.

The *leah* names begin with the fifth-century *Andredesleage* when the suffix clearly means woodland and is used in the same sense as *wald*, forest. We next encounter the suffix in charters of 680 and 780 A.D.[40] The Earnley charter of 780, which survives in the original, takes us out of the Weald temporarily, but this is relevant for the language of the charter indicates a change of meaning of *leah*. The phrase 'everything pertaining thereto in fields and woods' (*cum omnibus ad eum pertinentibus rebus, campis, silvis*)[41] suggests that the *-leah* in the peninsula of Selsey comprised both cleared land and woodland. This is confirmed by a further charter relating to Earnley in 930.[42] This therefore records an early use of *leah* to indicate cleared woodland for pasture and arable.

Returning to the Weald, the oldest *leahs* also have the sense of clearing or glade. Three are associated with heathen worship and in date they must take us back to the beginnings of the South Saxon land. Whiligh in Ticehurst and Whyly in East Hoathly, both deep into the Weald, are derived from Old English *weoh*, an idol or shrine. Such religious symbols were commonly established in natural clearings in woodland. Their existence does not necessarily imply permanent settlement in their localities; the seasonal swineherders may have worshipped there during the summer. In Bexhill there is a third 'clearing' of this type, *Thunoresleah*, which can be located by means of the boundary marks given in the charter of 772[43] to the lower edge of the spur of Barnhorne.

The early Saxon charters furnish the names of 11 *leahs* in the Weald, which indicates that the term was in active use from the eighth century. These names may not all mean the same. The *baere leage* at West Hoathly mentioned *c.* 765 (in a corrupt and later copy which nevertheless has an aura of authenticity)[44] is particularly significant for it means 'barley clearing'. Other clearings are indicated by two names in the Hazelhurst, Ticehurst, charter of 1018:[45] *fearnleges* 'the fern clearing' and *runanleages* 'clearing amidst the *brakes or thickets*', and another example is provided in the Washington charter of 947, *Yffeles leah* where it is compounded with a personal name.[46] The remaining *leahs* recorded in Saxon charters are denominated swine-pastures and probably the correct sense of the meaning is nearer the original 'wood' meaning of the fifth century: 'woodland glade' may be the most apposite, the degree of clearing, if any, being uncertain.

It is a long step from the eighth-century charters to Domesday when we discover that 15 Wealden *leahs* had been colonised by villeins and bordars to some extent. With the exception of Bexhill (*Bexlea*), a large manor, the other *leahs* seem to have been relatively small parcels of land, perhaps of between

150–500 acres. From other sources we know that another *leah*, Apsley in Thakeham, was also being farmed in 1073, and *Healdeleia* (Hairley farm in East Grinstead) was cultivated before 1103.[47] Only at this late date are we beginning to gather incontrovertible evidence of permanent Wealden settlement.

The Saxon achievement: a case study

We now have sufficient data to make at least a provisional measure of the stature of the Saxon achievement in clearing and colonising the Weald of Sussex. That the Saxon era was no mere passing phase, but was a formative period in the history of the Wealden landscape is clear from the story we can piece together from place-names and charters as to the origin of settlements. On the sites initially selected by South Saxons for pasture first arose temporarily-occupied huts and then permanent villages and farms. The widespread penetration of the Weald by occasional Saxon herdsmen from far-away coastal villages is fully supported by the evidence we can draw together, but how general was *permanent* occupation in the Saxon Weald? For reasons of space an ideally complete study of this matter cannot be attempted here, but the case study of an arbitrarily chosen area, meant to be suggestive rather than final, may help to bring the problem into clearer focus. The test case selected is the small tract of land extending in an arc around the northern edge of Ashdown Forest, and comprising the headwaters of the river Medway. The tract is small enough to permit us, so to speak, to make a tour of the Saxon farms and hamlets, and in imagination to follow the wood-paths and droveways leading to far-off manors. With the assistance of Domesday, some virtually contemporary evidence, and the testimony of place-names we can minutely explore this little Saxon agrarian landscape and retrospectively catch a glimpse of the collective work actually going on (Fig. 8).

The tract chosen for study in this way is the geographical centre of *Andredesweald*. It was one of the most inaccessible and therefore presumably one of the least attractive of the farming districts of Saxon Sussex. Its hilly topography and thickly-wooded valleys would justify us in believing that we shall be entering a great expanse of woods, unrelieved by cultivation. Nothing is further from the truth. An advance guard of agriculturalists, probably clearing their way westwards up the Medway and northwards up the Ouse and its tributaries, had made many openings and, in the language of the country, had made their *tye* (Old English *teag*, a close, a small enclosure). By the end of the eleventh century the Saxon colonists, who appear to have originated mainly in the coastal manors between the Ouse and Cuckmere, had established themselves in appreciable numbers in this heavily tree-clad and ill-drained countryside. This South Saxon penetration into a borderland of civilisation was evidently of great antiquity, for the county boundary between Sussex, Surrey and Kent in this district is drawn so much in favour of Sussex that it passes well beyond the watershed of Ouse and Medway occupied by Ashdown Forest and even beyond the main headwater of the Medway itself. Further evidence of ancient settlement lies in the element *tye* (*teag*) which is only found in South Saxon and Kent Charters.[48]

For many generations in this district farming doubtless partook of the character of pioneering. We need to endow villeins working a family farm with generous land. A virgate of 100–150 acres, which would have included much uncleared and rough land, is not excessive. Holdings of this size would give a maximum density of settlement of about four-to-six farms a square mile, a thinly-peopled countryside perhaps even by Saxon standards, but probably the limit of the capacity of the High Weald to support in a primitive stage of development. This is not pure conjecture, for the custumal of Rotherfield manor (1346), one of the estates we shall consider, explains that its large virgates, then sub-divided into more intensively-worked farms, were originally each held singly,[49] and similar evidence of a partition of large virgates comes from the adjoining manor of South Malling.

But let us return to the agrarian landscape itself. We shall start at Rotherfield, a royal estate mentioned in the wills of Alfred in 899[50] and of Athelstan Atheling in 1015,[51] and the site of a church dedicated to St. Denis in the eighth century by the monastery of that name.[52] By the time of Domesday, when this great record tells us that 14 villeins working with ploughs inhabited the place, it had at least three centuries of development behind it and the slow process of hewing farms out of the forest had made some headway. A sign of this maturity is the existence of a chapel at its daughter settlement of Frant.[53] When Domesday tells us that each villein had his own plough we presumably have Rotherfield and the dependent settlement at Frant, as doubtless we ought, but we can do this for *c.* 1200, when the amount of villein-held land had not greatly increased above that of Domesday. The important difference between Rotherfield of *c.* 1200 and the place in the fourteenth century is that there was no nucleated village at the earlier date. In Saxon times an 'island' of cleared land wrapped around the parish church, which was probably almost isolated from the pioneer farms in the manor which did not share its hill-top site but were scattered here and there at lower elevations along the sides of the valleys, where spring water, deeper soils and narrow strips of water meadow were at hand. We have, therefore, the somewhat unusual circumstance that many of the relatively outlying, peripheral settlements in the parish of Rotherfield are older than the central nucleated village, the reverse of the 'normal' development in England generally, but the prevailing rule in the High Weald. The origin of such villages warns us against assuming that even a medieval village had been a village from the first.

We now pass north-westwards in our imaginary journey through the past, skirting the park of Rotherfield mentioned in Domesday, into the upper Medway valley. Here we shall never be far from civilisation, for along the banks of this now lovely basin settlers had scattered their habitations uninterruptedly on the natural 'shelves' midway up the valley slopes. Some of these little places are recorded in Domesday itself, or in contemporary, or near contemporary, documents: *Wildene* (probably Withyham), *Apedroc* (Parrock), Brambletye, Hartfield, Standen, and farms set back in a second range to the north—Shovel-strode, *Berchelei* (in Fellbridge), Warley, Hazelden, Brockhurst, Walesbeach, and Fairlight. Several un-named places and a few unidentified places should be added. The total recorded population in Domesday for this little district is a minimum of 44 villeins, 18 bordars, and two serfs, and we have been unable to add any population collectively recorded under larger estates with headquarters elsewhere.

If we now pass on into West Hoathly and its contiguous parishes there are a half dozen place-names of such great antiquity as to imply that the Saxon was amongst the first pioneers up in these hills, stringing out his fences and building some form of house and barn in the woods. The unfolding drama of Saxon forest clearance is illustrated by such names as Selsfield (open land marked by a hall); Tickeridge (ridge of land with an enclosure, *teag,* on it); Burleigh (clearing with a manor house on it), Cuttinglye (Cuþela's clearing). It is worth considering how these names originated. A number appear to have been attached to farms and freshly-turned furrows rising into the view of an observing drover or shepherd, doubtless casting a jealous and uneasy eye on these ominous harbingers of a new way of life. How invaluably these early Saxon names evoke to our mind the small worlds or islands within the greater world of waste in which the pioneers led their lives—the newly-yoked oxen, yellow stubble in newly-fenced enclosures on the hillsides, the breaking of ground and the sowing of crops in the rough surroundings, the loneliness, the dull thud of an axe denoting the building of some sort of house over the hill. It was only as generations passed and the world widened about them that the woodmen also changed. These place-names of the Saxons, their houses, their food and their doings were all such as only the frontier brings.

General conclusions

The cumulative evidence we have been narrowly considering in this case study points clearly to an early Saxon encroachment on the deep Weald. After the lapse of several centuries, this emerges at the end of the eleventh century as a thinly, but fairly evenly, scattered group of permanent pioneer farms on the edge of the un-won waste of Ashdown Forest. So much for the foreground. What of the remaining landscape of the Weald, the largest woodland in Anglo-Saxon England, spreading before us? Do we receive the impression that in the various other districts the stature of the Saxon achievement in forest clearance grows or diminishes?

We cannot yet answer this question with any assurance, for whereas for most parts of England Domesday provides some idea of the extent of clearings at the end of the eleventh century, the Sussex folios are not an adequate source for Sussex settlement history, for they do not separately enumerate colonists in the outlying Wealden parts of manors based on the coastal plain or at the foot of the downs. Yet circumstantial evidence that agriculture had made considerable strides on the basis of a permanently-settled population in these large patches of darkness is impressive. Of special importance is the evidence that churches had been founded in Wealden parishes.

Taking central Sussex as an example, we learn from sources virtually contemporary with Domesday that churches existed in Ardingly, Balcombe, Chiddingly, Cuckfield, East Grinstead, Henfield, Lurgashall, Shipley, Slaugham, West Hoathly, and Wivelsfield. In Domesday itself are mentioned churches at Bexhill, Hamsey, Thakeham, and Woodmancote; *ecclesiola* ('little churches') at Catsfield, Hove, Sedlescombe, and Shermanbury; priests (no churches) at Brambletye (East Grinstead), Broomhill (Catsfield), and Wartling. We have earlier mentioned the eighth-century church at Rotherfield and its chapel in Frant, and the church in Mayfield with which Archbishop Dunstan is associated was built in the tenth century.[54] The surviving architectural features of existing churches at Bolney, Horsted Keynes, and Worth make it evident that these were Saxon built. This information implies that a considerable well-distributed cultivation and its attendant population must have existed in central Sussex by about 1100.

This evidence reinforces Reginald Lennard's injunction that 'we must not be too ready to fill the vacant spaces of the Domesday map with imagined woodland or marsh'.[55] His conclusion that places with large numbers of peasants assigned to them in the Sussex Domesday incorporate particulars of unmentioned places in the outlying Weald is almost certainly correct. We are not straining facts if we even out a little by eye the 94 ploughs and more than 300 peasant households assigned to the manor of South Malling, or the 36½ ploughs and 151 peasants recorded for the manor of Washington; or the 39 ploughs and 129 peasant households; or the 40 ploughs and 132 peasants assigned to Northease and Rodmell respectively, to take but a few examples: we shall have more than enough to provide the Saxon *dens, wicks* and *folds* with busy farmers. There is therefore every reason to believe that the South Saxons had begun to clear and settle the Weald in earnest before Domesday which so inadequately records their achievements.

This does not necessarily mean that the eleventh-century clearings had developed beyond an initial stage when they were insufficient to maintain more than a small group of families in still retarded frontier districts shouldered out by the wilderness. This certainly must be the judgement on the more inaccessible High Weald where colonists were still striking out into the wilder, uninhabited, countryside between 1086 and 1348. The Saxon achievement was to break up the unsettled areas into isolated bodies of settlement. Every generation saw the change deepened, broad woodlands ever encroached upon by peasant clearings. In the process the High Weald became frayed at the edges. On the Low Weald of west Sussex the impact of the expanding Saxon peoples was probably more far-reaching. On the basis of the case study conducted, it is likely that the clearings created by summer grazing on the Low Weald had become permanent farms before Domesday, for their natural environment is better than the sites in the more broken country around Ashdown Forest and they were altogether more accessible from the parent villages. The winning of the wilderness of the Low Weald would not have amounted to a dense settlement, but the foundations of peasant society and the broad outline of settlement distribution was probably laid down in this process. Certainly few new farms appear to have been established on the Low Weald after *c.* 1·150, an important terminal date in its evolution. We are perhaps near the truth if we regard the colonisation of the Sussex Weald as being in two main phases more or less distinct from one another both in time and space, that of the Low Weald being substantially a Saxon achievement, whilst that of the High Weald as primarily to be assigned to the later period of population growth in the twelfth and thirteenth centuries. It would be wrong, however, to assume that the Low Weald Saxons had left their successors nothing to do in the way of forest clearance. As the accompaniment, more or less, of every farm scene, we can probably visualise the oldest worked fields nearest the barns on the 'rising lands' assuming a more garden-like appearance with the greater thoroughness of cultivation in the period between 1086 and 1300, while remoter woods on the lower, wetter clays along the farthest farm-tracks were being grubbed as *rudings* (Middle English, *ridde,* to grub up trees). This impression of the turning of the Sussex Low Weald to greater account is the one we receive from the contemporary documents of the twelfth and thirteenth centuries.[56]

Professor P. H. Sawyer has recently questioned the traditionally held thesis of the slow and continuous process of growth that went to the making of England generally between the fifth and thirteenth centuries.[57] As far as the Weald is concerned, the Saxon place-names and other evidence we have been considering supports the 'conventional' view of persistent growth rather than Professor Sawyer's. It imparts a sense of a countryside in movement, being subjected to a continuous alteration by slow degrees, over the course of centuries. This change cannot all be regarded as having everywhere formed part of a single Saxon endeavour because the remaining wilderness of the Weald was still being fast driven back after the Norman Conquest. Infinitely more labour had to be expended before the Weald was capable of sustaining a considerable population, but the hardest work was the first, and this was a Saxon achievement.

It is against this dynamic situation in the Wealden countryside, and not *in vacuo,* that Professor Glanville Jones's thesis needs to be examined. This postulates that the loosely-grouped cluster of small family farms on shared yardlands of customary land in a thirteenth-century rental of the Archbishop's manor of South Malling are rooted in Celtic *clachans.*[58] An alternative origin for these hamlets can be postulated, however, based on a cycle of development associated with an expanding young frontier community. This evolution is clearest in the neighbourhood of Rotherfield where a number of organically similar hamlets evolved from a single pioneer holding of a named yardland (or its equivalent) as an accompaniment of population increase and the gradual improvement of the farmland by successive generations during a period so relatively recent that it was within the knowledge or experience of a mid-fourteenth-century scribe.[59] Such an evolution is consistent with the known population increase and regional inclination towards land clearance apparent in the Sussex Weald between A.D. 900 and *c.* 1280–1325. This alternative hypothesis relates the Wealden hamlets to the later stages of the settlement processes initiated in the Saxon Age which we have previously considered. The superficial resemblance of the Rotherfield hamlets to Celtic *clachans* is perhaps not surprising when it is considered that both types of hamlet probably resulted from a basically similar process, the reclamation of waste by a group of pioneer farmers.

A better understanding of the problems presented by the Wealden hamlets, re-opened first by J. E. A. Jolliffe and now by Professor Jones, will eventually lead us closer to an apprehension of the realities of the Saxon past. Although the main lines of the later story of man's colonisation of the Weald are well enough known, much more work is needed to penetrate the obscurity which still hides in so many various ways the story of the South Saxon as the foe of the desolate primeval landscape of the Weald. The task will need the co-ordinated approach of archaeology (including field archaeology), history, and place-name studies on the lines envisiged by F. T. Wainwright, and also set out so convincingly, and with such elegant simplicity, by J. H. Round in his pioneer paper on the Sussex place-names written as long ago as 1899.[60]

VII

THE CHURCH IN SAXON SUSSEX

D. P. Kirby

THE HISTORY of the Saxon Church in Sussex, which is generally regarded as beginning with the missionary activity of St. Wilfrid among the South Saxons in the 680s, and the founding of the see of Selsey, was brought to an end in 1070 when Aethelric, bishop of Selsey, was deposed by William the Conqueror and his advisers at Windsor in the presence of a papal legate—uncanonically, according to one chronicler, for he had not committed any crime[1]—and placed in confinement by the king at Marlborough. At this time there was a purge of leading Anglo-Saxon secular and ecclesiastical lords, many of whom were indeed potential rebels, and some of the prelates had compromised themselves either by previous uncanonical actions or by association with resistance to the Conqueror— or the Bastard, as contemporaries called him. William may not have wished to leave the South Saxon diocese, so strategically close to the continent (as the career of William himself had demonstrated), in the hands of any native bishop. Aethelric was replaced by one of William's chaplains, Stigand (1070-87), who moved his see from the old Saxon centre at Selsey[2] to the larger town of Chichester in 1075.[3]

No Saxon remains now survive at Selsey, and the only possible Saxon work at Chichester occurs in part of the south wall of what was the church of St. Olave.[4] The greater part of the fabric of the cathedral church of Holy Trinity, Chichester, dates to the time of Bishop Ralph (1091-1108) who built the first Norman cathedral apparently on the site of an existing Saxon church, a rather austere construction with very little in the way of embellishment or decoration.[5] D. Talbot Rice suggested that the famous Chichester panels, one of which depicts the raising of Lazarus, the other Martha and Mary greeting Christ at Jerusalem, may date to c. 1050 and might have been brought from Selsey to the new cathedral at Chichester.[6] Nevertheless, although A. W. Clapham maintained that the panels had 'few points of contact with post-Conquest sculpture' and dated to 'the late Saxon period',[7] it is clear that Talbot Rice's own reasoning, which led him to admit French influence and gravitate finally to a date c. 1080,[8]

160

precluded a Saxon Selsey origin. T. D. Kendrick, in fact, considered the 'heavy' treatment of the figures and the ponderous draperies to be non-Saxon, and, from continental analogies, likely to belong to the first half of the twelfth century,[9] a dating with which G. Zarnecki agreed, noting derivations from Anglo-Saxon art certainly, but emphasising rather analogies with the St. Alban's Psalter of the period 1119–45.[10]

Sussex, however, has a relatively high number of Anglo-Saxon churches, that is churches containing in their existing stone fabric surviving features of a pre-Conquest building. H. M. and J. Taylor provide a total list, with accompanying descriptions, of 26 churches in Sussex in origin at least of Anglo-Saxon date on the evidence of architectural style, and another five which are more doubtful if not, in some cases, wholly post-Conquest.[11] On a county basis only Norfolk (with 54 and 11 doubtful), Lincolnshire (47 and two doubtful), and Kent (36 and one doubtful) have higher figures. E. A. Fisher[12] included the five regarded as doubtful by the Taylors as revealing Anglo-Saxon traces, and actually added *another* thirty. Now this is a serious discrepancy, and it must be apparent immediately that the observer who is not an architectural historian must proceed carefully. The Taylors' list of 26 must be regarded as basic, and any addition to this list viewed with very marked circumspection. Whereas, for example, E. A. Fisher could write of St. Cross church, Bignor, that 'doorways, chancel arch, font and parts at least of the walling may well be Saxon',[13] the Taylors comment that at Bignor 'there are no distinctive features to fix a pre-Conquest date'.[14]

The problem is partly a tendency to see as pre-Conquest, architectural features which may not be. Only the *lower* part of the tower of Singleton church dates from *c.* 950–1000, not the tower as a whole,[15] and similarly the four receding stages of roughly equivalent height in the tower of Bishopstone church are not a typically Saxon feature, and the belfry openings are not of the usual Saxon double type 'but exemplify a typically Norman arrangement, namely a large round-headed single opening subdivided only on the exterior wall face'.[16] The Saxons constructed tall, narrow doorways, and there is one such doorway at Wivelsfield. Although including Wivelsfield church as one of their 26, the Taylors nevertheless comment: 'On the strength of this doorway, we would not wish to claim a pre-Conquest date or Anglo-Saxon style. We would rather say that the date is uncertain and the style shows Anglo-Saxon affinities'.[17] It is clear that some features are really dateless to within 50 or more years either side of 1066. The Taylors were aware of this. 'This is one of the several Sussex two-cell churches which are so difficult to date with certainty', they write of St. Andrew's, Tangmere,[18] and they relegated Tangmere to the 'doubtfuls'. How difficult the matter can become is revealed by their comment on Ford church, in which they were inclined to accept a Saxon element, 'although the church has no feature which would by itself be conclusive'.[19]

The problem is more particularly that of 'the Saxo-Norman overlap'. For a period of time before and after 1066, no differences of construction necessarily emerged to distinguish pre- from post-Conquest. Dr. Fisher himself was aware, naturally, of this dilemma, observing, 'some writers describe as early Norman churches which have no specifically Saxon features even though they may have no Norman features either'.[20] Of the church of St. Botolph, Hardham, the Taylors comment that it is 'difficult to date with certainty because, although a number of original features have survived, yet these are all of the type that could belong either to the late Saxon period or the early Norman'.[21] In a conservative area, and this was the basis of Fisher's position, a church could be loosely described as 'Saxon' in style as late as *c.* 1150, but many of the churches of the mid-eleventh or mid-twelfth century possessed features neither 'Saxon' nor 'Norman': 'they are simply examples of vernacular stone-building methods unaffected by changes in major building styles or of political overlordship'.[22] In such a situation, precise 'Saxon' or 'Norman' dating will indeed be very difficult, if not impossible. While accepting the presence of several such churches in Sussex, any discussion of ecclesiastical architecture in Sussex before the Conquest must necessarily relate to those churches which have retained undeniable Anglo-Saxon details.[23]

And here we are dealing with a mere handful compared with the number of churches in existence in Sussex in 1066—the existence of probably about 100 is revealed by Domesday Book, to which figure many more should certainly be added[24]—and conspicuous by their absence are the majority of those which appear in the historical records. The church of St. Andrew, Steyning, where King Aethelwulf, the father of Alfred the Great, was buried, is an obvious example.[25] Very many early churches, of course, like that at Mayfield with which Archbishop Dunstan in the tenth century is associated, will have been wooden constructions.[26] In the greater proportion of instances, pre-Conquest building has been destroyed by subsequent renovation.[27] Of St. Andrew's, Jevington, E. A. Fisher commented: 'The nave and western tower are at least in part Saxon but were so drastically over-restored in 1873 that many original features have been destroyed or obscured'.[28] The Taylors, more cautiously and more bluntly, declared that the church 'has unfortunately suffered so heavily at the hands of nineteenth-century restorers that its Anglo-Saxon features are almost unrecognisable'.[29] The church at Bishopstone, also dedicated to St. Andrew, affords an excellent illustration of the process by which an originally fairly simple Saxon church was transformed during the Middle Ages. The original west doorway was blocked up by Norman builders prior to the addition at the west end of a tower. In the twelfth century the pre-Conquest chancel was demolished in order to extend the nave eastward. Later, in the period of transition to Early English, the Norman chancel was extended further eastward, and a north aisle was added to the nave. Finally, in the thirteenth century, the chancel arch and the north arcade seem to have been rebuilt in the Early English style.[30]

Sussex is poor (because of its chalk) in native building stone and no 'schools of stonecraft' developed in early Sussex: Sussex masons were not particularly highly skilled 'and this may account for the severely plain, rather primitive looking churches, almost, if not quite, free from ornament'.[31] Most of the Saxon churches in Sussex before the Norman Conquest do appear to have been simple and basic in design. Such basic simplicity, therefore, is not necessarily an indication in Sussex of great antiquity. The only church in Sussex for which any appreciable antiquity within the Anglo-Saxon period can perhaps be claimed is that of St. Peter, Westhampnett, near Chichester, on the Roman Stane Street from Chichester to London, where the original early walling was 'of stone and flint rubble, with a liberal admixture of Roman tiles laid in herring-bone fashion'. The arched head of the chancel arch is 'wholly built of Roman tiles' and Roman tiles were used 'liberally in the surrounding walling'. Such a profuse use of Roman tiles is rather unusual and implies a date early enough for them to have been in plentiful supply.[32] Otherwise, a simple structure may belong to the late Saxon period. The church of St. James, Selham, is 'a particularly interesting example of the small, simple parish church which originally consisted of a rectangular nave with an almost square chancel'.[33] St. John the Baptist, Clayton, 'does not now look very different from the aisleless nave and chancel that were built about nine hundred years ago'.[34] Note that 900 years ago implies a late Saxon date, *c.* 1000 or after. St. Botolph's church, Hardham, which could even have been built after 1066, 'has preserved its original form almost unchanged, except for the addition of a porch to protect the north door; and it still consists of the original aisleless square-ended chancel, and aisleless rectangular nave'.[35]

Anglo-Saxon churches[36] were distinguished by thin, high walls, often imperfectly orientated or irregularly laid out, fabric of flint and rubble, high narrow doorways and narrow (in their basic form) single-splayed windows, large quoins and by their (again in basic form) single two-cell structure (chancel and nave). A conspicuous feature often seems to have been the chancel arch. The arguments in favour of the church of St. Mary, Chithurst, which have been variously dated pre- and post-Conquest, possessing features of Anglo-Saxon workmanship 'are the tall, thin walls; the large quoin stones; the tall, narrow chancel arch; and the simple window with its inner splay continued right through the wall'.[37] So also the external evidence of pre-Conquest date for Clayton church are 'the massive quoins and the disproportionate height of the walls'.[38] The north doorway of St. James, Selham, 'is a tall narrow opening, cut straight through the wall', but the most elaborate and distinctive feature of the church is the fine chancel arch.[39] At St. Nicholas, Worth, two very tall narrow doorways in the side walls of the nave 'are extreme examples of the Anglo-Saxon love of tall narrow openings, for their height is about four times their width', while 'The chancel arch is one of the most impressive that survive from before the Conquest. The whole composition is thoroughly Anglo-Saxon in all its somewhat incongruous but nevertheless impressive components'.[40]

By 1066 a proportion of ecclesiastical buildings in England were becoming increasingly elaborate. There had, of course, been richly decorated exceptions in the pre-Viking period (as at St. Wilfrid's, Hexham)—with chapels, and eastern, central and western towers, and a cruciform plan with transepts (not all features, of course, necessarily together). The Saxon churches of Sussex do not appear to have been among the most developed of the cruciform design with tower and transepts, but a number have interesting examples of one or other of these elaborations. Some may have been obscured by later developments. The Saxon church of St. Nicholas, Old Shoreham, *did* have transepts and a west tower, only the Saxon west tower has now disappeared, almost—but fortunately not quite—without trace: 'There seems little doubt that the thicker-walled western part of the nave was formerly an Anglo-Saxon west tower . . . It also seems reasonable to assume that the Normans lengthened the nave by absorbing the Anglo-Saxon west tower into it, and that they created a new tower over the Anglo-Saxon chancel, and then built a new chancel further to the east'.[41] Here again a fascinating glimpse of the process of transformation is presented. At Bishopstone, a south chapel or *porticus* balanced by a north *porticus* represented a degree of elaboration in the Saxon period.[42] Baldwin Brown was disposed to date Bishopstone to the early tenth century.[43] At Bishopstone perhaps, but certainly at Worth, there was the noteworthy absence of the west wall of the 'crossing' between two *porticus* or two transepts.[44] Worth, regarded (with Bosham and Sompting) as among the more distinguished of early Sussex churches,[45] was a late-Saxon transeptal church,[46] the walls of the transepts, however, being only half the height of those of the nave.[47] St. Mary, Stoughton, which was held by Earl Godwin in the time of Edward the Confessor and which has remarkable similarities to Bosham church, particularly in its chancel arch, was also transeptal, and built on 'an unusually large and ambitious scale'.[48]

The church of Holy Trinity, Bosham, near Chichester, has acquired a unique reputation among the Saxon churches of Sussex because of Earl Harold's association with it in the 1060s before his fateful visit to William of Normandy, and its subsequent, albeit stylised, representation in the Bayeux Tapestry. It was not a transeptal church, but it is comparable in scale to Stoughton (without the transepts, of course), well-built (despite odd angles), possessing a striking chancel arch, and a west tower, the walls of which are almost 55ft. in height.[49] The church shows no fabric earlier than the eleventh century, though its history, of course, goes back into the seventh.[50] In the eleventh century it was one of the richest churches in England. Edward the Confessor granted it to Osbern, his kinsman, later bishop of Exeter (1072–1103). The church of St. Mary, Sompting, near Worthing, is another church of importance, with a tower, 75ft. in total height and a very fine tower arch.[51] This church, as is well known, is 'unique in possessing a pre-Conquest form of shingled pyramidal spire', now in the form of a Rhenish helm (so-called from the development of the form in the Rhineland), consisting of a four-sided gabled roof, the only Saxon tower to have retained its early roof form.[52]

Whether pre-Conquest Norman influence 'would probably be more strongly felt in Sussex than in most parts of England outside London'[53] is debatable. This is a matter which would require very careful consideration with reference to the evidence (and possible destruction of it) in other south-eastern counties. Certainly too much should not be made of the use of Caen stone in the years before 1066.[54] An Anglo-Saxon sundial on Bishopstone church inscribed with the name 'Eadric' (whom it would be hazardous to try to identify), however, is of Caen stone from Normandy. The decorative motifs in Sussex churches of the Saxon period are conventional. There is nothing about what survives to indicate the *avant garde*. Oddly enough, Bosham, where elaborate Saxon decoration might be expected, exhibits nothing remarkable. For what there is, one must look elsewhere. At Selham the northern impost of the chancel arch seems to be 'a section of re-used Roman string-course or architrave, still bearing its original classical mouldings',[55] while much of the remaining decorative work in the church is typically Anglo-Saxon with inter-laced creatures and leaf-patterns ('linked acanthus or palmette leaves').[56] In fact, the capitals of the chancel arch 'are square in plan above and circular in plan below, so as to conform to their supporting shafts. In the northern capital, the transition from the square to the circle is effected by the traditional artifice of volutes at angles, but in the southern capital, a typically Anglo-Saxon device is used, whereby heads of monsters occupy the upper corners, while their interlaced bodies cover the lower parts'.[57] Saxon pilaster strips (functional as well as decorative), common in Saxon churches, but rarely surviving in Sussex, occur in the walls of the tower at Sompting.[58] The tower arch at Sompting is decorated with Anglo-Saxon foliated ornamentation with large volutes or horns, reflective of Scandinavian Ringerike art, on the capitals 'whose scrolls are placed at the top, enclosing circular areas that are filled with representations of bunches of grapes'.[59] A series of carved stones also at Sompting may have formed part of the pre-Conquest church, perhaps as an altar-front or reredos. They now represent three portions of a wall-arcade of semi-circular arches, eight lengths of friezes of palmette ornament, a fragment of a scrolled ornament, and a figure of a nimbed abbot.[60] All these features, together with its 'Rhenish' helm give Sompting a special place among the Saxon churches of Sussex. Another carving of interest—and uncertain date—is to be found in Jevington church, 'a full-length nimbed figure of Christ carved in relief . . . holding a cross-headed shaft, and standing above a curiously interlaced snake-like animal, or pairs of animals in the "Urnes" style'.[61] This is 'One of the few remaining pieces of Saxon sculpture in England showing the Scandinavian Urnes type of ornament. The two grotesque animals at the feet of Christ consist almost entirely of complicated Urnes interlace'.[62] T. D. Kendrick dated the slab to about 1100, Talbot Rice to *c*. 1050.[63] Kendrick comments that it 'can only have been because native art had nothing more satisfactory to offer that the matured "snake" Urnes style' was deemed 'an intelligible symbol of the animal form that could without incongruity be paraded before Englishmen in Sussex as the companion of a figure of Christ'.[64]

A glimpse of how the South Saxons in the eleventh century saw Christianity may be afforded by the wall paintings at Plumpton, Hardham and elsewhere, and more particularly at Clayton. The paintings at Hardham and Clayton have been dated, on the one hand, as late as 1125 and after,[65] and, on the other, to the time of William of Warenne, who held the Rape of Lewes under the Conqueror, *c*. 1080.[66] While Anglo-Saxon characteristics are detectable in these murals, continental influences, particularly from Flanders, are more so, but their probable proximity in date to pre-Conquest Sussex and their high artistic quality reveal something of what the men of Sussex were expected to comprehend when they went inside these Saxon churches. At Hardham, 'the complete story of salvation' is 'clearly and systematically presented' in scenes from the Infancy of Christ, the Passion, Christ in Majesty, and the Torments of the Damned.[67] The paintings of St. John the Baptist, Clayton, have been most graphically described. The Last Judgement is represented above the chancel arch with Christ as the central figure and processions of adoring figures on either side. He is clearly sitting in judgement. On the upper zone of the north wall appear to be depicted the fall of Anti-Christ and the Reception of the Blessed (which usually forms part of a Last Judgement composition) who are approaching the Holy City where stands St. Peter to welcome them. The paintings on the lower zone of the north wall represent the Resurrection. On the upper zone of the south wall (those on the lower have been destroyed), the paintings evidently refer to the end of the world and the Last Judgement, with the juxtaposition of the Cross and the figure of Death in relation to the procession so placed as to indicate that the figures in the procession are saved by coming to the Cross from Death and Damnation.[68] 'No example of a similar juxtaposition of the Cross and Death has been found in either medieval art or literature'.[69]

This, then, was the Christian message in Sussex as Anglo-Saxon art was being transformed by new Romanesque influences in the period of the Saxo-Norman overlap while England moved from the Germanic Baltic world into a new French feudal Europe. Whence did the Christian message originate in Sussex? It originated, of course, with Wilfrid, exiled bishop of York, long before, in the seventh century, for the Christian alternative of Salvation or Damnation will have been as starkly presented by him among the pagan South Saxons as it was by the murals of Clayton which, as a connoisseur of fine art, he would surely have admired.

*   *   *   *   *   *

The career of Wilfrid, bishop of York has recently been studied from several different viewpoints.[70] The *Life of Wilfrid* written by the priest, Stephen, regarded generally as Eddius Stephanus,[71] compiled at an uncertain date after the death of Wilfrid, probably requires further source-criticism before it can be fully exploited. It is, however, a unique literary source from the age of Bede. Bede's own *Ecclesiastical History of the English People,* compiled in 731,[72] is much more other-worldly, but dominates the historical achievement of Bede's own time. Eddius Stephanus was concerned to vindicate Wilfrid, to demonstrate how the persecutions of kings and the hardships of exile had been caused, not by any fault on Wilfrid's part but rather by the jealous envy of wicked enemies. For Bede, Wilfrid was a part, if a stormy part, of the golden age of the English Church as Bede saw it, the age of the Conversion. And it is when Wilfrid comes in his life as a missionary exile into Sussex that the historian is provided with his most vivid glimpse of the early South Saxon kingdom and nascent Christianity within it.

Following his expulsion from Northumbria in 678 and his first appeal to Rome, Wilfrid was again driven out of Northumbria and came by way of Mercia and Wessex into Sussex. During a sea journey from Gaul to England in 666,

Wilfrid had apparently been driven ashore on the Sussex coast. The region was, it is said, quite unknown to Wilfrid and his companions, but the receding tide left ship and men stranded. The pagan inhabitants of the vicinity gathered, led by a pagan chief priest, intending to seize the ship, plunder it, slay any who resisted and lead the remainder into slavery, for they regarded everything the sea cast onto the shore as theirs. A stone from the sling of one of Wilfrid's companions slew the chief priest, which seems to have been the signal for open warfare. Three times the defenders on the ship repulsed their assailants. As the pagans were preparing for their fourth attack and their king had arrived, the ship was able to sail again on the incoming tide, and so Wilfrid and his party escaped with few losses.[73] The incident is a vivid one and well told. How unfortunate that the name of the king is not given, but probably neither Wilfrid nor his companions knew it. The story was not included in the *Life* to shed light on the pagan South Saxons, of course, but to emphasise the miraculous power of a saintly Wilfrid. The crux of the episode for the writer of the *Life* is that God sent the tide back sooner than usual in answer to Wilfrid's prayers. H. Mayr-Harting has drawn attention, moreover, to the 'phenomenal use of the Old Testament' in the *Life of Wilfrid,* and in this episode on the shores of Sussex 'the guns of the Old Testament flash and pound'. Wilfrid is like Gideon; the sling expert like David to the pagan priest's Goliath; Wilfrid's followers numbered 120 only, one, as the *Life* states, for each year in the life of Moses, a number which constituted that 'of the primitive Church who received the Holy Spirit'; Hur and Aaron, Joshua against Amalek, and the forces of the Midianites are also mentioned in the course of the narrative. 'The story of the Sussex beach makes very good allegorical sense in the light of all this': the *Life* is seeing Wilfrid essentially in the garb of an Old Testament prophetic figure.[74] The literary and scriptural gloss on the event in Sussex naturally means that the account in the *Life* is not necessarily wholly historical. But there is no reason to doubt that Wilfrid did indeed have an unpleasant experience on the coast of Sussex, and 'the heathen who from his high mound cursed the company of Christians with St. Wilfrid seems to be directly related to the prophesying from a high place' (a 'howe' or mound) 'by the Scandinavian *völva* (seeress)'.[75] Here may well be a glimpse of Old English paganism.

A further glimpse is afforded in the account of Wilfrid's actual mission to the South Saxons in the period 681-6, following his exile from Northumbria. Bede records that for three years before Wilfrid's arrival in Sussex no rain had fallen in those parts so that a most terrible famine assailed the people and destroyed them. Forty or fifty men, wasted with hunger, would go together to some precipice or to the seashore where they would join hands and leap into the sea, perishing either by falling or by drowning. But, continues Bede, on the very day that the people received Christian baptism from Wilfrid a gentle rain fell, the earth revived, the fields once more became green, and a fruitful season followed.[76] The rather grim story has a nevertheless charming conclusion. There are, however, certain points to notice about it. Bede, of course, probably thought that he was describing the suicide of starving people.

He was, but their act of suicide possessed a pagan significance no doubt unappreciated by Bede. These unfortunates were almost certainly sacrificial offerings. The Scandinavians are known to have conducted ritual suicides in times of famine, when men and women would hurl themselves over cliffs believing that they were going to Valhalla by so doing.[77] This was the pagan world in Sussex which the early missionaries found.

A second point about this story, however, is that, sensational though the circumstances of the famine would seem to be and impressive the miracle of the rain at baptism, the *Life of Wilfrid* does not include it. The famine and the juxtaposition of the revival of fruitfulness with the acceptance of Christianity savour rather of a miracle-story grafted on to traditions about Wilfrid in Sussex and not at first part of the original tradition. Wilfrid was granted land during his stay in Sussex at Selsey where he founded a monastery[78] which seems to have enjoyed a lively sense of the visionary and the miraculous.[79] The elaboration of the miraculous details of the conversion of the South Saxons could well have originated in the monastery of Selsey. Certainly from wherever Bede derived this episode, it was not from the *Life*.[80] A further point to notice is that Bede proceeded immediately to relate how, though the sea and rivers abounded with fish, the South Saxons on his arrival knew only how to catch eels: Wilfrid and his followers taught them how to fish with their eel-nets, so winning the hearts of all, temporal blessings increasing the hope of heavenly ones.[81] Admittedly Bede, by his literary expertise, has interwoven this second story into the account of the famine and drought so skilfully as to give the superficial impression of a single whole: but it looks very much as if he is offering here what was in origin a quite separate, earlier explanation of Wilfrid's missionary success in Sussex. Devoid of miraculous overtones, it appears to reflect a less developed stratum of tradition, a stratum in the process of being depressed by the more dramatic story of the rain on the day of baptism. The account of this instruction in fishing is not in the *Life* either.

What does the *Life* report of Wilfrid's activities in Sussex? According to the *Life of Wilfrid*, following his expulsion from Northumbria, there was only one place where Wilfrid could enjoy safety from his enemies, the area of Sussex which, we are told, dense forests and a rocky coast had saved from conquest by other kingdoms (a detail of interest for the political history of early Saxon Sussex). The country had remained persistently heathen. Wilfrid sought out the king, Aethelwealh, and threw himself on his mercy. Aethelwealh granted Wilfrid his protection. Wilfrid, not unnaturally delighted, gave thanks to God and began gently to persuade the king and queen to accept the word of God: then, with royal permission, he preached to the people who had never before heard the Gospel. Hosts of pagans, some freely, some (it is interesting to discover) at the king's command, numbering many thousands, were baptised in one day, and the king gave up his own estate to Wilfrid for an episcopal seat to which he later added land at Selsey.[82] The last detail is striking. The episcopal seat of the South Saxons was clearly intended at first to be elsewhere than at Selsey. Selsey was simply a secondary foundation, which Bede indeed refers to, not as a bishopric in his account of Sussex, but as a monastery.[83] Bede describes Selsey as on a peninsula, surrounded on all sides by the sea except on the west where it could be approached by a narrow strip of land. The 250 male and female slaves whom Wilfrid found on his 87 hides of land at Selsey and freed are an indication of the probably very high percentage of slaves in England at this time.

It is recognised that the *Life of Wilfrid* is extremely partisan. Its purpose is to magnify Wilfrid as well as vindicate him. This is quite evident in its account of Wilfrid in Sussex. Bede knew that Aethelwealh and his queen, Eabe, were already Christian. Aethelwealh had been baptised in the midland kingdom of Mercia, in the reign of and at the suggestion of Wulfhere, king of Mercia, indeed in his presence, probably on the occasion of his marriage to Eabe, a Christian princess from among the Hwicce (of Worcestershire and bordering counties). The date of Aethelwealh's marriage and baptism will have been before 675, for King Wulfhere died in that year.[84] Wulfhere, who dominated the political scene in southern England by the end of his reign, detached the Isle of Wight and the province of Meonware (in Hampshire, opposite Wight) from Wessex and gave them to Aethelwealh.[85] It was this act which was subsequently to bring down the vengeance of Caedwalla of Wessex upon Aethelwealh.

Bede would seem to have been having difficulty reconciling the tradition that Sussex was wholly heathen when Wilfrid arrived there, with this previous baptism of the king and queen. After describing Aethelwealh's baptism, his reference to Eabe leads him to state that apart from her the South Saxons were ignorant of Christianity, but he had just declared that Aethelwealh's ealdormen and *gesiths* were cleansed with him in the holy fount of baptism. It is conceivable that Aethelwealh and his entourage lapsed into paganism on their return to Sussex, or on the death of Wulfhere, but there are other indications of a dilemma. Not only did Bede know of an Irish Monk, Dícuill, and his companions living a life of pious austerity at Bosham—though the dominant tradition from Wilfridian circles that Sussex was steadfastly pagan obliged him to declare that none of the natives followed the way of life of these Irish pilgrims or listened to their preaching—but he adds that after the baptism of Aethelwealh and his marriage to Eabe, the priests, Eappa, Padda, Burghelm, and Eddi, baptised the rest of the common people 'either then or later on'. Wilfrid's contacts with Wulfhere had evidently been very close:[86] it is unlikely that Wulfhere would have allowed Aethelwealh to return to his own kingdom without a supporting missionary task-force.[87] The suspicion must be quite strong that the kingdom of the South Saxons was not quite as totally pagan on Wilfrid's arrival as Wilfridian tradition sought to maintain. The sending of priests 'then' as well as 'later on' appears to derive from Mercian or more probably Hwiccian tradition (it is certainly quite independent of the *Life*), uncontaminated by Wilfridian publicity and reaching Bede probably via the monastery of Whitby, from whence Oftfor, former bishop of the Hwicce in the 690s, had come and about whom Bede learnt a considerable amount, as he did also about his predecessors, another of whom also came from Whitby.[88] If, as seems not impossible, the Eddi who worked among the South Saxons is to be identified with the Eddius Stephanus who accompanied Wilfrid to Northumbria in the 660s, it is perhaps odd that the *Life* does not record in greater detail the conversion of the South Saxons. This is but one of many details which may well necessitate a reappraisal of the traditional view of the authorship by Eddius of the *Life of Wilfrid*. What is immediately relevant here, however, is that the history of Wilfrid's mission to the South Saxons is not free from problems. It is likely that Wilfrid did conduct missionary work in the kingdom in the 680s, but it is also probable that he was accelerating the activity of already established Christian communities rather than introducing Christianity for the first time; and there is every reason to suspect that some at least of the traditions regarding his personal participation in evangelising should be treated circumspectly as the later hagiographical legend of Wilfridian circles. It could be that Christianity secured a foothold very early in Sussex, if the South Saxon, Damian, bishop of Rochester, *c.* 660,[89] was first converted in his native kingdom: but unfortunately there can be no certainty here, for he might well have been South Saxon by birth but (for reasons we do not know) brought up in Kent.[90]

The history of the Christian communities in Sussex after the conversion is extremely obscure. Sussex is poor even in local hagiographical cults which could have shed some light on its ecclesiastical history. If the legend of St. Lewina, whose relics were found at or near Seaford in 1058 has a historical basis at all, she is more likely to have perished during the Viking raids than in pre-Christian times: but it would be unwise to seek to comment definitively on the evidence available.[91] Though probably more historical, St. Cuthman, whose devotion to his invalid mother with whom he tramped the countryside pushing her in a barrow, is a conspicuous feature of his legend, is really associated only with the church of Steyning, which he built, perhaps in the ninth century.[92] It would not be surprising if a pagan relapse occurred when the West Saxon exile, Caedwalla, slew King Aethelwealh, detached Wilfrid from Sussex, and gained the support of Wilfrid for himself, re-annexed Wight and the Meonware, slew one of Aethelwealh's successors, Berhthun, and brought the kingdom under a West Saxon domination which his successor, Ine (688–726), maintained.[93] This sequence of events must have caused considerable dislocation. Moreover, internal divisions within Sussex may have rendered the growth of the Church in different parts variable. Wilfrid's monastery at Selsey enjoyed an uninterrupted existence,[94] but the oppression of Caedwalla and Ine was so harsh, apparently, that the kingdom had no bishop of its own, being subject to the authority of Winchester.[95] Sussex, however, is not at all rich in surviving pagan place-names,[96] which is a testimony not to the initial strength or weakness of South Saxon paganism, but to the activity of the missionary Church,[97] whether from established Christian communities within Sussex (not necessarily all Wilfridian) or from ecclesiastical centres (like Winchester) outside the kingdom. Irish influence may have continued as an effective force, despite Bede's indifference to Dícuill.[98] The south of England generally was a principal overland route for travel from Ireland to the continent.

*   *   *   *   *   *

It was probably while Aldhelm was bishop of Sherborne (705-9), and the West Saxon diocese had been finally partitioned, not after his death,[99] that the South Saxons were given an episcopal see of their own and Eadberht was consecrated first bishop: he had been abbot of Selsey and it was natural for him to retain Selsey as his see.[100] Eadberht was present at the council of *Clofesho* in 716.[101] His successor, Eolla, who was also formerly abbot of Selsey, had died some years before Bede completed the *Ecclesiastical History,* and the see was still vacant (731).[102] What caused this break in succession is not known. Perhaps West Saxon pressure was again serious. In 733, however, Archbishop Tatwine consecrated Sigeferth bishop,[103] and the names of successive bishops are known from surviving episcopal lists.[104] No further firm dates for South Saxon bishops occur until Aethelgar (subsequently to become archbishop of Canterbury in 988) was consecrated, according to the *Anglo-Saxon Chronicle* C on May 2, 980, except for Beornhaeth who became bishop of Sussex in 909 on the great reorganisation of the Church in southern England that year. Their approximate dates have to be inferred from the appearance of their names in the witness lists of Anglo-Saxon diplomas or charters.[105] Gislhere, Wihthun, Aethelwulf and Coenred are the first bishops of Selsey regularly to attend great councils and witness charters from the 780s to the 830s, soon after which a decrease tends to occur in the total number of Saxon diplomas, 'but when the regular flow is resumed about 930 the bishops of Selsey are revealed as taking a frequent part in the councils of the king'.[106]

There is a certain dearth of documents, however, from early Sussex itself. The Saxon charters which do survive are rarely contemporary texts or even pre-Conquest,[107] which makes it impossible to reconstruct a detailed history of the Church among the South Saxons before 1066. 'If the church of Selsey had kept a record comparable to the *Liber Vitæ* of Durham, or if its charters had been preserved like those of Canterbury and Rochester, many of the more serious difficulties in the interpretation of Sussex place-names would never have arisen'.[108] The same is true of the fullness of our knowledge of ecclesiastical developments. Despite attempts to infer details of Church organisation from Domesday Book, H. Poole declared 'the D.B. data do not appear to me to indicate any "ecclesiastical organization" at all', only that churches were better recorded in the richer south of the area than in the poorer wooded north: and he concluded that geological structure and settled conditions played a greater part in the distribution of early churches than ecclesiastical organisation, even 'that the existence or non-existence of a church depended largely on the landholder',[109] in which respect he was almost certainly correct. A few early grants to churches and monasteries (including Selsey) have been preserved.[110] In 714 Nunna, king of the South Saxons, granted land to the brethren at Selsey.[111] Another interesting, if brief, early charter relating to Selsey records the grant of land at Highleigh, Sussex, to Eadberht, abbot of ('the island which is called') Selsey, *c.* 700, by a South Saxon *dux*, clearly a leading member of the nobility, witnessed by King Nunna and King Watt.[112] A further document gives 'a complete and interesting— indeed unique— history of the land of Peppering almost throughout the eighth century'.[113] Political domination by Mercia, of course, becomes very apparent in the charters from the eighth century. No South Saxon charters are confirmed by Aethelbald of Mercia (716–57), but Offa (757–96) certainly made his influence felt.[114] A grant in 770 by Osmund, king of the South Saxons, of land at Henfield to the church of St. Peter, Henfield, was confirmed by Offa.[115] Another grant in the same year by Oslac, ealdorman of the South Saxons, made at Selsey to a church of St. Paul in Sussex in the time of Bishop Gislhere, was not confirmed by Offa until between 786–96 in the time of Bishop Wihthun. It is a document of peculiar interest, being the earliest South Saxon charter to survive in contemporary form and reveals the local script as crude by comparison with the later Mercian endorsement.[116] By now the kings of Sussex had been reduced to the status of *duces* by Offa. Between 772 and 787 Offa confirmed a grant of wooded land to the church of St. Peter, Selsey, by Ealdwulf, *dux* of the South Saxons,[117] and in (probably) 791 a grant by the same Ealdwulf to Wihthun, bishop of Selsey, for the church of St. Andrew, Ferring.[118] In 801 Cenwulf, king of Mercia, Offa's eventual successor, evidently after a dispute over ownership, confirmed land at Denton in Sussex, which had been given previously by Abbot Plegheard who had received it from King Offa, to Wihthun and the church of Selsey.[119] The Mercian rulers behaved quite autocratically in their dealings with the Church, and from 817 there was a major quarrel between Cenwulf and Wulfred archbishop of Canterbury, which Cenwulf's successors were not able finally to resolve until 825 or even 827.[120] The Church in Sussex was not unaffected. After Cenwulf's death, one very interesting document relates, 'Many discords and innumerable quarrels' arose in the Church, in the course of which Coenred, bishop of Selsey, lost the property at Denton which Cenwulf had confirmed as his, probably to Cenwulf's brother and successor, Ceolwulf I (821–3). The matter was settled in favour of Selsey at *Clofesho* in 825 at the same time as a settlement with Wulfred was being arranged.[121]

The defeat of the Mercian forces at *Ellandun* (Wroughton) in Wiltshire in 825 marked the beginning of permanent West Saxon supremacy over south-east England, including Sussex. Successive kings of Wessex must have made many grants to the episcopal see at Selsey. Alfred the Great possessed estates in Sussex and first received Asser, who was eventually to write the *Life* of Alfred, at West Dean. His father, King Aethelwulf, who died in 858 was first buried in the church at Steyning. In 930 King Athelstan, Alfred's grandson, gave land at Medmerry and Earnley in Sussex to Beornhaeth, bishop of Selsey. King Edmund, Athelstan's brother, completed a complicated transaction with Alfred, bishop of Selsey in 945,[123] and in 988 Aethelred II (the Unready) in a little-known document[124] granted land to Aethelgar of Selsey who was to become in that year archbishop of Canterbury. A considerable amount of land which the church at Selsey had lost was restored to Selsey under Bishop Brihthelm by King Eadwig, son of Edmund, in 957.[125]

But if these deeds were not untypical of other unrecorded transactions, there is some evidence also that lands in Sussex were used as much to enrich other churches as to benefit those in the diocese of Selsey. This is a feature of the period of the Benedictine monastic revival. There were no great revived Benedictine houses in Sussex. The reforming bishop, Aethelwold of Winchester, might exchange land in Sussex for land elsewhere,[126] but land in Sussex was granted by the king, Edgar, Edwig's successor, to Aethelwold's monastery at Abingdon[127] and to Aethelwold as bishop of Winchester in 963.[128] Cnut (1017-35) gave land in Sussex to Aelfstan, archbishop of Canterbury, in 1018.[129] Over the centuries Christ Church, Canterbury, was acquiring sizeable holdings in Sussex. By 1066 the archbishop of Canterbury held a collection of vills known as the archbishop's manor of South Malling, within the Rape of Pevensey, originating in land granted by Bealdred, last king of Kent under the Mercians and confirmed, in the hope of securing the support of Canterbury, by Ecgberht, king of Wessex, in 839.[130] Under Lanfranc, Canterbury reacted sharply to interference by clerks of Stigand, bishop of Chichester (1070-89) in estates in Sussex belonging to Christ Church.[131] Both Cnut and Edward the Confessor also granted lands in Sussex to the church of Fécamp in Normandy.[132] The fact that Sussex was uninvolved in the mainstream of monastic revival in the late Old English period meant that there was no lavish endowment of the South Saxon Church at that time. In the eleventh century three bishops were from Christ Church, Canterbury—Aethelric I (*c.* 1032-8), Grimketel (1039-47) and Aethelric II (1058-70).[133] But the cathedral remained a secular minster and was not transformed by the introduction of a monastic chapter, despite the fact that Aethelric I 'was probably from Dunstan's circle'.[134] Bishop Heca (1047-57), in fact, was a royal priest. Monastic cathedral chapters were relatively rare in England as a whole, but Selsey had been a monastic foundation at its beginning, probably observing—since it was a Wilfridian church—the Benedictine rule. During the dark period of the breakdown of monastic life in the ninth century in England, this monastic character must have been lost. It was never reconstituted, and in 1066, as Domesday Book reveals, Selsey was one of the poorest English sees.[135] Ironically, however, in the 1070s when Lanfranc accused the Conqueror's brother, Odo of Bayeux, Earl of Kent, and others, of robbing the extremely rich (monastic) archiepiscopal see of Canterbury of some of its lands, among those present at the trial on Penenden Heath, near Maidstone, was Aethelric II, ex-bishop of Selsey and last Saxon bishop of the see, 'a man of great age and very wise in the law of the land, who, by the command of the king, was brought to the trial in a wagon in order that he might declare and expound the ancient practice of the laws'.[136]

VIII

THE ORIGINS OF THE SAXON TOWNS

D. Hill

'491. In this year Aelle and Cissa besieged Andredesceaster, *and killed all who were inside, and there was not even a single Briton left alive!'*

THUS THE *Anglo-Saxon Chronicle*, drawing perhaps on some earlier epic poem of the deeds of Aelle, records the obliteration of civilised town life in Sussex. This annal has had a great importance for Anglo-Saxon studies far beyond the confines of Sussex and has coloured the views of generations of students about the end of Roman Britain. It is in many ways a snare and a delusion. *Anderida* (the later *Andredesceaster* or Pevensey) was a Saxon Shore fort and not a town, and it was held for nearly three-quarters of a century after the 'departure of the Legions', presumably by some sub-Roman successor state of unknown dimensions. Whatever the role of *Anderida* it was certainly not a town by 491, whatever definition is adopted. Nor had 'town-life' in Roman Britain flourished for well over a century, for the withdrawal of the Legions did not signify the end of town-life in Roman Britain. It was in all but a few centres effectively dead by the end of the fourth century. What remained were central places of defence or administration, not centres of trade and urban civilisation, and it is a mistake to picture the towns of 410 as full of lively, civilised, Latin-speaking traders and townsfolk with a council and municipal organisation. Nor is it true that the end for the towns came in fire and slaughter. The evidence is scanty in the extreme, but a good case has been made for the transfer of power in many centres from the native, sub-Roman, leaders to the Germanic element which had already been garrisoned in the area, usually as some form of mercenaries. Biddle's model for Winchester is an example.[1] If this model of Biddle's has a general relevance there are only three centres in Roman Sussex for us to concern ourselves with: *Anderida* (Pevensey), *Noviomagus Regnenses* (Chichester), and, perhaps, Hastings.

The problem of Hastings should be dealt with first, for here our evidence is so slender as to be almost transparent. When Hastings emerges into the record

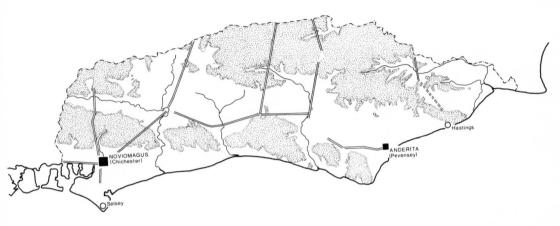

Fig. 9 Roman roads and centres in Sussex

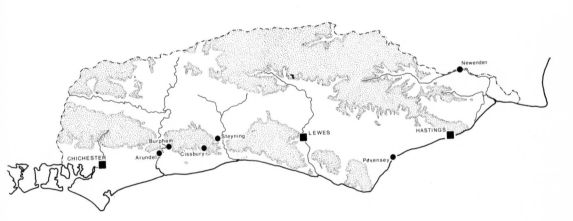

Fig. 10 Early Saxon centres in Sussex

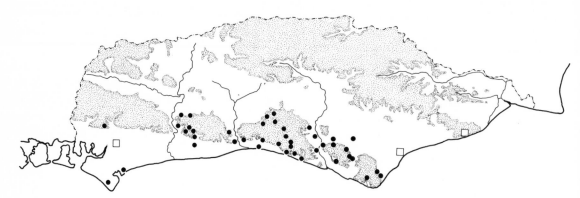

Fig. 11   Distribution of pagan Saxon burials

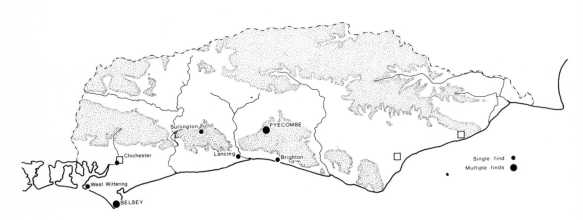

Fig. 12   Distribution of Sceatta findspots

it is known as *Hastingaceaster*. Now the Saxon site of the defences of Hastings is unknown, but the suffix *-ceaster* applied to the sites of Exeter, London, Winchester, Leicester and Dorchester, for example, almost invariably indicates a Roman fortified site, or as the compiler of the *English Place-Name Elements* translates it, 'the old fortification'.[2] The erosion of the coast at Hastings is so extreme that we have no real idea of what may have been there in Roman times and to have survived until the tenth century. We should simply bear in mind the possibility of a fort or fortified settlement, and considering that Hastings was a port in Roman times, served by its own road to Rochester and London, and standing as it did on an exposed coast where every comparable settlement was fortified, the idea of Hastings as a fort is not completely fanciful.

Anderida's extremely strong fortifications, overlooking a fine harbour, obviously made a place of refuge for the sub-Roman inhabitants until their annihilation came in 491 (the only one recorded in the *Chronicles* and therefore perhaps an exceptional event). The only real Roman town is Chichester. The presence there of a late-Germanic garrison, perhaps as part of considerable numbers of *foederati*, has been suggested by the discovery of a zoomorphic buckle of 'late military type' in the upper filling of a disused sewer. As the sewer seems to date from, or from later than, the late fourth or early fifth century, according to the ceramic evidence, this has been taken as an indicator of the use of the town at a late period in the Roman era.

Of the rest of the take-over of the area by the Germanic peoples, in particular of any association of these peoples with the town, or of Pevensey or Hastings, we can say nothing. It should be noted that the first recorded version of the place-names of the town owes nothing to the Roman name. In France it is usual for the place-names of the *civitas* capital to survive into the present day with the tribal part of the name forming the basis of the new form, as with Paris and Rheims. The continuity may also be direct, thus *Londinium* to London, *Lindum* to Lincoln. The most common type of Saxon place-name derived from the Roman is the addition of *-ceaster* to a modified form of the Roman. For example, we have Isca *-ceaster* to Exeter, Venta *-ceaster* to Winchester, and Glevum *-ceaster* to Gloucester. Unfortunately, the only Roman town in Sussex does not have a name which has any connection with its Roman original so that no measure of continuity can be claimed in this respect. This could be taken as an indication that the incoming Saxons had no contact with their predecessors, but this is most unlikely. In fact, the two of the towns with the best claim to some form of continuity in England, Rochester and Canterbury, also lack the connection. As we leave the period of the migrations we have then to consider what possible evidence we can adduce to disperse the haze over the Anglo-Saxon period. The total number of genuine references to the towns of Sussex before Domesday are less than five. This means that we must use every source and compare it with the developing pattern in the rest of the country to try and understand the towns of a shire which is less well provided than any other southern county (Figs. 9 and 10).

There are other problems associated with the study of the rise of towns, for we first have to define and distinguish those settlements that are towns from other large settlements. To do this we are drawn willy-nilly into the debate which has yet to reach an agreed conclusion. A useful set of definitions has been offered[3] but for the present purpose it has been thought best to deal with those sites which have *any* of the three attributes which Stenton saw as making an Anglo-Saxon town; a wall, a mint and a market. If we had to await the appearance of all three attributes in one site, or satisfy all the criteria demanded by many scholars for a town, we would find ourselves dealing with only the last years of the reign of Edward the Confessor, and with only three sites.

When we plot the places that succeed in satisfying any of the mentioned criteria it can be seen that there are a considerable number of sites of varying types and histories.

There are nine sites for which we have evidence, but this all dates from the close of the reign of Alfred the Great or later. The development of towns seems to start only some 400 years later than the recorded fall of Pevensey. There are a few fragments which might be used as evidence to fill the intervening years. Sussex was the last of the Saxon kingdoms to be converted to Christianity, it still being heathen in 681, over 80 years later than Kent. That means that for the first half of the period for which we have no records any town life would have to be heathen, and if there is one thing that should signify a town it is a concentration of population. If Chichester, or Hastings, or Pevensey survived as important centres then one would expect some concentration of the one type of Anglo-Saxon archaeology which is well recorded, the pagan burials. The town, if occupied in early Saxon times, should form the centre of a concentration of rich graveyards (Fig. 11).

The missing burials around Chichester are quite remarkable, but that they are mirrored by a lack of pagan burials in conjunction with the site of Hastings makes it even more surprising. The same phenomenon has been noted by Wheeler for London and led him to suggest a 'christian wedge' around that city. Nevertheless, Biddle points to a different pattern around Winchester and his model is of early Saxon domination of the towns. Until we have more archaeological evidence we simply cannot postulate any Dark Age history for the Sussex towns, but we should note that the shred of evidence provided by the one zoomorphic buckle of the late military type found in Chichester would point to a pattern such as the one suggested for Winchester.[4] The changing of the place-name from *Noviomagus* to Chichester involves the name of the son of the shadowy founder of the kingdom of Sussex, but what one may deduce from this is unclear at present.

The annals of the Conversion do not mention sites in Sussex that have any relevance to us, nor is there any archaeological material until we arrive at the history of St. Wilfrid and the surprisingly late conversion of the kingdom. This conversion centres around the royal family of Sussex, as with all conversions of this period, and led to the gift of Selsey by the king to St. Wilfrid as a seat for his bishopric. It is not explicitly stated that this was the king's residence originally. If it was a king's residence before it was a bishop's seat then it would already have been a centre. The concept of 'central-place' used by the geographers is here very useful to us. By calling a site a 'central place' we do not pre-judge a site in the same way as we would if we had labelled it 'town', nor do we beg the question by calling it a 'proto-urban site'. Obviously the royal residence is a central place for administration. If it was at Selsey then we may note that it was important in the late Iron Age, and in Selsey was the *Cymenesora* where Aelle and his three sons landed in 477. The importance is confirmed in 681 by its use, which continued throughout the rest of the Anglo-Saxon period, as the seat of the Sussex bishopric. That it was a central-place for ecclesiastic administration is obvious, and that it was probably more is indicated by the earliest coin distribution.

It is obvious that it is dangerous to read too much into coin find spots, but in a period of four and a half centuries without solid evidence for towns and trade we must examine all possibilities. It is clear that in times of even the most restricted trade and with 'self-contained' village communities, there was always some trading, and thus some trade routes. Sussex is fortunate in that it had both iron and salt available within the kingdom, but other metals are missing and were needed by the Anglo-Saxon economy. Millstones were imported, as were hones and wine and oil needed by the church. If we consider the distribution of the find spots of the early small flan silver deniers called *sceattas* we can see that there is a small concentration of findspots around Selsey. If, and it has been denied, the concentration of findspots of coins reflects concentrations of trade, as they would appear to do at Southampton, then there is a central-place for some sort of trade at Selsey (Fig. 12).

Now this slim evidence does point to some trade at least passing through Chichester, and it also shows the beginnings of commercial activity in the century from *c*. 670 to *c*. 750. This has been discussed by Metcalf in his note 'A coinage for west Sussex in the early eighth century?'[5] It should be noted that Metcalf here bravely suggests that the inscription *R-x Cic* might be interpreted as *Rex Cicestriae*. It may be as well to note the suggestion and the slender evidence.

Whatever it is that is happening in Chichester in *c*. 720, its vital road system and the state of the walls surviving must have made it a remarkable landmark to the Saxons in the eighth and ninth centuries. It is difficult to believe that its walls did not shelter people and armies in time of strife. Fowler has also pointed to the wide re-use of hillforts all over the south and west in the post-Roman period, including Sussex. Their fortifications together with those of the Roman circuits rendered them useful at various times. Nevertheless, this *fluchtburh* aspect, important as it is as a central-place for refuge, is not well defined in Sussex, although it must have existed. What is certain is that when we finally, and very late in the period, arrive at certainty it is within the Roman walls that we find it (Fig. 13).

The *Anglo-Saxon Chronicle* for 894 records:

> And when the Danish army which had besieged Exeter turned homewards, they ravaged up in Sussex near Chichester, and the citizens put them to flight and killed many hundreds of them, and captured some of them, and captured some of their ships[6]

It is clear that the sentence referring to Chichester '*þa hergodon hie up on Sud Seaxum neah Cisse ceastre,* ⁊ *þa burg ware hie ge fliemdon*' makes Chichester a *burh,* a fortified enclosure for all the people, and that it has what Whitelock calls citizens, but are more properly called the garrison. The various aspects of the Anglo-Saxon town as defined by Stenton now comes into consideration: wall, mint and market. Here we have a garrison, clearly tied to the *burh* but also these people are not too clearly permanent residents, for we are also told by the *Chronicle* (*sub anno* 893) 'The king had divided his army into two, so that always half its men were at home, half on service, apart from the men who guarded the boroughs'.[7] So these *burhware* may well have been attached to the town only for military purposes. However, it is likely that there were was a mercantile element. Even if Chichester was only a pale imitation of Winchester at this time, the analysis of its early medieval town plan does have some interesting things to say and some suggestions to make. The town of Winchester is dated to the close of the reign of Alfred, and there is a documentary reference to work refurbishing London in 886. There is a less reliable reference to the foundation of Shaftesbury

Fig. 13   The early topography of Chichester

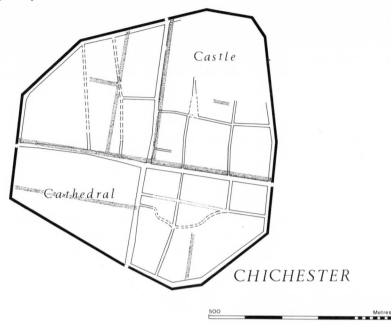

Fig. 14 Chichester: the origin of the street plan (Roman streets shown stippled)

in 880. It is therefore possible to see the town plan of Chichester as belonging to the same period as that of Winchester. The plan is clearly rectilinear, and has often been quoted as an example of the continuity of the Roman pattern, but the pattern which is known from the Middle Ages, and shown on Speed's map, is conditioned by Roman features but is early medieval in date. The phenomena have been extensively discussed[8] and it has been argued that the main crossing streets are where they are because they connect the gates, or at least the gaps where the gates had been, the causeways leading to those gates and the Roman roads bringing traffic to the town. Chichester's early pattern consists of four components, the main street, the intra-mural lane, the north-south streets, and the back streets parallel to the main street (Fig. 14).

Chichester has had its pattern disturbed more than most of this series of planned towns with a rectilinear pattern by the insertion of the castle, of the cathedral, the sokes of private jurisdiction, and by the dereliction of the north-western quarter of the town in the late Middle Ages. Nevertheless, the pattern does show just enough of a parallel with the type site of Winchester to allow us to discuss the two together, and to regain from that street plan the intention of the engineer who set it out at the end of the eighth century. The purpose of the intra-mural street is, as it was throughout the Middle Ages, to allow the free access of garrison troops defending the wall and also for effecting repairs. The High Street reflects the through traffic, but also is the *Ceap* Street, the main market of the town. The north-south streets and the back lanes should be regarded as one unit; they are difficult to discern except in the eastern half of the town. They should be seen, not in terms of the pattern of streets and lanes, but in the two sizes of blocks which they delineate. The blocks nearest to the High Street were perhaps meant for merchants needing direct access to the main market, the larger blocks being left as hedged areas, originally *haga*, and forming the areas into which fugitives from the countryside fled. For Chichester was a *fluchtburh,* even if this was only one of its roles in the last years of the ninth century. There would be no point in a *fluchtburh* which was already full of houses and merchants. Additional room would be needed and it is in the *hagas* in the back areas that we should see the country people sheltering. Maitland noted over 75 years ago the link between town and country discernible in Charters and in Domesday and thought that it was for military service. This garrison theory, German in origin, has passed out of favour, but there are, in several towns around the country, links between specific estates and parts of the towns to which they are linked. We should see the pattern in Sussex too. We should also be ready to define some part of the shire depending, for defence at least, on this *burh.* In the reign of Athelstan the burghal district was important as a judicial area, but we cannot discuss these areas in Sussex, certainly not until the Burghal Hidage gives us the list of sites which were centres to those districts. It is sufficient to say that Chichester would seem to be organised for defence, for trade and for refuge, by 894.

Although it would be dangerous to allow the achievement of (and sources for) the reign of Alfred the Great to blind us to the possibility of occupation and urban activity of both Chichester and Lewes, it is in the reign of Alfred that the evidence would begin to appear.

The next scrap of evidence for the towns of Sussex is the fascinating document known as the Burghal Hidage, the sole survivor apparently of a whole class of administrative documents. It has been extensively discussed and the most recent version[9] suggests a date of *c.* 919. The document can be shown to be carefully organised on a topographical basis, the mathematics are internally consistent, and the whole document may yet reveal new insights into the workings of late Anglo-Saxon administration. For us it is important to know that it lists the *burhs* of Wessex and assigns to them a number of hides. The list starts in Sussex and probably read originally:

> Three hundred hides belong to *Eorpeburnan* and twenty-four hides
> And at Hastings belong five hundred hides
> And to Lewes belong thirteen hundred hides
> And to Burpham belong seven hundred hides and twenty hides
> And to Chichester belong fifteen hundred hides . . .

These five places then are defences belonging to a system so organised that no village in Wessex was more than 30 miles from a refuge. The system must have started in the reign of Alfred, and from the topographical setting of the document it is clear that the first site is in the extreme east of the shire beyond Hastings. This site, *Eorpeburnan*, would seem to be the site referred to in Asser and the *Chronicle.* The *Chronicle, sub anno* 892, states that:

> They (the Danes) rowed their ships up the river (Lympne) as far as the Weald, four miles from the mouth of the estuary, and there stormed a fortress. Inside that fortification there were a few peasants, and it was only half made . . .[10]

and it is to an episode like this, if it is not the same episode, that Asser was referring when he wrote:

> But if, among these exhortations of the king, his orders were not carried out because of the slackness of the people, or things begun late in time of need were unfinished and of no profit to those who undertook them—for I may tell of fortresses ordered by him and still not begun, or begun too late to be brought to completion—and enemy forces broke in by land and sea, or as often happened, on every side, the opponents of the royal ordinances then were ashamed . . . by the loss of their fathers, wives, children, servants, slaves, handmaids, their labours and all their goods . . .[11]

Brian Davison has identified this site with that of Castle Toll at Newenden.[12] The other sites appear for the first time in history as fortifications in the Burghal Hidage. But it would be unwise to assume that the system of *burhs* was completed by Alfred the Great and then remained unaltered. The fort at Portchester in Hampshire did not come into royal hands until the reign of Edward the Elder, for example, and we know of *burhs* of the reign of Alfred which do not figure in the Burghal Hidage.

Next to the information that there were five defended places maintained by the king and people in the shire, the most enthralling glimpse comes from the ending:

> For the maintenance and defence of an acre's breadth of wall sixteen hides are required, if every hide is represented by one man, then every pole of wall can be manned by four men. Then for the maintenance of twenty poles of wall eighty hides are required . . . If the circuit is greater, the additional amount can easily be deduced from this account, for 160 men are always required for one furlong, then every pole of wall is manned by four men.

Amongst many things that could be deduced from this account it is possible to calculate the length of wall for each of the listed *burhs* from the hidage and this, in itself, has implications. For if we know the size of the wall we can state that, in *c.* 919, this was the size and area of the *burh*. Some of these measurements have been calculated and they appear to work out satisfactorily (Fig. 15).

If one considers that for all the cases where we know the circuit of the walls only two wall lengths seem wildly wrong, *prima facie,* then we should consider if the information has anything to tell us of the development of the Sussex towns. Firstly it has been demonstrated convincingly for three sites, Lyng,[13] Southampton, and Portchester[14] that only the *dry length of the ditch* appeared to count in most cases for the calculations. Secondly, it is clear that the various reports of lengths or hidages were assembled by different people, most rounding up the totals to the nearest hundred.

Davison has shown that the measurement at *Eorpeburnan* fits convincingly, Hastings, or its Roman fort of which we know nothing,[15] and Burpham was probably covered by marsh, reclaimed in modern times, on its southern and

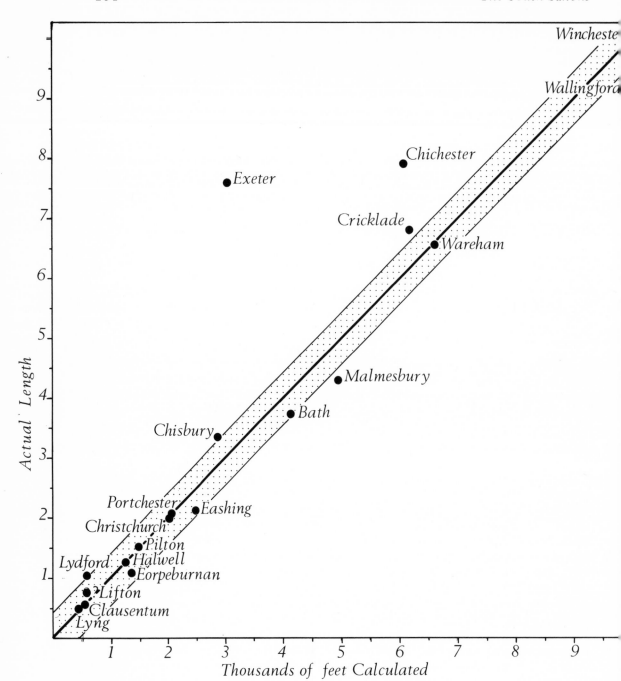

Fig. 15 The burghal hidage: correlation of wall lengths
        (The stippled area represents the 'rounding up' of 50 hides)

western sides. Only Lewes and Chichester seem difficult to reconcile in this county. The calculated length of the walls of Chichester is 6,187 feet, whereas the medieval and Roman circuit is actually 7,800 feet. The immense danger here is being over-inventive and being carried away by one's own wish to make the calculations work. However, I believe that the southern part of the wall was covered by marsh and the little river Lavant. Thus 1,612 feet are not included. This suggestion fits the topography and soils.

In view of the other correlations, however, it is possible to look at the circuit of Lewes in an entirely different way. Lewes is not Roman, and the site is a spur or promontory *burh*. These sites are very common at this period and consist of a site, strongly defended on three sides by slope, river, marsh or ravine, the fourth side covered by a considerable bank. *Eorpeburnan* and Burpham are both of this type. The circuit of the walls of medieval Lewes are at the foot of the promontory and not on the crest where one would expect them, neither do they fit the Burghal Hidage calculation. A calculated circuit would fit snugly on the crest of the promontory and against the known cutting-off bank. There is a parallel case postulated by Ralegh Radford for Shrewsbury where the original circuit was on the top and spread down the slope in later medieval times. This guess, or what in modern parlance is called a 'model' would fit all the known facts and in particular fit the otherwise surprising and confusing information yielded by the recent excavations (Fig. 16).

It should not be thought that these five *burhs* are, in some way, all the same. In essence they should be divided at this stage, around *c.* 919, into at least two clear groups. This has been done usually by size: the small area *burhs* are forts and the large area *burhs* are fortified towns. It can be argued that the area enclosed is an index, not of importance, but of the expectations of the king when the *burh* was set up. On this basis Chichester and Lewes are meant for fortified towns and *Eorpeburnan* and Burpham are intended as forts. The circuit of Hastings is unknown and so this sort of reasoning cannot be applied.

Inside the two forts one would expect on the analogy of the other known sites little more than the storehouses, and even these may be absent, unless the site was already, as at Portchester, the centre of an estate. The evidence from the recent excavations of Sutermeister at Burpham would point at this sort of situation at Burpham.[17] Davison found no internal features at *Eorpeburnan*. The role of Chichester has been discussed and would appear to have been that of refuge (*fluchtburh*), defence, market centre and mercantile settlement. It is also possible to apply the parallels to Lewes to elucidate the maximum information out of the town plan. To do this one first has to accept that the '*primary burh*' concept is acceptable and then compare the site with another promontory *burh* of the same period, such as Lydford. Here, too, one can see the street plan, which also has been distorted by the addition of a castle. But the pattern does show the elements High Street, 'north-south' streets, back lanes and intra-mural streets. In Lewes the last element seems entirely lacking. The other three elements are still there, but only on the south side of the High Street. The only dating that is available for this pattern is the clear curve visible in the High Street caused by the insertion of the castle. If this type of town-plan analysis

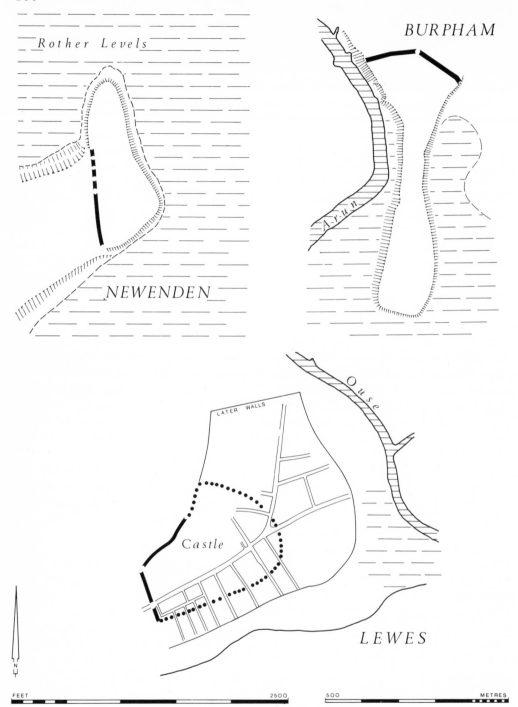

Fig. 16 The town plans of Newenden, Burpham and Lewes

is valid then Lewes, too, shows all the aspects of market, mercantile centre, refuge and defence that Chichester has. However, only with the most careful observation and excavation in the relevant areas will the plan emerge and just one good excavation may disprove this particular model.

In the last 150 years we have a great deal happening in the development of towns that we can actually demonstrate from the sources. In the reign of Athelstan great changes took place in the arrangement of towns and *burhs*. It is to this reign that the laws which associate *burh*, or defence, with market and mint, are promulgated. At the same time those small *burhs* which are forts disappear from the record, so that we can postulate that *Eorpeburnan* and Burpham are dismantled as centres for defence in this reign. However, the other three sites, Hastings, Lewes and Chichester, flourish. *Burhs* become in this reign administrative centres and the heart of a burghal district, although it would be a brave man who suggested the districts attached to the *burhs* of Sussex. The coinage of Athelstan has been well served by a recent study[18] and it may be of some indication of the relative importance of the Sussex mints that the Grately decrees of Athelstan record that:

> In Canterbury (there are to be) seven moneyers . . . In Rochester three . . . in London eight, in Winchester six; in Lewes two; in Hastings one; another at Chichester . . .

These three sites then had mints, two moneyers at Lewes, of whom the names of both are known, Wilebald and Eadric, whose coins travelled far enough to appear in the Forum hoard in Rome. There is a point of interest, too, in that these coins bear the inscription LAE VRB, one of the rare uses of *Urbs* on these coins. Chichester's one moneyer was Ioahan and the mint signature was CISSAN. No coins have survived of Hastings. Thus we have three major *burhs* in Sussex, the basis of the medieval and modern pattern for the county (Fig. 17).

Although the pattern was now set there were still to be some dislocations to the peaceful development of urban life in the last century of the Anglo-Saxon kingdom. In the reign of Ethelred II a terrible wave of Viking attacks disrupted the country. They continued for some 25 years and in some strange way the blame for them appears always to be laid at the door of the unfortunate king stigmatised as 'the Unready' or more properly 'the Counsel-less'. In fact Ethelred was always taking counsel and some of his plans were excellent, but the fabric of society was under considerable stress and they often came unstuck. One of his schemes was to replace the weaker fortifications and the *burhs* abandoned under Athelstan with a series of major *burhs* which would complement the stronger walled towns. We only know of three sites, although we have the names of several others as yet unrecognised. These three are all re-used hillforts on inaccessible hilltops: South Cadbury, Old Sarum and Cissbury. Whilst the author is still slightly unhappy about the identification of Cissbury, the case has been carefully argued.[19] It has been pointed out that, apart from a re-fortification and strong gates, these sites probably only contained the minimum of buildings, and the minting activites that took place in them were probably to service a market that was moved to the site in an attempt to familiarise the

Fig. 17 Mints of late Saxon England (the size of the symbols represents the relative importance of the mints)

populace with their new refuge centre. With the accession of Cnut in 1016 these sites passed out of use. Whilst it would be interesting for the identification of Cissbury to be checked by excavating a section of the walls to check for a refurbishing in the early eleventh century, any other finds would appear unlikely.

The other phenomenon of the late Saxon period, and particularly of the eleventh century, is the secondary market centres that were founded for it should be clearly realised that all these places of which we are speaking were foundations. (To speak of 'springing up' or 'appearing' is simply avoiding the issue.) These sites are usually called 'weak ports' because they lacked strong defences and were mainly 'ports', i.e., Anglo-Saxon markets. There are three in Sussex. Steyning is evidenced first from its mint in the reign of Cnut. The issue is dated ????? and would actually follow on nicely from the closure of the Cissbury mint which strikes in the issue before. The other two places are Arundel and Pevensey, both seaports, which are first evidenced as existing borough in Domesday. We should not expect much from these sites in the way of urban life even in 1066 as they were intended as filling places in the pattern of trade at a time when that trade was expanding, and when population was also increasing.

The sites are examples of the economic exploitation of the large royal estates which in the reign of Edward the Confessor, were in the hands of the Godwin-sons. That they do not form an important part of the trade, at least at this period, is perhaps to be found from Domesday, from which the following populations have been calculated:

Chichester	..	..	..	..	1,200–1,500
Lewes	..	..	..	..	2,000
Hastings	..	..	..	..	No description
Pevensey	..	..	..	..	500
Steyning	..	..	..	..	600
Arundel	..	..	..	..	No estimate[20]

There is another way of demonstrating the relative importance of the various late-Saxon towns, although it depends on the fact that all the major towns were also mints. If we compare the number of moneyers we can work out the proportion to the total moneyers, and thus arrive at a comparison. The importance of using moneyers in this way is that the vagaries of survival means that one coin surviving from a moneyer has as much weight as a considerable run. It also helps to overcome any distortion caused if a particular moneyer struck a large amount of coinage as a special striking for the king or for Danegeld, a situation that results in large runs of coins appearing in Scandinavian hoards.

When one considers the pattern so arrived at, it is clear that none of the towns are of the first rank, but that the three major *burhs*, founded before 919, formed the basis of the pattern. Steyning is a minor site and Pevensey and Arundel did not mint.

By 1066 the towns of Sussex are well established and full of life, and it should be remembered that the towns in 1066 contained 10 per cent. of the population of the country. They were genuine urban centres.

THE DOMESDAY RECORD OF SUSSEX

Dennis Haselgrove

'. . . What is the name of the manor? Who held it in the time of King Edward? Who now holds it? How many hides are there? How many teams—in demesne and of the tenants? How many villeins, cottars, serfs? How many free men and sokemen? How much wood, meadow, pasture? How many mills? How many fisheries? How much has been added or taken away? How much was the whole worth? How much is it worth now? How much had each free man or sokeman? . . . If more can be had than is had?'

Inquisitio Eliensis *(translation)*

KING WILLIAM'S great survey, the record of which we know as Domesday Book, was for its period an administrative undertaking of unprecedented scope. The inquisition, at least in some areas, was more comprehensive than the main record that survives. Thus for the West Country, in the 'Exon Domesday' version, and also in the second final Domesday volume, which covers only Essex, Suffolk and Norfolk, but in more detail, we have details of livestock which are not available for other counties. For most counties, including Sussex, the record corresponds closely with the question set out above, in the preamble of the *Inquisitio Eliensis,*[1] which seems to be a copy made a few years afterwards, of the Domesday returns for lands of the Abbey of Ely. Domesday Book, which was probably written out in its present form at the Exchequer at Winchester, has been popularly known by this name since the twelfth century, since it was a record from which, as from the Last Judgement, there could be no departing.[2]

Domesday Book has been intensively studied and there is a vast literature to which all present students are heavily in debt.[3] During the past century much has been made clear and is common ground among historians, but many problems of understanding and interpretation remain. It has long been accepted that Domesday, basically a record of established landholdings with a minimum of topographic detail, cannot of itself provide a clear picture of the underlying contemporary patterns of society and settlements. Of these, certainly in Sussex, all too little is yet known with certainty, and perhaps too much has been inferred from slender evidence. It is essentially late Saxon England that Domesday records. The survey was carried out in an alien environment, and the uniform plan and terminology hide the distinctive features and way of life of the different English provinces. But our knowledge of the period and of the preceding evolution of Saxon England is slowly being increased; not only, for example, by documentary and place-name studies, but especially by greater understanding of the evolution of the landscape itself, and man's impact upon it. Archaeologists are refining their techniques of discovery and interpretation. The wealth of the Domesday evidence needs continuously to be brought to bear in all studies of the period, but it is necessary to realise that in many ways the significance and real meaning of Domesday have still to be discovered and demonstrated.

Sussex has already been well served both in Domesday studies and in pioneer work on the historical landscape. Although written more than 70 years ago the introduction to the *Sussex Domesday* and annotated translation which were contributed by J. H. Round and Louis Salzman to the first volume of the *Victoria County History of Sussex*[4] were based on exhaustive knowledge of the documentary sources of national and local history in all periods and of the county's topography, and it is doubtful whether there is much that Salzman would have wished to change after a lifetime of further study. Much more recently the Sussex chapter by Dr. S. H. King, in Professor Darby's *Domesday Geography*,[5] is a model of detailed analysis and visual presentation. The pioneer study by Professor S. W. Wooldridge and F. Goldring of a vast landscape in *The Weald*[6] and Dr. E. M. Yates's detailed investigation of the development of two Sussex parishes, Harting and Rogate,[7] provide inevitable contrasts in aims and method. Recently Dr. P. F. Brandon has given an overall view of the development of the Sussex landscape as a whole.[8] All these, with many other contributions, provide essential guidelines. It may also be expected that by the time the present essay is in print the original Latin text of the *Sussex Domesday*, with translation, will have been made available in convenient form by Dr. John Morris. In a volume devoted to Sussex before the Norman Conquest it is appropriate, and may be opportune, to attempt to review briefly the nature of the Domesday evidence as a whole and perhaps point towards aspects of it that may be rewarding in future work.

The making of Domesday Book

The survey was carried out in 1086, a bare 20 years after the Battle of Hastings. Domesday reflects clearly King William's doctrine of the legitimacy of his own position as the successor of Edward the Confessor and that of his followers to whom he had given the succession to the lands and rights of their English predecessors. Harold is not recognised in Domesday as having been king. We are given the name of the holder of each 'manor', the territorial and jurisdictional unit on which the survey was based, 'in the time of King Edward', as well as at the time of the survey. We are also given the pre-Conquest 'hidage' or assessment of the manor and any change made subsequently, and its value in King Edward's time, at the time it was reviewed by its new owner and at the time of the Domesday survey itself. Other details are for the date of the survey only.

The purpose of the undertaking, from King William's point of view, has not been recorded. Professor Stenton concluded that it is unnecessary to go behind the contemporary opinion that the survey was carried out because William wished to know more about England.[9] The emphasis is on resources, and these could have been compared at the Exchequer with the liabilities, previously and currently, to taxation under the established English system of assessment by hidage. Military organisation can never have been far from William's mind, and invasion from Denmark had been threatened in 1085. Another aspect may have been the need to resolve outstanding disputes about holdings although, probably because of the nature of the jurisdictions established in Sussex, this seems hardly to have arisen here.

Historians agree that Sussex formed part of a 'south-eastern' circuit of the teams of commissioners who were sent to different areas of England to conduct the survey.[10] This circuit also included Kent, Surrey, Hampshire and Berkshire. Thus, while the accounts of other counties often have different or distinctive features, the information returned for the counties adjoining Sussex is generally on a comparable basis. There has been much controversy about how the information recorded was obtained and compiled, but it is difficult to believe that it could have been obtained in the first instance otherwise than directly from the holders of the manors and their agents. The preamble of the *Inquisitio Eliensis* also declares that the inquisition was made 'by the oath of the sheriff and of all the barons and of all their Frenchmen and of the whole hundred, of the priest, the reeve and six villeins of each vill'.[11] Thus, in Cambridgeshire and, as Domesday itself shows, in other areas, there was a verification procedure which made use of the established system of shire and hundred courts which seems to have survived the Conquest without significant change. Nothing is known of the resources of local administration in the shire or hundred at this time, but written records may have been limited to hidage assessment lists.

There must be some doubt about the reliability of a record derived largely from returns by interested parties. However, although the surviving text of Domesday Book may frequently be convicted of error or carelessness, both internally and where independent evidence is also available, the overall impression is of a generally comprehensive and consistent result within the evident limitations of what would have been feasible. Contemporary references suggest that the project was viewed with the utmost seriousness, and one source indicates that the procedure included a check by second teams of commissioners who were sent to areas in which they were not personally known.[12] It also appears that the whole undertaking was carried out under great pressure and with maximum speed, so that possibly most of the returns were received at Winchester within a twelvemonth of the decision to make the survey.[13]

The survey's content and terminology

The manors are listed, county by county, under the names of 'tenants-in-chief'. In Sussex, apart from King William himself, who retained only part of Bosham and Rotherfield, these comprised only seven ecclesiastical holders of lands, the Norman lords of the five 'rapes' (Roger of Montgomery at Arundel, William of Braose or Briouze at Bramber, William of Warenne at Lewes, Roger of Mortain at Pevensey, and the Count of Eu at Hastings), and two Englishmen, Ode of Winchester (a pre-Conquest treasurer) and his brother Eldred, who, however, had only two small holdings in West Sussex. Each of the tenants-in-chief held directly from the king, and the lords of the rapes kept some important holdings in their own hands. Within this arrangement the individual manors are assigned to hundreds; sometimes in Sussex and elsewhere, the hundredal heading is misplaced or omitted by the clerks who compiled the final record. The origin of the rapes in Sussex and the nature of the hundreds are matters of major historical importance, to which it will be necessary to return. Although the unit of the survey is the manor Domesday also recognises and reports to a limited extent on the boroughs, which in Sussex passed after the Conquest from the jurisdiction of the king to that of the appropriate tenant-in-chief. Failure, due probably to jurisdictional or administrative difficulties, to give an adequate account of the boroughs is a serious loss.

The term translated by 'manor' was not used in England before the Conquest, and in the pre-Conquest use it may be better to write 'estate' or 'holding', although to do so obscures the complex and varied relationships involved in land and personal superiorities in Saxon England. On the Sussex evidence it does not seem possible to do otherwise than follow Maitland's view that the Domesday manor, and its Saxon predecessor, was a land-holding for which there was a direct individual assessment for payment of *geld* or tax.[14] Such a holding might be very small or it might be vast. The king's own 'royal estates' were included and in Sussex assessed in hides, although their liability in practice was still sometimes merely providing for a night's maintenance for the royal household. The nature of the individual holdings is the crux of the geographical problems of Domesday Book. Some at least of them comprised widely separated lands and probably, like their medieval successors, also individuals owing services. Frequently a large element of historical continuity extending into the better-documented medieval period may be seen. Tenure by one individual did not involve unity of his holdings as a single manor. In Sussex a notable and often informative feature of the Domesday evidence arises from the fact that it was considered appropriate after the Conquest to divide the lay estates whose lands fell into more than one of the rapes. Where a holding had been detached from a parent estate it may be described as having 'lain' (*iacuit*) in it, and an assigned hidage was deducted from that of the parent estate.

A manor is usually named from a 'vill' (*villa*) in which its centre, sometimes referred to as a hall, was located. It appears that 'vill' may mean a settlement or group of settlements of any kind, large or small, including examples such as the dispersed Mardens in the Western Downs. More than one manor may appear under the same place-name, but in other cases no place-name may appear. Thus the Domesday record of place-names, of which in Sussex there are 337, is haphazard. What may have been quite large villages may not appear because they were part of a manor with a different name. Conversely, we often find the names of what may have been no more than hamlets or single farms. Some obscure or now lost place-names may obscure the existence already, or at any rate the continuity, of a settlement which has survived under a different name. Many Domesday names are those of medieval parishes and modern villages and towns, but there may not always have been continuity on the same site.

The economic basis of life over most of Saxon England was arable. Certainly in Domesday Book the main emphasis throughout is on the arable resources and cultivation. But we are told nothing about the organisation, apart from a consistent division, as in other counties, of the resources of 'ploughs' between the demesne and the dependents of a manor. Ploughs are generally accepted to represent full notional ploughing teams of eight oxen. Sometimes individual oxen are referred to, and there is even, though not in Sussex, a remarkable *semibos*. The division of the teams between the demesne and the tenants does not necessarily imply a system of cultivation of infield and outfield. Nor does Domesday provide evidence to show how far a communal system of agriculture based on the sharing out of acres or furlongs, including demesne land and in common fields, as was widespread in medieval times, had been developed in different parts of Sussex by the late Saxon period. Thus the probable annual capacity of a Domesday 'plough' is difficult to assess, even in general terms. Although the question does not appear in the *Inquisitio Eliensis* the commissioners were, however, evidently also required to ascertain the number of 'ploughlands' of each manor. The criteria to be used are not indicated, and it is not perhaps surprising that the matter presented difficulty. In some cases the figure was left blank. Probably the intention was that a current deficiency or surplus of teams should be shown, but in many cases equation of the ploughlands to the actual number of teams seems to have provided the answer.

Much has been written about the 'hide', with which the obviously important initial question 'How many hides?' was concerned. Description of land grants in terms of hidage goes back to the earliest charters of the time of Archbishop Theodore in the seventh century. Bede's Latin indicated that the hide in English usage was the possession of a family.[15] He also wrote that Sussex was a territory of 7,000 hides,[16] thus giving the same figure as that in the early Mercian tribute list known as the Tribal Hidage.[17] There is abundant evidence that over the years the hide continued as the basis of a sophisticated system of assessment over much of England for levies for defence and taxation, including payment of *danegeld,* and that the system continued up to and after the Conquest. Much confusion, however, arises from the fact that the hide, with its sub-divisions of virgates or 'yardlands' and acres, also retained its reality as a basis of land measurement, although the basis differed in various parts of the country. The official assessments imposed on estates, or in some parts of the

country, as in areas of the Danelaw after its recovery, on hundreds and constituent vills, were necessarily to some extent arbitrary. Whatever the attempts
that may have been made to ensure realistic or equitable treatment there were
also numerous examples of exemptions or other forms of beneficial assessment,
as is noticeable, for example, after the Conquest in reduced assessments for some
of the Sussex manors, especially in the rape of William of Braose. In the agricultural context, on the other hand, people probably had no difficulty in
recognising what was meant locally by a hide or a virgate of land, but in general
there is little evidence surviving to indicate the reality. Although, however, the
Domesday hides and their sub-divisions are fiscal and thus a matter of interest
primarily in an administrative and historical context, nevertheless Sussex seems
to be a case of special interest, since not only do many individual assessments
of holdings appear to be carefully calculated, but there is also a degree of
coincidence, in totals of about 3,200, between the assessed hidage in the time of
King Edward and the total number of plough teams (and also the apparent
number of ploughlands as estimated) found in the survey, though there is no
close correlation for many individual manors.[18] Nevertheless, it appears essential
to abandon the view which was formerly prevalent that the Domesday hide,
whether divided into 120 acres, as in Cambridgeshire and elsewhere or 40 to 48
acres, as in Wiltshire and Dorset, provides a firm basis (even in terms of the
smaller customary acres which persisted in Sussex and elsewhere into comparatively modern times) for estimating the extent of the arable.

In recording population, Domesday Book lists for 1086 what appear to be
the numbers of those bound to give agricultural services to each manor. Of over
9,500 in all enumerated in Sussex nearly 6,000 are *villani,* literally 'men of the
vill', but usually translated as 'villeins', who evidently had reasonably large shares
of land of their own and whose individual share of the hidage assessment seems
often, from evidence from other counties, to have been one virgate. Most of the
remainder were 'bordars' or 'cottars' of inferior status (these terms being used
indiscriminately in Sussex) who had little or no land of their own, and there was
a relatively small total, compared with many other counties, of some 400 *servi*
or 'serfs', who were presumably bound to work continuously on the demesne
lands or on other duties, but appear only for a limited number of manors. All
those enumerated must probably be considered realistically as heads of households, but it seems doubtful how far the figures provide a basis for an assessment
of the total population. It is possible that considerable groups of people, such
as craftsmen, household or casual workers and occupants of religious houses
were omitted altogether. Uniquely, 10 shepherds are mentioned in what was
previously Harold's estate of Patcham, north of Brighton. Burgesses and other
people are also mentioned in connection with some of the boroughs, but the
totals may be far from complete, and a notable feature in Sussex is the enumera-
tion of properties, but rarely of people, in the boroughs belonging to rural manors
over wide surrounding areas.[19]

It is likely that the uniform description of villeins, bordars and cottars in
Domesday Book conceal considerable differences in conditions and status, but

in practice the status of many people seems likely to have been seen as formally reduced after the Conquest. Domesday shows that before the Conquest in many parts of Sussex named individuals, or often anonymous 'free men' had held small independent holdings, but by 1086 many of these had been absorbed into larger units. Thus 'Wyke' (Rumboldswyke), close to Chichester, had been held by five free men 'as five manors' and neighbouring Hunston by six free men. By 1086 the free men have disappeared. In this way Domesday notably sheds light on conditions before the Conquest, and clearly the record of small holdings in late Saxon times alongside the large estates is of great interest. They appear often to have been concentrated in particular areas. such as the hundreds of *Benestede* (Binstead, or later Avisford) in the coastal plain west of the Arun. Larger sub-holdings which previously already formed parts of the larger estates appear generally to have been kept unchanged, but the names of the holders in 1086 show that nearly all, like the independent manors, had been taken over by new Norman occupiers.

Domesday records manorial resources of meadow, pasture and woodland, and the comparative maps in the *Domesday Geography*[20] are of great interest. Meadow, which would primarily have supported the ploughing oxen, is generally described in terms of 'acres', but again there must be doubt as to what was meant by an acre. Pasture, which is relatively rare in the *Sussex Domesday,* and woodlands, which were evidently widespread, are generally in terms of 'swine renders', emphasising the importance of pigs in the economy. Generally, because the indications of the sub-holdings in the Weald are mostly fortuitous, Domesday fails to reflect the longstanding possession by estates in the more populated areas in the southern parts of the county of distant woodlands in the Weald, taken initially, as swine pastures, as evidenced in charters of the Saxon period. Nor, apart from the single reference at Patcham, is there evidence as to the importance of sheep raising. In Essex, Suffolk and Norfolk, for which Domesday provides details of livestock, sheep accounted for 70 per cent. of the livestock population.[21]

Manorial resources also regularly recorded in Sussex, as required by the version of the commissioners' instructions in the *Inquisitio Eliensis,* are mills and fisheries, and also 'salt pans'. Often a monetary return to the manor is indicated, suggesting that some of these perquisites were 'farmed' by people who may have been excluded from the recorded population. Geographical locations are, of course, lacking. However, mills of the period were water-mills, operated on streams and rivers.[22] Fisheries, too, should be understood generally as fresh-water fisheries. Returns from herring fishing are recorded separately, but only at Brighton and from certain estates adjoining the Ouse. Recorded salt pans are very numerous, and must have absorbed a fair amount of labour, and it seems possible that a surplus was produced for trading outside Sussex. Although inevitably based entirely on the place-names of the manors, large or small, which possessed them, the maps in the *Domesday Geography*[23] showing salt pans and fisheries also provide an indication of the extent of tidal penetration of the principal rivers at this period.

About the exploitation of other resources we are given little information. Quarries are referred to at Stedham, Iping and Grittenham (and for mill stones), Bignor, all in West Sussex, and a single iron-working establishment (*ferraria*) in East Grinstead hundred in the High Weald which was associated with the former royal estate of Ditchling. Churches which were manorial property produced revenue for their owners, and just over 100 churches and chapels are recorded in Sussex, but not always in the most populated estates. Independent evidence, as similarly in Kent and other counties, shows that there were probably many others already existing. It may be that in regard to incidental sources of manorial revenue the guidance given to the Domesday commissioners was vague or altogether lacking, and the references may be fortuitous.

Finally the annual value of each manor had to be reported, not only at the date of the survey but also in King Edward's time, and when it passed into the hands of the new owner. Figures were obtained, and provide a fairly consistent pattern, expressed often on round numbers of pounds, but sometimes necessarily in shillings. The amounts are often large. After showing a fall after the Conquest they have usually recovered at the time of the survey to the pre-Conquest level or even higher. As an example, the medium-sized manor of Shoreham had been worth £25, but fell to £16. In 1086 it had apparently been let to farm by William of Braose for £50, yet, so the record states, it could not produce more than £35. There is no indication that in Sussex, apart from local effects of wastage, mainly in the Hastings area, the Conquest had produced any serious economic consequences. The special importance which William evidently attached to its secure defence and its situation astride the most direct routes between Normandy and many parts of England probably had a contrary effect. There is, of course, much independent evidence in Sussex that the new Norman lords were able, almost immediately, to devote considerable resources to the endowment of religious houses and the building of churches.

Domesday Sussex

Despite the wealth of material, the evidence of Domesday Book for the distribution of population and settlements in late Saxon and early Norman Sussex is obscured by the lack of geographical detail and of knowledge of the kind of organisation involved, in particular, in the large estates, for which the information is consolidated.

Certain general features are readily apparent. The manors are almost entirely outside the Weald, pointing to a heavy concentration of settlements in the southern and central parts of the county. Nevertheless, there are clear indications in Domesday itself, which are reinforced by independent documentary and place-name evidence and by architectural features in some churches, that there was fairly extensive settlement in at least some parts of the Weald. In the more populous areas in the south there were many small settlements and probably many quite large villages. But we are seriously in need of further evidence of the extent to which, in different parts of Sussex, people at this time lived either in 'nucleated' villages or in scattered hamlets or farms. There appear to have been large concentrations of population particularly in parts of the West Sussex coastal plain and also around the Downs and in the Chalk valleys. However, it is difficult to form a view how far the settlements in and around the Downs represent a stage in a process, for example, of retreat from the Chalklands, or rather of advance due to increasing population. The size, population and activity of the boroughs, which were also seaports, must be largely a matter of guesswork. The answers to problems such as these must be sought primarily by large-scale archaeological fieldwork and excavations in areas where they may still be found. Clearly, in all parts of Sussex, the Domesday evidence should have a continuing major role to play. However, the thesis here is that the historical and institutional evidence which is reflected in Domesday should be considered equally as important as that which is of geographical significance, and this seems to apply particularly to the patterns both of hundreds and of large estates which are revealed by the *Sussex Domesday*. It must be accepted that in the problems of the development of the boroughs Domesday does not give a great deal of help. Each of these, in any case, has an individual history.

Rapes and hundreds

The unique Sussex institution of large territorial rapes, which forms the basis of the non-ecclesiastical tenurial arrangements in the *Sussex Domesday* and which continued to be a feature of the county's organisation, has been long debated. They have been compared with the apparently similar lathes of Kent which as institutions of local organisation go back far into early Kentish history. From a few apparent references to the rape in Domesday in a pre-Conquest context,[24] our only documentary evidence apart from the fact of the use of this Saxon word, it is possible to argue that the rapes were necessarily a pre-Conquest institution. Salzman was convinced that, at least in the sense of the territorial divisions, which we recognise as lordships, they were not.[25]   He showed incontrovertibly, and has been followed in further work by J. F. A. Mason,[26] that the rape of William of Braose based on Bramber was a creation of slightly later date than the territorial lordships assigned by the Conqueror in the first instance. This established a jurisdiction on both sides of the Adur, which uniquely cut through the hundredal organisation. Thus both Roger of Montgomery at Arundel, and William of Warenne at Lewes, lost lands. The latter seems also at about the same time to have lost the areas in the Weald around East Grinstead to his neighbour at Pevensey, Roger of Mortain, and he was compensated by the grant of additional estates in Norfolk.[27]

It may readily be accepted that the Hastings territory, which became the rape of Hastings east of the Pevensey Levels, was still a province somewhat apart. Although it is clearly part of Sussex in Domesday Book, it has been referred to, in the *Anglo-Saxon Chronicle* not long since, separately from both Sussex and Kent.[28] Features of the rape of Hastings in Domesday Book are particularly small hundreds, relatively low assessments and use of a hide of eight virgates, in contrast with the usual four, all of which may be held to reflect features of Kent, where the assessments were based on a different system of sulungs and yokes, and not in hides. But if the rape of Bramber did not exist, little remains of an overall system of territorial divisions (the separate rape of Chichester was a twelfth-century post-Domesday creation by division of the rape of Arundel). J. E. A. Jolliffe in important studies,[29] considered, from the evidence of the organisation and pre-Conquest assessment of the five rapes of Domesday and features of tenurial custom and manorial organisation in the eastern and northern parts of the county in medieval times, that the whole of Sussex shared with Kent and Hampshire as far west as the Avon, common influences of early post-Roman settlement attributable to Jutes and Franks, as well as later Saxon settlement based on the West Sussex coastal plain. But it does not appear that the existence of the rapes we find in Domesday should be used to support such a view, even if it is allowed, as Jolliffe suggested, that the term 'rape' may have been significant in relation to the imposition in Sussex of hidage assessments.

If a significant territorial division of Sussex in later Saxon times at least, is to be sought, it should almost certainly as Salzman suggested, be at the Adur. This was indeed the boundary adopted in the institution of the Sussex arch-deaconries, which perhaps took place shortly after the Conquest and before the creation of the rape of William of Braose, though, as Mason pointed out, it is difficult to fit in such a time sequence.[30] It has also long been realised that the pre-Conquest hidage assessment of Sussex divides approximately equally at the Adur, with about 1,600 hides on either side (including the rape of Hastings). Encouraged by Salzman and working on this basis, David Clarke in 1933[31] worked out geographical groupings by which the apparently haphazard hidage assessments of the Sussex hundreds are made to form multiples of 80 hides, a figure which is undoubtedly significant in the Sussex assessments, as well as in relation to the assessments in Kent. Apart from assessment of the rape of Hastings at about 160 hides, however, the scheme does not entirely carry conviction as it stands. The figures include the scattered estates of the Archbishop of Canterbury and the Bishop of Selsey, whereas these seem to be assessed under a separate system. It can hardly be coincidence that west of the Adur the pre-Conquest assessments of their estates in Domesday each total 108 hides, divided up on a duodecimal system (which also appears in West Sussex to a limited extent in the assessments of Earl Godwin's estates). East of the Adur, on the other hand, the Bishop's estates, assessed in multiples of five hides, together provide an 80-hide unit which corresponds with the assessment of the Archbishop's large estate at Malling.[32]

Irrespective of the origin of the rapes or other major pre-Conquest divisions of Sussex, the constitution of the Sussex hundreds, as reflected in Domesday Book appears as a matter of considerable historical interest. The system in Sussex is distinctive, and parallels with the adjoining counties are not easily seen. For the most part the hundreds are small, so that they are exceptionally numerous. But there are some which are notably large and populous. Apart from Clarke's suggestions of their possible grouping for assessment, their individual hidage varies greatly, both in total and in sub-division, so that no overall system is apparent, such as appears in many other counties. In some Sussex hundreds with major ecclesiastical holdings, though by no means always, exclusive ecclesiastical jursidiction had been secured. Clearly in such cases, and apparently in a number of others, the hundred is related to the existence of a single large estate, and it is possible that the origin of many of the hundreds should be seen in individual landholdings, particularly royal estates.

It is difficult to see from the evidence of Domesday Book how far there were defined hundredal boundaries, as in medieval times. Boundaries are more likely to have been those of the constituent estates or holdings which were subject to their jurisdiction. Very often, however, boundaries of hundreds as well as of estates seem to be formed by the principal rivers, although exceptionally Climping, west of the Arun, is assigned to *Risberg* (later Poling) hundred east of the river. While there appears to have been substantial continuity, both major and minor differences are apparent from the medieval hundreds. However, in Domesday the basis already appears to be mainly geographical, so that a hundred primarily formed a compact and convenient grouping of settlements. A complication is that many estates possessed land outside the general area of the hundred to which they were assigned, as often also in medieval times when, in consequence, detached parts of both hundreds and parishes are found. Our view of the pre-Conquest discrete holdings is made a good deal clearer by Domesday's evidence of the post-Conquest doctrine that lay estates should fall entirely within the rape, since numerous examples are recorded in which separation had been effected on this basis. With the qualification that the drawing of geographical boundaries of hundreds based on the assignments in Domesday Book and later hundredal and parish boundaries may be partly misleading, it has nevertheless been thought worthwhile in seeking to take an overall view of *Domesday Sussex,* to give in the Appendix brief notes on the individual hundreds on a geographical basis, with relative details for 1086 of numbers of households, plough teams, annual value and approximate area, so as to provide a general basis of comparison.

The differences and similarities may be seen as primarily related to the terrain, but further limitations of the evidence, particularly as to penetration and settlement in the Weald, have also to be borne in mind. The extent to which Domesday holdings appear in the Weald is largely accidental, due, as will be suggested below, to the changes brought about by the establishment of the jurisdiction of the five rapes. So far as the hundreds themselves are concerned, we seem to see a system of some antiquity, possibly organised or imposed at a particular time but developed to take account of changing conditions. Whether, in Sussex, the hundreds were established in conformity with legislation in the tenth century by King Edgar or one of his immediate predecessors,[33] when their status as administrative units seems to have been formalised, or whether they had effectively developed earlier, cannot be said at present. In the last resort the history of the developing pattern of settlement in Sussex will be able to be deduced only when we have recovered firm evidence of the history of individual settlements in different areas and of their surrounding landscape.

Settlements, estates and colonisation

The *Sussex Domesday* reveals a great variety of individual holdings, large, medium, and sometimes very small. In all there are some 400, of which 40 were assessed at 20 hides or more. Their distribution in different parts of the county and within the areas of the different hundreds must clearly reflect the evolution of Sussex through many generations in the Saxon period.[34] In Domesday the large estates, whatever their history within the pattern of development as a whole, present the more difficult problems of understanding. Moreover, we see both estates which independent documentary evidence shows to have been very ancient and others which may have been formed only recently. The not inconsiderable estates which in King Edward's time were in the hands of the king himself, Queen Edith (who was the daughter of Earl Godwin) and his sister, the Countess Goda, and some of the ecclesiastical estates also, were probably mostly of great antiquity. The immensely larger estates shown to have been in the hands of Earl Godwin and other members of his family may largely have been taken over from others (some of them undoubtedly from the church) or may partly have been recent creations. The fact that many estates are shown as having been in the hands of Countess Goda and Earl Godwin, though they had both died in 1053, shows that the information which the Domesday commissioners obtained about the pre-Conquest ownership of estates were not necessarily up to date for the end of King Edward's reign.

Domesday shows some evidence of the widely scattered nature of some of these estates. Leaving aside the matter of distant holdings in the Weald, the evidence that holdings, which fell into more than one of the rapes after the Conquest were divided, shows that even in the populated areas extensive lands had been regarded as parts of distant estates. The most notable case is that lands at Plumpton and Saddlescombe due west of Lewes, which are assessed at as much as 47 hides, had been part of Bosham in West Sussex. There were numerous other such cases, although the location of the individual holdings is often not explicit. After 1066, because of the rape boundaries, estates at Broadwater and Beeding both lost lands at Aldrington, Kingston Buci at Hangleton, and Hurstpierpoint, and at Lancing. The situation was evidently complex, and there is no evidence to show how these discrete units were formed, or for what purpose, or over what period. On the other hand many estates probably included mainly large compact blocks of territory. Earl Godwin's large estate of Singleton in the Western Downs must have included the adjoining large territories of West Dean and East Dean. Bosham also included Funtington, Chidham, West Thorney, and West Stoke, although only West Thorney is named. Domesday states that it had also previously included one hide at Itchenor, but fails to reveal that it probably also included Apuldram, as in the medieval period. The Archbishop of Canterbury's hundred of Pagham included a large area around Pagham and also the separate area of Tangmere. All these must have embraced numerous individual settlements or farms.

The royal estates in Sussex of King Edward, Queen Edith and Countess Goda, as listed in Domesday, were strategically centred in fertile areas throughout the county, but totalled only approximately 400 hides of the county's total of eight times this amount. They were exceeded by the possessions of Earl Godwin and members of his family with a total of about 1,200 hides, and also by the estates in the hands of the church. King Edward himself held Lyminster, Steyning (in part), Beeding, Ditchling, Beddingham, Eastbourne, and *Filsham* (Pilesham), near Hastings. A corresponding list of estates 150 years earlier in King Alfred's will[35] comprised the first five of these, together with Felpham and Aldingbourne, which, with the greater part of Steyning, had passed into the hands of the church, Angmering and Rotherfield, which in Domesday Earl Godwin had acquired (the former in part) and Sutton and Beckley, which may or may not have been in Sussex. Bishop Asser[36] in Alfred's time knew also in Sussex the royal estate of 'Dene', believed to have been Westdean in East Sussex, which seems in Domesday to have been split up. The distribution and redistribution of lands by the king was no doubt a continuous process through the centuries of the Saxon era, but Domesday provides a view of the situation at its close. It seems likely that there was no great disruption of landholdings in Sussex in the ninth century during the period of the Danish attacks, or, if there was, that the situation was later restored. The earliest documented example of a Sussex grant is, of course, that by King Aethelwealh in the seventh century to Bishop Wilfrid of the royal estate centred at Selsey,[37] remarkable for Bede's statement that it had a population of 250 male and female slaves; part only of this seems to have been retained by the bishopric in Domesday Book. The estate of Denton, which according to texts in the diocesan archives was separated from the royal estate and church of Beddingham in the time of King Offa of Mercia,[38] seems almost certainly to have been in Domesday the bishop's estate of Bishopstone.

The estates of Earl Godwin and members of his family are found in Domesday Book in all parts of Sussex, as well as many outside the county, but there is little evidence of how or when they were acquired. Some estates were gained by Godwin a year before his death when Archbishop Robert was ousted,[39] but cannot be identified. The Confessor granted a large part of the great Bosham estate to his Norman chaplain, Osbern, afterwards Bishop of Exeter, and in Domesday the remainder had been held by Godwin, but there is no actual evidence that Bosham had previously been a royal estate in the time of King Canute, or that, as tradition also relates, it was obtained by Godwin from the Archbishop by a trick. Charter evidence[40] shows that the large estate of Harting, which in Domesday was in the hands of Godwin's wife, had been returned to King Edgar in 970 by the Bishop of Winchester, in exchange for lands at Ely. In Saxon times the lordship of an estate could be as rapidly taken away as obtained. Thus Harold, after he became king, did not scruple to take back from the Abbey of Fécamp the large part of the Steyning estate which had been granted by King Edward. Churchmen had early developed the practice of obtaining grants by charter to provide the best possible defence of their rights, and so later did laymen.

Comparison of the extant Sussex charter texts with Domesday Book provides evidence not only of long continuity in holdings of the church but also continuity of their hidage assessments. The important qualification that must be made is that most of the charters survive only in late copies: it was not considered wrong to adapt or indeed fabricate ancient texts to support what were actually, or were believed to be, the facts, and even the making of a spurious claim might have been considered a pious act. In the case already mentioned Denton was 25 hides in the ninth century when the bishop's claim to it was disrupted,[41] and Bishopstone is assessed at the same figure in Domesday. Henfield, described in an apparently genuine charter dated 770[42] as 15 hides, is again 15 hides in Domesday. Such continuity may indeed be considered as possible support for identifications which have been in doubt. The very early text in the diocesan records[43] in probably a tenth-century copy, by which King Nunna of Sussex granted the bishop 20 hides at 'Hugabeorgum' and 'Dene', seems likely, as was also suggested by R. Forsberg[44] on topographic and place-name grounds, to refer to the bishop's Domesday estate of Preston, near Brighton, also of 20 hides, rather than, as generally assumed the area of East Dean in West Sussex; and Aethelstan's grant of 12 hides to the Archbishop at 'Derantune'[45] (whose identification as Durrington has been disputed) seems likely to have nevertheless been the major part of the Archbishop's 18-hide Domesday estate of West Tarring. But there were also changes in the assessments. The earliest grant, that of Selsey to Bishop Wilfrid, described by both Wilfrid's biographer, Eddius, and Bede[46] as an estate of 87 hides, appears in King Edward's time in Domesday, with Sidlesham and Wittering, at what was undoubtedly a quite arbitrary figure of 36 hides, one-third of the bishop's assessment west of the Adur. Harting is recorded as 60 hides in the exchange of 970, but 80 hides in Domesday. In the grant of Pagham,[47] which also purported to be made in the seventh century to Bishop Wilfrid, but is now usually considered a tenth-century fabrication, Pagham is 70 hides and Tangmere 10 hides, but in Domesday Pagham is reduced to 50, although Tangmere is unchanged.

As to the actual distribution of population within the large estates, the charter texts, notably the two grants purporting to be made to Bishop Wilfrid, provide earlier evidence of the existence of scattered settlements within an estate, but Domesday is entirely unhelpful. It is not possible to tell how far the sub-holding listed in such estates were separate, although probably they often were. Some of the Domesday population figures are large. On what had been Earl Godwin's very large estate of Singleton in the midst of the Western Downs there were in 1086 86 villeins, 52 bordars and 17 serfs. There were also five small sub-holdings, one held by 'the clerks of the church' (possibly Earl Roger's foundation at Arundel), with a further total of three villeins, six bordars and three serfs, but there is no indication of their nature. However, the estate must undoubtedly have included the areas of the medieval parishes and modern villages of West Dean and East Dean, and there is also the hamlet of Charlton. Professor Finberg[48] drew attention to places throughout England with this name (or a variant) as likely to represent subordinate settlements of a working population vital to the economy of a large estate. In some cases the names go back at least to the tenth century. In Sussex the name 'Charlton' is also found in the vicinity of Pagham (now lost), Steyning, West Firle, and Westdean (East Sussex), all of which were centres of large estates in the Saxon period.

The nature of the Domesday estates needs also to be examined from the point of view of the possible date of the founding of churches or chapels, most of which were provided in the first instance by the owner of the estate (with a view often to financial profit) and the formation of parishes. The process was a continuing one, probably from the time of Bishop Wilfrid's mission the later part of the seventh century until the Middle Ages were well advanced. Unusually Domesday mentions the existence of as many as five churches at unknown places in the Abbey of Fécamp's large manor of 'Rameslie', which included a considerable area in the vicinity of Hastings, Winchelsea and Rye. In Domesday the areas of many medieval parishes, such as, for example, Oving and Eartham within the Bishop of Selsey's estate of Aldingbourne, are hidden within the territories of the large estates and include places such as West Dean (in Singleton), West Stoke (in Bosham), and Poling, where substantial work of Saxon date is considered to survive in the church fabric. On the other hand, there are also areas, for example around Chichester and along the scarpfoot of the Downs, where a close relationship will be found between the incidence of Domesday place-names related to small manors and the pattern of medieval parishes. Charter evidence which is closely contemporary with Domesday Book, in the form of grants by William of Braose[49] and William of Warenne,[50] shows patterns of settlements in a few areas which are un-named in Domesday and in the latter case the existence by the end of the eleventh century of churches at remote places in the Weald, such as Ardingly, Balcombe, Cuckfield, West Hoathly, and Wivelsfield. H. Poole,[51] in his study of the Sussex churches actually named in Domesday Book, reached the conclusion, largely on architectural grounds, that some of them were first built, in at any rate their surviving form, in a new impetus of church buildings in the years immediately after the Conquest.

Provision of a church, whether in Saxon or post-Conquest times, suggests that there was a community, however scattered, to serve. A church, once established, is likely to have remained, although it cannot necessarily be supposed that it will then have attracted a larger population to its vicinity. Indeed, in the medieval period and later, the sites of some churches became deserted.

Domesday provides at least a strong implication that the large estates were managed and controlled as units for the profit of their owners. This is also supported by the evidence that activity was organised in the Weald.

Penetration and colonisation of the Weald

At first sight a map of place-names recorded in Domesday shows virtually a a blank in the northern parts of Sussex compared with closely settled areas elsewhere. Closer inspection shows some names in the High Weald, but that the extensive areas mainly of Weald Clay to the west, although fringed with settlements of the Lower Greensand strata, are almost void. Yet the evidence of a number of early charters shows that the Weald was used from early Saxon times extensively at least for the raising of pigs.

There can be little doubt that Domesday reflects a situation in which the settlements in much of the Weald, such as they were, were still dependent on the holdings in the settled parts of the county and were not separately recorded. The pattern of the hundreds, and many parishes also, as they developed in the medieval period, bears this out. Extending northwards the hundreds of Bury, Easewrithe and Burbeach, for example, covered very large tracts of the Weald. A large area of the north formed a detached part of Steyning. But Domesday already shows exceptions. Two separate small hundreds of 'Grenestede' had been formed, corresponding with the later West and East Grinstead. In the High Weald there were Domesday hundreds of Rotherfield and Hartfield, with numbers of settlements. Rotherfield had indeed been a royal estate even in King Alfred's time. The Archbishop of Canterbury's hundred of Malling extended from Lewes to the Kentish border and Domesday shows that there were a number of separate holdings, but the only places named were Framfield and Little Horsted, forming an enclave which had been detached. Two settlements at Ifield, near Crawley, constituted a tiny hundred of 'Tifeld' which, if it was not the result of a clerical mistake, nevertheless does not appear again, since the area became part of Burbeach hundred. The remote holding of Worth, with a magnificent church considered by most authorities to be largely pre-Conquest in date, is assigned in Domesday to the hundred of 'Cherchefelle' (Reigate) in Surrey.

There is a single direct reference in the *Sussex Domesday* to apparent colonisation after the Conquest at an un-named place in 'Iswerit' (Easewrithe) hundred, previously a pasture of a Storrington estate, where there was now a plough team and a mill. Fortuitously, however, we have a much clearer picture of extensive settlement in the East Grinstead area. This occurs solely because the area was transferred from the rape of Lewes to that of Pevensey and it was necessary to record the settlement there, since they had been separated from their parent estates. Thus, 13 small settlements, all but one of them named, were separately recorded in 1086.

A similar fortuitous view of colonisation, to which attention was first drawn by Round and Salzman,[52] appears in the rape of Hastings in the hundreds of 'Hauchesberie' (Hawksborough), 'Shoeswelle' (Shoyswell), and 'Henhert', and to some extent also in 'Hailsaltede' (Netherfield). The parent estates had been in the Lewes-Seaford-Eastbourne triangle in the rape of Pevensey, and had been largely in the hands of King Edward, Countess Goda, Wilton Abbey, and Harold. This looks like a co-operative and organised venture, but there is no evidence of the period of the settlement. The area was probably heavily wooded. Dr. Brandon[53] has suggested possible interest in exploiting the iron-bearing deposits, but there is no evidence as yet to support this.

Boroughs

Domesday shows the existence as boroughs of Chichester, Arundel, Steyning, Lewes, Pevensey, Hastings and another un-named but recently-established place in the rape of Hastings, which is generally thought to have been Rye. All were seaports—there is independent contemporary evidence that ships sailed up the Adur to St. Cuthman's port, or market, at Steyning.[54] Chichester, Lewes and Hastings had probably had their origins as defensive 'burhs' of Alfred or Edward the Elder, as listed in the Burghal Hidage,[55] and seem likely to have been the largest places. Unfortunately, a Domesday account of Hastings is omitted, and for all the boroughs the information given is minimal. Chichester, Lewes, Pevensey, and Hastings all had pre-Conquest moneyers, but Domesday mentions mints only at Lewes and Pevensey.

The features of pre-Conquest boroughs were royal grants of privileges, including markets, and of burgage tenures which permitted the holders to engage in crafts, trading or similar activities. There are no relevant pre-Conquest documents for Sussex.

Of Chichester we are told no more than that in King Edward's time there were 97½ enclosures and three crofts, and that at the time of the survey there were 60 more houses than before. At Lewes there had been 127 burgesses in King Edward's time, and there were now 39 inhabited messuages and 20 unoccupied. But these details, whatever their precise meaning, related only to the property held from the king or, after the Conquest, from the lord of the rape. The accounts of individual outside manors produce, in 1086, a further total in Chichester of 135 enclosures and nine burgesses. All these manors were west of the Arun. At Lewes 197 enclosures, 53 burgesses and 18 messuages are similarly shown, mainly belonging to manors in the rape of Lewes, but including Laughton and Alciston in Pevensey.[56] By 1086 Lewes had become the seat of William of Warenne and Chichester that of the bishopric, previously at Selsey.

At Pevensey in 1086 the number of burgesses had risen to 90, some of them similarly belonging to outlying estates. For Hastings there is mention only of dependents of the manors of Bexhill and 'Rameslie'. Both Pevensey and Hastings had also become the headquarters of the lords of the respective rapes. Steyning had been historically the centre of a royal estate, of which King Edward had granted the larger part to the Abbey of Fécamp. After seizure by Harold, this was returned to the Abbey by King William. Steyning was evidently a sizeable place, with 123 properties in 1086 and a large agricultural population, but William of Braose elected to build his castle at Bramber. Roger of Montgomery also chose a new site for his castle at Arundel. Domesday shows that in King Edward's time there was virtually nothing there, but by 1086 four burgesses could be recorded and 13 enclosures belonging to manors in the vicinity. Finally it was recorded that a 'new town' had been established in the Abbey of Fécamp's estate at 'Rameslie', and there were 64 burgesses, together with 104 dependent villeins and four cottars. This has been generally considered to have been Rye.

The general impression is thus that at the time of Domesday the boroughs were becoming places of considerable importance. Perhaps the most significant information is the role they were fulfilling as centres of interest for the surrounding estates. As seaports they were no doubt depots for both coastal and overseas trade, and connections with Normandy particularly would be developing. Their new roles in some cases after the Conquest as the seats of the bishop and the feudal lords must have provided an added impulse in urban development.

Domesday Book and Saxon Sussex

The question may again be posed—what was the real significance of Domesday? It is easier to say what Domesday was not. It was not a population census. Nor was it a gazetteer or description of the English shires and their settlements, or of their resources, actual or potential. It was not a roll of barons and knights who could be called out to fight with their retinues. It was not strictly a *geld* roll or tax book. Yet it combined something of all these purposes.

Whoever devised the plan and its details, the king or one of his advisers, he was concerned mainly about government and the control of the kingdom, its leading men and its resources. He well knew that King Edward and his predecessors had not been ineffective as rulers, and that England had not been lacking in the arts of a civilised kingdom. Perhaps, after 20 years, William felt himself frustrated, having encountered in England little more than rebellion, grudging support and quarrels among his own family and followers. Because of his death the following year no effective use was made of the survey, but it remained as an authentic record of late Saxon land tenure and the assignments to the invaders.

From our own viewpoint Domesday seems to show Sussex at a crucial period of its development. It appears still as a primarily maritime and rather isolated province, and we cannot yet see clearly the picture which emerges in the Middle Ages of an intensive advance into the Weald, cultivation of difficult land and inroads into the forests, development of new towns and communications and revival of the extensive iron-working industry of the Roman period. Nevertheless, Sussex towards the close of the Saxon period was not entirely a province apart. Godwin, Earl of Wessex, we believe to have been primarily a Sussex man. He almost dominated the kingdom, and his son was chosen as the last Saxon king. Important Sussex estates were held from outside the county, by the New Minster at Winchester and the Wiltshire abbeys of Wilton and Shaftesbury, and by leading men of Kent.[57] On any interpretation of Domesday statistics the more populous parts of Sussex were as densely settled as any part of England.

The questions we put to Domesday Book today are not the same as those of King William. Eighty years ago, in 1897, Maitland, in the last sentences of *Domesday Book and Beyond,* already expressed the conviction that 'A century hence . . . Those villages and hundreds which the Norman clerks tore into shreds will have been reconstituted and pictured in maps . . .'. The century is far advanced but the detailed picture does not yet readily appear, and we may also believe rather that the Norman clerks did no more than record what was reported to them. We have yet to find on the ground in Sussex the pattern of a late Saxon village and its fields, or of the nucleus of an estate.

It may now be time to seek a new approach and perhaps turn attention more closely to some, at least, of the hundreds and compare all our Domesday and

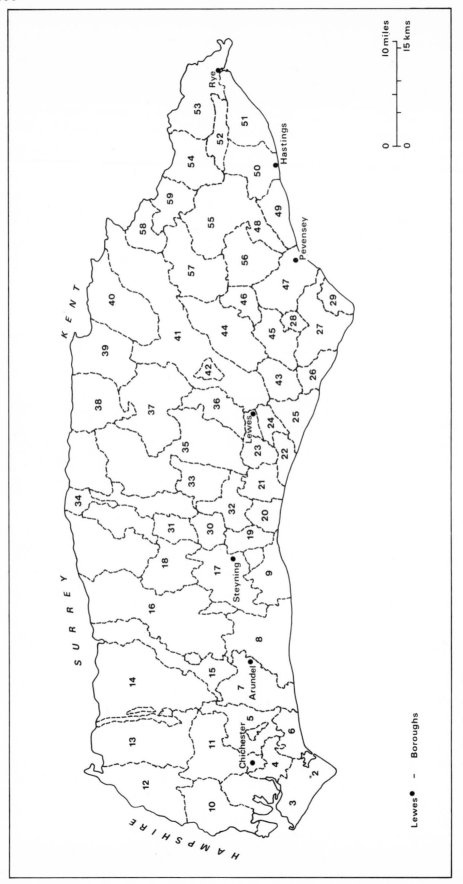

Fig. 18 The Domesday Hundreds of Sussex

other evidence with the pattern within them of the Sussex landscape, where it still survives. May such a focus, neglecting no detail, begin to reveal a corresponding pattern of settlements and livelihood to that recorded in Domesday? And even if we may believe that in Sussex the organisation of the hundredal system was initially arbitrarily imposed, perhaps as late as the tenth century, it may be possible to see a little more clearly the pattern of settlements as it existed also at that time, in a process of slow evolution. The Domesday text, despite its difficulties, provides the sole and vital link between medieval Sussex, of which we know much and are learning much more, and the still relatively obscure centuries of the Saxon era.

*   *   *   *   *   *

APPENDIX

THE DOMESDAY HUNDREDS OF SUSSEX

In this Appendix brief notes and statistics are given for the individual Sussex hundreds of Domesday Book.

The hundreds in the eleventh century are unlikely to have had fixed territorial boundaries. The tenurial arrangements probably resulted in the existence of numerous detached areas or enclaves of population. Nevertheless, an overall geographical view of the hundreds and their constituent estates or holdings may serve to provide a generalised indication of patterns of tenure, settlement and population in Sussex at the close of the Saxon era.

The pre-Conquest hidage assessments in the time of King Edward (T.R.E.) are also included for comparison. These are generally as estimated by David Clarke[58] on a basis of fiscal liability, rather than geographical incidence.

The areas, in square kilometers (km.^{2}), are estimated very approximately, mainly on the basis of later hundredal and parish boundaries.

The statistics of households (i.e., villeins, bordars, cottars and serfs), plough teams and annual value are calculated from those given in Domesday for 1086, the year of the survey. No account is taken of the population of the boroughs. It must be assumed that possibly a not inconsiderable part of the population was settled, especially in the Weald, outside the general area of the hundreds in which it was enumerated.

The arrangement of the individual hundreds is by broad geographical regions of the county rather than by rapes, but those in the compact Hastings territory, which became the rape of Hastings, are obviously grouped together. To facilitate reference the names of the hundreds as they appear in Domesday Book are given alphabetically in the following list, which shows the numerical order in which they have been dealt with. The relevant numbers also appear on the map (Fig. 18), p. 208.

Avronelle (later part of Longbridge)............28
Babinrerode (later Gostrow)........................52
Baldeslei (Baldslow).....................................50
Battle—*see* Hailsaltede
Benestede (Binsted) (later Avisford)............ 7
Bercheham (Barcombe)...............................36
Berie (Bury)..15
Bexelei (Bexhill)...49
Bocse or Bosgrave (Boxgrove)..................... 5
Borne (Eastbourne)....................................29
Boseham (Bosham).................................... 1
Botingelle (Buttinghill)..............................33
Bradfota (Brightford)................................. 9

Burbece (Burbeach).....................................19
Colespore (Goldspur)..................................53
Edivestone (later Shiplake)..........................44
Eldritune (Aldrington) (later Fishersgate)....20
Eseburne (Easebourne)...............................13
Estrat (Streat)...35
Falemere (Falmer) (later Younsmere)..........23
Flexberge (Flexborough) (later also Bishop-
    stone) 26
Folsalre (Foxearle)......................................56
Framele (Framfield).....................................42
Gestelings (Guestling)..................................51
Ghidentroi (later Westbourne)....................10

Grenested (East Grinstead)...........................38
Grenestede (West Grinstead).......................18
Hailsaltede (later Netherfield and Battle).....55
Hamesforde (later Dumpford)....................12
Hamfeld (Henfield)....................................30
Hauchsberie (Hawksborough).....................57
Henhert (Henhurst)...................................59
Hertevel (Hartfield)...................................39
Homestreu (Holmestrow)...........................25
Iswerit (later West and East Easewrithe)......16
Latille (Dill)..46
Mellinges (Malling)...................................41
Nerefelle (Ninfield)...................................48
Pagham (later Aldwick)............................. 6
Pevensel (Pevensey)..................................47
Poninges (Poynings)..................................32
Presteton (Preston) (later part of Whales-
    borne) 21
Redrebruge (Rotherbridge)........................14

Reredfelle (Rotherfield)..............................40
Risberg (later Poling)................................. 8
Ristone (later Rushmonden).......................37
Shoeswelle (Shoyswell)...............................58
Silletone (Singleton)..................................11
Soaneberge (Swanborough).........................24
Staninges (Steyning)..................................17
Staple...54
Stocbruge (Stockbridge).............................. 4
Summerleg (Somerley) (later part of Man-
    hood) 2
Tifeld (later part of Burbeach)....................34
Totenore (Totnore).....................................43
Wandelmeistre (later Alciston)....................45
Welesmere (later Whalesborne)...................22
Westringes (Wittering) (later part of Man-
    hood) 3
Wildene or Willendone (Willingdon).............27
Windham 31

A.—THE WEST SUSSEX COASTAL PLAIN

1. *Boseham* (Bosham) (T.R.E. 121½ hides, excluding 47 in East Sussex).
    Households, 197; teams, 70½. value, £69 5s. 0d. (as much as £340, in all, before the Conquest); area, *c.* 50 km.[2]
    Domesday shows that the large estate of Bosham was divided in King Edward's time between Earl Godwin and the king's Norman chaplain, Osbern, later Bishop of Exeter, and probably included the parishes of Bosham, Funtington, Apuldram, Chidham, West Thorney and West Stoke, with land also in Itchenor (Westringes hundred) and at Plumpton (Estrat hundred) and Saddlescombe (Poninges hundred), both in East Sussex. No intrusive holdings were named in the Bosham area. There is no Domesday evidence of Wealden outliers, but in the Middle Ages land was held in Kirdford. Bosham was not actually called a hundred in Domesday.
2. *Summerleg* (Somerley) (T.R.E. 36 hides)
3. *Westringes* (Wittering) (T.R.E. 6½ hides) (later Manhood).
    Households, 143; teams, 40½; value, £43; area *c.* 55 km.[2]
    The territories of the two hundreds cannot be distinguished. Somerley comprised the Manhood estates of the Bishop of Chichester (formerly Selsey), divided into Selsey, Sidlesham, and Wittering. The cathedral canons held 16 additional hides (unlocated). Westringes consisted of four small estates held by laymen, including Itchenor, which had been part of Bosham. The area suffered much later coastal erosion.
4. *Stocbruge* (Stockbridge) (T.R.E. 33 hides).
    Households, 102; teams, 21½; value, £31 5s. 0d.; area, *c.* 21 km.[2]
    Within the hundred there were small estates west and south of Chichester in Donnington, New Fishbourne, Wyke (Rumboldswyke), North Mundham and Hunston, possibly largely coinciding with these parishes. Before the Conquest Wyke and Hunston were respectively divided into holdings of five and six 'free men'.
5. *Bocse*, or Bosgrave (Boxgrove) (T.R.E. 112 hides).
    Households, 235; teams, 40; value, £52 6s. 0d.; area, *c.* 52 km.[2]
    The hundred extended eastwards to Upwaltham (the route of Stane Street), Eartham and Aldingbourne. Apart from the Bishop of Chichester's 36 hide estate of Aldingbourne, which probably included most of Oving and Eartham, this was an area of small or very small holdings, often described as having been in the hands of 'free men', which were partly consolidated after the Conquest.

6. *Pagham* (later Aldwick) (T.R.E. 60 hides).

Households, 184; teams, 36; value, £66; area. *c.* 34 km.[2]

The Archbishop of Canterbury's estate of Pagham included South Bersted, South Mundham and Tangmere, the latter forming an enclave in Bosgrave hundred. Charter evidence (probably tenth century)[59] referred to sheep pastures at 'meos dune', which it has been suggested was Levin Down. Some later coastal erosion was experienced, including loss of a settlement named Charlton.

7. *Benestede* (Binstead) (T.R.E. 95¼ hides) (later Avisford).

Households, 346; teams, 74; value, £91 2s. 6d.; area, *c.* 73 km.[2]

This was the area eastwards to the Arun, including South Stoke, but, if the Domesday text is accurate, specifically excluding Climping. The only sizeable estate was Felpham, held by the Abbey of Shaftesbury, of 21 hides. Most of this partly clayey area was split into very small holdings. There has been severe later coastal erosion.

8. *Riseberg* (T.R.E. 158 hides) (later Poling).

Households, 625; teams 149½; value, £197; area, *c.* 86 km.[2]

The estates are generally medium-sized, and there are indications of probable breaking up of much of the ancient royal estate of Lyminster. Although assessed before the Conquest at only 20 hides this was still the most important estate in the hundred, with 113 households and 44 teams. 'Nonneminstre', another important estate, had been held from King Edward by two priests and may have been based on West Preston.[60] The Archbishop of Canterbury held Patching, and Domesday's statement that it was used for the clothing of the monks at Canterbury may indicate sheep raising. The Bishop of Chichester held Ferring. Climping, west of the Arun, was an important estate, which had been held by Earl Godwin. After the Conquest it was given to the Abbeys of Almènesches and Séez, but the Domesday entries, which are identical may have been duplicated in error. Estates at Angmering and Goring lost lands to the east on the formation of Bramber rape. Place-name evidence, for example Pallingfold in Rudgwick and Goringlee in Thakeham, suggests that there were Wealden holdings established from estates in this area,[61] but Domesday provides no evidence. The area has suffered much coastal erosion.

9. *Bradfota* (Brightford) (T.R.E. 113½ hides).

Households, 268; teams, 70½; value, £89 15s. 0d.; area, *c.* 42 km.[2]

The hundred extended to the Adur. The estates are of moderate size and before the Conquest were mostly sub-holdings from the king or Earl Godwin or members of his family. (West) Tarring was held by the Archbishop of Canterbury. Other important estates were at Broadwater, Sompting and Lancing, and all these after the Conquest lost lands which were in the rape of Lewes. On the other hand, other land in Lancing had been part of Earl Godwin's estate of Hurstpierpoint. In Domesday Book Findon and Clapham in the Downs gap formed part of Staninges (Steyning) hundred, though they were later in Brightford. In medieval times the Archbishop's estate included holdings at Shipley, Horsham and Rusper in the Weald. There has been severe coastal erosion in this hundred also.

B.—THE WESTERN DOWNS

10. *Ghidentroi* (T.R.E. 105½ hides) (later Westbourne).

Households, 281; teams, 69¼; Value, £117 15s. 0d.; area, *c.* 65 km.[2]

The hundred embraced the western Downland valleys, with the major holdings before the Conquest based on Westbourne and Stoughton (each 36 hides) and Compton (10 hides), all of which were in the hands of Earl Godwin. Westbourne also included Warblington, which was in Hampshire, west of the Ems, and in Domesday this was returned as part of that county.

11. *Silletone* (Singleton) (T.R.E. 135½ hides).

Households, 237; teams, 62; value, £149 and one mark of gold; area, *c.* 70 km.[2]

This was the area of the Lavant valley, with three estates in Lavant and two in Binderton and the very large estate of Singleton, held before the Conquest by Earl Godwin, which would have included West Dean and East Dean. Singleton's assessment of 97½ hides was the largest undivided pre-Conquest assessment in Sussex. The Archbishop of Canterbury held East Lavant as 18 hides.

C.—THE VALLEY OF THE WESTERN ROTHER

12. *Hamesforde* (T.R.E. 117 hides) (later Dumpford).
    Households, 274; teams, 82; value, £128; area, *c.* 91 km.[2]
    Holdings were based on the scarpfoot and the river, and no doubt, like the medieval parishes, extended south on to the Downs and north on to the Weald Clay. By far the largest estate was Harting (80 hides) held before the Conquest by Earl Godwin's wife, Countess Goda, who also held Trotton. Treyford and Chithurst were held by Earl Godwin. Elsted had been given to Osbern, the later Bishop of Exeter. Harting probably included the whole of Rogate, and probably Terwick was included in Trotton, and Didling in Treyford. Hamesford is shown in Domesday as including a number of estates which were later in Easebourne hundred, perhaps in error; they are here assigned to Easebourne.
13. *Easeburne* (Easebourne) (T.R.E. 64 hides).
    Households, 193; teams, 53½; value, £61 5s. 0d.; area, *c.* 120 km.[2]
    There were smallish estates, based on the scarpfoot or the river, at Stedham, Cocking, Linch Farm, Buddington, Selham, Bepton, Todham, Graffham, Woolbeding and Iping. Before the Conquest Earl Godwin was prominent among the holders. It is curious that there is no Domesday holding of Easebourne, although Todham is in Easebourne parish. This might be an accidental omission. There are no Domesday names on the Weald Clay, and the medieval parishes ran northwards in strips, with some detached areas. Linch, now a Wealden parish, was originally a scarpfoot settlement at Linch Farm. The strip of North and South Ambersham belonged to a Hampshire estate; this featured in a grant by King Edgar in 963.[62] The strip of Lodsworth, which was retained after the Conquest by 'Chetel the huntsman', is oddly assigned in Domesday to Woking hundred in Surrey, and has also been excluded here.
14. *Redrebruge* (Rotherbridge) (T.R.E. 59¼ hides).
    Households, 286; teams, 66; value, £78 4s. 0d.; area, *c.* 164 km.[2]
    The hundred was formed of mainly small estates, some of them divided before the Conquest among numbers of 'free men'. These extended along the scarpfoot and the river as far east as Sutton and Stopham, although the latter was possibly isolated by a strip of 'Berie' (Bury) hundred extending northwards. Tillington and Grittenham are included in Domesday in Easebourne hundred, but were later in Rotherbridge, and have been included here. Petworth and Tillington, both north of the river, had considerable populations of 44 and 45 households respectively, but the extent of the medieval parishes indicates that probably there was a minimum of settlement on the Weald Clay. The hundred has been taken to include also the large Wealden parishes of Kirdford, North Chapel (part of Petworth) and Lurgashall, as in the medieval period, though none of these appear in Domesday. The name of the hundred means 'oxen bridge'; the river name is a later back-formation.[63]

D.—NORTH OF THE DOWNS TO THE ADUR

15. *Berie* (Bury) (T.R.E. 25 hides).
    Households, 99; teams, 29; value, £33; area, *c.* 83 km.[2]
    In Domesday there were three estates only: Bignor, Bury and Hardham, of which Bury, which had been held by King Edward's sister, Countess Goda, was the most

important. The medieval hundred extended northwards as a strip across the Weald Clay, including Egdean, Fittleworth, Wisborough Green and part of Alfold (Surrey), and this area has been included, although Domesday shows no settlements. Felpham had early swine pastures in Fittleworth,[64] and there was a detached part of the medieval parish of Bignor about 13 km. distant, at Buddington in Easebourne.

16. *Iswerit* (Easewrithe) (T.R.E. 107 hides) (later West and East Easewrithe).
    Households, 333; teams, 95; value, £97 17s. 0d.; area *c.* 187 km.^{2}

The hundred name appears in Domesday in different spellings. The medieval hundreds embraced the catchment area of the Arun, including the large Wealden parishes of Pulborough, Billingshurst, Rudgwick, Slinfold, and Itchingfield. The division into two separate hundreds arose from creation of the rape boundary between Arundel and Bramber. The most important Domesday estates were Amberley, held by the Bishop of Chichester (24 hides), Thakeham, which had been held of King Edward by Brixi,[65] and Pulborough. There were numerous smaller estates in the Lower Greensand belt, but the only example of a named estate in the Weald Clay area was 'Moha', probably Muntham in Itchingfield, with a population of 11 households, which may originally have been a dependent of Muntham in Findon. There is a Domesday reference to an apparent very recent example of colonisation in mention of an un-named holding with a single plough team, which had previously been pasture belonging to one of the estates of Storrington.

17. *Staninges* (Steyning) (T.R.E. 258½hides).
    Households, 795; teams, 199; value, £289 16s. 4d.; area, *c.* 90 km.^{2} and a further detached area of *c.* 90 km.^{2} in the Weald.

This was by far the largest Sussex Domesday hundred in terms of hidage assessment and population. It included Washington, Wiston and Steyning in the scarpfoot zone, the Downland estates of Findon and Clapham, and the adjoining areas west of the Adur. Most of the royal estate of Steyning (99 hides) had been given by King Edward to the Abbey of Fécamp, though he kept a part of it in his own hands. It was afterwards seized by Harold, but restored to Fécamp after the Conquest. Washington (59 hides) was held by Harold's brother, Earl Gurth, and Findon (30½ hides) by Harold. The smaller estates were mostly held from King Edward or Earl Godwin. Findon and Clapham lost land to the west after the creation of the rape of Bramber, the Clapham land being part of Lyminster.

In medieval times a large detached area in the north of the county, comprising Horsham, Nuthurst, Warnham, and Rusper, was part of Steyning hundred (later hundreds of Horsham and Singlecross). Charter evidence shows that there were swine pastures of Washington in the Horsham area in the tenth century,[66] but there are no Domesday holdings shown in that area.

A number of places not named in Domesday are among those documented as grants of tithes by William of Braose to his new church at Bramber,[67] where he built his castle. Bramber is described in Domesday as 'one hide of Washington', which is some distance to the west. Although Steyning apparently enjoyed borough status, its population was enumerated as villeins, bordars and serfs, and these have been included.

18. *Grenestede* (West Grinstead) (T.R.E. 3½hides).
    Households, 8; teams, 2; value, £2; area, *c.* 57 km.^{2}

A single estate, 'Etune', is assigned in Domesday to this hundred, and is generally identified as Eaton's Farm on the Hythe Beds, east of Ashurst. Fulking in Lewes rape is described in Domesday as an outlier of 'Sepelei' (Shipley), but Shipley does not otherwise appear, though it is one of the places named in William of Braose's grant of *c.* 1073 to the church of Bramber.[68] It was presumably part of another estate in Steyning or Easewrithe. The name probably means 'sheep clearing', and the present village is on the Weald Clay area on the western arm of the Adur. The area of the hundred has been taken to approximate to the parishes of West Grinstead and Shipley.

E.—THE EASTERN DOWNS

19. *Burbece* (Burbeach) (T.R.E. 54 hides).

Households, 233; teams, 59½; value, £98 10s. 0d.; area, *c.* 29 km.[2], together with a further 42 km.[2] (Lower Beeding).

The royal estate of (Upper) Beeding, centred in the scarpfoot and east of the Adur, was held by King Edward and assessed at 32 hides. Aldrington in *Eldritune* hundred (q.v.) had been part of it. It may be inferred that the estates of Erringham and Shoreham in Burbeach, which were held from King Edward, had similarly also been part of it at one time. Beeding lost 10 hides to the east when Bramber rape was formed, but in 1086 included former 15 hides of 'Berth', generally considered to have been in Hurstpierpoint, and Rodmell, near Lewes. Tottington had been part of Harold's Findon estate.

Upper Beeding parish in medieval times included the large detached area of Lower Beeding in the High Weald, which was also part of the medieval Burbeach hundred. This seems clearly to reflect early dependence of a large tract of the Weald. Burbeach also absorbed the Domesday hundred of 'Tifeld' (q.v.). No Domesday names appear in Lower Beeding.

20. *Eldritune* (Aldrington) (T.R.E. 52¾ hides) (later Fishersgate).

Households, 182; teams, 38; value, £48 19s. 6d.; area, *c.* 22 km.[2]

Two estates named 'Kingston' (Kingston Buci) had been held from Harold, one of 21 hides by Azor, who also held Hangleton (14¼ hides), stated to be part of Kingston, from the king; and the other, of seven hides, which was probably in the Southwick area, by Gunnild, a woman. Nine hides at Aldrington had been held as part of Broadwater, but a further seven hides were held from the king by villeins as part of Beeding. The hundred was divided by the establishment of the rape of Bramber.

21. *Presteton* (Preston) (T.R.E. 80 hides) (later part of Whalesborne).

Households, 278; teams, 109; value, £98; area, *c.* 30 km.[2]

The 60-hide Downland estate of Patcham had been held by Harold. Uniquely 10 shepherds are mentioned. The Bishop of Chichester held the remainder as Preston. The hundred probably included West Blatchington and Hove.

22. *Welesmere* (T.R.E. 33¼ hides) (later Whalesborne).

Households, 113; teams, 16½; value, £47; area, *c.* 26 km.[2]

The Domesday hundred comprised a number of small holdings under the names of Brighton, Ovingdean and Rottingdean. The Rottingdean holding had been part of one in Alfriston (Frog Firle) and Queen Edith's Ovingdean holding had had an outlier in the same area. This looks like an exchange of lands. There were herring renders from Brighton. This has been an area of later coastal erosion.

23. *Falemere* (Falmer) (T.R.E. 51 hides) (later Younsmere).

Households, 101; teams, 50; value, £43 16s. 0d.; area, *c.* 23 km.[2]

The hundred included the estates of Falmer (21 hides), held by Wilton Abbey, and Stanmer (20 hides), which was held from the Archbishop of Canterbury by the canons of Malling. Three hides of Falmer were stated to be in Pevensey rape, where Wilton Abbey also held the large estate of West Firle. A Canterbury charter,[69] apparently of the late eighth century, associates extensive Wealden holdings in the areas of Wivelsfield and Lindfield with Stanmer. In Domesday a holding in East Grinstead hundred had been associated with Bevendean.

Reorganisation in the medieval period created the hundreds of Youngsmere, which also included Ovingdean, Rottingdean and Kingston-by-Lewes.

24. *Soaneberge* (Swanborough) (T.R.E. 80½ hides).

Households, 154; teams, 50½; value, £45 1s. 0d.; area, *c.* 18 km.[2]

The hundred virtually consisted of Queen Edith's major holding of 'Niworde' (Iford), but a substantial part of this had been in the rape of Pevensey. There were small holdings from King Edward at Winterbourne and Ashcombe. The important royal estate of

Ditchling is also assigned in Domesday to this hundred, but this may well be a clerical error, and it has been placed here in the hundred of 'Estrat' (Streat), (q.v.), as subsequently.

25. *Homestreu* (Holmestrow) (T.R.E. 124 hides).

Households, 224; teams, 70; value, £63, area, *c.* 29 km.[2]

Harold had held the major estate of 'Ramelle' (Rodmell) (79 hides, of which, however, 15 lay east of the Ouse in Pevensey rape). The New Minster at Winchester (later Hyde Abbey) held 'Suesse' (Southease) (28 hides), which produced an annual render of 38,500 herrings. Meeching (Newhaven), Piddinghoe, and Telscombe are not named. However, a New Minster grant purporting to be made by King Edgar included Telscombe, with its church.[70] Churches at Piddinghoe and Meeching were among those named as presented by William of Warenne to his newly-founded Priory of St. Pancras at Lewes.[71] These places may have been included in the unidentified Domesday holdings of 'Herbertinges' and 'Laneswice' in this hundred.

26. *Flexberge* (Flexborough) (T.R.E. 51 hides) (later also Bishopstone).

Households, 105; teams, 53; value, £38 10s. 0d.; area, *c.* 26 km.[2]

This hundred covered much of the Downland east of the Ouse as far as the Cuckmere. The main estate of Bishopstone (25 hides), which included Denton, belonged to the Bishop of Chichester. There were three holdings of 'Ferles', the same name as that of the major estate of West Firle (see Totenore hundred), but these have been generally thought to have been at Frog Firle in Alfriston. They possibly included the general area of Seaford, Sutton and Chynting, none of which is named in Domesday. Two Alfriston holdings were in the hundred of *Wandelmestrie*.

27. *Willendone* or *Wildene* (Willingdon) (T.R.E. 117 hides).

Households, 241; teams, 74½; value, £117 4s. 0d.; area, *c.* 50 km.[2]

East of the Cuckmere this hundred mainly comprised numerous small Downland holdings in the parishes of Westdean, Friston, Eastdean, Jevington and Willingdon. The large estate of Willingdon (51½ hides) had been held by Earl Godwin, but most of the small estates were held from King Edward, and may represent the breaking-up of a former royal estate of Westdean, thought to be the most likely identity of the Sussex estate of 'Dene' which was visited by Bishop Asser in King Alfred's time. The estates in this hundred, including Willingdon, were involved in the colonisation of the Hastings backwoods. More than 20 of their assessed hides are identified in Domesday as being in that area.

28. *Avronelle* (T.R.E. 20 hides) (later part of Longbridge).

Households, 39; teams, 13½; value, £16; area, *c.* 13 km.[2]

In this hundred there were only two small holdings in Wilmington and Folkington.

29. *Borne* (Eastbourne) (T.R.E. 55 hides).

Households, 101; teams, 41; value, £49 5s. 0d.; area *c.* 18 km.[2]

In this hundred there was the important royal estate of 'Borne' (46 hides, of which two hides were in the rape of Hastings). Other small estates were held directly from King Edward or by 'free men'.

F.—NORTH OF THE DOWNS FROM THE ADUR TO PEVENSEY

30. *Hamfeld* (Henfield) (T.R.E. 23 hides).

Households, 75; teams, 24; value, £16 12s. 0d.; area, *c.* 26 km.[2]

The estate of the Bishop of Chichester at Henfield, in the Lower Greensand zone east of the Adur, was assessed at 15 hides. Other holdings in the hundred were at Wantley Farm in Henfield and at Woodmancote. Due to folding of the geological strata the Lower Greensand areas here are further north than to west of the Adur.

31. *Windham* (T.R.E. 8¼ hides).

Households, 26; teams, 8¼; value, £9 19s. 0d.; area, *c.* 36 km.[2]

In this hundred there were small holdings in Henfield, Shermanbury and Twineham in the Adur valley, in an area partly of Weald Clay.

32. *Poninges* (Poynings) (T.R.E. 62½ hides).

Households, 106; teams, 59½; value, £49; area, *c.* 23 km.[2]

The hundred included the scarpfoot and adjoining Downland in the Fulking, New-timber, Poynings and Pyecombe areas. These were small populous holdings, which had been mainly held direct from King Edward or Earl Godwin. Saddlescombe on the Downs, assessed at 17 hides, had been part of Bosham. The medieval strip parishes in this area included scattered hamlets.

33. *Botingelle* (Buttinghill) (T.R.E. 65 hides).

Households, 135; teams, 60½; value, £32; area, *c.* 47 km.[2] in Hurstpierpoint, Clayton and Keymer, and *c.* 71 km.[2] in Cuckfield, Slaugham and Crawley. Worth is excluded.

The largest estate was 'Herst' (Hurstpierpoint), held by Earl Godwin, but of its 41 hides before the Conquest 19 were to the west in Bramber rape and three to the east in Pevensey. The other estates were Wickham in Hurstpierpoint, Clayton and Keymer. The strip parishes of the hundred run northwards across the Lower Greensand to the Weald Clay. The medieval hundred included the Wealden areas of Ardingly, Balcombe, Bolney, Cuckfield, West Hoathly, Slaugham, Twineham, and Worth, but earlier it appears that Ardingly, Balcombe, West Hoathly, and Twineham had been associated with the royal estate of Ditchling (see 'Estrat' hundred).

The ground is hilly, rising from the Adur towards the Forest Ridge, and there were areas of marl, clay and sand. The only Wealden holding in the area listed in Domesday is the small holding of Worth in the far north, but this is assigned to 'Cherchefelle' (Reigate) hundred in Surrey. The existence here of the fine church, apparently of Saxon date, is not easily explained. But that the area as a whole was devoid of settlements at the time of the Domesday survey is disproved by apparently genuine grants in the Lewes cartulary in which William of Warenne grants churches at Ardingly, Balcombe, Cuckfield, and (West) Hoathly to the Priory.[72]

34. *Tifeld* (T.R.E. 1½ hides) (later part of Burbeach).

Households, 10; teams, 1½; value, £1 6s. 0d.; area, *c.* 18 km.[2]

Two very small holdings in 'Ifeld' (Ifield) in the Crawley area in the extreme north of the county are assigned to a hundred of 'Tifeld'. One of these is stated to have been part of Shoreham. There is no later reference to this hundred, and the area became part of Burbeach.

35. *Estrat* (Streat) (T.R.E. 117½ hides).

Households, 367; teams, 162½; value, £123 12s. 0d.; area, *c.* 73 km.[2] with *c.* 86 km.[2] in Wivelsfield, Ardingly, Balcombe, and West Hoathly.

Before the Conquest the most important holding in the area was the royal estate of Ditchling, assessed at 46 hides. In Domesday Book this is placed in 'Soaneberge' (Swanborough) hundred, but this appears likely to be a mistake. In medieval times the parishes of Ditchling, Westmeston, Streat, Plumpton, and Chailey formed strips extending northwards from the Downs across the Lower Greensand to the Weald Clay, but large parts of the manor of Ditchling were in Ardingly, Balcombe, and West Hoathly. Wivelsfield, where a church was given by William of Warenne to Lewes Priory,[73] was afterwards a chapelry of Ditchling and was part of the medieval hundred. The only iron-working establishment in Sussex referred to in Domesday had also been associated with Ditchling and was in 'Grenested' (East Grinstead) hundred (q.v.).

The large holding of Plumpton (32 hides) was part of Bosham before the Conquest and was held by Godwin, a priest.

The area between the Adur and the High Weald appears as a likely scene of substantial early penetration of the Weald, but Domesday provides virtually no evidence. In an eight-century charter Wivelsfield and Lindfield were named as swine pastures of Stanmer.[74]

36. *Bercheham* (Barcombe) (T.R.E. 44 hides).

Households, 73; teams, 27½; value, £22; area, *c.* 39 km.[2]

In the Ouse valley above Lewes, there were two small holdings in Allington, now part of Lewes, an important one of 25 hides at Hamsey, which had been held from King Edward by Ulveva, a woman, and Barcombe, which was held from Earl Godwin by Azor.

Seven hides of Hamsey had been in Pevensey rape, including four hides in Horsted Keynes, and a little less than four hides were remarkably in the rape of Arundel.

37. *Ristone* (T.R.E. 9 hides) (later Rushmonden).

Households, 63; teams, 24½; value, £11 11s. 0d.; area, *c.* 73 km.[2]

This appears to have been a rather dispersed hundred made up of small holdings in the Fletching, Horsted Keynes, Lindfield, and Maresfield areas. There were sub-holdings from Hamsey and Barcombe. The hundred became part of Pevensey rape.

38. *Grenested* (East Grinstead) (T.R.E. 1 hide).

Households, 36; teams, 12½; value, £6 9s. 0d.; area, *c.* 50 km.[2]

Before the Conquest a single one-hide holding at Brambletye was assessed to pay *geld*; in 1086 there were 15 households here with one team, and it was unusually noted that there was a priest. However, transfer of the territory from William of Warenne to Roger of Mortain[75] made it necessary to show the holdings which had previously been dependent, so that in 1086 there were in all 12 named holdings and one un-named, totalling about 12 hides. Parent estates included Willingdon, Allington, and the Archbishop of Canterbury's holdings at Wootton, Falmer and East Lavant, and the un-named holding had depended on the royal estate of Ditchling and provides the sole Domesday reference in Sussex to iron working.

39. *Hertevel* (Hartfield) (T.R.E. 3 hides).

Households, 31; teams, 18½; value, £10 12s. 0d.; area, *c.* 75 km.[2]

There were only five small holdings, but to judge from the numbers of households and teams reported in 1086 they were fairly well established. An un-named holding, which had belonged to Earl Godwin, had been part of Rodmell, and 'Wildene', held by Harold, was probably a sub-holding of Willingdon.

40. *Reredfelle* (Rotherfield) (T.R.E. 9 hides).

Households, 48; teams, 31½; value, £17 13s. 0d.; area, *c.* 127 km.[2]

Rotherfield was a royal estate in King Alfred's will. The pre-Conquest charters of the Abbey of St. Denis, near Paris, which claimed Rotherfield, appear to be forgeries.[76] In King Edward's time Earl Godwin is shown in Domesday as holding this estate. Later, apart from part of Bosham, it was the only estate in Sussex which King William kept in his own possession. An estate possibly at Maresfield is also assigned to this hundred, and there is one un-named. Settlement in this area of the High Weald, if sparse, seems nevertheless to have been long-established.

41. *Mellinges* (Malling) ⎫
42. *Fremele* (Framfield) ⎭ (T.R.E. 80 hides).

Malling: Households, 310; teams, 94; value, £70; area, *c.* 220 km.[2]

Framfield: Households, 27; teams, 12; value, £5 15s. 0d.; area, *c.* 9 km.[2]

The Archbishop of Canterbury's large holding of Malling, which may go back to the early ninth century,[77] covered a large belt of the Weald extending from Lewes to the Kent border in Wadhurst. It included the areas of Glynde, Ringmer, Mayfield, Wadhurst, Buxted, Framfield, Hadlow Down, Isfield, and Uckfield. The Domesday entry suggests that there were several main settlements, but does not name them. After the Conquest an area around Framfield, comprising two holdings in Little Horsted which had been held independently from King Edward by laymen, was separated and constituted as 'Framele' hundred. Their assessment, totalling eight hides, was reduced to five hides.

43. *Totenore* (Totnore) (T.R.E. 152½ hides).

Households, 225; teams, 109; value, £102; area, *c.* 34 km.[2]

East of the Ouse the royal estate of Beddingham was based on the scarpfoot of the Downs. A little to the east the large estate of 'Ferle' (West Firle) was held by Wilton Abbey. Beddingham was assessed at 52½ hides, and Firle at 48. There were various smaller estates, extending to Sherrington in Selmeston and Tilton in Alciston. Some, like Itford and Preston in Beddingham, had been held from King Edward before the Conquest, and it is likely that they were part of a formerly much more extensive royal estate. Probably Denton (later Bishopstone) had also been detached from it in the eighth century,[78] and it seems possible that Queen Edith's large holding west of the Ouse at

Iford (Swanborough hundred) and her holdings at 'Ferle' (usually placed at Frog Firle in Alfriston) were at one time similarly part of a single great estate.

It is not known when Wilton Abbey acquired Firle. The estate was involved, with others in the area, in pre-Conquest settlement in the Hastings backwoods.

44. *Edivestone* (T.R.E. 61½ hides) (later Shiplake).

Households, 84; teams, 42½; value, £33 11s. 0d.; area, *c*. 86 km.[2]

The area around the Ouse levels east of Lewes and of the backwoods in Chalvington, Chiddingly, East Hoathly and Waldron seems to show a dispersed pattern of settlements, with relatively small holdings. The most important were Ripe (22 hides, of which eight were in the rape of Hastings) and 'Lestone' (Laughton). The former had been held by Harold and the latter by Earl Godwin. Several estates in the area were similarly involved in the Hastings settlements.

45. *Wandelmestrie* (T.R.E. 63 hides) (later Alciston).

Households, 129; teams, 49; value, £50 11s. 0d.; area, *c*. 47 km.[2]

This hundred was primarily the large scarpfoot estate of Alciston (assessed at 50 hides), which before the Conquest was held by 'Alnod cild', identified as probably Ethelnoth of Canterbury.[79] Probably it included the adjoining East Blatchington, as in the medieval period. After the Conquest William gave it to his foundation of Battle Abbey. Other small estates in the hundred were in Alfriston, 'Sidenore' (a lost site in Selmeston) and Sessingham in Arlington. Arlington and Berwick were later in Longbridge hundred.

46. *Latille* (Dill) (T.R.E. 1½ hides).

Households, 5; teams, 3½; value, £1 2s. 1d.; area, *c*. 47 km.[2]

This was the clayey and probably heavily wooded area north of Hailsham, including Hellingly and probably part of Heathfield, the remainder of which was in the rape of Hastings. Two small holdings are listed in Hellingly. Later evidence shows that the Bishop of Chichester's Bishopstone estate had extensive detached holdings of woodland in Heathfield and Hellingly in the medieval period.[80]

47. *Pevensel* (Pevensey) (T.R.E. 23½ hides).

Households, 33; teams, 12½; value, £18 0s. 5d.; area, *c*. 39 km.[2]

About 20 very small holdings are shown in the area around the borough and port of Pevensey, where the Wealden strata reach the coast. Six were in Westham and two in Hailsham.

G.—THE HASTINGS AREA (RAPE OF HASTINGS)

48. *Nerefelle* (Ninfield) (T.R.E. 4½ hides).

Households, 100; teams, 63½; value, £37 10s. 0d.; area, *c*. 32 km.[2]

The hundred formed a strip rising from the Pevensey East Stream to the Battle Ridge, including the modern parishes of Hooe, Ninfield and Catsfield. Earl Godwin had held 12 hides at Hooe, which in 1086 contributed as many as 71 households and 40½ teams, but it was part of his Willingdon estate. The figures are included above. The holdings at Ninfield and Catsfield were small, but Domesday records chapels at both.

49. *Bexelei* (Bexhill) (T.R.E. 25 hides).

Households, 131; teams, 45½; value, £25 9s. 0d.; area, *c*. 29 km.[2]

The hundred included only the Bishop of Selsey's pre-Conquest estate of Bexhill, with a sub-holding at Bollington. The charter text setting out Offa's grant of 772[81] gives boundaries and shows that there were detached holdings in the backwoods at Icklesham in Guestling hundred and Crowhurst in Baldslow. After the Conquest the estate was taken by the Count of Eu and not restored to the bishopric until 1148.

50. *Baldeslei* (Baldslow) (T.R.E. 36½ hides).

Households, 181; teams, 99½; value, £44 17s. 0d.; area, *c*. 49 km.[2]

This was the area generally to the north of Hastings itself, including Crowhurst, Hollington, Ore and Westfield. King Edward had held an estate of 'Filsham' (Pilesham in Hollington) for 15 hides, with 88 households and 50 teams in 1086. The other holdings were small, but this was a closely-populated area.

51. *Gestelinges* (Guestling) (T.R.E. 31½ hides).

Households, 151 (excluding 14 bordars in Hastings); teams, 70; value £74 3s. 0d.; area, *c.* 49 km.[2]

The hundred later comprised Guestling, Fairlight, Icklesham and Pett. Fairlight, Guestling and Pett are named as Domesday holdings in the hundred, and also 'Rameslie', the important holding of 20 hides which had been given to the Abbey of Fécamp by King Canute[82] in fulfillment of a promise by Aethelred the Unready, who obtained refuge there. The grant was annulled by Earl Godwin and restored by King William. The site of 'Rameslie' has not been established. The estate had five churches, and Domesday adds that there was a 'new town', with 64 burgesses, which is generally thought to have been Rye. It had four burgesses and 14 bordars in Hastings (not included above). Domesday records that 'Rameslie' itself in 1086 had 107 households and 46 teams and was worth £52 4s. 0d. (£34 before the Conquest). It was later partly included in the manor of Brede in Gostrow hundred, so that its lands probably extended into that hundred and also Baldslow.

52. *Babinrerode* (T.R.E. 6½ hides) (later Gostrow).

Households, 25; teams, 17; value, £9; area, *c.* 26 km.[2]

The hundred later comprised Brede and Udimore. The land rises from the River Brede to about 100m. Udimore in Domesday was a six-hide estate, which had been held from Earl Godwin by a certain Algar. The other holding, 'Checeha', may have been in Peasmarsh, later in Goldspur hundred.

53. *Colespore* (T.R E. 6 hides) (later Goldspur).

Households, 50; teams, 18; value, £9 9s. 0d.; area, *c.* 70 km.[2]

This was the most easterly Sussex hundred, mainly low-lying land between the Rivers Tillingham and Rother and bordering Romney Marsh. It later included Beckley, Peasmarsh, Iden, Playden, and East Guldeford. Broomhill was in Kent. Excluding 'Checeha' (*see* 'Babinrerode'), there were five small Domesday holdings, of which the largest was Playden. Beckley was possibly named in King Alfred's will.[83]

54. *Staple* (T.R.E. 12½ hides).

Households, 115; teams, 59½; value, £25 8s. 0d.; area, *c.* 52 km.[2]

The hundred included areas bordering the rivers Rother, Brede and Tillingham, but was also partly hilly. Later it comprised Northiam, Ewhurst, Bodiam and Sedlescombe, but the Domesday hundred may have extended into Brede, Salehurst and other adjoining parishes. There were numerous small holdings.

55. *Hailsaltede* (T.R.E. 7 hides) (later Netherfield and Battle).

Battle: Households, 49 (and four unlocated); teams, 18½ + 2; value, £5 19s. 0d. (+ £1); area, *c.* 18 km.[2]

Hailsaltede: Households, 65; teams, 38½; value, £17 12s. 0d.; area, *c.* 65 km.[2]

The area is hilly and largely sandy territory of the Hastings Beds around Battle. After the Conquest King William's foundation of Battle Abbey was given all the land within a radius of a little over 2 km. (1½ miles), and Domesday shows that this included 12 small parcels totalling a little under six hides, some of which had belonged to distant estates such as Hooe and 'Filsham'. The abbot's own holding was assessed at 2½ hides.

Some 14 holdings remained in 'Hailsaltede', including relatively small holdings in Netherfield, Whatlington, Mountfield, Brightling and Dallington. They also included four small former sub-holdings of Chalvington and Heighton in the rape of Pevensey.

56. *Folsalre* (Foxearle) (T.R.E. 15 hides).

Households, 147; teams, 75; value, £37 6s. 0d.; area, *c.* 55 km.[2]

The ground rises from the low-lying areas adjoining the Pevensey Levels in Wartling and Herstmonceux to the ridges well above 100 m. in Ashburnham. In Domesday Wartling and 'Herste' (Herstmonceux) were well populated holdings, though each was assessed for only five hides. There were two smaller holdings in Ashburnham and others un-named.

57. *Hauchesberie* (Hawksborough) (T.R.E. 1 hide).

    Households, 101; teams, 79½; value, £18 8s. 6d.; area, *c.* 86 km.[2]

    This was one of the three hilly hundreds of the Hastings backwoods, which are seen clearly in Domesday to have been settled from estates in the rape of Pevensey, although the date at which this occurred does not appear. 'Hauchesberie' probably comprised Warbleton, Burwash and part of Heathfield. Only a single one-hide holding of Countess Goda was directly assessed before the Conquest. Domesday lists 25 further holdings totalling about 20 hides which had been part of estates in the rape of Pevensey. Prominent among the former owners were Countess Goda, Harold and Wilton Abbey. The settlement, which was also in 'Shoeswelle' (Shoyswell) and 'Henhert' (Henhurst), appears as a major co-operative venture, but may have been carried out over a considerable period.

58. *Shoeswelle* (Shoyswell) (T.R.E. 4½ hides).

    Households, 54; teams, 43; value, £17 1s. 4d.; area, *c.* 34 km.[2]

    The area is around Ticehurst. The only estate assessed before the Conquest was one at Hazelhurst, held by the Bishop of Selsey from King Edward. The Pevensey subholding listed in this hundred, totalling about six hides, largely originated from estates of Countess Goda and Wilton Abbey.

59. *Herhert* (Henhurst) (T.R.E. 4½ hides).

    Households, 101; teams, 52½; value, £20 19s. 0d.; area, *c.* 42 km.[2]

    The area of the hundred is in Salehurst and Etchingham. There were six small holdings already separately assessed before the Conquest, of which the only one given a location was a small holding of Countess Goda at Salehurst. The estates in the rape of Pevensey to which the further holdings had belonged were largely those of King Edward and Countess Goda. They totalled a little more than eight hides.

X

SAXON SUSSEX: SOME PROBLEMS AND DIRECTIONS

Barry Cunliffe

FROM THE FORMAL END of the Roman province of Britannia in 410 to the beginning of Norman rule in 1066, the social and economic structure of the communities of southern Britain underwent one of the greatest upheavals recognisable in the development of the country. Plunged into anarchy with the collapse of Rome, it emerged, six and a half centuries later, totally reformed, as a stable and increasingly powerful element in a new Europe. The study of any period of change and innovation cannot fail to be both fascinating and demanding. Sussex in particular lends itself to such a study, for not only is it a neatly contained geographical entity, but two centuries of intense archaeological and historical activity have yielded a wealth of data. The moment is opportune for a stocktaking of what we know, and perhaps more important, what we can hope to know.

In the preceding papers the disparate strands of evidence are neatly displayed: each has something to add to the story, but each is beset by distinct and often insuperable limitations. Documentary references are few, third-hand and usually biased; place-name evidence is coarse-grained and still notoriously difficult to interpret with any degree of accuracy;[1] cemeteries, though numerous, have on the whole been badly excavated on a limited scale and are ill-published; settlement excavation is in its infancy; and large-scale intensive field-work has hardly begun. But even so there is probably more varied evidence now available about Sussex than about any other part of Saxon Britain. The scholars, whose individual papers are presented in this volume, not only explore the present state of knowledge in their own fields, but each has attempted to relate his particular speciality to its associated disciplines. The result is the first integrated and thoroughly up-to-date study of the development of a Saxon Kingdom.

It is the purpose of this brief conclusion to comment on the strengths and weaknesses of our present knowledge and to suggest some directions for further research. It does so from the point of view of an archaeologist interested in culture-process. Having admitted this, however, it is fair to add that significant advances in our understanding of the earlier period (fifth to eighth century) will rest almost entirely upon the intensification of archaeological and topographical activity. Even for the later period most of the questions now raised require the archaeological dimensions to be filled out before further progress can be made.

Settlements

Central to our understanding of the situation in the fifth and sixth centuries are the problems posed by the size, distribution and organisation of the late Romano-British population. Here our archaeological evidence is at its weakest. In Chichester, the relevant levels have for the most part been destroyed or disturbed by post-Roman activity, while Pevensey is virtually unexplored. In the countryside the development of a few villas has been recorded in the west of the county, and some work of a very high quality was carried out on the distribution of rural sites in the 1930s, but beyond this we are almost entirely ignorant. The reason seems to be that the late Roman period is at present an unfashionable area of study. Yet the potential exists for a systematic programme of field survey aimed, in the first instance, at attempting to define the density of settlements, their size and the duration of their occupation. Where this has been carried out in the Chalton area on the Downs of East Hampshire,[2] it is possible to demonstrate a range of settlement type, from small farms to villages, densely spaced out in a well-ordered landscape of fields, trackways and pasture. In so far as it is possible to say, there appears to have been a nucleation of population in the third and fourth centuries, giving rise to the development of settlements of considerable size. If this pattern is repeated on the Sussex Downs it has significant implications for the later period.

We know practically nothing of these late Roman rural settlements. In Wessex[3] and at Chalton the larger villages were carefully laid out, some of them along village streets, while the individual houses, known only at Chalton and Park Brow, were rectangular and timber built. More than this it is impossible to say; indeed, we know less about late Roman rural settlement than we do about early Saxon sites. How can we begin to understand the dynamics of the invasion period without a clearer understanding of what immediately preceded it?

The end of Roman rule brought with it the breakdown of centralised government and the complete collapse of its complex market economy. It is hardly surprising, therefore, that the institutions depending upon them, the towns, the centralised industries and the villa system, should rapidly disintegrate. Those villas which have been adequately examined seem to have been abandoned in the late fourth or early fifth century, while a sufficiently large area of Chichester has now been excavated to suggest that urban life in all its aspects ceased. But what of the very substantial rural population, which would have greatly outnumbered the town and villa dwellers? Famine, pestilence, a decline in birth rate, and slaughter, would have reduced it to some degree, but there can be little reasonable doubt that the sub-Roman rural population remained considerable throughout the fifth century and may well have greatly outnumbered the immigrants. We should no longer under-estimate the potential influence of the indigenous communities on the culture of the invaders.

Martin Welch has gone some way towards raising this problem historically by defining a region of early Germanic settlement between the Rivers Ouse and Cuckmere,[4] and the present writer has expanded this approach in a tentative model to cover the rest of the county.[5] But the definition of potential areas of initial settlement is only a preliminary step: it is the interaction of the immigrant population with the indigenous inhabitants we should now be considering. How many Romano-British villages continued in use into the Saxon period? Were those Saxon settlements, which were established *de novo,* like Rookery Hill[6] and Chalton, sited on marginal land in such a way as to suggest infilling in an already densely populated landscape? To what extent does the British Saxon house type, which differs so dramatically from the three-aisled type common in the Saxon homeland, reflect the rapid adoption of local styles of construction and, more to the point, what percentage of the inhabitants of Rookery Hill and Chalton were the direct descendants of the rural population of the Roman period? Admittedly, it is easier to ask questions than to provide answers, but the very formulation of these problems helps to focus attention on crucial areas of study which have hitherto been totally neglected. There is no doubt that with an integrated campaign of excavation and intensive field-work considerable advances could be made.

Another matter which requires attention is the relationship of the Roman villa estates to the early Saxon settlement pattern. One of the best regions in which to examine this problem is the Upper Greensand bench which foots the scarp slope of the Downs. By no means all of the villas have yet been found, but those which are known are clearly optimally sited to exploit the varied resource potentials of the region, the fertile farmland of the Greensand with the chalk downs and Weald on either side providing pasture and pannage. One would expect the villa estates to have included the full range of these resources, extending for some distance north and south but being packed closely together along the ridge. This is precisely the form of the early medieval parishes which no doubt reflect the territorial divisions of the preceding Saxon period. Given nucleated settlement on the Greensand bench, in any period, some such pattern is likely soon to have developed. In other words, the geomorphological constraints imposed by the environment probably affected communities in the same way over considerable periods of time. It would be interesting, therefore, to examine to what extent, if at all, the potential territories of the villas corresponded to the earliest definable boundaries of the Greensand parishes. If the villa estates continued as viable entities both economically and in terms of land holding into the Saxon period, then some kind of correlation might reasonably be expected. The problem is not an easy one to approach and would require intensive field-work, but it is potentially capable of some degree of elucidation.

So far we have been concerned with the effects of Roman settlement on the later period, but we know pitifully little about the early and middle Saxon settlement pattern, as Martin Bell so clearly demonstrated in his survey of the evidence (pp. 38–55). Yet there can be little doubt that settlements were numerous and that they can be discovered by careful field-work. The parish of Chalton has so far yielded evidence of six different settlement locations of early or middle Saxon date and comparable figures are now available for several Northamptonshire parishes, where sufficient field-work has been undertaken. Evidently the total number of sites occupied at one time or another during this period was far more numerous than had been anticipated even a few years ago, but as to the nature of these settlements, their size and duration of occupation, we know practically nothing. The excavations at Chalton and Rookery Hill are providing superb evidence of nucleated hill-top 'villages', but these are likely to represent only one type of inhabited location. It would be wrong to believe that the only unit of rural settlement in the Saxon period was the village. While this may be so in some areas, the possibility of there being scattered farmsteads in addition should be seriously considered. Strictly, what is now required is the thorough survey of a number of parishes, in order to discover their Saxon settlements, followed by the selection of one or more of the smallest for total excavation.

The need for intensive field survey has been emphasised several times in the above discussion, but the discovery of Saxon sites in field walking depends on a number of factors, among which the survival, recovery and recognition of pot-sherds are among the most important. The fact that early and middle Saxon pottery is uncommon even on intensively-occupied sites, and friable when exposed to weathering, means that only the most thorough programme of field walking involving the constant re-examination of the same area under different conditions is likely to be of value in discovering sites. Survival of the evidence is by no means even. Ploughing over many years could easily have destroyed all Saxon pottery at a particular location, while the survival of quantities of pottery of earlier or later date may obscure the odd small sherd of Saxon ware. This is a particular hazard in the case of a Roman site continuing into the Saxon period, or a Saxon site continuing to develop into medieval times. It was only after 15 years of constant collection in and around the medieval village of Chalton that the first early-middle Saxon sherds were found.

The dating of sites, in the absence of distinctive metalwork poses particular problems which can most readily be solved by the establishment of one or more pottery sequences in different parts of the country. Little progress has yet been made in this field, but the excavations at Chichester can now provide a tolerably complete series forward from the ninth or late eighth century, and future work may allow it to be extended back even further,[7] while the Portchester Castle[8] sequence is of some relevance at least for the west of Sussex. For the east of the county there is nothing. Pevensey Castle has, however, a considerable potential and if, after the old finds have been carefully re-examined, some Saxon material is recognised, a very good case could be presented for carrying out a limited programme of research excavations here. Until this is done it is difficult to see how further advances can be made unless a complex stratified site is found by accident.

Population

The problem of population dynamics is notoriously difficult for the archaeo-logist or historian of the Saxon period to approach. By the time of the Domesday Survey, however, it is usually assumed that the population of Britain was approaching one and a half million. There had been a tendency in the past to suppose that the population of Roman Britain therefore had to be less, but Frere has suggested that it had probably reached a figure of two million by the end of the second century,[9] roughly comparable to the estimated population of England and Wales by about A.D. 1200. More recently, field surveys in various parts of Britain have shown that the density of settlement in the Iron Age and Roman period was far more considerable than had previously been supposed, and a guess (estimate is too grand a word) of about four million for the late second century might be nearer the truth. If this is so, something dramatic must have happened between 300 and 1100. The late Roman world is known to have suffered a serious decline in the birth rate and it is therefore a distinct possibility that the downward trend in Britain was well underway during the fourth century, only to be exacerbated by the transfer to Europe of three large armies, recruited in the province in the last 30 years of Roman rule. Add to this plague and barbarian attack, together with the general malaise which must have accompanied the collapse of the Roman economic system, and it is not unreasonable to suppose that the downward trend became further accentuated after 400 with a momentum which may have caused it to reach a trough well below a million by the beginning of the sixth century. After a period of stabilisation there would have been a slow but steady rise to the Domesday level. Vague and inaccurate though these figures are, the general trends at least must approximate to the truth. Any attempt to understand the social and economic development of the Saxon period must take cognisance of these matters.

In crude terms, the Domesday population density for Sussex has been estimated at 9.4 persons per sq. km.,[10] which would suggest a total figure for the county in the order of 35,000 by A.D. 1100. Thus, if we are broadly correct in our assumptions, the Saxon period would have seen a steady rise from about 25,000 or less to 35,000 over a period of 650 years.[11]

Allowing for considerable margins of error, two points deserve emphasis: first, the population was very small throughout, and second, in a situation of rising population communities situated on good land would soon expand to utilise fully the available resources. This would in turn lead to the establishment of boundaries and, subsequently, to the colonisation of hitherto unexploited environments. In theory, then, one might postulate two stages in settlement dynamics: the first of unrestricted growth continuing all the time that the population was below a certain level, to be followed, once this threshold had been passed, by a phase of territorial definition. It was presumably at this later stage that the boundaries, which were to become the medieval parish boundaries, were established, and there may well have been some degree of settlement reorganisation at the same time. This would appear to be the implication of the settlement pattern in and around the village of Chalton, Hants.,[12] where the

Saxon settlement on Church Down seems to have been abandoned at about the time when three neighbouring villages began to develop. A consideration of the medieval parish boundaries suggests that they represent the division of a single large territory within which the Church Down settlement had been centrally sited.

The study of parish boundaries and of Saxon estate boundaries from a topographical point of view clearly offers one way of approaching the problem of population and settlement dynamics. It is a field which holds out the prospect of real and significant advances in our understanding, but one which has so far been sadly neglected.

Population increase and the development of the church from the beginning of the eighth century would together have contributed to a situation in which further change was inevitable, since both would have demanded a greater degree of centralisation than had hitherto been necessary. It was factors of this kind which led to the development of 'central-places' for trade and exchange, for government, and for religious observances. Where all three aspects coalesced at a single location urban life, which had died at the beginning of the fifth century, was once more re-created. This re-emergence of urban centres in Sussex is discussed in some detail by David Hill (above, pp. 174–189), where the evidence, sparse though it is, is carefully considered. What stands out so clearly from Hill's paper is that we have gone as far as we reasonably can using the available documentary and numismatic evidence. For further advances to be made we need a new range of archaeological evidence, in particular from the three principal towns of Chichester, Lewes and Hastings. Fortunately, the programme of excavations in Chichester is now beginning to fill a serious gap in our knowledge, but a great deal more work requires to be undertaken before the social and economic development of our Saxon urban centres can begin to be understood. The smaller, subsidiary markets of Pevensey, Steyning and Arundel, each with a fascinating potential, have hardly been considered.

The papers which constitute this volume present in detail a range of evidence and draw from it a number of interim conclusions about the nature and development of Saxon Sussex. Together they represent all that can reasonably be said, at a certain level, about the subject: they bring us hard up against the limits of reasonable inference. What I have attempted in this chapter is to offer some suggestions as to how we might advance our understanding beyond its present limitations. In the past, it has been possible for the lone scholar to make considerable contributions to knowledge by working and re-working existing data. In Saxon studies, however, the point is now fast being reached when the questions now being asked require the co-operation of a number of scholars, working together over a period of years having first formulated a clear-cut research design. The publication of this volume not only marks an anniversary, it sums up our present state of knowledge and prepares the way for a new era of research.

ABBREVIATIONS AND REFERENCES

Antiq. J.	*Antiquaries' Journal*
Arch. J.	*Archaeological Journal*
B.C.S.	W. de Gray Birch, *Cartularium Saxonicum* (1885)
E.H.R.	*Economic History Review*
Med. Arch.	*Medieval Archaeology*
S.A.C.	*Sussex Archaeological Collections*
S.N.Q.	*Sussex Notes and Queries*
S.R.S.	*Sussex Record Society*

Chapter I: The Saxon Heritage

1. J. Morris, 'Dark Age dates' in M. G. Jarrett and B. Dobson (eds.), *Britain and Rome: essays presented to Eric Birley* (1965), pp. 145-185. Idem, *The Age of Arthur* (1973), pp. 28-9
2. For a recent examination of the continental homeland of the English see W. Davies and H. Vierck, 'The contexts of Tribal Hidage: Social aggregates and settlement patterns, *Frühmittelalterlich Studien*, vol. 8 (1974), pp. 242-249
3. William Morris, *Address*, Birmingham Municipal College of Art (1894), p. 11
4. See, for example, Peter Reynolds, *Farming in the Iron Age* (1976)
5. Below, p. 225
6. The Exeter Book, Riddle 22. Some scholars take the ox to be the subject of this phrase. See Frederick Tupper, *The Riddles of the Exeter Book* (1910), p. 115
7. Below, pp. 154-9
8. Peter Brandon, *The Sussex Landscape* (1974), p. 73. A detailed reconstruction of the droveways of mid-Sussex is in preparation by the author.
9. Ruth Tittensor, 'The History of the Mens', *S.A.C.*, vol. 116 (1977)
10. Gaston Roupnel, *Histoire de la Campagne Francaise* (1932 edn.), pp. 134-5
11. Gordon Ward, 'The Haeselersc Charter of 1018', *S.A.C.*, vol. 77 (1936), pp. 119-129
12. Peter Brandon, *op. cit.*, p. 82
13. Peter Brandon, *op. cit.*, p. 80
14. E. M. Yates, 'The *Meare* Marsh of Merston', *S.A.C.*, vol. 113 (1975), p. 118
15. The Venerable Bede, *The Ecclesiastical History of the English People* (1935 edn.), p. 123
16. W. H. Blaauw, 'Letters to Ralph de Nevill, Bishop of Chichester, 1222-1244', *S.A.C.*, vol. 3 (1850), pp. 35-76
17. J. N. L. Myres, in R. G. Collingwood and J. N. L. Myres, *Roman Britain and the English Settlements* (2nd edn., 1937), p. 441
18. J. E. A. Jolliffe, *Pre-Feudal England: the Jutes* (1933)
19. J. N. L. Myres, *Arch.J.*, vol. 90 (1933), p. 159
20. W. D. Peckham, 'Customary acres in South-West Sussex', *S.A.C.*, vol. 66 (1925), p. 155
21. G. R. G. Jones, 'Settlement patterns in Anglo-Saxon England', *Antiquity*, vol. 35 (1961), pp. 221-232
22. J. H. Round (ed.), *Calendar of documents preserved in France* (1898), p. 91
23. Peter Brandon, 'Cereal yields on the Sussex estates of Battle Abbey during the later middle ages', *Econ. H. R.*, second series, vol. 25 (1972), pp. 403-20
24. Richard Hamer, *A choice of Anglo-Saxon verse* (1970), p. 195
25. Leslie Alcock, *Arthur's Britain* (1973 edn.), p. 80

Chapter II: Early Anglo-Saxon Sussex

1. *Historia ecclesiastica gentis Anglorum* (abbreviated hereafter to *H.E.*)
2. *Vita Sancti Wilfridi* (abbreviated hereafter to *V.S.W.*)

227

3.   *The Anglo-Saxon Chronicle* (abbreviated hereafter to *A.S.C.*)
4.   *De exidio et conquestu Britanniae* (abbreviated hereafter to *D.E.*)
5.   *Historia Brittonum* (abbreviated hereafter to *H.B.*)
6.   *A.S.C.*, 477
7.   *V.S.W.*, Ch. XLI
8.   For discussions of Roman Sussex see S. S. Frere, *Brittania* (2nd edn., 1974); B. Cunliffe, *The Regni* (1973); J. Wacher, *The towns of Roman Britain* (1974)
9.   M. G. Bell, 'The excavation of an early Romano-British site and Pleistocene landforms at Newhaven, Sussex', *S.A.C.*, vol. 114 (1976), pp. 218–305
10. H. Cleere, 'The Roman iron industry of the Weald and its connexions with the *Classis Britannica*', *Arch. J.*, vol. 131 (1974), pp. 171–199
11. *Med. Arch.*, vol. 15 (1971), p. 134
12. S. Johnson, *The Roman forts of the Saxon shore* (1976)
13. Ammianus Marcellinus, *Rerum cestarum libri qui supersunt*, Book XXVII, Ch. 8
14. Zosimus, *Histories*, Book V, Chs. 5 and 6
15. Procopius, *de bello Vandalico*, Book 1, Ch. 2, 38
16. *D.E.*, Ch. 25
17. Constantius, *Vita Germani*, Chs. III and V
18. Patrick, *Confessio*
19. *D.E.*, Ch. 23
20. *H.B.*, Ch. 31
21. Asser, *De rebus gestis Aelfredi*, Ch. 2
22. *A.S.C.*, 514
23. For a detailed discussion see H. M. Chadwick, *Origin of the English nation* (1924), pp. 111–36
24. F. Tischler, 'Der Stand der Sachsenforschung, archäologisch gesehen', *Bericht der Römisch-Germanischen Kommission*, vol. 35 (1954), pp. 21–215
25. W. Haarnagel, 'Die Ergebnisse der Grabung Feddersen Wierde im Jahre 1961', *Germania*, vol. 41 (1963), pp. 280–317; P. Schmidt, 'Die Siedlungskeramik von Mucking (Essex) und Feddersen Wierde (Kr. Wesermünde)—Ein Formenvergleich', *Berichten van de Rijksdienst voor het Oudheidkundig Bodemonderzoek*, vol. 19 (1969), pp. 135–144; a useful English summary of the early phases is contained in M. Todd, *The northern barbarians 100 B.C.–A.D. 300* (1975), pp. 103–06, Fig. 18
26. W. A. van Es, Wijster, 'A native village beyond the imperial frontier, 150–425 A.D.', *Palaeohistoria*, vol. 11 (1967)
27. S. E. West, 'The Anglo-Saxon village of West Stow', *Med. Arch.*, vol. 13 (1969), pp. 1–20; S. E. West, 'Pagan Saxon pottery from West Stow, Suffolk', *Berichten van de Rijksdienst voor het Oudheidkundig Bodemonderzoek*, vol. 19 (1969), pp. 175–82
28. P. V. Addyman and D. Leigh, 'Anglo-Saxon houses at Chalton, Hampshire', *Med. Arch.*, vol. 16 (1972), pp. 13–31; P. V. Addyman and D. Leigh, 'The Anglo-Saxon village at Chalton, Hampshire: second interim report', *Med. Arch.*, vol. 17 (1973), pp. 1–25
29. M. G. Bell, *S.A.C.*, vol. 115 (1977)
30. H. W. Bohme, *Germanische Grabfunde des 4. bis 5. Jahrhunderts zwischen unterer Elbe und Loire* (1974), p. 240, Taf. 28
31. All charters are listed under their numbers in W. de Gray Birch, *Cartularium Saxonicum* (1885)
32. B. Cunliffe, *Excavations at Portchester Castle, Hants., 1961–71*, vol. 2: Saxon (1976)
33. *Proceedings of the Society of Antiquaries*, 2nd series, vol. 19 (1901–03), pp. 125–29; F. Aldsworth, 'The pagan Saxon Cemetery at Droxford', *Hampshire Newsletter*, vol. 2 (1975), pp. 105–07
34. M. G. Welch, *Highdown Hill and its Saxon cemetery* (Worthing Museum 1976)
35. E. C. Curwen, *The journal of Gideon Mantell, surgeon and geologist* (1940), p. 76; G. A. Mantell, *A day's ramble in and about the ancient town of Lewes* (1846), pp. 134–35;

N. E. S. Norris, 'Miscellaneous researches 1949-56', *S.A.C.*, vol. 94 (1956), pp. 11-12; V. I. Evison, *The fifth century invasions south of the Thames* (1965), p. 21 and map 7, 2

36. See footnote 30 and reports by D. Thomson in *Med. Arch.*, vol. 12 (1968), p. 161, and vol. 13 (1969), p. 240; V. I. Evison, 'Quoit brooch style buckles', *Antiquaries Journal*, vol. 48 (1968), p. 244, Fig. 2e

37. A. F. Griffith and L. F. Salzman, 'An Anglo-Saxon cemetery at Alfriston, Sussex', *S.A.C.*, vol. 56 (1914), pp. 16-51; A. F. Griffith, 'An Anglo-Saxon cemetery at Alfriston, Sussex', Supplemental Paper, *S.A.C.*, vol. 57 (1915), pp. 197-208

38. *The Times*, 6 Sept. 1963

39. T. W. Horsfield, *The history and antiquities of Lewes and its vicinity*, vol. 1 (1824), pp. 48-49

40. M. J. Swanton, *The spearheads of the Anglo-Saxon settlements* (1973), pp. 40-45, Fig. 7c

41. E. T. Leeds, *The archaeology of the Anglo-Saxon settlements* (1913), p. 46

42. *H.B.*, Ch. 44

43. *A.S.C.*, 455, 456-7, 465 and 473

44. *H.B.*, Ch. 46

45. Dr. J. Morris, 'Dark Age dates' in M. G. Jarrett and B. Dobson (eds.), *Britain and Rome* (1966), pp. 157, 167-8, n. 88

46. *Ibid.*, p. 151 and n. 31

47. C. E. Stevens, 'Gildas Sapiens', *E.H.R.*, vol. 56 (1941), pp. 353-73

48. *Monumenta Germaniae Historica, Anctorum Antiquissimorum*, vol. IX (1892), p. 660

49. *H.E.*, Book II, Ch. 5

50. *A.S.C.*, 829; E. John, *Orbis Britanniae* (1966), p. 7

51. *D.E.*, Ch. 26

52. J. N. L. Myres, *Anglo-Saxon pottery and the settlement of England* (1969), p. 112

53. M. A. Cotton and P. W. Gathercole, *Excavations at Clausentum, Southempton, 1951-1954* (1958), p. 45 and Fig. 12, 5

54. I am grateful to Mrs. S. Hawkes, the excavator of this unpublished cemetery, for informing me of her current views on its chronology

55. B. Cunliffe, *The Regni* (1973), pp. 132-39 and Fig. 46

56. M. G. Welch, 'Late Romans and Saxons in Sussex', *Britannia*, vol. 2 (1971), pp. 232-37

57. H. Surrrell, 'Antiquarian notes on the district of the Eastbourne Natural History Society', *Transactions and Reports of the Eastbourne Natural History Society*, new series, vol. 1 (1881-6), pp. 30-31; H. M. Whitley, 'Notes on the history and topography of Eastbourne', *Transactions and Reports of the Eastbourne Natural History Society*, new series, vol. 2 (1886-94), p. 111; H. M. Whitley, 'Recent archaeological discoveries in the Eastbourne district', *S.A.C.*, vol. 37 (1890), pp. 112-13; *S.N.Q.*, vol. 1 (1926-27), p. 112; *S.N.Q.*, vol. 2 (1928-29), p. 193 and pl. opp. p. 184; *S.N.Q.*, vol. 15 (1958-62), p. 250

58. J. Sawyer, 'Important discovery of Anglo-Saxon remains at Kingston, Lewes', *S.A.C.*, vol. 38 (1892), pp. 177-83

59. E. T. Leeds, 'The distribution of the Angles and Saxons archaeologically considered', *Archaeologia*, vol. 91 (1945), p. 94, Fig. 12: in the British Museum, formerly in the Fenton Collection

60. Unpublished, in Chichester Museum

61. H. R. E. Davidson and L. Webster, 'The Anglo-Saxon burial at Coombe (Woodnesborough), Kent', *Med. Arch.*, vol. 11 (1967), p. 31, Fig. 8, g-j

62. 'Bronze strap ends, in Chichester Museum', *S.N.Q.*, vol. 14 (1954-57), p. 214; K. M. E. Murray and B. Cunliffe, 'Excavations at a site in North Street, Chichester, 1958-9', *S.A.C.*, vol. 100 (1962), p. 110

63. This cemetery, excavated in 1974 by the Oxfordshire Archaeological Unit, has not been published at the time of writing. I am grateful to David Miles and David Brown for permission to examine this material

64. H. F. Bidder and J. Morris, 'The Anglo-Saxon cemetery at Mitcham', *Surrey Arch. Coll.*, vol. 56 (1959), pp. 50-131

65. A. W. G. Lowther, 'The Saxon cemetery at Guildown, Guildford, Surrey., *Surrey Arch., Coll.*, vol. 39 (1931), pp. 1–50

66. M. Hyslop, 'Two Anglo-Saxon cemeteries at Chamberlain's Barn, Leighton Buzzard, Bedfordshire', *Arch. J.*, vol. 120 (1963), pp. 161–200

67. A. L. Meaney and S. C. Hawkes, *Two Anglo-Saxon cemeteries at Winnall* (1970)

68. See footnote 57 and P. M. Stevens, 'Ocklynge Saxon Cemetery', *S.A.C. Newsletter*, vol. 4 (1971); *Med. Arch.*, vol. 15 (1971), p. 134

69. E. W. Holden, V. I. Evison and H. B. A. Ratcliffe-Densham, 'The Anglo-Saxon burials at Crane Down, Jevington, Sussex', *S.A.C.*, vol. 107 (1969), pp. 126–34

70. G. M. White, 'A settlement of the South Saxons', *Antiq. J.*, vol. 14 (1934), pp. 393–400

71. *S.N.Q.*, vol. 14 (1954–57), pp. 123–25

72. *Proceedings of the Society of Antiquaries*, 2nd series, vol. 26 (1913–14), pp. 133–34; two other pieces are in the British Museum and one fragment in the Ashmolean Museum, Oxford

73. *Antiq. J.*, vol. 4 (1924), pp. 49–50; J. Werner, 'Byzantische Gurtelschnallen des 6. und 7. Jahrhunderts aus der Sammlung Diergardt', *Kölner Jahrbuch für Vor- und Frühgeschichte*, vol. 1 (1955), pp. 36–48

74. G. M. Knocker, 'Early burials and an Anglo-Saxon cemetery at Snall's Corner, near Horndean, Hampshire', *Proceedings of the Hampshire Field Club and Archaeological Society*, vol. 19 (1958), pp. 117–70

75. See footnote 28 above

76. J. P. Williams-Freeman, *Field archaeology as illustrated by Hampshire* (1915), pp. 286–93; *Proceedings of the Hampshire Field Club*, vol. 9 (1920–24), pp. 411–12; F. Aldsworth, forthcoming study of Anglo-Saxon settlement in Hampshire

77. *V.S.W.*, Ch. XLI (villam suam propriam, in qua manebat); see also *H.E.*, Book IV, Ch. 13

78. J. McN. Dodgson, 'Place-names from *ham*, distinguished from *hamm* names, in relation to the settlement of Kent, Surrey and Sussex', in P. Clemoes (ed.), *Anglo-Saxon England*, vol. 2 (1973), pp. 1–50

79. H. M. Colvin (ed.), *The History of the King's Works*, vol. 1 (1963), pp. 2–5, Fig. 1

80. D. M. Metcalf, 'The 'Bird and Branch' Sceattas in the light of a find from Abingdon', *Oxoniensia*, vol. 37 (1972), p. 65; A. de Belfort, *Description Générale des Monnaies Mérovingiennes*, vol. IV (1894), p. 214f, no. 5756; Dr. S. Rigold still maintains, however, that B.M.C.3a sceattas are minted at London, see S. Rigold, 'The two primary series of sceattas', *British Numismatic Journal*, vol. 30 (1960–61), p. 23

81. *H.E.*, Book IV, Ch. 15

82. *H.E.*, Book III, Ch. 20

83. *H.E.*, Book IV, Ch. 13

84. *Ibid.*

85. *A.S.C.*, entry for 675; S. C. Hawkes, H. R. Ellis Davidson and C. F. C. Hawkes, 'The Finglesham Man., *Antiquity*, vol. 39 (1965), p. 32 n. 62

86. *H.E.*, Book II, Ch. 15

87. *H.E.*, Book II, Chs. 3 and 5; Book III, Chs. 22 and 30

88. *V.S.W.*, Ch. XIII

89. *H.E.*, Book IV, Ch. 13

90. W. Davies and H. Vierck, 'The contexts of Tribal Hidage: Social aggregates and settlement patterns', *Frühmittelalterliche Studien*, vol. 8 (1974), pp. 223–93

91. *H.E.*, Book IV, Ch. 15

92. William of Malmesbury, *De gestis regum Anglorum*, Book I, Ch. 34

93. N. Brooks, 'Anglo-Saxon charters: the work of the last twenty years', in P. Clemoes (ed.), *Anglo-Saxon England*, vol. 3 (1974), pp. 211–31

94. P. Chaplais, 'The origin and authenticity of the Royal Anglo-Saxon Diploma', *Journal of the Society of Archivists*, vol. 3 (1965–69), p. 50 n. 24; P. Chaplais, 'Some early Anglo-Saxon diplomas on single sheets: originals or copies?', *Journal of the Society of Archivists*, vol. 3 (1965–69), p. 316

95. P. Chaplais, 'Some early Anglo-Saxon diplomas on single sheets: originals or copies?', *Ibid.*, pp. 333–35
96. J. E. A. Jolliffe, *Pre-feudal England: the Jutes* (1933)
97. J. McN. Dodgson, 'The significance of the distribution of the English place-name in *-ingas, -inga* in south-east England', *Med. Arch.*, vol. 10 (1966), pp. 11–12, 14–16
98. Simeon of Durham, *Historia Regum*, Ch. 47
99. C. T. Chevallier, 'The Frankish origin of the Hastings tribe', *S.A.C.*, vol. 104 (1955), pp. 56–62
100. See footnotes 78 and 97; also M. Gelling, 'English place-names derived from the compound *wicham*', *Med. Arch.*, vol. 11 (1967), pp. 87–104; B. H. Cox, The significance of the distribution of English place-names in the Midlands and East Anglia', *Journal of the English Place-Name Society*, vol. 5 (1972–73), pp. 15–78
101. *A.S.C.*

Chapter III: Saxon Settlements and Buildings in Sussex

1. I am grateful to Dennis Haselgrove and Eric Holden for their criticism of an earlier draft of this paper, and to Brenda Westley for her help with its preparation
2. A conservative estimate based on sites on the *Ordnance Survey Map of Southern Britain in the Iron Age* (1975)
3. J. McN. Dodgson, 'The significance of the distribution of the English place-name in *-ingas, -inga*, in south-east England', *Med. Arch.*, vol. 10 (1966), pp. 1–29
4. M. G. Welch, 'Late Romans and Saxons in Sussex', *Britannia*, vol. 2 (1971), pp. 232–237
5. M. Bell, 'Excavations at Bishopstone, Sussex', *S.A.C.*, vol. 115 (1977)
6. I am grateful to Mr. Thomson for discussing his excavations with me
7. V. I. Evison, 'Quoit brooch style buckles', *Antiq. J.*, vol. 48 (1968), pp. 231–246
8. Directed by the writer for the Sussex Archaeological Field Unit in association with the Brighton and Hove Archaeological Society
9. Structure numbers include Iron Age buildings not discussed here. Two of the buildings, of which little remained, are not marked on Fig. 1
10. B. Hope-Taylor, 'The boat-shaped house in northern Europe', *Proc. Cambridge Antiquarian Society*, vol. 55 (1962), pp. 16–22
11. D. R. Wilson, 'Roman Britain in 1970', *Britannia*, vol. 2 (1971), pp. 284–5
12. P. V. Addyman and D. Leigh, 'The Anglo-Saxon village at Chalton, Hampshire: second interim report', *Med. Arch.*, vol. 17 (1973), Figs. 9 and 10
13. W. H. Zimmermann, 'A Roman Iron Age and migration settlement at Flögeln, Kr. Wesermünde, Lower Saxony' in T. Rowley (ed.), *Anglo-Saxon settlement and landscape* (1974), pp. 56–73
14. P. V. Addyman, 'The Anglo-Saxon house: a new review', in P. Clemoes (ed.), *Anglo-Saxon England*, vol. 1 (1972), pp. 273–307
15. P. V. Addyman and D. Leigh, *op. cit.*, (1973), pp. 1–25
16. E. Fletcher, 'Anglo-Saxon architecture in the seventh century', *Transactions of the London and Middlesex Archaeological Society*, vol. 21, pt. 2 (1967), pp. 89–97; W. H. Godfrey, 'The parish church of St. Andrew, Bishopstone', *S.A.C.*, vol. 87 (1948), pp: 164–183
17. W. de G. Birch, *Cartularium Saxonicum* (1885–93), nos. 302 and 387
18. P. H. Sawyer, 'Early medieval English settlement', in P. H. Sawyer (ed.), *Medieval Settlement* (1976), p. 1
19. P. H. Sawyer, 'Anglo-Saxon settlement: the documentary evidence', in T. Rowley (ed.), *op. cit.*, (1974), p. 108
20. W. de G. Birch, *Cartularium Saxonicum* (1885–93), no. 1000. A translation of the charter with notes was provided by Mr. J. McN. Dodgson. The fieldwork by Mrs. B. Westley confirms that this charter refers to South Heighton rather than to Heaton, Hampshire (see R. Forsberg, *Nomina Germanica*, vol. 9 (1950), p. 208)

21.   A. F. Griffith and L. F. Salzmann, 'An Anglo-Saxon cemetery at Alfriston, Sussex',
      S.A.C., vol. 56 (1914), p. 26 and supplemental paper in *S.A.C.*, vol. 57 (1915), p. 199
22.   N. E. S. Norris, 'Miscellaneous researches 1949–56', *S.A.C.*, vol. 94 (1956), pp. 10–12.
      The sherd, which is not published, is in Lewes Museum, Acc. No. 53.48
23.   A. E. Wilson, 'Report on the excavations on Highdown Hill, Sussex, August 1939',
      S.A.C., vol. 81 (1940), pp. 173–203, and 'Excavations on Highdown Hill, 1947', *S.A.C.*,
      vol. 89 (1950), pp. 163–178
25.   E. C. Curwen, 'Perforated rim-lugs from Friston, Sussex', *Antiq. J.*, vol. 21 (1941),
      pp. 62–64
26.   *S.A.C.*, vol. 8 (1856), p. 297
27.   Worthing Museum, Acc. No. 58/261
28.   J. McN. Dodgson, 'Place-names in *ham*, distinguished from *hamm* names, in relation to
      the settlement of Kent, Surrey and Sussex', in P. Clemoes (ed.), *Anglo-Saxon England*,
      vol. 2 (1973), pp. 1–50
29.   J. McN. Dodgson, *op. cit.*, (1966)
30.   B. W. Cunliffe, 'Saxon and medieval settlement pattern in the region of Chalton, Hamp-
      shire', *Med. Arch.*, vol. 16 (1972), pp. 1–12
31.   Fishbourne: B. W. Cunliffe, 'The Saxon culture-sequence at Portchester Castle', *Antiq. J.*,
      vol. 50 (1970), p. 77; Lancing: C. Ainsworth, personal communication
32.   G. C. Dunning in 'Anglo-Saxon pottery: a symposium', *Med. Arch.*, vol. 3 (1959), pp. 56
      and 57
33.   J. G. Hurst in 'Anglo-Saxon pottery: a symposium', *Med. Arch.*, vol. 3 (1959), pp. 23–5.
      I am grateful to E. W. Holden for information on Sussex loomweights
34.   E. W. Holden, 'Excavations at Old Erringham, Shoreham, West Sussex: part 1, a Saxon
      weaving hut, *S.A.C.*, vol. 114 (1976), pp. 306–321
35.   E. W. Holden, 'Saxo-Norman remains at Telscombe', *S.N.Q.*, vol. 16 (1963–67), pp. 154–158
36.   W. de G. Birch, *Cartularium Saxonicum* (1885–93), No. 1191
37.   Writer's fieldwork at TQ.383026
38.   Recorded in the unpublished *Journal of G. P. Burstow*, 19 and 22 October 1950. A small
      cup from the burial site is in Barbican House Museum, Lewes, Acc. No. 51.3
39.   Finds in Chichester Museum and information from E. W. Holden
40.   Barbican House Museum, Lewes, Acc. No. 27.80
41.   Barbican House Museum, Lewes, Acc. No. 55.47
42.   H. Sutermeister, 'Burpham: a settlement within the Saxon defences', *S.A.C.*, vol. 114
      (1976), pp. 194–206
43.   D. J. Freke, 'Further excavations in Lewes, 1975', *S.A.C.*, vol. 114 (1976), pp. 176–193
44.   Denton find at TQ.455025; Bishopstone at TQ.472011, both Brighton Museum; Bramber
      Castle, *S.N.Q.*, vol. 16 (1967), pp. 333–5; Newhaven, *S.A.C.*, vol. 112 (1974), pp. 154–5
45.   A. Barr-Hamilton, 'The excavation of Bargham church site, Upper Bargham, Angmering,
      Sussex', *S.A.C.*, vol. 99 (1961), pp. 38–65
46.   G. M. White, 'A settlement of the South Saxons', *Antiq. J.*, vol. 14 (1934), pp. 393–400
47.   V. L. Gregory, 'Excavations at Becket's Barn, Pagham, West Sussex, 1974', *S.A.C.*,
      vol. 114 (1976), pp. 207–217
48.   A. H. Collins, 'Saxon cinerary urn from Pagham churchyard', *S.N.Q.*, vol. 14 (1955),
      pp. 123–5
49.   L. F. Salzman, 'Excavations at Selsey 1911', *S.A.C.*, vol. 55 (1912), pp. 56–62
50.   A. E. Wilson, 'Chichester excavations 1947–50', *S.A C.*, vol. 90 (1952), p. 164
51.   Nyetimber, *S.A.C.*, vol. 90 (1952), p. 173. I have not been able to trace this material;
      Aldingbourne: M. W. Pitts, personal communication
52.   E. and E. C. Curwen, 'A Saxon hut site at Thakeham, Sussex', *Antiq. J.*, vol. 14 (1934),
      p. 425
53.   D. Wilson and D. G. Hurst, 'Medieval Britain in 1968', *Med. Arch.*, vol. 13 (1969), p. 267
54.   A. E. Wilson, 'The end of Roman Sussex and the early Saxon settlements', *S.A.C.*, vol. 82
      (1941), p. 46

55.   A. Meaney, *A Gazetteer of early Anglo-Saxon burial sites* (1964), p. 255. Further excavations by Mr. David Thomson are not yet published.

56.   Finds in Lewes Museum, Acc. Nos. 39.9; 39.22; 51.51; 55.5

57.   G. C. Dunning, 'Report on pottery from ditch under Balsdean chapel', *S.A.C.*, vol. 91 (1953), pp. 63–68

58.   B. W. Cunliffe, *op. cit.*, (1970)

59.   A. J. F. Dulley, 'Excavations at Pevensey, Sussex, 1962–6', *Med. Arch.*, vol. 11 (1967), pp. 209–232

60.   Durhamford, *Transactions of the Battle and District Historical Society*, 1952–4, p. 28. (I have not examined this material.) The other finds are in Lewes Museum. Bignor Acc. No. 51.6; Barcombe Acc. Nos. 61.5; 73.9

61.   E. W. Holden, 'Excavations at the deserted medieval village of Hangleton, Part 1', *S.A.C.*, vol. 101 (1963), p. 59

No references to Chapter IV: Place-Names in Sussex

Chapter V: The Sussex Mints and their Moneyers

The following abbreviations are used to refer to publications most frequently cited:
B.M.C.: British Museum Catalogues: C. F. Keary and H. A. Grueber, *Catalogue of English Coins in the British Museum, Anglo-Saxon Series*, I (1887) and II (1893); G. C. Brooke, *Catalogue of English Coins in the British Museum, Norman Kings* (1916)
B.N.J.: British Numismatic Journal
Num. Chron.: Numismatic Chronicle
S.C.B.I.: Sylloge of Coins of the British Isles

1.   Chancton find, B. V. Head in *Num. Chron.* 1867, pp. 63–126 (J. D. A. Thompson, *Inventory of British coin hoards*, no. 81); Oving, D. M. Metcalf in *Num. Chron.* 1957, p. 198 (Thompson —); Offham, *S.A.C.*, vol. 21 (1869), p. 219 (Thompson 297)

2.   For a colour photograph, see frontispiece to R. H. M. Dolley, *Anglo-Saxon pennies* (1964). C. S. S. Lyon, in *B.N.J.*, vol. 38 (1969), p. 208, has suggested that the three late Saxon gold coins may each have been designed to weigh three times a contemporary silver penny, giving (at a gold:silver ratio of 10:1) the value of 30d. as represented by the *mancus* of the records. See 1. Stewart, 'Anglo-Saxon Gold Coins', in R. A. G. Carson (ed.), *Scripta Nummaria Romana: Essays presented to Humphrey Sutherland* (1978)

3.   I would like to record my gratitude to Miss Marion Archibald, Mr. Christopher Blunt and Mr. Stewart Lyon, who have saved me from many of the errors and omissions otherwise inevitable in a paper so hastily written and without whose ready assistance and advice this paper could not have been completed at all in the time available. I am also indebted for comment on various points to Miss Frances Colman, Prof. Michael Dolley, Prof. Philip Grierson, Mr. F. Elmore Jones, Dr. Gay van der Meer, Mr. Peter Mitchell, Mr. Hugh Pagan and Mrs. Veronica Smart.

4.   The British Museum contains some Sussex coins from two nineteenth century finds buried in the 1040s. From the 1853 Wedmore (Somerset) hoard (Thompson 374), which ends with type 13, there are B.M.C. Cnut 33–4 (Chichester), 258–9 and 261–2 (Lewes) and Harold 42 (Lewes). From the 1832 Thwaite (Suffolk) hoard (Thompson 360, see *B.N.J.*, vol. 28 (1955–7), pp. 414–6), which was dominated by, and ended with, type 16, there are two Lewes coins (B.M.C. 573–4) but none of the other Sussex mints (Kentish mints are better represented). The Milton Street hoard (Thompson 270; and see *Numismatic Circular* Feb. 1971, pp. 54–6) ended with type 18 and some of the Sussex coins from it were in a parcel sold by Sotheby on 24 June 1970 (lots 63–77); this provenance perhaps supports the reattribution to Lewes of a type 7 coin (listed as Chester) reading PVLFEH :MM LEE, or LEC (lot 63; cf. King 149b, which is from the same obv. die, of London style)

5. W. A. Raper and E. H. Willett in *S.A.C.*, vol. 33 (1883), pp. 1–38 (Thompson 327). A parcel from this hoard is published by Dolley, *B.N.J.*, vol. 30 (1960–1), pp. 76–81

6. There is no need to regard this hoard as connected with the Hastings mint itself, as suggested by Dolley and Metcalf in Dolley (ed.), *Anglo-Saxon Coins* (1961), p. 158. A similar local dominance over a number of types is that of the York mint in the Bishophill hoard (Thompson 386; Dolley, 'The mythical Norman element in the 1882 Bishophill (York) find of Anglo-Saxon coins', *Annual Report* (1971) of Yorkshire Philosophical Society, pp. 88–102)

7. Thompson 255; Willett in *Num. Chron.* 1876, pp. 323–94. Other hoards of this period were not adequately recorded. For Denge Marsh, Kent (1739) see *Num. Chron.* 1957, p. 186. From the 1851 find at Soberton, Hants., there are two Lewes coins of Harold II in B.M.C. (nos. 43 and 45), but none from Sussex mints of Edward or William.

8. Thompson 323; R. Carlyon-Britton in *B.N.J.*, vol. 12 (1915), pp. 15–32 (the so-called 'War Area' hoard), but for find-spot see Dolley in *B.N.J.*, vol. 28 (1955–7), pp. 650–1

9. Thompson 37; for a convenient summary see *B.N.J.*, vol. 2 (1905), pp. 103–4

10. Thompson 350. See also C. E. Blunt and B. H. I. H. Stewart, 'A parcel from the Shillington (1871) hoard?', *Numismatic Circular*, Sept. 1977, p. 354, for information about a very important find (Thompson 330) of the mid-Norman period

11. *Coin Hoards* I, 1975, no. 359

12. B.M.C., pp. xxvi–xxxi; also the South Kyme hoard (Thompson 337; L. A. Lawrence in *Num. Chron.* 1922, pp. 49–83) and the 1972 Prestwich find (*Coin Hoards* I, no. 360)

13. B. E. Hildebrand, *Anglosachsiska Mynt* (3rd edn., 1881)

14. *S.C.B.I.*, vols. 4, 7, 13 and 18

15. See note of principal references, B.M.C.

16. *S.C.B.I.*, vols. 1; 2; and 9 and 12

17. *B.N.J.*, vol. 28 (1955–7), pp. 60–74 (Bramber, Chichester, Pevensey and Rye); pp. 249–63 (Hastings and Steyning); and pp. 518–36 (Lewes); addenda and corrigenda, vol. 29, pp. 190–1, 415, and vol. 30, p. 188. Two earlier papers by King also contain relevant comment: 'The Steyning mint', *B.N.J.*, vol. 24 (1941–4), pp. 1–7, and 'Two numismatic journeys to Scandinavia', *B.N.J.*, vol. 27 (1952–4), pp. 173–4

18. H. B. A. Petersson, *Anglo-Saxon currency* (Lund, 1969). Of these he weighed nearly 35,000 (pp. 240–1)

19. Thompson 71; P. W. P. Carlyon-Britton in *B.N.J.*, vol. 19 (1927–8), pp. 93–107. This find is usually known as the Canterbury hoard, but the concentration of coins of Winchester, Twynham, Shaftesbury and Dorchester would support the tradition of an origin in the area of Bournemouth or Poole. See Stewart, 'The Bournemouth Find (*c.* 1901) of coins of Henry I', *Num. Chron.* 1977, pp. 180–3

20. Thompson 372; J. Rashleigh in *Num. Chron.* 1850, pp. 138–65

21. For differing interpretations of how the system worked see R. H. M. Dolley and D. M. Metcalf, 'The reform of the English coinage under Eadgar', in *Anglo-Saxon Coins* (ed. Dolley, 1961), pp. 136–68; Petersson, *op. cit.*; C. S. S. Lyon, 'Variations in currency in late Anglo-Saxon England', in R. A. G. Carson (ed.), *Mints, Dies and Currency* (1971), pp. 101–20

22. Because of advances in knowledge none of the earlier classifications are suitable for the purpose of discussing chronological developments, such as the activity of mints over a period or the careers of individual moneyers; as explained in the relevant sections, the types from Edgar's reform to the Conquest have therefore been numbered in sequence, from 1 to 23, for simple reference, as set out in Stewart, 'A numeration of late Anglo-Saxon coin types', *B.N.J.*, vol. 45 (1975), pp. 12–18

23. G. C. Brooke, 'Quando moneta vertebatur', *B.N.J.*, vol. 20 (1929–30), pp. 105–16

24. The Lincoln hoard confirms that the relative abundance of Henry I types VII and X is not due to the chance of finds: see M. M. Archibald, 'English medieval coins as dating evidence', in Casey and Reece (eds.), *Coins and the archaeologist* (1974), pp. 234–71 (at p. 250)

25. Where hoard evidence is lacking, the number of specimens recorded by King have been used. It should be noted that in his lists King excluded coins in provincial museums (except Brighton), foreign museums (except Stockholm) and private collections (except his own) unless 'the coin is the only or nearly the only specimen known to me'; this limitation of listed material has little practical effect in the rarer issues

26. Stewart, 'Reflections on some Wessex mints and their moneyers', *Num. Chron.* 1975, pp. 219-29; for a general discussion, see H. R. Loyn, 'Boroughs and Mints', *Anglo-Saxon Coins*, pp. 122-35

27. E.g. in the *First Hand* and *Last Small Cross* types of Ethelred and *Quatrefoil* of Cnut

28. Type 7, Lefa, King 150; type 18, Oswold, King 244

29. King 36

30. King p. 536

31. The reading *Laewude* on a die of type 8 probably does not represent this mint; see infra

32. E.g. in Hildebrand: Canterbury, Ethelred 1820, Cnut 3871, Edward 34; Cadbury, Ethelred 118; Leicester, Cnut 1307, 1339, 1364, 1387; and Lincoln, Ethelred 1810

33. Norden 1595; Speed, 1610

34. R. H. M. Dolley and F. Elmore Jones, 'The mints 'aet Gothabyrig' and 'aet Sith(m)estebyrig', *B.N.J.*, vol. 28 (1955-7), pp. 270-82

35. F. Elmore Jones, 'The Stephen mint of 'Bran . . .': a new attribution', *B.N.J.*, vol. 25 (1945-8), pp. 119-24

36. W. J. Andrew, 'The mints of Rye and Castle Rising in the reign of Stephen', *B.N.J.*, vol. 20 (1929-30), pp. 117-22; R. Seaman, 'The Rye mint', *Numismatic Circular*, Jan. 1977, p. 9

37. V. J. Smart, 'Moneyers of the late Anglo-Saxon coinage, 973-1016', *Commentationes de nummis saeculorum IX-XI in Suecia repertis*, II (Stockholm, 1968), pp. 193-276 (see p. 271)

38. *Ibid.*, 214-5

39. M. Biddle (ed.), *Winchester in the early middle ages: an edition and discussion of the Winton Domesday* (1976)

40. I owe this suggestion to Professor Peter Sawyer; Birch, *Cart. Sax.* 951

41. See Stewart, *The Exeter mint and its moneyers*, in Glendining sale catalogue of Brettell collection, 28 Oct. 1970, pp. 3-37 (especially 28-30)

42. No systematic attempt has been made in this paper to trace possible identities of moneyer between Sussex mints and mints outside the county except Winchester), although they could exist (e.g. with Southampton, a mint which shared moneyers with Winchester), as the Pevensey-Sandwich example demonstrates in the Norman period.

43. For Athelstan's coinage see the comprehensive study by C. E. Blunt, 'The coinage of Athelstan, 924-939, survey', *B.N.J.*, vol. 42; Chichester, pp. 73-4; Lewes, p. 70; chronology p. 57

44. B.M.C., type V; Blunt 181

45. B.M.C., type I; Blunt 108

46. B.M.C., type VIII; Blunt 267

47. Edmund, C. E. Blunt collection (no. 3 of plate accompanying this paper); Eadred, British Museum, acquired 1957 (no. 4 of plate). The reverse of the Edmund coin was illustrated by Fountaine, *Numismata Anglo-Saxonica* etc. (1705), pl. v, 14

48. Blunt 159 (no. 2 of plate)

49. Blunt 71

50. E.g. Glendining sale 16 May 1929, lot 90 (illustrated); see no. 1 of plate

51. The entry under Edmund in Blunt, p. 73, is an error based on a mis-reading, corrected by Blunt in *B.N.J.*, vol. 40 (1971), p. 18

52. B.M.C., type III (no. 185); see no. 5 of plate

53. Belfast; *B.N.J.*, vol. 29 (1958-9), pl. I, 1

54. Examples are: Edmund (Siedeman, Siademan), Forum hoard 369, B.M.C., 127; Eadred (Sideman), *S.C.B.I.*, Edinburgh 255; Eadwig (Sedeman), B.M.C., 32; Edgar (Sedeman),

B.M.C., 135, *S.C.B.I.*, Edinburgh 501, Copenhagen 813, Ashmolean 401, etc. Edgar's Sedeman is one of only four moneyers, all with southern connections, recorded of B.M.C., type Ib, the extremely rare variety of the two-line type with crosses instead of trefoils above and below the name (*B.N.J.*, vol. 35 (1966), pl. xiv, 12)

55. See King, Chichester nos. 41 and 48; Hastings nos. 16 and 18–9; Lewes nos. 60–1, 103–4, 108–9, 114 and 119–20

56. Lyon, *op. cit.*, 110

57. The numbers depart from King's lists in the following respects: Chichester, Wunstan (type 2) is distinguished from Dunstan (type 6); Hastings, Aelwine (type 3), noted only from a sale catalogue (L. E. Bruun, Sotheby 18 May 1925, lot 135) is omitted from totals; Lewes, B.M.C., 127 (*First Hand*, 'Eadgar') is in fact of Theodgar; Wine is omitted (? = Leofwine, *B.N.J.*, vol. 27, p. 174). The Lewes Leofstans of types 2 and 6 are presumably separate

58. This chain of die-links was discovered by Mr. Lyon when working with Prof. Dolley in Stockholm in 1962; I am greatly indebted to him for his generous suggestion that I might publish them here. The coins are all listed by Hildebrand except one from a subsequent Swedish hoard (Inv. 14565–61). Six obverse dies are involved: (a) with reverses of AElfwerd (H.1407), Godeferth (H.–), Liofwine (H.1459) and Siric (H.4312); (b) with reverses of Godeferth (H.1409, 1414 and 118 'Cadbury') and Liofwine (H.1458); (c) with reverses of Godeferth (H.1413 and 1416); (d) with reverse of Liofwine (H.1457); (e) with reverses of Leofnoth (H.1435) and Siric (H.4311); and (f) with reverses of AElfwerd (H.1405 and 1408) and Siric (H.4310). The reverse die-links are: Godeferth, H.1409 = H.– and H.1413 = 1414; Liofwine, H.1457 = 1458 = 1459; and Siric, H.4310 = 4311·= 4312

59. For these links, also discovered by Mr. Lyon, see *B.N.J.*, vol. 39 (1970), pp. 202–3 and pl. IX. Other cases of dies not used at the mints named on them have been published by M. M. Archibald, *Mints, dies and currency*, p. 153 and Stewart, *ibid.*, p. 272

60. Dolley, 'Hiberno-Norse coins in the British Museum', *S.C.B.I.*, 8 (1966), p. 122

61. Of Lewes, King 197–8 (Edwerd and Northman) have bust right and K.199 and 200 (Northman and Wulfric) bust left

62. See no. 10 and plate. A few coins of type 10 also (but none from Sussex) have the name Cnut, which here too may represent Harthacnut

63. Hild. 1286; King 168. The two latter are from a Norwegian find—Årstad, Rogaland, 1836 (C. A. Holmboe, *De Nummis medii aevi in Norvegia nuper repertis* I–II (Christiania, 1836-7); H. Holst, *N.N.Å.* (1943), p. 80, no. 60d

64. Cf. Hild. 64

65. There are distant outliers, e.g. Bath; see L. V. Grinsell, *The Bath mint* (1973), pl. II, no. 23. The curious reading CNVT . . /EX ANG, with a trefoil replacing the R of Rex, is characteristic. The two *Laewude* coins weigh only 0.84 g. and 0.87 g. against a range of 0.95-1.16 g. and an average of 1.06 g. for the 11 undamaged Lewes coins of the same type in Copenhagen

66. King 149a, *B N.J.*, vol. 29 (1958–9), p. 190; *S.C.B I.*, Copenhagen, nos. 4229–30. Mr. Lyon remarks that some odd styles are found at the Sussex mints at this period (e.g. Onlaf's dies of type 6 are of East Anglian style—cf. *S.C.B.I.*, Cop. 467 with 1211 of Thetford), and it is possible that the Onlaf coins of type 7 are English (cf. *S.C.B.I.*, Cop. 1330–2)

67. King 35

68. Hild. 1108–9, King 33 and 47 (types 7 and 8)

69. King records only eight Sussex coins of the type, of which one (K.16) has been shown by Mr. Hugh Pagan to be a modern forgery (*B.N.J.*, vol. 40, p. 157)

70. O. von Feilitzen and C. E. Blunt, 'Personal names on the coinage of Edgar' in P. Clemoes and K. Hughes (eds.) *England before the Conquest* (Cambridge, 1971), pp. 183–214 (at pp. 210–1). The alternative interpretation, that these two names might have belonged to the same person, and have been used either together or separately, has not found

favour with philologists in spite of the other double names at Winchester which appear to denote single persons at this period and of another case (*Aestan Loc*) where the second name as well as the first is sometimes found alone.

71. Wulfric's Hastings entry under type 18 rests on a single coin (with an apparently clear reading, ON HAESTI) recorded in the report of the Sedlescombe hoard, but unverified since.

72. King in *B.N.J.*, vol. 24 (1941-4), p. 3; P. J. Seaby, 'The sequence of Anglo-Saxon coin types, 1030-50', *B.N.J.*, vol. 28 (1955-7), pp. 111-46

73. The parallel run of types is nevertheless suggestive and at both mints they end with the Conquest; if the type 14 Chichester fragment (Hildebrand 56) is of this moneyer, it would complete the sequence.

74. The unverified Chichester entry depends on a coin recorded in the report of the Walbrook hoard (*Num. Chron.* 1876, p. 347). For type 17 of Lewes (King −) see no. 11 of plate.

75. E.g., all the other four occurrences of Wulfric in the later part of the reign are scattered: Lincoln, London, Rochester, Shaftesbury.

76. Cf. Aelfric in Devonshire (Stewart, 'The Barnstaple mint and its moneyers' in Glendining's sale catalogue, R. P. V. Brettell collection, 18 June 1975)

77. Archibald, *op. cit.*, p. 249. Brooke was following P. W. P. Carlyon-Britton (in *B.N.J.*, vol. 2) as to both sequence and regnal division

78. In the totals I have included Godwine of Chichester in type 34, although the mint reading of the coin concerned (Lockett lot 1022) is open to doubt (B.M.C., p. ccvi suggests London). I have omitted Edwine at Chichester in type 28 but this attribution of *S.C.B.I.*, 21 (York) no. 1210 is a possibility.

79. Metcalf and F. Schweizer, 'The metal contents of the silver pennies of William II and Henry I (1087-1135)', *Archaeometry*, vol. 13 (1971), pp. 177-90

80. Archibald, *op. cit.*, 248-9

81. For Colbrand, type IV, see *B.N.J.*, vol. 28 (1955-7), pp. 536 and 652; Brand, type VI, recorded by Andrew (p. 158) but current whereabouts unknown; Brand, type VII, see *B.N.J.*, vol. 28 (1955-7), p. 536, but there seems little doubt about this attribution.

82. Known−Hastings 4, Chichester 3, Lewes 1; new types for moneyers−Hastings 3, Lewes 3; new moneyers−Hastings 2, Lewes 2; total−Hastings 9, Lewes 6, Chichester 3, Pevensey 0. Miss Archibald has kindly supplied me with the latest tally of Sussex coins from the Lincoln hoard−Chichester: Brand, XIV (1); Godwine, XIII (1), XIV (1). Hastings: Dunninc, X (1), XIV (3); Sperling, VII (1), X (1); Boneface, X (1), XIV (5); Rodbert, XIV (1); Wulnot X (1); Ailmer X (1−presumably this mint but reads hA only). Lewes ?, Winf(raed ?) X (1−possibly this moneyer; no mint signature); Alfward, VII (1); Edmund, X (3), XIV (2); Ordmaer, X (2); Oswald X (3), XIII (1−no. 15 of plate)

83. W. J. Andrews, 'A Numismatic history of the reign of Henry I' (*Num. Chron.* 1901) Brand, pp. 153, 156-7; Boneface, pp. 206, 208-9

84. The Lincoln figures are supported by those of the Bournemouth hoard, in which all three Hastings coins were of this moneyer. A type XIV coin in the L. A. Lawrence sale (lot 339), supposed to read −VNERIC, 'unpublished moneyer', is presumably of BVNEFACE

85. This was Andrew's arrangement (cf. B.M.C., p. cxlviii)

86. The Prestwich hoard contained 10 Stephen type I coins of Chichester, 8 of Hastings (3 Rodbert, 5 Sawine) and 7 of Lewes (3 Herrevi, 3 Osbern, 1 Willem). There were none of Ryè or by Wenstan of Hastings (for which moneyer see *Num. Chron.* 1922, pp. 53 and 71, regarding a coin from the South Kyme hoard with full name but no mint; another with mint name (h?)AS(.) is in the British Museum ex L. A. Lawrence, cited in B.M.C., p. ccxiii)

87. *B.N.J.*, vol. 37 (1968), pp. 31-2

88. Chichester, Prestwich hoard, moneyer illegible but presumably Godwine; bar across chin to sceptre. Hastings, Nottingham hoard: see *B.N.J.*, vol. 37 (1968), p. 59 and R. P. Mack, 'Stephen and the Anarchy', in *B.N.J.*, vol. 35 (1966), no. 155

89. For a full study of this issue, which is only sketchily treated in B.M.C., see F. Elmore Jones, 'Stephen Type VII', *B.N.J.*, vol. 28 (1955-7), pp. 537-54

90. D. F. Allen, B.M.C., *Henry II*, p. cxxi-ii. Rawulf's known coins of Rye are listed and mostly illustrated by R. Seaman in *Numismatic Circular*, Jan. 1977, p. 9. The I/II mule, wrongly stated by Mack (no. 52) to be in the Fitzwilliam Museum, is in Corpus Christi College, Cambridge (no. 161 in P. Spufford's MS catalogue of the Lewis collection). For type VII see *B.N.J.*, vol. 30 (1960-1), p. 188

91. There is a coin of B.M.C. type VI, mint illegible, of a moneyer Aelfwine (Mack no. 95), but the difference in spelling limits the likelihood of a Pevensey attribution. Felipe might be supposed to have been a Lewes moneyer of Henry II on the basis of the reading (F. L. . . .) given by King for his no. 341 but in the view of Mr. Elmore Jones, the present owner, no trace of a moneyer's name is visible at all on this coin (Carlyon-Britton log 1519 = B.M.C. 374a)

92. This coin is in the British Museum, from the South Kyme hoard (*Num. Chron.* 1922, pp. 58 and 75)

93. *B.N.J.*, vol. 25 (1945-8), pp. 119-24. The unique coin of Rodbert is in Moscow, probably from a Baltic hoard (*B.N.J.*, vol. 36 (1967), p. 90). For a possible fourth moneyer see *B.N.J.*, vol. 28 (1955-7), p. 552 and pl. xxxi, 28

94. It does, however, recall the comment of Professor Dolley about the name Osferth which appears at three mints in another very rare type, Ethelred's *Benediction Hand* (Smart, *op. cit.*, p. 218)

Chapter VI: The South Saxon *Andredesweald*

1. For a full bibliography of the Sussex place-name material see in this volume John McNeil Dodgson, 'Place-names in Sussex: the material for a new look', pp. 54-88

2. H. C. Darby, 'Place-names and the geography of the past', in Arthur Brown and Peter Foote (eds.), *Early English and Norse Studies* (1963), p. 13

3. Dorothy Whitelock, et al. (eds.), *The Anglo-Saxon Chronicle* (1965), p. 11

4. *Ibid.*, pp. 30-31

5. *Ibid.*, p. 54

6. *Ibid.*, p. 91

7. R. du Boulay, *The lordship of Canterbury* (1966), p. 138

8. Dorothy Whitelock, *op. cit.*, p. 98

9. Bertram Colgrave (ed.), *The life of bishop Wilfrid by Eddius Stephanus* (1927), pp. 81-82

10. Edwin Guest, 'On the early English settlements in South Britain', *Proceedings of the Royal Archaeological Institute*, Salisbury meeting, 1849 (1851), pp. 28-72. The map, also published in Edwin Guest, *Origines Celticae* (1883), facing p. 147, is reproduced as Fig. 7 in this volume

11. John Richard Green, *A short history of the English people* (1892 edition), p. 18

12. H. A. Wilcox, *The woodlands and marshlands of England* (1933)

13. A. Mawer and F. M. Stenton, *The place-names of Sussex*, English Place-Name Society vols. 6-7 (1929-30)

14. H. C. Darby, *op. cit.*, 6-18

15. S. R. J. Woodell, 'Changes in vegetation at Shakenoak', *Excavations at Shakenoak*, III, A. C. C. Broadribb, A. R. Hands and D. Waller (printed privately) (1972), pp. 158-59; W. R. Fisher, 'Forestry protection', *Dr. Sclich's Manual of Forestry*, vol. IV (1895), pp. 37, 42-3, 78, 79

16. L. F. Salzman (ed.), *The chartulary of the priory of St. Pancras at Lewes*, Part 1 (1932), Sussex Record Society, p. 119

17. C. F. Tebbutt, 'The prehistoric occupation of the Ashdown Forest area of the Weald', *S.A.C.*, vol. 112 (1974), pp. 34-43; idem, 'Garden Hill camp, Hartfield', *S.A.C.*, vol. 108 (1970), pp. 39-49

18. The names, other than those recording swine, used for this study are: *horse*: Horsham, Horse Eye, Horsted Keynes, Little Horsted, Warnham; *goat*: Gotwick (Rusper), Gotham

(Durrington charter); *cattle*: Cowfold, Keymer, Rotherfield, Rotherbridge Hundred; *sheep*: Sheffield, Shipley

19. A. Mawer, *Problems of place-name study* (1929), p. 125
20. W. de Gray Birch, *Cartularium Saxonicum* (1892), (hereafter B.C.S.), 702; Eric E. Barker, 'Sussex Anglo-Saxon charters, part 2', *S.A.C.*, vol. 87 (1948), pp. 115, 150-62
21. B.C.S. 898
22. A. Mawer, *op. cit.*, pp. 16, 55; E. Ekwall, *op. cit.*, p. 161
23. E. Ekwall, *op. cit.*, p. 162
24. A. Mawer, *op. cit.*, pp. 16, 81-2
25. E. Ekwall, *Studies of English place-names and personal names* (1931), pp. 44-5; A. Mawer, *op. cit.*, p. 58
26. A. Mawer, *op. cit.*, p. 18
27. B.C.S. 702, 834, 1134; Eric E. Barker, *op. cit.*, *S.A.C.*, vol. 89 (1948), pp. 15-00; *S.A.C.*, vol. 88 (1949), pp. 64-70, 89-92
28. J. H. Round, 'The settlement of the South and East Saxons', in J. H. Round, *The Commune of London* (1899), pp. 1-27. Round's paper was amongst the earliest to be devoted to Sussex place-names and for sheer readability it is still unmatched
29. E. Ekwall, *Old English WIC in place-names* (Lund, 1964), p. 44
30. A. H. Smith, *English place-name elements*, English Place-Name Society vol. 26, part 2 (1956), pp. 152-3
31. William Marshall, *The rural economy of the southern counties* (1798), vol. 2, p. 48
32. John Ruskin, *Seven lamps* (1849 edition), p. 185
33. B.C.S. 702, 834, 1114; Eric E. Barker, *op. cit.*, *S.A.C.*, vol. 87 (1948), pp. 150-162; *S.A.C.*, vol. 88 (1949), pp. 64-70, 89-92
34. B.C.S. 834; Eric E. Barker, *S.A.C.*, vol. 88 (1949), pp. 64-70
35. B.C.S. 702; Eric E. Barker, *S.A.C.*, vol. 87 (1948), pp. 150-162
36. P. A. Nicklin and E. G. Godfrey-Fausset, 'On the distribution of place-names in Sussex', *S.A.C.*, vol. 76 (1935), pp. 220-21
37. Margaret Gelling, *The place names of Berkshire*, E.P.N.S. vol. 51, part 3:11, pp. 836, 926-7
38. A. Mawer and F. M. Stenton, *The place-names of Sussex*, vol. 7 (1930), p. 458
39. B.C.S. 702; Eric E. Barker, *S.A.C.*, vol. 87 (1948), pp. 150-162
40. B.C.S. 1334, 669; Eric E. Barker, *S.A.C.*, vol. 86 (1947), pp. 98-100; *S.A.C.*, vol. 87 (1948), pp. 139-148
41. B.C.S. 50, 1334; Eric E. Barker, *op. cit.*, pp. 98-100
42. B.C.S. 694; Eric E. Barker, *S.A.C.*, vol. 87 (1947), p.
43. B.C.S. 208; Eric E. Barker, *S.A.C.*, vol. 86 (1947), pp. 90-95
44. B.C.S. 197; Eric E. Barker, *S.A.C.*, vol. 86 (1947), pp. 85-90
45. Eric E. Barker, *S.A.C.*, vol. 88 (1948), pp. 109-133
46. B.C.S. 834; Eric E. Barker, *S.A.C.*, vol. 88 (1948), pp. 64-70
47. L. F. Salzman, *The chartulary of the priory of St. Peter at Sele* (1923), p. 4; idem, *The chartulary of the priory of St. Pancras at Lewes*, Part 1 (1932), Sussex Record Society, p. 119
48. A. Mawer, *op. cit.*, (footnote 19), p. 53
49. Sussex Archaeological Trust, Barbican House, Lewes, MS LB34
50. F. E. Harmer, *Select English historical documents of the ninth and tenth centuries* (1914), pp. 13-19
51   *Ibid.*, p. 51
52. The charter is a blatant forgery but J. H. Round noted that the witnesses 'seem genuine enough' and that 'it is difficult to resist the impression that the first parish church must have been erected when Rotherfield belonged to the monks of the abbey'; J. H. Round, 'A note on the early history of Rotherfield church', *S.A.C.*, vol. 41 (1898), pp. 49-53
53. J. H. Round (ed.), *Calendar of Documents in France* (1898), p. 471
54. W. Stubbs (ed.), *Memorials of Saint Dunstan* (Rolls series, 1894), p. 97

55. R. Lennard, *Rural England, 1066–1142* (1959), p. 9
56. See P. F. Brandon, 'Medieval clearances in the east Sussex Weald', *Trans. Institute of British Geographers*, vol. 48 (1969), pp. 135–153
57. P. H. Sawyer, 'Early medieval English settlement', in P. H. Sawyer (ed.), *Medieval settlement: continuity and change* (1976), pp. 1–7
58. G. R. G. Jones, 'Multiple estates and early settlements', in P. H. Sawyer, *op. cit.*, pp. 26–35
59. Sussex Archaeological Trust, Barbican House, Lewes, MS LB34
60. J. H. Round, *op. cit.*, (footnote 28)

Chapter VII: The Church in Saxon Sussex

1. B. Thorpe (ed.), *Florentii Wigorniensis monachi Chronicon ex Chronicis* (1849), vol. II, p. 6
2. General reference may be made to E. Heron-Allen, *Selsey Bill: historic and prehistoric* (1911)
3. H. Mayr-Harting, *The Bishops of Chichester 1075–1207: biographical notes and problems*, The Chichester Papers, no. 40 (1963). A number of other Norman bishops also transferred their sees in the 1070s: F. Barlow, *The English Church*, 1000–1066 (1963), pp. 164–5
4. L. Fleming, *The little churches of Chichester*, The Chichester Papers, no. 5 (1957), p. 7. The three other churches he discusses are not now generally regarded as containing Saxon work
5. *Victoria County History, Sussex*, vol. 3, pp. 105 ff. Cf. W. D. Peckham, *The chartulary of the High Church of Chichester*, Sussex Record Society, vol. 46 (1942–3), and a recent paper on architectural matters, idem, 'Some notes on Chichester Cathedral', vol. 111 (1973), pp. 20–6
6. D. Talbot Rice, *English Art 871–1100* (1952), pp. 110–11
7. A. W. Clapham, *English Romanesque Architecture before the Conquest* (1930), p. 138
8. D. Talbot Rice, *op. cit.*, p. 110 ff.
9. T. D. Kendrick, *Late Saxon and Viking Art* (1949), pp. 52–4
10. G. Zarnecki, *English Romanesque Sculpture 1066–1140* (1951), p. 6
11. H. M. and J. Taylor, *Anglo-Saxon Architecture* (1965), vol. II, p. 730. The Taylors cite references to earlier papers by previous writers in the case of each individual church with which they deal
12. E. A. Fisher, *The Saxon Churches of Sussex* (1970)
13. H. M. and J. Taylor, *op. cit.*, vol. I, p. 40
14. *Op. cit.*, vol. II, p. 715
15. Cf. E. A. Fisher, *The Greater Anglo-Saxon Churches* (1962), p. 375, with H. M. and J. Taylor, *op. cit.*, vol. II, p. 548
16. D. Parsons, reviewing E. A. Fisher, *The Saxon Churches of Sussex*, in *Arch. J.*, vol. 127 (1970), pp. 305–6. H. M. and J. Taylor, *op. cit.*, vol. I, pp. 72–3, regard the tower at Bishopstone as Norman
17. H. M. and J. Taylor, *op. cit.*, vol. II, p. 681
18. *Ibid.*, vol. II, p. 721
19. *Ibid.*, vol. II, p. 718
20. E. A. Fisher, *The Saxon Churches of Sussex* (note 12), p. 13
21. H. M. and J. Taylor, *op. cit.*, vol. I, p. 283
22. D. Parsons, reviewing E. A. Fisher, *The Saxon Churches of Sussex*, in *Arch. J.*, vol. 127 (1970), p. 306
23. Cf. D. Parsons, 'A note on the east end of Roche Abbey church', *Journal of the British Archaeological Association*, vol. 38 (1974), 123, observing that the double-splayed clerestory windows are characteristic in their double-splaying of the Anglo-Saxon architectural type, but 'an insistence on this stylistic attribution, however, would lead to ludicrous results'
24. E. A. Fisher, *op. cit.* (note 12), pp. 12–13, 228 ff.; H. Poole, 'The Domesday Book churches of Sussex', *S.A.C.*, vol. 97 (1948), pp. 30–76, is extremely useful

25. P. M. Johnston, 'Steyning church', *S.A.C.*, vol. 57 (1915), pp. 149–61. The church contains two stones with incised crosses, commonly regarded as associated with the Saxon church if not with the shrine of Aethelwulf
26. W. Stubbs (ed.), *Memorials of Saint Dunstan* (Rolls series, 1874), p. 204
27. For a study of the demolished old church of St. John-sub-Castro (Lewes), postulating an original Saxon nave, see R. Gilbert, 'Evidence for Tower transepts at the old Church of St. John-sub-Castro, Lewes', *S.A.C.*, vol. 112 (1974), pp. 44–47
28. E. A. Fisher, *The Greater Anglo-Saxon Churches* (1962), p. 374
29. H. M. and J. Taylor, *op. cit.*, vol. I, p. 349
30. *Op. cit.*, vol. I, p. 71
31. E. A. Fisher, *op. cit.* (note 12), p. 13
32. H. M. and J. Taylor, *op. cit.*, vol. II, pp. 644–5
33. *Ibid.*, vol. II, p. 536
34. *Ibid.*, vol. I, p. 159
35. *Ibid.*, vol. I, p. 283
36. A. W. Clapham, *English Romanesque Architecture before the Conquest* (1930) is an informative and attractive survey but, of course, G. Baldwin Brown, *The Arts in Early England: Ecclesiastical architecture in England from the conversion of the Saxons to the Norman Conquest* (1903) still remains fundamental, if heavy, reading
37. H. M. and J. Taylor, *op. cit.*, vol. I, p. 157
38. *Ibid.*, vol. I, p. 159
39. *Ibid.*, vol. II, p. 537
40. *Ibid.*, vol. II, pp. 691–2. Cf., on possible relationships between manuscript illustrations and architectural practice, in the context of a date in the second quarter of the eleventh century, with reference to the doorways at Worth, D. Parsons, 'The Saxon doorways of the Church of St. Nicholas, Worth', *S.A.C.*, vol. 107 (1969), pp. 12–13
41. *Ibid.*, vol. II, p. 544
42. *Ibid.*, vol. I, p. 71
43. G. Baldwin Brown, *op. cit.*, p. 288
44. A. W. Clapham, *op. cit.*, p. 100
45. E. A. Fisher, *op. cit.* (note 12), pp. 14, 218. Whether these churches were built by masons from Normandy (*ibid.*, 14) is another matter altogether
46. H. M. and J. Taylor, *op. cit.*, vol. II, pp. 688 ff.
47. *Ibid.*, vol. II, p. 692
48. *Ibid.*, vol. II, pp. 581–3
49. *Ibid.*, vol. I, pp. 81 ff. E. A. Fisher, *op. cit.* (note 15), p. 373, described the chancel arch as 'one of the finest in the country', and 'magnificient'
50. *Ibid.*, vol. 1, p. 81. E. A. Fisher thought (on the basis of an old tradition about the burial of one of Cnut's daughters in the church) that the present building might have been erected in the time of Cnut; *The Greater Anglo-Saxon Churches*, p. 370 ff. Stressing the imperfect alignment, Fisher comments that 'The church is badly set out, in true Saxon Manner' (p. 371). Cf. H. M. and J. Taylor, *op. cit.*, vol. 1, p. 84: 'The tower is very irregularly laid out'
51. E. A. Fisher, *op. cit.* (note 15), pp. 376 ff. and H. M. and J. Taylor, *op. cit.*, vol. II, p. 558 ff. Cf., for interest, an account of a visit to the church and description by A. W. Clapham, *Arch. J.*, vol. 92 (1935), pp. 405–9
52. E. A. Fisher, *op. cit.* (note 15), p. 380 and *op. cit.*, vol. II, p. 588. Cf. A. W. Clapham, *op. cit.*, p. 120: 'This was a common form of roof in the Rhineland, but whether or not it was the normal method of covering a small Saxon tower we do not know.' Clapham assigns it by decorative features to the first half of the eleventh century
53. H. M. and J. Taylor, *op. cit.*, vol. II, p. 580
54. E. A. Fisher, *op. cit.* (note 12), p. 14
55. H. M. and J. Taylor, *op. cit.*, vol. II, p. 537
56. *Ibid.*, vol. II, p. 539

57. *Ibid.*, vol. II, p. 538

58. E. A. Fisher, *op. cit.* (note 15), p. 377, and *op. cit.* (note 12), p. 176; cf. H. M. and J. Taylor, *op. cit.*, vol. II, pp. 558–60

59. H. M. and J. Taylor, *op. cit.*, vol. II, pp. 561–2: A. W. Clapham, *op. cit.*, p. 135

60. H. M. and J. Taylor, *op. cit.*, vol. II, p. 562. E. A. Fisher saw the figure as a bishop or an apostle: *op. cit.* (note 15), p. 381, describing it as 'very primitively Anglo-Saxon in execution', (cf., *op. cit.* (note 12), p. 181). There has been debate over the date of the figure, but it is now generally placed in the first half of the eleventh century: see in particular, A. W. Clapham, 'Sompting church', *Arch. J.*, vol. 92 (1935), pp. 405–9, and D. Talbot Rice, *English art 971–1100* (1952), p. 107

61. H. M. and J. Taylor, *op. cit.*, vol. I, p. 350

62. E. A. Fisher, *op. cit.* (note 15), p. 374. Cf. *op. cit.* (note 12), p. 134. On the Urnes style from Scandinavia, see T. D. Kendrick, *op. cit.* (note 9), p. 110 ff.

63. T. D. Kendrick, *op. cit.*, p. 120; D. Talbot Rice, *op. cit.*, p. 95

64. T. D. Kendrick, *op. cit.*, p. 120

65. M. Rickert, *Painting in the Middle Ages* (Pelican History of Art: 1954), p. 89. Cf. C. Bell, *Twelfth century Paintings at Hardham and Clayton* (Lewes, 1947), p. 10

66. A. Baker, 'Lewes priory and the early group of wall paintings in Sussex', *Walpole Society*, vol. 31 (1942–3; London, 1946), pp. 1–44; cf. H. M. and J. Taylor, *op. cit.*, Vol. I, p. 160, on the date. Note in general, E. W. Tristram, *English medieval wall painting: the twelfth century* (1944), pp. 27 ff., on the Lewes school with reference to Hardham and Clayton. In a paper, Audrey M. Baker again discusses 'The wall paintings in the church of St. John the Baptist, Clayton', *S.A.C.*, vol. 108 (1970), pp. 58–81 (with plates), retaining the hypothesis of a connection with the de Warenne family (though not with Lewes) and accepting (apparently) a more flexible date of 'late 11th or early 12th centuries'

67. M. Rickert, *op. cit.*, pp. 89–90

68. A. Baker, *art. cit.*, 4 ff.

69. *Ibid.*, p. 15

70. D. P. Kirby (ed.), *St. Wilfrid at Hexham* (Newcastle-upon-Tyne, 1974)

71. B. Colgrave (ed.), *The Life of Bishop Wilfrid by Eddius Stephanus* (Cambridge, 1927)

72. B. Colgrave and R. A. B. Mynors, *Bede's Ecclesiastical History of the English People* (1969), cited here henceforth as *H.E.* (*Historia Ecclesiastica*)

73. *The Life of Bishop Wilfrid, c.* 13

74. H. Mayr-Harting, *The Coming of Christianity to Anglo-Saxon England* (1972), pp. 139–42

75. W. A. Chaney, *The Cult of Kingship in Anglo-Saxon England* (Manchester, 1970), p. 104

76. *H.E.*, IV, p. 13

77. E. O. G. Turville-Petre, *Myth and Religion of the North* (1964), p. 254; W. A. Chaney, *op. cit.*, p. 166

78. *H.E.*, IV, p. 13

79. *H.E.*, IV, p. 14

80. The suggestion that he obtained the story from Daniel, bishop of Winchester (*Bede's Ecclesiastical History of the English people*, 374, n. 2), is probably incorrect. Daniel did tell Bede about Sussex (*H.E.*, Preface), but probably with reference more to the warfare between Caedwalla of Wessex and the South Saxons and the fact that Sussex had fallen under his episcopal jurisdiction. On the transmission of material in the *H.E.*, see D. P. Kirby, 'Bede's Native Sources for the *Historia Ecclesiastica*', *Bulletin of the John Rylands Library*, vol. 48 (1966), pp. 341–71 (cf. p. 368). That the story of the drought and the miraculous rain developed in the circle of Wilfrid's companion, Acca, later bishop of Hexham and Bede's diocesan, is an alternative possibility (cf., *ibid.*, p. 366). On balance, it is most likely to have originated in Sussex, and to have been relayed to Bede from Selsey by Acca (cf. *H.E.*, IV, 14)

81. *H.E.*, IV, 13, 14

82. *The Life of Bishop Wilfrid, c.* 41. The copy of the charter purporting to be a record of Æthelwealh's grant of Selsey to Wilfrid (cf. W. D. Peckham, 'The text of Caedwalla's

Charter', *S.N.Q.*, vol. II (1928–9), pp. 45–7 (*C.S.*, no. 64), is discussed by M. Roper, 'The Territorial Possessions of St. Wilfrid and their influence upon his career' (unpublished University of Manchester M.A., 1958), pp. 130 ff., together with other early charters relating to Wilfrid and Sussex. Though he favours an authentic base for Aethelwealh's charter, he does comment that until all South Saxon diplomas are properly edited 'it will be impossible to pronounce final judgement on any South Saxon charter' (*The Territorial Possessions of St. Wilfrid*, p. 187). Mr. Roper is editing the charters of Saxon Selsey as part of a corpus of Anglo-Saxon charters sponsored jointly by the British Academy and the Royal Historical Society

83. *H.E.*, IV, 14

84. It *is*, therefore, 'too much to suggest that the conversion of Aethelwealh himself may have been stimulated by a desire to seek relief from the famine by turning to a God more effective than the tribal deities who failed to alleviate it' (W. A. Chaney, *op. cit.*, p. 166), for even if the famine had lasted three years this would not carry its commencement back into Wulfhere's reign

85. *H.E.*, IV, 13

86. *The Life of Bishop Wilfrid, c.* 15

87. Cf. how Wulfhere intervened to re-convert the East Saxons after the pagan relapse of 664–5; *H.E.*, III, 30

88. *H.E.*, IV, 23. For a survey of the early history of Hwicce, and a possible Northumbrian element in the evolution of the kingdom, see H. P. R. Finberg, *The Early Charters of the West Midlands* (1961), pp. 167–90

89. *H.E.*, II, 20

90. His predecessor, Ithamar, had been of Kentish birth (*H.E.*, III, 14). Ithamar and Damian were both among the earliest of the native Saxons to receive consecration as bishops. Cf., Deusdedit, a West Saxon, consecrated archbishop of Canterbury (by Ithamar) in 655 (*H.E.*, III, 20): he, too, must have been brought up in Kent.

91. Cf., for convenience, H. Thurston and D. Attwater (eds.), *Butler's lives of the Saints*, (1956), vol. III, pp. 174–5

92. *Ibid.*, vol. I, pp. 280–1. Cf., on the church, P. M. Johnston, 'Steyning Church', *S.A.C.*, vol. 57 (1915), pp. 149–61

93. *H.E.*, IV, 15, 16: *The Life of Bishop Wilfrid, c.* 42. Any idea that Wilfrid would not really have abandoned Aethelwealh rests on sentiment rather than on the historical evidence which actually leaves Wilfrid's role in the conflict between Aethelwealh and Caedwalla obscure (allowing for some exaggeration of the pagan Caedwalla's early reliance on Wilfrid in the *Life, c.* 42). Wilfrid is likely, however, to have been completely unscrupulous. On unfamiliar territory, he would need to be on the winning side to safeguard himself and his possessions. Moreover, Caedwalla was a scourge also of Centwine, king of the West Saxons, whom Wilfrid (cf. the *Life, c.* 40) had no reason to cherish

94. *H.E.*, IV, 13, 14. Caedwalla too, apparently was generous to Selsey, as was a contemporary sub-king, Ecgwald, if B.C.S. 50 possesses an authentic base

95. *H.E.*, IV, 15: V, 23

96. Cf., A. Mawer and F. M. Stenton (Eds.), *The place-names of Sussex*, (English Place-Name Society vol. 6: Cambridge, 1929), xviii–xix, and M. Gelling, 'Place-names and Anglo-Saxon paganism', *University of Birmingham Historical Journal*, vol. VIII (1961), pp. 7–25 (p. 15)

97. M. Gelling, *art. cit.*, and cf., 'Further thoughts on pagan place-names', in F. Sandgren (ed.), *Otium et Negotium* Studies in Onomatology and Library Science presented to Olof Von Feilitzen), (1973), pp. 109–28

98. T. D. Kendrick, *op. cit.*, p. 86, was puzzled by the small grave-slab in Bexhill church, Sussex, dating to 11th century but representing a return, in his view, in spirit and type to the pre-Viking Hiberno-Saxon art in a district where this part-Irish, part-native Saxon style had not been previously pursued. 'How to explain this solitary archaizing sculpture, I do not know.' There may have been a more pronounced Irish strain in early Sussex than we appreciate.

99.   As G. W. Searle, *Anglo-Saxon bishops, kings and nobles* (Cambridge, 1899)

100. *H.E.*, V, 18

101. B.C.S. 91

102. *H.E.*, V, 18, 23. B.C.S. 145 indicates that he held the office of abbot at Selsey. For what may be his ring, see A. Anscombe, 'The Ring of Bishop Eolla', *Sn'.Q.*, vol. 1 (1926-7), pp. 136-9

103. *Bede's Ecclesiastical History of the English People*, pp. 572-3

104. See most recently, R. I. Page, 'Anglo-Saxon episcopal lists, parts I and II', *Nottingham Medieval Studies*, vol. 9 (1965), pp. 71-95, and 'Part III', *ibid.*, vol. 10 (1966), pp. 2-24

105. As M. A. O'Donovan has done in 'An interim revision of episcopal dates for the provence of Canterbury, 850-950: Part I', *Anglo-Saxon England*, vol. 1 (1972), pp. 23-44: Part II, *ibid.*, vol. 2 (1973), pp. 99-114. This can be done in the same way, of course, for other periods before the Conquest

106. E. Barker, 'Sussex Anglo-Saxon charters, Part I', *S.A.C.*, vol. 86 (1947), pp. 42-101 (p. 49)

108. *The place-names of Sussex*, vol. I, xix-xx

109. H. Poole, 'The Domesday Book churches of Sussex', *S.A.C.*, vol. 98 (1948), pp. 75-6

110. B.C.S. 132. See the catalogue in P. H. Sawyer, *Anglo-Saxon Charters: an annotated list and bibliography* (Royal Historical Society Guides and Handbooks 8: 1968), pp. 82-3 (noting the 'doubtful', 'dubious' and 'spurious' terms, of course). Reference needs also to be made to M. Roper, *op. cit.*, p. 130 ff. which will be superseded eventually (so far as Sussex is concerned) by his edition of the Selsey documents.

111. B.C.S. 132: Sawyer, 42; cf., B.C.S. 144: Sawyer, 43; B.C.S. 145: Sawyer, 44; B.C.S. 78: Sawyer, 45

112. B.C.S. 80: Sawyer, 1173 for a review of the opinions of diplomatists

113. E. Barker, *art. cit.*, 77, no. 25, commenting on B.C.S. 145: Sawyer, 44

114. F.M.Stenton, *Anglo-Saxon England* (3rd edn., 1970), 208 ff.

115. B.C.S. 206: Sawyer, 49. The existing church at Henfield has no Anglo-Saxon features

116. B.C.S. 1334: Sawyer, 1184. Cf., E. Barker, *art. cit.*, 87. F. M. Stenton, *Latin charters of the Anglo-Saxon period* (1955), pp. 37-38, and *E.H.D.*, vol. I, no. 76

117. B.C.S. 262: Sawyer, 1183

118. B.C.S. 261: Sawyer, 1178. The existing church at Ferring has no Anglo-Saxon features

119. B.C.S. 302: Sawyer, 158: cf., B.C.S. 387: Sawyer, 1435

120. B.C.S. 384: Sawyer, 1436. Cf., F. M. Stenton, *Anglo-Saxon England* (1970)

121. B.C.S. 387: Sawyer, 1435

122. B.C.S. 669: Sawyer, 403

123. B.C.S. 807: Sawyer, 506

124. E. Edwards (ed.), *Liber Monasterii de Hyda* (Rolls series: London, 1886), 238-42: Sawyer, 869

125. B.C.S. 997: Sawyer, 1291

126. B.C.S. 1131: Sawyer, 1377. This document is interesting for the sidelight it sheds on alleged witchcraft in England at this time, not actually in Sussex itself but in Huntingdonshire and the drowning of a widow accused of witchcraft at London Bridge: cf., also *E.H.D.*, vol. I, no. 112

127. B.C.S. 1124: Sawyer, 708

128. B.C.S. 1125: Sawyer, 714

129. W. B. Sanders, *Facsimiles of Anglo-Saxon manuscripts*, 3 vols. (Ordnance Survey: Southampton, 1878-84), vol. III, p. 39

130. B.C.S. 421: *V.C.H. Sussex*, vol. II, 3: and cf., M. S. Holgate, 'The Canons Manor of South Malling', *S.A.C.*, vol. 70 (1929), pp. 183-95, noting also her shorter communication, 'The Manors of the Archbishops in Sussex', *S.A.C.*, vol. 68 (1927), pp. 269-72

131. See, for instance, *E.H.D.* vol. II, no. 92, and for a detailed discussion of all Canterbury's holdings, F. R. H. du Boulay, *The Lordship of Canterbury*, (1966)

132. See D. J. A. Matthew, *The Norman monasteries and their English possessions* (1962), pp. 19-21

133. F. Barlow, *op. cit.* (note 3), p. 222; cf., 72, n. 3
134. *Ibid.*, 222, 239; and that Dunstan himself visited Sussex (supra footnote 26)
135. *Ibid.*, 222
136. See, for convenience, *E.H.D.* vol. II, no. 50 (p. 451) and bibliographical details given, p. 449

Chapter VIII: The origins of the Saxon Towns

1. M. Biddle, *Winchester Excavations* 4 (1974), pp. 20–24
2. A. H. Smith, *English place-name elements* English place-name Society, 1956)
3. C. M. Heighway, *The erosion of history* (Council for British Archaeology, 1972)
4. J. Wacher, *The towns of Roman Britain* (1974)
5. D. M. Metcalf, 'A coinage for West Sussex in the early eighth century', *Oxoniensia*, vol. 38 (1972), p. 65
6. D. Whitelock, D. C. Douglas and S. I. Tucker, *The Anglo-Saxon Chronicle: a revised translation* (1955)
7. *Ibid.*, p. 54
8. M. Biddle and D. Hill, 'Late Saxon planned towns', *Antiq. J.*, vol. 51 (1971), pp. 70–85
9. D. Hill, 'The Burghal Hidage: The establishment of a text', *Med. Arch.*, vol. 13 (1969), pp. 84–92
10. D. Whitelock, *English historical documents*, vol. 1, *c.* 500–1042 (1955), p. 54
11. D. Whitelock, D. C. Douglas and S. I. Tucker, *op. cit.*, p. 273
12. B. K. Davison, 'The Burghal Hidage fort of Eorpeburnan: A suggested identification', *Med. Arch.*, vol. 16 (1972), pp. 123–27
13. David Hill, 'The Burghal Hidage—Lyng', *Proc. Somerset Archaeol.*, vol. III (1967), pp. 64–6
14. David Hill, 'The Burghal Hidage—Southampton', *Proc. Hants. Field Club*, vol. 24 (1967), pp. 59–61
15. B. K. Davison, *op. cit.*, pp. 123–27
16. D. Freke, 'Excavations at Lewes, East Sussex' and 'Further excavations at Lewes, East Sussex', *Bulletin of the Institute of Archaeology*, 12 and 13 (1975 and 1976), pp. 52–8 and 34–9. See also D. Freke, 'Excavations in Lewes, 1974', *S.A.C.*, vol. 113 (1975), pp. 67–84
17. H. Sutermeister, 'Burpham: A settlement site within the Saxon defences', *S.A.C.*, vol. 114 (1976), pp. 194–206
18. C. E. Blunt, 'The coinage of Athelstan, King of England, 924–939', *B.N.J.*, vol. 43 (1974)
19. R. H. M. Dolley and F. Elmore Jones, 'The mints 'aet Gothabyrig' and 'aet Sith(M)esteby-rig'', *B.N.J.*, vol. 28 (1955–7), pp. 270–82
20. H. C. Darby and E. M. J. Campbell,

Chapter IX: The Domesday Record of Sussex

1. N. E. S. A. Hamilton (ed.), *Inquisitio Comitatus Cantabrigiensis . . . subjicitur Inquisitio Eliensis* (London, 1886). Translations of preamble in David C. Douglas and George W. Greenaway (eds.), *English historical documents*, vol. II, 1042–1189 (1953), p. 882 and Public Record Office, *Domesday re-bound* (1954), pp. 3, 7
2. Dialogus de Scaccario, I.16. Translation in *English historical documents*, vol. II, (note 1 above), p. 530
3. The classic works are J. H. Round, *Feudal England* (1895) (also reset with new Foreword 1964) and F. W. Maitland, *Domesday Book and beyond* (1897) (also Fontana Library (1960), with new pagination). Modern general works are V. H. Galbraith, *The making of Domesday Book* (1961); V. H. Galbraith, *Domesday Book: its place in administrative history* (1974); R. Welldon Finn, *The Domesday Inquest* (1961); R. Welldon Finn, *An introduction to Domesday Book* (1963); and R. Welldon Finn, *Domesday Book: a guide* (Chichester, 1973). A valuable summary is Public Record Office, *Domesday re-bound* (1954)

4. J. H. Round and L. F. Salzman, 'Domesday Book', in *Victoria County History of Sussex* (abbreviated hereafter to *V.C.H. Sussex*), vol. I (1905), pp. 351–451

5. S. H. King, 'Sussex' in H. C. Darby and Eila M. J. Campbell (eds.), *The Domesday geography of south-east England* (1962), pp. 407–82. *The Domesday geography of England* appeared in five volumes between 1952 and 1967 with, subsequently, an Index Volume for the whole of England (1975)

6. S. W. Wooldridge and Frederick Goldring, *The Weald* (1953)

7. E. M. Yates, 'History in a map', *Geographical Journal*, vol. 126 (1960), pp. 32–51; also E. M. Yates, *A history of the landscape of the parishes of South Harting and Rogate* (Chichester, 1972)

8. Peter Brandon, *The Sussex landscape* (1974)

9. Sir Frank Stenton, *Anglo-Saxon England* (3rd edn. 1971), p. 657

10. Summary in Public Record Office, *Domesday re-bound* (1954), Appendix II

11. Note 1 above

12. 'Robert Losinga, Bishop of Hereford (1079–95)'. Printed by W. H. Stevenson in *English Historical Review*, vol. 22 (1907), p. 74

13. *Anglo-Saxon Chronicle*, MS E, *sub anno* 1085. Dorothy Whitelock (ed.), *The Anglo-Saxon Chronicle: A revised translation* (1961)

14. F. W. Maitland, *Domesday Book and Beyond* (1897), pp. 199–28 (in Fontana Library edition (1960), pp. 154–63)

15. Bede, *H.E.*, Book I, ch. 25. Trans. L. Sherley-Price, *The Venerable Bede, history of the English church and people* (1955) (revised edition 1968)

16. Bede, *ibid.*, Book IV, ch. 13

17. Text in W. de G. Birch, *Cartularium Saxonicum* (abbreviated hereafter to B.C.S.), 3 vols. (1885–93), no. 297

18. *The Domesday geography of south-east England* (note 5 above), pp. 429, 431, 434

19. *Ibid.*, pp. 464–70

20. *Ibid.*, pp. 447, 450, 452

21. R. Welldon Finn, *An introduction to Domesday Book* (note 3 above), p. 202

22. The earliest documented windmill in Sussex appears to be that presented in 1218–22 by Bishop Ranulf at Bishopstone. W. D. Peckham (ed.), *The chartulary of the High Church of Chichester*, S.R.S., vol. 46 (1946), p. 47

23. H. C. Darby and E. M. J. Campbell (eds.), *op. cit.* (note 5), pp. 454, 457

24. *V.C.H. Sussex*, vol. I, p. 354

25. L. F. Salzman, 'The rapes of Sussex', *S.A.C.*, vol. 72 (1931), pp. 20–9

26. J. F. A. Mason, 'The rapes of Sussex and the Norman Conquest', *S.A.C.*, vol. 102 (1964), pp. 68–93

27. *Ibid.*, pp. 79–86

28. *Anglo-Saxon Chronicle*, MSS C, D and E, *sub anno* 1011 (note 13 above)

29. J. E. A. Jolliffe, 'The Domesday hidation of Sussex and the rapes', *E.H.R.*, vol. 45 (1930), pp. 427–35 and J. E. A. Jolliffe, *Pre-feudal England: the Jutes* (1933), pp. 73–97

30. J. F. A. Mason, *op. cit.*, pp. 87–89

31. David Clarke, 'The Saxon hundreds of Sussex', *S.A.C.*, vol. 74 (1933), pp. 214–25

32. The Bishop and the Archbishop also respectively held small estates at Hazelhurst and Wootton in East Sussex; the canons of Selsey and Malling also held separate estates

33. *The Hundred Ordinance*, often cited as I Edgar but probably a little earlier. Translation and discussion in Dorothy Whitelock (ed.), *English historical documents*, vol. I, *c.*500–1042 (1955), pp. 393–4

34. A view that the discrete Sussex estates of Domesday Book might reflect organisation going back to the pre-Roman Iron Age is in Glanville Jones, 'Settlement patterns in Anglo-Saxon England', *Antiquity*, vol. 35 (1961), pp. 221–32

35. B.C.S., 553. Text and translation, with commentary, in E. E. Barker, 'Sussex Anglo-Saxon charters', *S.A.C.*, vol. 86 (1947), pp. 42–101, vol. 87 (1948), pp. 29–76 and vol. 88 (1949), pp. 51–113 (cited hereafter as *Barker*), no. 24 (1948). Critical comment on the charters is briefly summarised in P. H. Sawyer (ed.), *Anglo-Saxon Charters* (1968)

36. Asser, *Vita Aelfredi*, ch. 79. Text and commentary in W. H. Stevenson (ed.), *Asser: Life of King Alfred* (1904)
37. Eddius Stephanus, ch. 41.B. Colgrave (ed.), *The Life of Bishop Wilfrid by Eddius Stephanus* (1927). Bede, *H.E.*, Book IV, ch. 13 (note 15 above)
38. B.C.S., 302 (*Barker* 20 (1948)) and B.C.S., 387 (*Barker* 21 (1948)). These were records of argument about the Bishop of Selsey's rights to 'Denton' at synods in 801 and 825
39. *Anglo-Saxon Chronicle*, MS C, *sub anno* 1052 (note 13 above)
40. B.C.S., 1265 (*Barker* 46 (1949)) and B.C.S., 1266 (*Barker* 48 (1949))
41. Note 38 above
42. B.C.S., 206 (*Barker* 12 (1947))
43. B.C.S., 144 (*Barker* 3 (1947))
44. Rune Forsberg, 'A contribution to a dictionary of Old English place-names' in *Nomina Germanica* 9, (Uppsala 1950), pp. 63–4
45. B.C.S., 702 (*Barker* 28 (1948))
46. Note 37 above
47. B.C.S., 50 (*Barker* 1 (1947))
48. H. P. R. Finberg, 'Charltons and Carltons', in his *Lucerna* (1964)
49. J. H. Round, *Calendar of documents preserved in France illustrative of the history of Great Britain and Ireland* (cited hereafter as Round, *France*), (P.R.O., 1899), vol. I, no. 1130, p. 405
50. L. F. Salzman (ed.), *The chartulary of the priory of St. Pancras of Lewes* (*S.R.S.*, vol. 38 (1933)), Part I, pp. 15–22
51. H. Poole, 'The Domesday Book churches of Sussex', *S.A.C.*, vol. 87 (1948), pp. 29–76
52. *V.C.H. Sussex*, vol. I, pp. 357–8
53. Peter Brandon, *op. cit.*, p. 81
54. Round, *France* (note 49 above), vol. I, no. 114, p. 38
55. B.C.S., 1335. Text and commentary in A. J. Robertson, *Anglo-Saxon charters* (1939), pp. 246–9. The larger hidage, totalling 4350 hides, assigned in the Burghal Hidage for the defence of the five Sussex 'burhs' in the time of King Alfred or, more probably, Edward the Elder, is a figure related to the need of men for manning the defences rather than an assessment on the county comparable with the Domesday pre-Conquest figure of approximately 3200 hides (page 194 above)
56. H. C. Darby and E. M. J. Campbell (eds.), *op. cit.*, pp. 464–70
57. *V.C.H. Sussex*, vol. I, pp. 370–1. Alnod, who held Alciston, is identified by Round and Salzman with Ethelnoth of Canterbury, sheriff of Kent, and Brixi, who held considerable estates in Sussex, probably with a Kentish noble of this name

Appendix

58. David Clarke, 'The Saxon hundreds of Sussex', *S.A.C.*, vol. 74 (1933), pp. 214–25
59. B.C.S., 50 (*Barker* 1 (1947))
60. A. Hadrian Allcroft, *Waters of Arun* (1930), pp. 97–107
61. A. Mawer and F. M. Stenton, *The Place-names of Sussex*, Part 1 (English Place-Name Society, vol. 6) (1929), pp. 134, 181, 196 n
62. B.C.S., 1114 (*Barker* 41 (1949))
63. *The Place-names of Sussex*, Part 1 (note 61 above), p. 7
64. B.C.S., 898 (*Barker* 35 (1949))
65. Note 57 above
66. B.C.S., 702 (*Barker* 28 (1948))
67. Round, *France* (note 49 above), vol. I, no. 1130, p. 405
68. *Ibid.*
69. B.C.S., 197 (*Barker* 13 (1947))
70. B.C.S., 1191 (*Barker* 44 (1949))
71. *The chartulary of the priory of St. Pancras of Lewes*, Part I (note 50 above), pp. 15, 21
72. *Ibid.*, pp. 15, 17, 22
73. *Ibid.*, p. 22

74. B.C.S., 197 (*Barker* 13 (1947))

75. Page 193 above

76. B.C.S., 252 (*Barker* 18 (1948)), B.C.S., 259 (*Barker* 19 (1948)), B.C.S., 494 (*Barker* 23 (1948)). In the will of Prince Aethelstan (*c.* 1015) land at Rotherfield is granted to 'the nuns' minster'. Dorothy Whitelock, *Anglo-Saxon Wills* (1930), no. 20

77. B.C.S., 421 (*Barker* 22 (1948)). Barker, however, considered that this charter probably did not refer to Malling in Sussex, since it was granted by a Kentish king

78. B.C.S., 202 (*Barker* 20 (1948)) and B.C.S., 387 (*Barker* 21 (1948)). See note 38 above

79. Note 57 above

80. W. D. Peckham (ed.), *Thirteen custumals of the Sussex manors of the bishop of Chichester and other documents*, *S.R.S.*, vol. 31, 1925; *custumal of Bishopstone*, pp. 96–8, and terrier (1327–8), p. 132

81. B.C.S., 208 (*Barker* 14 (1947))

82. *V.C.H. Sussex*, vol. 9 (Rape of Hastings) (1937), p. 49. Also, A. Mawer and F. M. Stenton, *The Place-names of Sussex*, Part 2 (English Place-Name Society, vol. 7) (1930), pp. vi–vii

83. B.C.S., 553 (*Barker* 24 (1948))

Chapter X: Saxon Sussex: some problems and directions

1.   See for example, Margaret Gelling, 'The place-names of the Mucking area', *Panorama* 19 (1975/6), pp. 7–20

2.   Some results of the Chalton Survey are briefly summarized in Barry Cunliffe, 'Chalton, Hants.: the evolution of a landscape', *Antiq. J.*, vol. 53 (1973), pp. 173–190

3.   For plans and a discussion see H. C. Bowen and P. J. Fowler, 'Romano-British rural settlements in Dorset and Wiltshire', in A. C. Thomas (ed.), *Rural settlement in Roman Britain* (London 1966), pp. 43–67

4.   M. G. Welch, 'Late Romans and Saxons in Sussex', *Britannia* II (1971), pp. 232–6

5.   Barry Cunliffe, *The Regni* (London 1973), pp. 126–139. See also Welch's comments above, p. 27

6.   See above, pp. 37–43

7.   The principal results are published by Alec Down in *Chichester Excavations* 3 (1978)

8.   Barry Cunliffe, *Excavations at Portchester Castle, vol. II: Saxon* (London 1976)

9.   S. S. Frere, *Britannia* (London, 1st edn., 1967), pp. 309–11

10. J. C. Russell, *British Medieval Population* (Albuquerque 1948)

11. The present population density in the county averages six times the Domesday figure

12. Barry Cunliffe, 'Saxon and medieval settlement pattern in the region of Chalton, Hampshire', *Med. Arch.*, vol. 16 (1972), pp. 1–12

INDEX

LIST OF SUBSCRIBERS

Mr. Geoffrey Edgar Nicholas Adams
P. V. Addyman
Mr. Paul Adorian
Leslie Alcock
F. G. Aldsworth Esq.
Mr. John C. Allen
L. Allen, D.Sc., F.Inst.P.
Trevor Charles Allen, B.A.
R. M. Allott
The Reverend and Mrs. A. B. de T.
  Andrews
C. J. Arnold
Miss M. A. Ash, M.A.
D. R. J. Barber
Prof. T. Barna, C.B.E.
Barr-Hamilton, Alec
Miss J. Barrowman
Mrs. J. Barry
Martin Batt
Battle and District Historical Society
  Museum
Thomas Baxendale Esq.
Dr. Archie Beatson
Mr. T. Beaumont
Mr. N. C. Beck
Martin Bell
W. H. C. Bell
Mr. L. W. Belton
Mrs. G. I. Beresford
Mr. W. R. Beswick
Edward H. Biffin, M.A.
D. G. Bird
Birmingham Public Libraries, History
  and Geography Department
Revd. J. H. Bishop, M.A.
Graham Black
Miss A. E. Blakeney
Christine G. Bloxham
John Boldero
W. G. D. Bone
M. W. Bone
Mr. and Mrs. P. F. Bonham
Mrs. Peter Booker
Mrs. B. M. Bourke
S. J. and P. M. Bracher
Mrs. D. E. Brandon
Dr. Peter Brandon
Mrs. E. R. Brewer, B.A.(Hist.Hons.)
  (London)
The Brotherton Library, University
  of Leeds
Mrs. E. Muriel Brown
Mr. L. A. Buckland
William Guy Budden
Sanseagh de Burca
Mrs. Bobby Burke
Dr. N. F. H. Butcher, M.A.
J. Campbell
D. J. T. Carter
Mr. C. Charman
Chichester Cathedral Library
Mr. I. B. Child
Dr. Terence Clark

P. F. Cockburn
Michael Coker
P. H. Cole, B.A.
Peter Cooper
Mr. J. C. K. Cornwall, M.A., F.R.Hist.S.
Mr. Alexander H. Corrie
Miss K. L. Cosway
The Hon. E. D. Courthope
Mr. M. J. Coviello
Paul Craddock
A. L. Crich, B.A., M.Ed.Psy.
Miss R. M. Crutch
J. M. N. Dame
Mrs. N. K. Daniel
Mr. J. M. J. Danzelman
Mrs. T. R. Davidson, B.A.
Mrs. Norma Dawlings
Miss Beryl Day
C. L. Deacon, B.Sc.
Department of Medieval and Later
  Antiquities, The British Museum
K. W. Dickins
Miss Janet M. Dods
Mr. J. C. Dove
Alec Down
Mrs. Sheila Doyle
Laurence Draper
Richard Dumbreck
Mr. K. A. Du Boisson
Mr. H. P. Durant
G. W. C. A. Durrant
Miss Enid Dyer
B. Dysterre-Clark
Pamela Edwards
Professor T. H. Elkins
Ms. Susan Ellis, B.A.
Julian Elloway
Mr. J. P. Elston
Emmanuel College Library,
  Cambridge
Mr. P. L. Everson
Mr. G. H. Farebrother
Sue and John Farrant
William Arthur Fisher
Fitzwilliam College, Cambridge
Frederick E. Ford, A.R.I.B.A.
Ford, Mr. Wyn K., F.R.Hist.S.
James Forsyth
K. Fossey, B.Ed.
Miss Jennifer Foster
Miss J. V. H. Fraser
W. A. D. Freeman Esq., M.A.
John A. Fryer, C.B.E.
Mr. P. J. Fynmore
The Viscount Gage, K.C.V.O.
Miss Brenda Gardner
Simon Garrett
Gates, Mr. J. S.
Miss M. F. W. Gates
Mr. P. S. Gelling
Geography Department, Bishop Otter
  College, West Sussex Institute
Mrs. J. E. Gibb

Dr. C. B. Giles, Ph.D., B.Sc. and
  Mrs. C. B. Giles, B.A.
Mrs. D. F. Giles, B.A.
Rev. J. P. Giles, M.A., B.D., B.Sc.
A. P. Glover, F.L.A.
Janet Goldsbrough-Jones
R. J. Goulden, B.A. Dip. Lib.
Graduate School in Arts and Social
  Studies, University of Sussex
K. Gravett
C. G. W. Green
The Reverend Canon R. T. Greenacre, M.A.,
  Chancellor of Chichester Cathedral
Mr. F. W. Greenaway
James I. Hadfield
Mr. Michael Hare, M.A.
Peter Harrington
Mr. H. J. Harrison
Dr. C. R. Hart
Mr. J. R. S. Hart
Mr. R. Hartridge
Mr. Alan W. Hastings
Mr. J. D. Helme
The Reverend Canon John Hester
Mr. G. A. Hillman
Dr. C. M. Hills
Mrs. C. M. Hills
Paul Trevor Hodge
Stanley Hodgson, C.B.E.
Mr. E. W. Holden, F.S.A.
Mr. E. E. and Mrs. R. K. Hole
Barbara H. Holland
Hollingdale, Miss E. A., A.L.A.
Mr. G. Holloway
Betiwyn Holmes, B.A.
Mrs. Margaret Holt
R. A. Hook
G. Hooker
John Houghton
Howard, Miss M. E.
Dr. T. P. Hudson
Dr. R. F. Hunnisett
D. M. Hurst
Mrs. Robert R. Jackson
Mrs. Patricia E. James
Mr. C. H. Jaques, M.A.
Mr. R. C. Jarvis
Colonel E. C. Johnson
K. R. Johnstone
Mrs. M. U. Jones, Mucking
  Excavation, Essex
Mr. G. W. Kearvell
Laurence Keen
J. R. Kellam
Frederick W. W. Kempton
Mr. Michael N. Kendall
David H. Kennett
Dr. Basil S. Kent, M.B., B.S., L.R.C.P.,
  M.R.C.S., D.A., F.F.A.R.C.S.
Dr. John A. Kiechler
D. Kingsley
J. S. Kirby
B. W. Knight